HENRY FIELDING
AND THE AUGUSTAN IDEAL UNDER STRESS

❋

'Nature's Dance of Death' and other Studies

C. J. Rawson

Professor of English, University of Warwick

Routledge & Kegan Paul
London and Boston

First published 1972
by Routledge & Kegan Paul Ltd
Broadway House, 68–74 Carter Lane
London EC4V 5EL and
9 Park Street,
Boston, Mass. 02108, U.S.A.

Printed in Great Britain
by W & J Mackay Limited, Chatham

ISBN 0 7100 7454 9

In Memory of
JOHN BUTT and PETER URE

CONTENTS

✸

The 'Nature' in my subtitle is that animating ideal or live fiction of order and coherence which was so essential a part of the Augustan sensibility, and to which Pope referred in a famous exhortation:

> First follow NATURE, and your Judgment frame
> By her just Standard, which is still the same.

The *Essay on Criticism*, where this couplet appears, reminds us that the model of order and of harmony evoked by the term 'Nature' had one of its most vivid emblems in the image of the dance. The image is an old one, and very pervasive, and had often been used in the service of time-honoured notions of a cosmic harmony. By the age of Pope and of Fielding, however, the more meaningful and potent applications of the image were less all-embracing, and had particularly to do with moral, and social, and aesthetic ideals of harmony, rather than with any truly active faith in a vast universal synthesis. The aristocratic colouring, the celebrated 'urbanity' of some eighteenth-century literary styles, notably Pope's and Fielding's, seem to us a richer and a truer expression of harmony than such more universalizing claims as those of the *Essay on Man*.

My main theme in this book, however, is that even these more limited harmonies were felt to be under threat, and that disruptive pressures and radical insecurities became evident in some of the seemingly most confident, and some of the most conservative, writing of the period. It is this which I seek to convey by the term 'Dance of Death': a sense of beleaguered harmony, of forms preserved under stress, of feelings of doom and human defeat ceremoniously rendered. My title does not, therefore, indicate a direct preoccupation with those medieval and post-medieval rituals and art-forms whose best-known example in art is Holbein's great series of engravings. But there is an association of ideas, and some of Rowlandson's illustrations to *The English Dance of Death*, although later than the period of which I write, make vivid the kind of connection I mean (one of these illustrations appears on the dust-jacket to this volume).

My chief example is Fielding, who for many reasons occupies a special, ambiguous position between an older world of aristocratic and neo-classic loyalties, and newer forces, one of whose literary manifestations is the novel-form itself. The first half of the book explores a crisis in stylistic 'urbanity', in 'True Ease in Writing', in the forms of couplet rhetoric. The second examines a crisis in mock-heroic, a favourite style of the period, and in itself an ambiguous expression of one of the oldest and most cherished cultural loyalties, to the heroic ideal and the epic poem. In this second section, the crucial text is *Jonathan Wild*, a work which in my view has extraordinary interest (though unequal value), and which has been greatly misunderstood.

I have tried not to suggest that there is here any simple, schematic thesis. I have been more concerned to explore a theme than to argue a case. In particular, I did not wish to present this study as a systematic, or neatly progressive, account of Fielding's 'development', although I have views about this development which are implied in particular contexts. This is one reason why I have violated chronological tidiness, leaving to my second half a work which is early, and dealing in my first with some of Fielding's last writings. A more important reason for this arrangement is that an understanding of the crisis in 'urbanity' which is discussed in Part One seems a better background for an understanding of what I try to show in Part Two than I could provide by a more orthodox and progressive procedure.

The various chapters of this book are, in some ways, separate studies, each exploring certain aspects of my theme in their own way, whilst being linked with the others by the common larger theme. There is some overlapping and repetition, because similar points, and the same Fielding passages, seemed to me to belong naturally to more than one exploration. There may even be some contradictions, because what might in one sense appear to be opposite views both seemed valid in the respective contexts of exploration. I believe that certain kinds of inconsistency or self-contradiction are truer to the many-sidedness of a literary text or topic than critical acts of reductive coherence. I prefer to think of this book as having certain faults of open-endedness and of doubt, than the virtues of a systematically articulated certainty.

The connections which I have suggested between Fielding and some writers of our own century do not imply 'influence' in the ordinary or traditional sense. But they seek to bring out, I hope without falsifying Fielding, certain features of which he cannot have been consciously aware, but which help to emphasize his live interest and significance in a cultural climate so different from his own. I have not sought, however, to rewrite him for our time. My chief purpose (whether or not I have succeeded in it) has been to try to understand him better, and to pay my tribute to him, as he is.

I am indebted to the learned journals, and the organizers of learned conferences, who invited, or found themselves putting up with, various individual portions or stages of what has now become this book.

Chapters I to III appeared, with minor differences, in *Eighteenth-Century Studies* (1967; 1970), and chapter VII in *Modern Philology* (1972). Acknowledgments are due to the publishers (University of California Press; University of Chicago Press) and the editors of these journals. To Robert H. Hopkins especially I owe more than anyone has a right to expect of an editor. Part of chapter III was also read as a paper at the annual conference of University Teachers of English at Nottingham in 1970, and I benefited from the discussion which followed.

A shorter version of chapter IV was delivered at the Second Nichol Smith Memorial Seminar in Canberra in 1970, and will appear in its shorter form in a volume of contributions to the Seminar, published by the Australian National University Press, and edited by R. F. Brissenden. To him and to Ian Donaldson, both of the Australian National University, I owe debts, scholarly and personal. To other members of the Seminar I am also indebted for their stimulating discussion of my paper.

Parts of chapters V and VI were read as a paper at the Third International Congress on the Enlightenment in Nancy in 1971.

Several friends have read parts or all of this book at various stages, adding information, correcting mistakes, and answering questions. In addition to those I have already named above, these are: G. K. Hunter, Jennifer Lorch, J. C. Maxwell, Jenny Mezciems, Henry Knight Miller, my wife Judy Rawson, Pat Rogers, John Saunders, Arthur H. Scouten, R. Hinton Thomas (who commented valuably on the discussion of Thomas Mann), Jonathan Weiss (who commented similarly on the discussion of Camus) and Martin Wright.

Keith Bullivant and Rolf Lass helped me in my difficulties with the German texts.

The staff of the University of Warwick Library has, as usual, been remarkable for its helpfulness and efficiency. Special thanks are due to Audrey Cooper, Alison Marsh and also to several successive library assistants who have dealt with inter-library loans. But special mentions do not exhaust my debt to the whole library staff, and to a Librarian who has created in a short time a better stocked and more variously efficient library than any new university could reasonably hope for.

To the University itself I owe gratitude for periods of sabbatical leave, and other assistance without which this book might not have materialized.

Ann Griffin and Joyce Pemberton gave heroic secretarial assistance with unruffled good-humour and tolerance, as well as expertise.

My debt to the two great scholars to whose memory this book is dedicated, is beyond words. To have known them was an education in itself.

❀

Except where otherwise noted, I have used the following texts of Fielding's writings:

Joseph Andrews (*J.A.*), ed. Martin C. Battestin, Riverside edn (Boston, 1961). Battestin's other, old-spelling, 'Wesleyan' edition (Oxford, 1967) has been consulted throughout, but I have preferred to quote from his modern-spelling text so as not to isolate *Joseph Andrews* artificially from Fielding's other novels, for which authoritative modern old-spelling editions are not yet available;

Tom Jones (*T.J.*), ed. R. P. C. Mutter (Harmondsworth, 1966);

Amelia, Everyman's Library (London and New York, 1966);

Covent-Garden Journal (*C.-G.J.*), ed. G. E. Jensen (New York, 1964) (abbr. Jensen in page-refs.);

Voyage to Lisbon, ed. Harold E. Pagliaro (New York, 1963).

For all other works by Fielding, I have used W. E. Henley's edition of the *Works* (London, 1903). This includes *Jonathan Wild* (*J.W.*), for which Henley's text is based on the revised edition of 1754. Any exceptions to this are noted in context. The abbreviation *Works* refers to this edition, with an exception involving Swift's *Works* (see below). References to Fielding's novels give Book and chapter, but not page numbers.

The abbreviations 'Cross' and 'Dudden' refer respectively to W. L. Cross, *The History of Henry Fielding* (New York, 1963), and F. Homes Dudden, *Henry Fielding, His Life, Works, and Times* (Oxford, 1952).

The abbreviation 'Swift, *Works*' (or merely *Works* if the context makes it clear that Swift is being quoted) refers to the edition by Herbert Davis and others of the *Prose Works* (Oxford, 1939–68). 'Swift, *Poems*' refers to Harold Williams's second edition (Oxford, 1958).

Quotations from Pope are from the Twickenham Edition. Details of the particular volume are given where necessary.

✹

NATURE'S DANCE
OF DEATH

CHAPTER I

GENTLEMEN
AND DANCING-MASTERS[1]

❊

In euery daunse, of a moste aunciant custome, there daunseth to gether a man and a woman, holding eche other by the hande or the arme, whiche betokeneth concorde. . . . A man in his naturall perfection is fiers, hardy, stronge in opinion, couaitous of glorie, desirous of knowledge, appetiting by generation to brynge forthe his semblable. The good nature of a woman is to be milde, timerouse, tractable, benigne, of sure remembrance, and shamfast. . . . Wherfore, whan we beholde a man and a woman daunsinge to gether, let us suppose there to be a concorde of all the saide qualities, being ioyned to gether, as I haue set them in ordre. And the meuing of the man wolde be more vehement, of the woman more delicate, and with lasse aduauncing of the body, signifienge the courage and strenthe that oughte to be in a man, and the pleasant sobrenesse that shulde be in a woman. . . . These qualities, in this wise beinge knitte to gether, and signified in the personages of man and woman daunsinge, do expresse or sette out the figure of very nobilitie; whiche in the higher astate it is contained, the more excellent is the vertue in estimation. . . .
    Nowe by cause there is no passe tyme to be compared to that, wherin may be founden both recreation and meditation of vertue, I haue amonge all honest passe times, wherin is exercise of the body, noted daunsinge to be of an excellent utilitie, comprehendinge in it wonderfull figures, or, as the grekes do call them, *Ideae*, of vertues and noble qualities.
                (Sir Thomas Elyot, *The Gouernour*, I, xxi–xxii)

I begin with a small class-conscious episode from *Amelia*. Sergeant Atkinson visits Mrs Ellison's house, where Booth, Amelia and Mrs Bennet are having tea. Atkinson is shy with women, and a social inferior. Mrs Ellison makes some condescending but welcoming remarks to the effect that 'a serjeant of the guards is a gentleman':[2]

... accordingly, the serjeant was ushered in, though not without
some reluctance on his side. There is, perhaps, nothing more
uneasy than those sensations which the French call *mauvaise honte*,
nor any more difficult to conquer; and poor Atkinson would, I
am persuaded, have mounted a breach with less concern than he
showed in walking across a room before three ladies, two of whom
were his avowed well-wishers.

Though I do not entirely agree with the late learned Mr. Essex,
the celebrated dancing-master's opinion, that dancing is the
rudiment of polite education, as he would, I apprehend, exclude
every other art and science, yet it is certain that persons whose
feet have never been under the hands of the professors of that art
are apt to discover this want in their education in every motion,
nay, even when they stand or sit still. They seem, indeed, to be
overburthened with limbs which they know not how to use, as if,
when Nature hath finished her work, the dancing-master still is
necessary to put it in motion.

Atkinson was, at present, an example of this observation which
doth so much honour to a profession for which I have a very
high regard. He was handsome, and exquisitely well made; and
yet, as he had never learnt to dance, he made so awkward an
appearance in Mrs. Ellison's parlour, that the good lady herself,
who had invited him in, could at first scarce refrain from laughter
at his behaviour. He had not, however, been long in the room
before admiration of his person got the better of such risible
ideas. So great is the advantage of beauty in men as well as women,
and so sure is this quality in either sex of procuring some regard
from the beholder.

The exceeding courteous behaviour of Mrs. Ellison, joined to
that of Amelia and Booth, at length dissipated the uneasiness of
Atkinson; and he gained sufficient confidence to tell the company
some entertaining stories of accidents that had happened in the
army within his knowledge, which, though they greatly pleased
all present, are not, however, of consequence enough to have a
place in this history.

So many of Fielding's attitudes, spoken and unspoken, are blended
into this passage, that it serves as an admirable starting-point for a
discussion of his views on 'politeness' and social rank, and of some
aspects of his style or tone of voice. Atkinson here combines some dis-
tinctive qualities of both Joseph Andrews and Tom Jones. Joseph is

4

described as handsome 'without the least clumsiness',[3] but he exhibits an embarrassed rigidity in his admittedly somewhat trying relations with the fair sex. Fielding treats this affectionately, but with an undercurrent of mockery: as with Atkinson, he values the great personal decency, while displaying an urbane humour about the lack of social freedom and grace. His attitude is well short of Chesterfield's obsessional patrician distaste for *mauvaise honte* (a favourite bugbear of courtesy-writers) and for 'awkwardness': 'Awkwardness and ill-breeding shock me to that degree, that, where I meet with them, I cannot find in my heart to inquire into the intrinsic merit of that person.'[4] Fielding spoke sympathetically in the *Covent-Garden Journal* of 'an awkward Sort of Politeness' as 'a Sort of good Breeding undrest',[5] and there is no doubt of his real sympathies when, in his satiric *Modern Glossary* of worldly usage, he sarcastically defines Modesty as 'Awkwardness, Rusticity'.[6] On the other hand, Fielding does not wholly share the feeling of some mid- and late eighteenth-century novelists that a certain kind of 'bashfulness' is to be cherished, 'sentimentally' and for itself, as something 'which the most delicate feelings produce', against the false politeness of a corrupt 'world'.[7] The check on such sentimentalization comes in part from an aristocratic outlook which Fielding, in a modified way, shared with Chesterfield. An amusing ambiguity concludes the slightly burlesque description (which parodies accounts of heroes in romances) of the handsome Joseph Andrews: 'Add to this the most perfect neatness in his dress, and an air which, to those who have not seen many noblemen, would give an idea of nobility.'[8] The remark alludes to a common assumption in romances that the true nobility of a hero, however disguised, will always show. One suggestion, here, however, is that real-life noblemen are a degenerate lot, hardly handsome and healthy like Joseph. But another implication is that only 'those who have not seen many noblemen' could possibly take this blushing footman for one.

Atkinson is also like Tom, though without Tom's ease and grace. This is not only because of his warm-hearted benevolence. Part of the similarity, as well as the difference, is contained in a useful phrase, 'natural gentility', which is used of Tom[9] as well as of Sophia Western and Joseph's Fanny. The exact overtones of this phrase vary according to the context: Fanny's 'natural gentility, superior to the acquisition of art'[10] differs subtly from Sophia Western's (about which much the same is said)[11] because the girls and their social background are very different. In one sense, the phrase clearly suggests a native kindness and innocence independent of politer graces, a 'Sort of good Breeding undrest'. At the end of his *Essay on Conversation*, Fielding says that ill-natured people of exalted rank are 'thoroughly ill-bred', while a good man, 'however low in rank' and 'however clumsy . . . in his figure or demeanour' can claim good-breeding 'in the truest sense'.[12] This posits an aristocracy of the heart, and Atkinson is in this sense clearly one of nature's aristocrats.

But to talk in metaphors of gentility readily involves subtle identifications of morals with social rank and with grace of manner. There is obviously no question of Fielding making crude equations on these matters. But the 'natural gentility' of Fanny and Sophia clearly has something to do with a graceful and delicate bearing. Sophia, 'the daughter of a country booby squire' who 'hath been in town about a fortnight, for the first time', gives Lord Fellamar the impression that 'she had been bred in a court'.[13] (The earlier passage about Sophia, like that about Atkinson, also celebrates, with an irony that is by no means simply dismissive, the charms of politer refinements.)[14] Sophia, moreover, like Tom, has gentility not only in the natural but also in the technical sense. In Tom's case 'natural gentility' might almost be a pun, for he turns out to be the illegitimate son of a gentleman. The fact that he is often taken for a gentleman in disguise clearly works in with all this. The old formula, guyed in the description of Joseph, according to which one's rank showed itself not only through disguises but through one's own ignorance of the facts of one's birth, clearly operates in *Tom Jones*. Strictly, this is also true of Joseph, who turns out to be the son not of Gaffar Andrews but of Mr Wilson. But Joseph's status, throughout most of the novel, as a mere footman, his extreme and somewhat comic chastity, and the residual tang of the anti-Richardsonian parody, conspire to dissipate the impression of an inborn gentlemanly grace.

Tom, on the other hand, grows up not as a servant but as an accepted member of Allworthy's household. At no point in the novel did Fielding need to imagine him, as he needed to imagine Joseph throughout, in a role which Fielding would instinctively regard as demeaning and slightly ridiculous. Fielding was able to think constantly of Tom as a gentleman of sorts, instead of merely knowing in the abstract, as with Joseph, that he would reveal technical gentility at the end. Thus while Joseph (and Atkinson) are undoubtedly nature's gentlemen in a way, this is even truer (and truer in a more live and active sense) of Tom, precisely because he is a gentleman in the more ordinary sense as well. There is certainly a correlation (partly unconscious perhaps) between this and Tom's natural charm and freedom of manner with women, which Atkinson so conspicuously lacks. Even Tom's illegitimacy is indirectly related to all this. The nastier characters in the novel despise him for this, but Fielding's more open-minded and large-hearted view strikes a note of easy patrician liberality. This aristocratic superiority to mere technicalities, and the characteristic moral generosity with which it is blended in Fielding's case, suffuses the novel and naturally rubs off on the hero.

It will not do to infer too much from Tom's illegitimacy. Probably, as Scott and others have pointed out,[15] its main function lies in the mechanics of the plot: if Miss Bridget Allworthy had been married to Tom's father, there would have been no need to keep his birth a secret, and thus no opening for the main plot-complications which follow. But at the same time it is hard to see why Tom could not have been made a legitimate foundling like Joseph Andrews. If the plot requires him to be related to Allworthy, any number of fictional arrangements not much more improbable than the one we actually have could surely have been devised: for example, Tom might have been born to Bridget legitimately, been abducted by gypsies like Joseph, and been returned incognito say a year later; or he might have been born to some other sister of Allworthy's, estranged from her brother and dying in childbirth, and been desposited on Allworthy's doorstep by a well-wisher who knew the facts. Such speculations are idle, of course, except to suggest that the situation as we have it was not quite as inevitable, in terms of plot, as is sometimes implied. One need not disagree that Fielding devised it because of the particular needs of his plot. But Fielding must have known that it was in some ways bold and unorthodox to make his hero a bastard and keep him so, and could have re-manipulated his opening if he had wanted to avoid this. We know, on the other hand, that Fielding particularly disliked sanctimonious and uncharitable attitudes on subjects involving illegitimacy. He had made the point before.[16] It is at least fair to say that the plot as he devised it offered exceptional play to a narrator of his temperament and moral sensibility. A situation in which patrician hauteur and moral charity are readily and relevantly congruent (Fielding certainly knew well that not all situations were of this sort) is one in which Fielding is most at home. In a novel in which the narrator's voice is always vividly present, it would be surprising if the atmosphere created by that voice did not also surround, though indirectly and perhaps illogically, the chief character celebrated there. It is at least half-true to say that Tom seems the more a gentleman because he is a bastard, as if a noble generosity on the subject of bastards made illegitimacy itself seem a noble thing. Henry James paid tribute to the way in which Fielding's storytelling voice injected qualities of its own, or at least an aura of such qualities, into a hero who strictly

7

speaking is a very different character.[17] Tom has none of Fielding's witty urbanity or sophistication, none of the Olympian assurance of voice, and by no means the same kind of knowledge of the world. But these qualities of Fielding's somehow support Tom's gentlemanly status in a way which would be unthinkable with Atkinson, just as Fielding's unsolemn tolerance of Tom's unchastities contributes an indirect patrician gloss to Tom's own entirely unselfconscious ease with women.

Atkinson lacks this ease, but there remains a sense in which the passage about him quoted at the beginning tells Tom's story in small:

> He was handsome, and exquisitely well made; and yet, as he had never learnt to dance, he made so awkward an appearance in Mrs. Ellison's parlour, that the good lady herself, who had invited him in, could at first scarce refrain from laughter at his behaviour. He had not, however, been long in the room before admiration of his person got the better of such risible ideas. So great is the advantage of beauty in men as well as women, and so sure is this quality in either sex of procuring some regard from the beholder.

Mrs Ellison is a nasty piece of work, but in this particular situation her readiness to be charmed by the awkward Atkinson does not detract from the value of his unconscious victory over an embarrassing moment. Tom had similarly, without conscious effort, charmed a variety of disreputable and snobbish women without being especially diminished in our eyes by this fact. Tom also had a lot of social disadvantages and personal difficulties to overcome, and the fact that he conquers many of them, without really trying, through natural goodness and charm is another aspect of his status as one of nature's aristocrats. In this sense, Atkinson is at this moment very like him. He overcomes a difficult social situation through sheer obvious decency and a handsome person: the two a little archly go together, because a good-natured character and sexual love (or sexual attraction, for there is nothing between him and Mrs Ellison except her slight response to his sex appeal) tend to belong with one another in the moral atmosphere of Fielding's novels.

There may seem something a little sentimental and unquestioning about this when baldly described, but Fielding's sexual ethic, as several critics have shown, is in fact a very elaborately articulated thing, intelligently and seriously thought out as well as held with passionate moral conviction. For the moment we should note how in the little vignette about Atkinson, as at many points in Tom's career, sheer worth conquers class inhibitions and class prejudice. Later in *Amelia*,[18] Atkinson is the subject of a conversation between Mrs Bennet (one of the ladies present in the earlier scene, and about to admit her secret marriage to him) and Amelia. Amelia says the sergeant has virtues especially rare 'in persons of his rank', to which Mrs Bennet vehemently insists that 'the lower order of mankind' are the equals of the higher. Mrs Bennet is an interested party, and something of a pedant by temperament, so Fielding mocks her dogmatism a little. But he accepts the valuation of Atkinson, and Amelia proceeds warmly to agree with the lady. Fielding even allows Mrs Bennet to express some very plausible doubts as to the power of a 'genteel education' to improve anybody's head or heart.

Fielding's own views on this question were by no means simple. He had moods in which he could readily endorse Mrs Bennet's scepticism, just as he would agree with her that there can be found 'instances of as great goodness, and as great understanding too, among the lower sort of people as among the higher'. But his mildly superior kindliness towards her is a condescension which prevents her from being taken with unqualified seriousness. It suggests something of the ambiguity, and of the many oscillations of emphasis, which run through Fielding's attitudes on questions of rank, social grace, and the like. Whatever the emphasis at any moment, the mood is almost never simple. For this reason, it is impossible to speak of inconsistency. But it is also dangerous to reduce Fielding's social outlook to a system, however complex, which is rationally coherent in all its parts. Nevertheless, it is worth surveying a number of aspects of the matter, and even rationalizing in places. This is not because the matter can or should be seen as a neat rational whole, but because some of the complexity needs to be made clear, or at least indicated for what it is. A proper attention to the implications of Fielding's style or tone of voice at any moment, and to its fluctuations, is unlikely to reveal a system of impregnable philosophical coherence. But it may suggest a broader coherence of moral sensibility, though one should perhaps be content if it made possible a fuller or more exact understanding of individual passages or works.

No 'genteel education' was complete without a dancing-master, and Atkinson's chief trouble, in the passage from *Amelia*, is that 'he had never learnt to dance'. The passage typically contains an implied deflation of 'those great polishers of our manners',[19] who are often the target of similar urbane mockery throughout Fielding's works. At the same time, Fielding genuinely means that Atkinson would have been better off for some dancing lessons.

Though I do not entirely agree with the late learned Mr. Essex, the celebrated dancing-master's opinion, that dancing is the rudiment of polite education, as he would, I apprehend, exclude every other art and science, yet it is certain that persons whose feet have never been under the hands of the professors of that art are apt to discover this want in their education in every motion, nay, even when they stand or sit still. They seem, indeed, to be overburthened with limbs which they know not how to use, as if, when Nature hath finished her work, the dancing-master still is necessary to put it in motion.

John Essex, who also gets a friendly if slightly patronising compliment in *Tom Jones*,[20] had actually said:[21]

altho' other Arts and Sciences have their peculiar Use in Life, and are valuable in Education; yet few, if any, are so Necessary and Advantageous as this, especially under a good Master ... So much therefore of Dancing as belongs to the Behaviour, and handsome Deportment of the Body, is not only useful, but absolutely necessary.

This may sound like mere professional inflation. Or one might, remembering Monsieur Jourdain, suppose it to be exclusively for the consumption of his descendants, tradesmen with social aspirations anxious to learn a few graces. But compare two further passages, of 1748 and 1751, almost exactly contemporary with *Tom Jones* and *Amelia*: 'But the greatest advantage of dancing well is, that it necessarily teaches you to present yourself, to sit, stand, and walk genteely; all which are of real importance to a man of fashion', and 'I have known very many genteel people who could not dance well; but I never knew anybody dance very well who was not genteel in other things.'[22] The speaker this time is neither a professor of dancing nor a social-climbing cit, but the arbiter of aristocratic manners, Lord Chesterfield himself. The unrelieved insistence with which Chesterfield nagged his son about his dancing lessons is one of the dispiriting experiences of reading the *Letters* in bulk, but its message is practical and usually unhighfalutin, and it is exactly the same as Fielding's. Johnson's famous comment on Chesterfield, that he taught 'the morals of a whore, and the manners of a dancing master', is partly an attempt (a familiar thing in the great Augustan writers, especially frequent perhaps in Pope) to outdo the nobles in patrician hauteur. As such (for the main sting is of course moral) it seems to miss the mark. Chesterfield may have partly deserved it, to the extent that the sheer detailed repetition lacks the element of *sprezzatura*. But the letters were, after all, private, and their recipient seems (forgivably enough) to have needed such things drumming in. In strict fact, dancing lessons were both a normal and a severely practical part of a 'genteel education'. Its ends were kept well in view, and they specifically excluded dancing like a dancing-master. Neither the professional expertise, nor the elaborate foppishness, would do for a gentleman. 'They say that Dancing Masters never make a handsome Bow, because they take too much Pains', reports the anonymous author of an *Essay on Wit* (1748).[23] Chesterfield said that 'whatever is worth doing at all, is worth doing well . . . down to the lowest things, even to dancing and dress.' He meant that neither should seem 'too negligent or too much studied': 'Custom has made dancing sometimes necessary for a young man; therefore mind it while you learn it, that you may learn to do it well, and not be ridiculous, though in a ridiculous act.'[24] These words restore a perspective. Dancing is important, as the world goes. But the one thing Chesterfield does not after all do is take it as seriously as Mr Essex. The attitude is practical, and detached, like Fielding's, though without Fielding's humour. For Fielding, the gap in Atkinson's education is real. The 'artificial' props of good-breeding help to make things easy all round. Tom Jones can sometimes get away without them. When his 'natural, but not artificial good breeding' leads him to give his address to Mrs Fitzpatrick instead of a servant, one feels a breath of fresh air sweeping over the rather fetid scene.[25] But the act remains a solecism, and, as we have already seen, what is good for Tom is not always good for Atkinson. Fielding knew very well the sterling worth of both men and was very clear that true good-breeding was not something a dancing-master could teach: Socrates, he says, was 'a well-bred man' although 'very little instructed' by pedagogues of this order.[26] But dancing-masters and their like retain their (strictly practical) uses. Both Fielding and Chesterfield readily tend, on these matters, to seesaw from essentials to technicalities, especially in their more informal thinking. But there is no evidence that they often mistook the one for the other.

The seesawing comes particularly easily because good-breeding is normally defined as the art of pleasing, of making people comfortable, avoiding embarrassment and offence, and so on. It is probably true, however, that Fielding's eyes are more firmly fixed on the essentials, while Chesterfield's are more on the technicalities. Allowance must be made for the fact that Chesterfield was frankly trying to teach the social graces to his son, and training him up for a diplomatic career, while

Fielding was expressing his whole sensibility at high creative pressure. But the fact is that Chesterfield exhibits a degree of concern with 'appearing to advantage', not appearing ridiculous, 'making a figure' (though not *cutting* a figure, that phrase 'being the very lowest vulgarism in the English language'),[27] which seems unthinkable in Fielding. There is visible relief all around when Fielding's Atkinson conquers his awkwardness and gains 'sufficient confidence to tell the company some entertaining stories of accidents that had happened in the army within his knowledge'. One suspects that for Chesterfield Atkinson could never have won through, and telling stories in company is in any case vulgar.[28] Fielding, half out of tenderness to his reader, omits to repeat the stories, 'which, though they greatly pleased all present, are not, however, of consequence enough to have a place in this history'. But the momentary effect in the novel is one of warmth and release. By comparison, Chesterfield's prescriptive obsessions with ease and freedom of manner come to seem constricting and inhibited. Chesterfield knows and frequently says that morals are more important than manners, but 'awkwardness and ill breeding' offend him so much that 'I cannot find in my heart to inquire into the intrinsic merit of that person'. Like Fielding and other courtesy-writers, Chesterfield knows that the function of good-breeding is to create well-being and avoid giving pain, but unlike Fielding he habitually stresses the personal advantage that one gains by it. Fielding's emphasis is entirely the opposite. He is always emphatic about the intimate connection between good-breeding and good-nature, good-nature being 'the very habit of mind most essential to furnish us with true good-breeding'.[29] His tendency is not merely to relate the two, but even to fuse them into one another. '*Good-breeding* then, or the *Art of pleasing in Conversation*, . . . may be reduced to that concise, comprehensive rule in Scripture: *Do unto all men as you would they should do unto you.*'[30] These words from the early *Essay on Conversation* are repeated in a pair of late essays in the *Covent-Garden Journal*: 'I have not room at present, if I were able, to enumerate all the Rules of good Breeding: I shall only mention one, which is a Summary of them all. This is the most golden of all Rules, no less than that *of doing to all Men as you would they should do unto you.*' In the next essay, Fielding remembers that he is after all talking here about manners rather than morals, so that 'on the present Occasion' a more low-pitched formulation is called for.[31]

Chesterfield, as it happens, often invoked the same Golden Rule, which seems to have been a commonplace in courtesy-literature.[32] But there is seldom any need, in the letters to his son, for the language to drop, because it is unlikely to rise in the first place. The emphasis is cool, practical, basically a matter of self-interested policy: 'Observe carefully what pleases you in others, and probably the same things in you will please others.'[33] Chesterfield's later letters, to his godson, give the Golden Rule a more attractive, softer, at times even a moral rather than tactical, emphasis.[34] These later letters are in general warmer, less hidebound, more vital. Chesterfield had perhaps mellowed, and, in old age, loved the small boy without the slightly chilling discomfort he perhaps felt at the illegitimacy of his own son. Certainly the illegitimacy caused repeated embarrassments and obstructed the son's career. Some of the tactical emphasis in the earlier set of letters may, as Bonamy Dobrée suggests, be due to this.[35] There is no unpleasant cant about illegitimacy in Chesterfield himself, any more than in Fielding, but also none of the fervour (however unfussy) with which *Tom Jones* is suffused: no doubt the differences between fiction and real life apply here particularly. And in general it remains true that the greatest part of Fielding's moral vision comes to us in the novels, where his whole being expresses itself in the fullness of imaginative creation, untrammelled by immediate practicalities, while Chesterfield is giving technical advice. But the last few quotations from Fielding come precisely from essays on good-breeding, concerned with roughly the same kind of technical instruction as Chesterfield's letters. Even here, Fielding is warmer, and naturally gets carried away into making high moral claims, so that on reflection he must pull himself down.

Chesterfield, on the other hand, seems frequently to feel the need to pull himself up. Voluminous instructions on the graces are punctuated by perfunctory reminders of the greater importance of the moral aspect ('I say nothing to you now as to honour, virtue, truth, and all moral duties, which are to be strictly observed at all ages and all times; because I am sure you are convinced of the indispensable necessity of practising them all').[36] Alternatively, some letters actually begin with a bluff, get-it-over-with disposal of 'important' things like 'religion and morality', before getting back to the real business.[37] Much of this has the dullness of the merely apologetic. Despite statements which assert the moral basis of manners (that 'humanity is the particular *characteristic* of a great mind', that considerateness and affability are parts of good-breeding, that it is bad-hearted to be impolite to one's inferiors),[38] Chesterfield seldom seems fired by the connection; and there are times when he will say that 'The solid and the ornamental united are undoubtedly best; but were I reduced to make an option, I should, without hesitation, choose the latter.'[39]

Except for some of the letters to his godson, which Johnson did not see,[40] that part of Johnson's charge which suggests that Chesterfield is more concerned with manners than with morals does largely stick. This is true in more than the obvious literal sense, that Chesterfield mainly *intended* to teach his son manners, which is a fair thing to want to do. The enormous insistence on manners goes, in Chesterfield, with a fairly low sense of their function. It is not that manners are rated higher than morals (except in a limited context of avowed expediency), but that they become an obsession and sometimes seem to exist in a self-enclosed world of stultifying reiteration. They appear, as it were, in a kind of moral void, effectively separated from the sort of role or function which might give all the insistence some show of self-respect, and which Fielding can indicate without the insistence. That *humanitas* to which Chesterfield paid lip service (as a word in which 'civility' becomes 'inseparable from humanity')[41] is seldom, in these letters, a very active force.

The measure of Fielding's difference from Chesterfield may properly be gauged from their treatment of two further topics. One fairly frequent piece of advice which Chesterfield was inclined to give, and which has become a bit notorious, was this: 'Address yourself to some woman of fashion and beauty, wherever you are, and try how far that will go. If the place be not secured beforehand and garrisoned, nine times in ten you will take it. By attentions and respect you may always get into the highest company.'[42] This is one of a whole series of statements about the civilizing properties of women of fashion, the entry they can offer into the best company, the importance to best companies of 'Women of fashion and character (I do not mean absolutely unblemished)',[43] the desirability of avoiding low debaucheries as distinct from the polite kind ('*l'honnête débauche*'), [44] and the undesirability of a young man being 'old' before his time. Most of this is cool, worldly, and unfussy, though occasionally stirred by a mildly voyeuristic note. It is nothing for us to get very worried about, though much more frequent than Chesterfield's defenders say;[45] and it is what Johnson meant when he said that Chesterfield taught 'the morals of a whore'. I do not think Fielding would have been troubled in Johnson's way because, though he had a due regard for chastity, it stopped well short of uncompromising rigour. Both he and Chesterfield clearly share a readiness, which may or may not be 'aristocratic', to overlook or even accept a certain amount of sexual misbehaviour. There is a remarkable passage in *Tom Jones* in which Fielding suggests that there may even not be enough sexual misbehaviour among persons of condition:

There is not indeed a greater error than that which universally prevails among the vulgar, who borrowing their opinion from some ignorant satyrists, have affixed the character of lewdness to these times. On the contrary, I am convinced there never was less of love intrigue carried on among persons of condition, than now. Our present women have been taught by their mothers to fix their thoughts only on ambition and vanity, and to despise the pleasures of love as unworthy their regard; and being afterwards, by the care of such mothers, married without having husbands, they seem pretty well confirmed in the justness of those sentiments; whence they content themselves, for the dull remainder of life, with the pursuit of more innocent, but I am afraid more childish amusements, the bare mention of which would ill suit with the dignity of this history. In my humble opinion, the true characteristick of the present *Beau Monde*, is rather folly than vice, and the only epithet which it deserves is that of *frivolous* (*T. J.*, XIV, i).

It is unnecessary to disentangle all the coils of the irony in order to feel the strength with which Fielding is saying that 'lewdness' is better than no love at all. The passage is backed by the whole moral atmosphere of *Tom Jones* in its feeling that sexual love, even in the case of some passing and occasionally some really disreputable amours, is to be valued to the extent that it carries warmth and mutuality of feeling: but one hardly requires the rest of the novel to sense the gist of the message. Chesterfield's passage, and others like it, would be unlikely to offend Fielding. But they lack any element of the humanity (the sense of the point of it all) with which the whole subject is suffused in Fielding, and what comes through most is their shallowness.

The second example is one in which Chesterfield advises his son to cultivate 'a frank, open, and ingenuous exterior':[46]

The height of abilities is, to have *volto sciolto* and *pensieri stretti*; that is, a frank, open, and ingenuous exterior, with a prudent and reserved interior; to be upon your own guard, and yet, by a seeming natural openness, to put people off theirs. Depend upon it, nine in ten of every company you are in will avail themselves of every indiscreet and unguarded expression of yours, if they can turn it to their own advantage. A prudent reserve is therefore necessary as a seeming openness is prudent.

How far this is from the 'glaring' unselfconsciousness of Parson Adams or the undesigning honesty of Tom Jones need not be insisted on. But one may compare it with some passages in Fielding's *Essay on the Knowledge of the Characters of Men*: 'that open disposition, which is the surest indication of an honest and upright heart, chiefly renders us liable to be imposed on by craft and deceit, and principally disqualifies us for this discovery'.[47] And again, after discussing falsely smiling countenances which do not indicate goodness, Fielding continues:[48]

> But I would not be understood here to speak with the least regard to that amiable, open, composed, cheerful aspect, which is the result of a good conscience, and the emanation of a good heart; of both which, it is an infallible symptom; and may be the more depended on, as it cannot, I believe, be counterfeited, with any reasonable resemblance, by the nicest power of art. . . .
> The truth is, nature doth really imprint sufficient marks in the countenance, to inform an accurate and discerning eye; but, as such is the property of few, the generality of mankind mistake the affectation for the reality.

Fielding is concerned to warn innocent, undesigning people against imposition, since they are its likeliest victims. This is a recurrent theme in his work. But there is no reservation in his warm respect for the sincere and honest 'open disposition'. He is warning against the snares of wicked men, not against 'losing the advantage' (as Chesterfield puts it in the next sentence of his letter) in a social confrontation.[49] When Fielding adds that 'a more subtle hypocrisy will sometimes escape undiscovered from the highest discernment', it is not too much to say that he is partly warning against the kind of prudent 'seeming openness' that Chesterfield recommends.[50]

Fielding, unlike Johnson, did not see Chesterfield's letters, for they were not published, and many had not been written, in his lifetime. He praised Chesterfield's good-nature in his poem 'Of Good-Nature',[51] and his self-effacing affability and his liveliness in the *Essay on Conversation*.[52] These references have the air of routine compliments to a patron or potential patron, though there is no reason to suppose that Fielding did not think they were true, or that they *were* not, in a way, true. There is no doubt, as we have seen and shall see further, that he shared many of the assumptions and attitudes that are revealed in Chesterfield's *Letters*, including, when all is said, an occasional recoil from 'awkwardness'[53] and plenty of patrician superiority. But the writings of both men suggest that, for all that, they lived in very different moral worlds. It is at least true to say that in those very considerable areas of feeling where they seem logically in agreement, the difference in the quality of the feeling is radical. If the codes and even the underlying assumptions are often the same, the cumulative effect of Chesterfield's *Letters* is to suggest that the code was, for him, something of a mental prison. There is a cool rootedness in the writing which one seldom finds in Fielding: the qualifications which sometimes invite a larger view or remind us that morals are more important than manners are not insincere, but they sound like not much more than routine good sense, and they occur much less often than the opposite emphasis. For Fielding, not only is the moral basis of manners always kept in close view, but there is often a note of disturbed oscillation, of passionate self-doubt, in the mental debate he conducted with himself on these matters throughout the entire period of his mature writings. If there was a prison for him, he was a strenuously recalcitrant inmate. The liberations, the explosions away from the constrictions of the 'polite' code, as in the glowing endorsement of Parson Adams, are many and triumphant. So are the places where the aristocratic voice, instead of closing in on itself, opens out into the largest-hearted benevolence.

Fielding must not, however, be over-sentimentalized at Chesterfield's expense. There are moments (not in every way attractive to a twentieth-century sensibility) when, in the works of both men, the concern with manners and refinement assumes an importance and urgency which transcend not only a mere pleasure in 'the graces', but also the simpler moral rationalizations of the code of manners. One such moment occurs in an essay on good-breeding which Chesterfield wrote, not as a private letter, but for publication in Edward Moore's periodical, *The World*:[54]

> Courts are unquestionably the seats of GOOD-BREEDING; and must necessarily be so; otherwise they would be the seats of violence and desolation. There all the passions are in their highest state of fermentation. All pursue what but few can obtain, and many seek what but one can enjoy. GOOD-BREEDING alone restrains their excesses. There, if enemies did not embrace, they would stab. There, smiles are often put on, to conceal tears. There, mutual services are professed, while mutual injuries are intended; and there, the guile of the serpent simulates the gentleness of the dove.

There is a curt intensity about this, a proud and fierce insecurity, as of a whole civilization under siege from its own destructive energies. Such urgencies are rare in Chesterfield, and even this one is allowed to peter out in the smug patness of the words which immediately follow: '. . . all this, it is true, at the expence of sincerity; but, upon the whole, to the advantage of social intercourse in general.' This sentiment follows logically from the rest, though the ease of the transition in the tone of voice seems demeaning. Still, the earlier portion offers a glimpse, not easily cancelled, of a strength of feeling that is neither frivolous nor glib, and whose object is powerfully realized. The passage may be compared with one from Fielding, whose prose sense is likely for once to offend a modern reader more than that of Chesterfield's. Fielding is describing the scene of his boarding the boat which is to take him on his fatal voyage to Lisbon. He is crippled with disease and his infirmities have been the object of heartless jeers from the sailors and watermen:[55]

> I think, upon my entrance into the boat, I presented a spectacle of
> the highest horror. The total loss of limbs was apparent to all who
> saw me, and my face contained marks of a most diseased state, if
> not of death itself. Indeed so ghastly was my countenance, that
> timorous women with child had abstained from my house, for
> fear of the ill consequences of looking at me. In this condition, I
> ran the gauntlope, (so, I think, I may justly call it) through rows of
> sailors and watermen, few of whom failed of paying their
> compliments to me, by all manner of insults and jests on my
> misery. No man who knew me will think I conceived any
> personal resentment at this behaviour; but it was a lively picture
> of that cruelty and inhumanity, in the nature of men, which I
> have often contemplated with concern; and which leads the mind
> into a train of very uncomfortable and melancholy thoughts. It
> may be said, that this barbarous custom is peculiar to the English,
> and of them only to the lowest degree; that it is an excrescence of
> an uncontroul'd licentiousness mistaken for liberty, and never
> shews itself in men who are polish'd and refin'd, in such manner
> as human nature requires, to produce that perfection of which it is
> susceptible, and to purge away that malevolence of disposition, of
> which, at our birth we partake in common with the savage
> creation (26 June, 1754).

If Chesterfield's passage irons itself out in self-satisfaction, he is not after all writing from the depths of an excruciating experience. Fielding's passage has all the power that comes from an understandable pained fury, but it is only fair to point out that *his* anguished eloquence is also followed by a kind of collapse, though in the opposite direction of a momentary, petulant near-hysteria:

18

This may be said, and this is all that can be said; and it is, I am afraid, but little satisfactory to account for the inhumanity of those, who, while they boast of being made after God's own image, seem to bear in their minds a resemblance of the vilest species of brutes; or rather, indeed, of our idea of devils: for I don't know that any brutes can be taxed with such malevolence.

What has disappeared here is the confident rising sweep of the rhetoric, the firm though angry control of argument and rhythm, the eloquent awareness of saving possibilities, that distinguishes the immediately preceding passage. It is as if the earlier effort proved exhausting, and the guard dropped for the helpless phrases ('this is all that can be said') and the weak second-thought intensives ('or rather, indeed, of our idea of devils') to take over.

But in both *main* passages, the minds of Chesterfield and Fielding are on the extreme situation, the point at which good-breeding does not merely make things pleasant, but is the quality without which man is reduced to brutalism. It is at moments like this that one senses the truly desperate importance, to some of the most representative Augustan writers, of that whole 'polite' civilization which is at other times taken for granted with such confidence and ease. This is no simple matter of 'the gloom of the Tory satirists',[56] resisting a boorish modernism of dunces and virtuosos, though both Fielding and Chesterfield were in fact of the class of Whigs who agreed with Pope and Swift on some specific cultural issues. But here (as often for Pope and Swift) the threat is still more fundamental, for the enemy is within, and ever present. This is a lesson that might have been learned from Hobbes, or La Rochefoucauld (whom Chesterfield particularly admired), or any number of lesser sources. Ideas of the natural depravity of man were certainly in wide circulation and could readily enter into certain moods or states of mind in writers who (like Fielding) mainly disliked Hobbes, or who did not think about such things at all in a systematic way. It is misleading and oversimple to account for these passages in terms of beliefs in particular philosophical ideas. Their force, their whole atmosphere, is that of anguished constatations, momentary starknesses in which the writers sensed with particular vividness the precariousness, as well as the immense importance to them, of the forms of Augustan culture. Whatever their philosophical beliefs, Fielding and Chesterfield had many other moods, as well as often speaking of similar things with other and less disturbing emphases. Perhaps the only great writer of the century whose style is fairly consistently charged (even in its gayer moments) with a note of anguished yet passionately committed loyalty to cherished values under threat is Swift. Of the three, Swift is certainly the only one who is ever inclined to sustain a note of desperation for any length; and the strange collapses which follow both Fielding's and Chesterfield's passages suggest that both men were temperamentally ill-adapted to living with their starkest thoughts. That Chesterfield's passage collapses into smugness and Fielding's into a flustered over-intensity may be a measure of the difference between them. Fielding's prose sense may be less attractive, but the somewhat unbalanced anger might imply how much he really cared. Too much should not be made of this, for the contexts are really very different. Nor should the analogy with Swiftian anguish be pressed too far. Not only are these passages notably unsustained, but they still assert, in their best moments of stark constatation, a degree of confidence in the staying power of the system, which is often absent in Swift. 'Politeness' may have some terrifying savagery to contend with, but Chesterfield's passage shows it as actually, and Fielding's as potentially, in control: we are a long way from Swift's *Digression on Madness*.

In one of his essays on good-breeding, Swift warned, as Chesterfield, Fielding, and other courtesy-writers often warned, against that pedantry in manners which consists of excesses of ceremony:[57]

> There is a pedantry in manners, as in all arts and sciences; and sometimes in trades. Pedantry is properly the overrating any kind of knowledge we pretend to. And if that kind of knowledge be a trifle in itself, the pedantry is the greater. For which reason, I look upon fidlers, dancing-masters, heralds, masters of the ceremony, &c. to be greater pedants, than LIPSIUS, or the elder SCALIGER.

Swift continues with brilliant description of those to whom good-manners are a trade, from gentleman-usher to gentleman-porter (and taking in, presumably, gentleman dancing-master):

> With these kind of pedants, the court, while I knew it, was always plentifully stocked: I mean from the gentleman-usher (at least) inclusive, downward to the gentleman-porter: who are generally speaking, the most insignificant race of people, that this island can afford, and with the smallest tincture of good-manners; which is the only trade they profess. For being wholly illiterate, and conversing chiefly with each other, they reduce the whole system of breeding within the forms and circles of their several offices: and as they are below the notice of ministers, they live and die in

court under all revolutions, with great obsequiousness to those who are in any degree of favour or credit: and with rudeness or insolence to every body else. From whence I have long concluded, that good-manners are not a plant of the court growth.

In this passage, 'the whole system of breeding' becomes disembodied, an end in itself, detached from its humane function. Fielding would have understood it well, but it is characteristic of the difference between the two writers that Swift's intensest energies are trained on the negative side of the issue. For Fielding, but not often for Swift, a positive union of good-nature and good-breeding was something that could be imagined, with power and conviction, as actively possible. This is true even at times when, as in the passage about sailors in the *Voyage to Lisbon*, he feels most anguished and bitter. As to Chesterfield's parallel Hobbesian vision, its complacent opening statement that 'Courts are unquestionably the seats of GOOD-BREEDING' is (however qualified by what follows) vividly shown up by Swift's: 'From whence I have long concluded, that good-manners are not a plant of the court growth: ...' There is no need to labour the point that Swift is a greater writer than Chesterfield, and probably than Fielding; or that his vision is more uncompromisingly disturbing. Fielding, lacking Chesterfield's smugness,[58] also lacked the full depth of Swift's bitter understanding. But he did share Swift's ever vivid sense of the full *humane* function of manners. That he found it possible to be, with conviction and without smugness, more hopeful than Swift, was a great moral strength. It did not exclude his having, like Swift though less fiercely, a hurt insight, actively felt, into the negative side, those yawning disconnections between manners and their *raison d'être*, which Chesterfield only criticized in principle, and when not actually guilty of them himself.

Though Fielding has many moods which differ radically from the *Voyage to Lisbon* extract, and though the particular intensity of that extract is itself unusual, the sentiment which it expresses occurs often enough. It is in this sense that I mean Fielding should not be over-sentimentalized. He not only frequently notes the natural malignity of man, but usually charges his reflections on this topic with what would seem, to a present-day sensibility, an offensive class-consciousness. A reference to 'that Malignity which is the rankest and most poisonous Weed that disgraces human Nature', in a *Covent-Garden Journal* essay not in itself concerned with distinctions of rank but with malicious slander in general, is immediately followed by an explanation that 'This is that *malignant Temper* which Horace attributes to the Vulgar, when he says *he despises them*'.[59] It would also be wrong to suppose that such sentiments belong only to the later, more embittered, phase of Fielding's life. Mr Wilson speaks in much the same way in *Joseph Andrews*, though the particular objects of his wrath in this case are 'the lower class of the gentry, and the higher of the mercantile world':

> there is a malignity in the nature of man, which, when not
> weeded out, or at least covered by a good education and politeness,
> delights in making another uneasy or dissatisfied with himself.
> This abundantly appears in all assemblies, except those which are
> filled by people of fashion, and especially among the younger
> people of both sexes whose birth and fortunes place them just
> without the polite circles; I mean the lower class of the gentry,
> and the higher of the mercantile world, who are, in reality, the
> worst-bred part of mankind (*J.A.*, III, iii).

Mr Wilson has just been describing his bitter experience of the way 'men of business' treat poets, and his particular comment here is related perhaps to that special form of patrician hauteur which values the noble and the beggarman, and scorns fumblers in the greasy till.[60] The example of Yeats makes one feel that this is a special hauteur of poets who cherish an aristocratic ethos while only half-belonging to a real aristocratic world. Allowing for all manner of biographical differences, Fielding was in some ways a parallel case, and Mr Wilson in his scrivener's garret evokes something of Fielding's uneasy and hurt pride at being a poor relation to noble families and engaged in the vulgar trade of authorship. Garrets were more acceptable in Yeats's day than Fielding's, and the professional poet's calling needed less defensiveness.[61] On the other hand, though Yeats moved easily in some great houses, he was not, like Fielding, related to an earl.[62] The emotional need of both men to find an aristocratic voice that expressed some of their strongest aspirations was complicated in each case by very different factors: but something of the same grandiose, ambiguous edginess was the result. Chesterfield speaks like a grandee, coolly and without fuss, but also without the glow that one finds in the hauteurs of Pope or Fielding or Yeats: the proud conversational sweep of Pope's verse has more in common with Yeats than Yeats would have cared to admit.[63] Many eighteenth-century writers felt a special need to identify themselves with an aristocratic ethos, because there was still (especially in the first half of the century) a strong sense in which the canons of taste were appreciably bound up with the values of a literate and politically powerful nobility. Yeats lived in an age when noble houses no longer dominated the cultural scene, and his hankerings after the great age of Swift and Burke are partly an index of the affinity I am suggesting.[64]

Yeats's figure of the beggarman involves a mystique which Fielding would not have understood. He would not consciously have understood, as Yeats claimed Swift and some others understood ('whether they knew [it] or not'), 'that wisdom comes of beggary'.[65] He often regarded beggars as a social nuisance, as for that matter did Swift, and his thinking on such questions was usually low-pitched and literal-minded. There are many accounts of the depravity of the very poor, but where he tended to celebrate them he would speak in a familiar sentimental way about the 'plainness, honesty, and sincerity'[66] in which they excel the politer classes. It is all very well meant, though no doubt may be thought patronizing: I am not sure that there would be much to choose between Fielding and Yeats in that respect. But the fact is that Fielding seldom permits himself to heighten the issue with the Yeatsian rhetoric of beggar and prince. On rare occasions when such terms are used, the argument remains fixed at the normal sentimental-mundane level.[67] Thus Booth (for Fielding himself might be charier of such high language, though he approves the sentiments) says to Miss Matthews:

> Love, benevolence, or what you will please to call it, may be the reigning passion in a beggar as well as in a prince; and wherever it is, its energies will be the same.
> To confess the truth, I am afraid we often compliment what we call upper life, with too much injustice, at the expense of the lower. As it is no rare thing to see instances which degrade human nature in persons of the highest birth and education, so I apprehend that examples of whatever is really great and good have been sometimes found amongst those who have wanted all such advantages. In reality, palaces, I make no doubt, do sometimes contain nothing but dreariness and darkness, and the sun of righteousness hath shone forth with all its glory in a cottage (*Amelia*, III, vii).

This is mildly undercut by Fielding's mockery of Booth's doctrines about reigning passions. But it unquestionably expresses a powerful and sincere element in Fielding's outlook, and may be set alongside the passages from the *Voyage to Lisbon* and the rest to restore a balance. It is unfruitful to describe this as inconsistency, for we are not dealing with a philosophical system but with the intellectual and emotional oscillations of a many-sided man. Chesterfield may have had oscillations too, but his characteristic thoughts about courts and cottages are contained in

the testy admission that courts may contain 'falsehood and dissimulation
. . . but where are they not to be found? Cottages have them as well as
courts, only with worse manners.'[68]

Fielding's angers, in the passage about the sailors and in Mr Wilson's
speech, never lose sight of the assumption that the whole point of good-
breeding is to promote happiness and avoid distress. The correlation
between good-breeding and good-nature is one of the really unflinching
and ineradicable elements in Fielding's entire moral outlook. When Mr
Wilson speaks of certain classes of people as 'the worst-bred part of
mankind', there is no disguising the purely snobbish dimension; but the
remark is made in the immediate context of unkind and inconsiderate
acts. The comment on the sailors says literally, though at an extreme of
pained exacerbation, that lack of good-breeding leaves malice free play,
and the incident equally literally exemplifies it. If, as I said, passages like
this, and like Chesterfield's Hobbesian vision of the natural viciousness
which lies beneath the courtly forms, transcend the simple moral
rationalization of manners, it is only because of their starkness of
realization. The moral rationale is not in either case dismissed or
played down, but on the contrary clung to with an added urgency.
Both men strongly believed in the moral value of what Yeats called the
'household courtesy and decency'[69] of the gentlemanly way of life. But
Chesterfield tends to think of manners cynically as an external check,
whereas Fielding liked to think of them as in some ways an internal
growth (though taught by codified rules and even by dancing-
masters).[70] This means that he sometimes seeks to blur (in a deliberate
and positive sense) the distinction between morals and manners, so that
his language can slide into saying, as in the *Essay on Conversation*, that
the clumsiest and lowest-born persons may have true good-breeding
provided they are good-natured. Chesterfield will say instead that 'A
ploughman will be civil, if he is good-natured, but cannot be well-bred.
A courtier will be well-bred, though perhaps without good-nature, if
he has but good-sense.' The differences may in part be merely termino-
logical, but Fielding is unlikely ever to talk quite like this. Later in the
same essay (which is the one in which the Hobbesian piece occurs)
Chesterfield argues himself into saying that good-breeding is the only
lovable quality, which in strict logic means that 'a ploughman' cannot
be 'beloved'. Chesterfield presumably did not believe this crudely and
absolutely, but the logical trap is a small sign of the way his system was
a kind of mental prison.[71] On the rare occasions when he allows
himself some Fielding-like remarks about 'a natural good-breeding'
that goes with good-nature and is 'practised by a good-natured

American savage as essentially as by the best-bred European', he is so anxious to make qualifications and to pass on to the kind of good-breeding that really interests him, that such concessions may for practical purposes be ignored in the present argument.[72] Chesterfield readily speaks of good-breeding as *covering* faults, *supplying the want* of some virtues, *acting* good-nature.[73] Fielding can just about think in those terms, but his real claims are higher. Mr Wilson speaks of 'education and politeness' as things which *weed out, or at least cover* natural malignity.[74] It is as though Fielding would settle for the Chesterfieldian solution as second-best, but regards something deeper as not only desirable but possible. Similarly, the passage about the sailors speaks of 'purging away' an innate malevolence. When he speaks there of 'men who are polish'd and refin'd, in such a manner as human nature requires, to produce that perfection of which it is susceptible', the context makes clear that there is no glib optimism. But it is also clear that the ideal which is set up, and whose viability Fielding acknowledges even in this dark mood, assumes an inner growth through politeness to virtue, and not an outer veneer. A word like 'organic' in its Yeatsian sense would be foreign to Fielding's vocabulary (though its opposite, 'mechanical', was common to Chesterfield's), but he would, like Yeats, have felt that the connection between 'natural kindness', an education 'In courtesy . . . chiefly learned', and great houses 'Where all's accustomed, ceremonious', was a living and flowering thing. And it is not fanciful to say that the measure of his difference from Chesterfield is that, at his most exclusively patrician, he would have understood the spirit of Yeats's lines, 'How but in custom and in ceremony/Are innocence and beauty born?'[75]

It will be evident by now that Fielding's attitudes on matters of rank and virtue, morals and manners, good-nature and good-breeding, and the like, were hardly simple and clear-cut. The subject is pregnant with ambiguities, and these include confusions as well as fusions, violent oscillations of mood as well as smaller variations of emphasis, tones of voice at subtle variance with things said, and certainly some examples of what, in a logical system, would be inconsistencies and loose ends. The fact of ambiguity is not confined to Fielding, and seems present in many similar forms in many other writers of the period. Fielding's beliefs could be made to seem logically similar to Chesterfield's, including the reservations and illogicalities; they differ not in having complicated feelings but in the over-all character and atmosphere of these feelings. For this reason, because a whole atmosphere needs as far as

possible to be caught, it has been necessary to consider a large number
of examples. One of the most important themes, and one of the most
ambiguous, in Fielding's work, is snobbery itself, and we may, in
conclusion, glance at this. It is part of a larger question: again and again
in his writings, early and late, Fielding complains of that contemptuous
superiority between classes of men, of which a technical snobbery of
rank or status is only a part. Fielding devotes a large part of the *Essay
on Conversation* to a discussion of this vice in straightforward moral
terms, and with a comprehensive breadth of examples. At one climax
of the discussion, he says:[76]

> Lastly, the lowest and meanest of our species are the most strongly
> addicted to this vice. Men who are a scandal to their sex, and
> women who disgrace human nature; for the basest mechanic is so
> far from being exempt, that he is generally the most guilty of it.
> It visits alehouses and ginshops, and whistles in the empty heads
> of fiddlers, mountebanks, and dancing-masters.

This must be taken in the context of a much broader discussion, and,
even as a moment of particular intensity, needs to be balanced by such
another emotional climax (in the same essay) as this:[77]

> I have myself seen a little female thing which they have called My
> Lady, of no greater dignity in the order of beings than a cat, and
> of no more use in society than a butterfly; whose mien would not
> give even the idea of a gentlewoman, and whose face would cool
> the loosest libertine; with a mind as empty of ideas as an opera,
> and a body fuller of diseases than an hospital—I have seen this
> thing express contempt to a woman who was an honour to her
> sex, and an ornament to the creation.

The second passage makes clear that the first does not indicate any
simple snobbery from above on Fielding's part. Both passages, however,
preserve a characteristic patrician inflection, and one of the most biting
stings in the second is that My Lady's 'mien would not give even the
idea of a gentlewoman'. But just as here the concept of gentility slides
upwards from rank to virtue (or to some ideal fusion of virtue and
rank),[78] so in the first passage the meaning of 'lowest and meanest' slides
the other way from morals to rank. What begins as an indictment of
depraved men and women quickly attaches itself to base mechanics and
ends with fiddlers and dancing-masters. Into it goes not only the
tendency to identify vice with low rank which we have seen before, but
also the instinctive patrician scorn of the professionals. In this seesaw

between virtue and rank, mountebanks are perhaps the fulcrum, for they are frauds by occupation and enter logically into both kinds of thinking: but such considerations do not really enter, since the seesawing is instinctive and non-logical, or must be made to seem so (in this grandee mood one is superior to fine distinctions). Alongside this belong not only the doubts about My Lady's gentility, but also the serener transitions which surround a phrase like 'natural gentility' in the novels. That literal identifications of virtue and rank were insistently denied by Fielding, as by Chesterfield or any other rational person who thought about these things, only testifies to the strength of the opposite irrational feeling: why else would one want to assert the obvious? The feeling is perhaps atavistic, and is not in all its forms confined to nobles or would-be nobles. It clearly underlies certain old and recurrent patterns in the fictional arts. There is no mistaking its presence, or its specific uppish tang, in the tone and the content of the two Fielding statements we are now discussing, or the fact that it runs in a sense against the main message of his argument.

Though this argument asserts that we should not despise one another, it certainly does not mean that social gradations or distinctions of rank should be abolished. Fielding may tartly admit that possessors of titles are in no danger of forgetting the fact, or suggest that 'if men were to be rightly estimated' it would be 'according to the superior excellence of their several natures', but both statements occur within a paragraph of the outburst against My Lady. In the same place he reminds us that 'the most exact compliance' with gradations of rank is essential to good-breeding, as well as important in 'the policy of government'.[79] Rules of precedence should be interpreted tactfully and 'with as much seeming indifference as possible'[80] to avoid giving offence, and 'gentlemen' should 'be considered as equals', but only when they 'are not raised above each other by title, birth, rank in profession, age, or actual obligation'.[81] As to professions, however, not all were suitable for gentlemen, and there was something ungenteel about having one at all.

Being a gentleman meant having that 'liberality of spirit' which Fielding has 'scarce ever seen in men of low birth and education':[82] the professional was always to some extent a technician, his views limited by an element of demeaning specialism. The issue is complex, and largely beyond my present scope. But some professions were lower than others. 'Fiddlers . . . and dancing-masters' were obviously very low, mere trades really, but dancing-masters were a special and embarrassing case, because they were a necessary part of a 'genteel education'. Not only did one therefore see them a good deal, but they were professionals who taught gentlemen some of the marks of gentility. (Fiddlers were perhaps not quite in the same class: Chesterfield insisted that no gentleman should play musical instruments,[83] though all gentlemen must learn to dance.) The gentleman thus had a painful obligation to the dancing-master, and the dancing-master must have acquired pretensions of gentility which exacerbated the situation; the gentleman had to learn from a laboured specialist the graceful ease which was supposed to be his birth-right, and the dancing-master could feel that he did things better than his pupils. Hence part of the particular insistence that a gentleman should learn to dance well, yet not like a dancing-master,[84] and, more generally, the obsessional frequency with which writers of the period keep mentioning dancing-masters, often with edgily ambiguous or over-aggressive contempt. The title of Wycherley's *Gentleman Dancing-Master* must have derived much piquancy from this whole situation. In the plot itself, it only means that the hero disguises himself as a dancing-master in order to gain access to the heroine. What was thought of *real* dancing-masters in the play emerges in the first scene, when the heroine says that the Frenchified fop her father wants her to marry 'debases . . . civility and good breeding more than a city dancing-master'. Several decades later, however, the 'celebrated dancing-master John Essex', surveying the achievements of Mr Isaac, the dancing-master who had taught 'our late . . . Queen when a young Princess' and the rest of 'the first Quality', felt that Mr Isaac 'therefore might truly deserve to be called the Gentleman Dancing-Master'.[85] Wycherley's phrase was obviously a contradiction in terms, but gentlemen were, it seems, not permitted by their dancing-masters to be too absolutely sure of the fact. That Fielding (like some other writers) should lump them with fiddlers and mountebanks derives an added tang from this embarrassment of obligations and inflated claims. That dancing-masters did indeed make special claims for their status, above other caterers of gentility, comes out amusingly in an assertion of Fielding's that true good-breeding, not being 'confined to externals', cannot be 'furnished by a milliner, a tailor, or a periwig-maker; no, nor even by a dancing-master himself'.[86] But the obligations also remain real, and John Essex, who made some of the claims, is complimented with not altogether unfriendly irony on his expertise and the usefulness of his art in *Tom Jones*,[87] as well as in the passage from *Amelia* with which this chapter began. Fielding more than once laughed at the notion that 'those great polishers of our manners' taught 'what principally distinguishes us from the brute creation'.[88] But even here there is a piquancy in the fact that dancing-masters were, in their small way, an almost invariable part of that polite education which Fielding, in a most serious and urgent context, really did consider necessary in order to raise us above 'the savage creation'.[89] In this mincing, ambiguous figure, who nagged the imaginations of many men of letters and the lives of young or would-be gentlemen, the sublime and the ridiculous sometimes seem to meet, comically, uneasily. Fielding, Chesterfield, and many others, would agree that such a thought was absurd, but they knew that they half-believed in it too. Hence the readiness to see the dance as an emblem of moral and intellectual poise ('Do everything in minuet time, speak, think, and move always in that measure'), or, as for Pope, of literary excellence.[90] Subtle combinations of hauteur, humour, and loyalty towards dancing-masters contain, in small, much of the 'social outlook' of Augustan gentlemen. It is convenient to end this chapter, as it began, with dancing-masters, not least because the example helps us to see how gentlemen, like Fielding and Chesterfield, differ where they seem most to agree.

NOTES

1 This and the next two chapters are slightly revised versions of articles which appeared in *Eighteenth-Century Studies*, i (1967), 127–58; iii (1970), 307–38 and 491–522, under somewhat different titles.
2 *Amelia*, V, ii.
3 *J.A.*, I, viii.
4 Letter to his son [November 1749]. *The Letters of Philip Dormer Stanhope, 4th Earl of Chesterfield*, ed. Bonamy Dobrée (London, 1932), 6 vols, IV, 1439. Subsequent references to Chesterfield's letters are to this edition, and the recipient of each letter is assumed to be his son, unless otherwise noted.
5 *C.-G.J.*, No. 33, 25 April 1752, Jensen, I, 327.
6 *C.-G.J.*, No. 4, 14 January 1752, Jensen, I, 156.
7 Henry Mackenzie, *Man of Feeling* (1771), ch. XI.
8 *J.A.*, I, viii.
9 *T.J.*, XIII, ii.
10 *J.A.*, II, xii.
11 *T.J.*, IV, ii, *ad fin.*
12 *Works*, XIV, 277.
13 *T.J.*, XV, ii.
14 *T.J.*, IV, ii, *ad fin.*

15 Sir Walter Scott, *Lives of Eminent Novelists and Dramatists*, new edn, Chandos Classics (London, n.d.), p. 431; George Sherburn, 'Fielding's Social Outlook', *Philological Quarterly*, xxxv (1956), 8.

16 In the *Journey from this World to the Next*, I, vii, Minos refuses to admit into Elysium a man who 'had disinherited his son for getting a bastard' (*Works*, II, 241). *Tom Jones* was to be 'legitimated' in comic-opera in the 1760s: see F. T. Blanchard, *Fielding the Novelist* (New York, 1966), p. 174. For some of the jibes about Tom's illegitimacy among Fielding's contemporaries, see Blanchard, pp. 38, 41, 63, 68.

17 Preface to *The Princess Casamassima*, in *The Art of the Novel*, ed. R. P. Blackmur (New York, n.d.), p. 68.

18 *Amelia*, VII, x.

19 *T.J.*, IX, v.

20 *T.J.*, XIV, i.

21 John Essex, *The Young Ladies Conduct: or, Rules for Education* (1722), pp. 82–3.

22 Chesterfield, *Letters*, IV, 1234–5, 27 September 1748; and IV, 1748, 10 June 1751.

23 *An Essay on Wit: To which is annexed a Dissertation on Antient and Modern History* (1748), p. 17 (Augustan Reprint Society, Series I, No. 2, 1946). Cf. Chesterfield, *Letters*, III, 698, 19 November 1745: 'though I would not have you a dancer, yet, when you do dance, I would have you dance well, as I would have you do everything you do, well'.

24 *Letters*, III, 783, 9 October 1746.

25 *T.J.*, XIII, iv.

26 *Essay on Conversation*, *Works*, XIV, 248–9.

27 *Letters*, IV, 1414, 2 October 1749.

28 *Letters*, III, 1036, 16 October 1747, *et passim*.

29 *Essay on Conversation*, *Works*, XIV, 250.

30 *Ibid.*, p. 249.

31 *C.-G.J.*, Nos 55–6, 18 and 25 July 1752, Jensen II, 63–4.

32 See George C. Brauer, Jun., 'Good Breeding in the Eighteenth Century', *University of Texas Studies in English*, xxxii (1953), 37.

33 *Letters*, III, 1035, 16 October 1747; cf. IV, 1428, 3 November 1749; IV, 1762, 24 June 1751. See also S. Shellabarger, *Lord Chesterfield* (London, 1935), p. 347, for some pointed comments.

34 *Letters*, VI, 2409, 11 August 1762; VI, 2501, [1763]; VI, 2540, 26 September 1763; VI, 2636, 15 December 1764; VI, 2673, 31 October 1765 (all to his godson).

35 *Letters*, I, 208–9.

36 *Letters*, II, 479, 4 November 1741.

37 *Letters*, IV, 1251, 29 October 1748; IV, 1427–8, 3 November 1748; IV, 1481, 8 January 1750. The usual arguments given for not going into these things at length are that they are obvious, that the young man possesses

or understands about virtue anyway, and that, if not, he has a professional tutor to teach him. That these points may have been true does not invalidate the point about the curiously perfunctory and embarrassed nature of the reminders, or about the cumulative effect of the letters as we have them and as the son received them. Equally, Chesterfield's vaguely apologetic awareness of his own repetitiveness on a few shallow topics does not exorcize the dispiriting, lapidary fact.

38 *Letters*, II, 432, [1740]; II, 446, [1741]; II, 380, [1739].

39 *Letters*, IV, 1680, 11 February 1751. See also IV, 1700, 18 March 1751: 'Your sole business now is to shine, not to weigh. . . . You had better return a dropped fan genteely, than give a thousand pounds awkwardly; and you had better refuse a favour gracefully, than grant it clumsily. Manner is all in everything; it is by manner only that you can please, and consequently rise.' Chesterfield is here talking specifically about political advancement, and his admirers will no doubt be content to say that it is all just common sense.

40 A few letters to the godson were published in the *Edinburgh Magazine and Review* in 1774, but the first substantial collection is Lord Carnarvon's in 1890 (*Letters*, I, xvii–xviii).

41 *Letters*, II, 526, [1742].

42 *Letters*, V, 1845, 5 March 1752.

43 *Letters*, VI, 2688, 4 December 1765 (to his godson).

44 This phrase occurs in *Letters*, V, 2045, 3 October 1753.

45 See Dobrée, in *Letters*, I, 167: 'only eight times in some four hundred and thirty letters to his son'. I gave up counting after twenty, and the topic also occurs in letters to and about his godson, and to Lord Huntingdon.

46 *Letters*, IV, 1248, 19 October 1748.

47 *Works*, XIV, 283.

48 *Works*, XIV, 287-9.

49 Chesterfield's exact point here is that one should be careful to 'look people in the face' so as not 'to lose the advantage of observing by their countenances what impression your discourse makes upon them'.

50 Chesterfield of course stresses that he does not recommend outright knavery, and more than once makes the distinction between 'dissimulation', which is permissible, and 'simulation', which is not. Dobrée, *Letters*, I, 164 ff., surveys the question, offering a defence of Chesterfield which seems to me rather smug in its 'commonsensical' shallowness. The real objection, it seems to me, is not that Chesterfield recommends any diabolical villainy, but that he should be quite happy to say, for example, something like this (which may be compared with the last quotation from Fielding): 'A cheerful, easy countenance and behaviour, are very useful at Court; they make fools think you are a good-natured man; and they make designing men think you an undesigning one'. ('Maxims', enclosed in letter of 15 January 1753, *Letters*, V, 2002.)

51 *Works*, XII, 261; also XII, 257 ('Of True Greatness').

52 *Works*, XIV, 251, 276. For other compliments to, and political collaborations with, Chesterfield, see Cross and Dudden, *passim*.

53 See, for example, *C.-G.J.*, No. 56, 25 July 1752, Jensen II, 67, where he mocks the affected awkwardness of a country girl. There is, characteristically, a corresponding jibe at court affectation in the same sentence; and the sting is anyway at least as much against affectations of worldliness in the country gentlewoman, as against the awkwardness itself.

54 *The World*, No. 148, 30 October 1755, in *British Essayists*, ed. A. Chalmers (1817), XXVIII, 229–30. This is a rewording of a passage in *Letters*, IV, 1383, 21 August 1749.

55 *Voyage to Lisbon*, pp. 44–5.

56 The useful phrase is, of course, Louis Bredvold's, and I borrow it for convenience and without wishing to impute to him any views of mine he might not share. Bredvold's fine essay with this title occurs in *Pope and his Contemporaries: Essays Presented to George Sherburn*, ed. James L. Clifford and Louis A. Landa (Oxford, 1949), pp. 1–19.

57 Swift, *Works*, IV, 215–16. This essay, 'On Good-Manners and Good-Breeding', was published posthumously in 1754.

58 On courts, see especially Fielding's statement in the Preface to the *Miscellanies*, *Works*, XII, 243: 'Without considering Newgate as no other than human nature with its mask off, which some very shameless writers have done, a thought which no price should purchase me to entertain, I think we may be excused for suspecting, that the splendid palaces of the great are often no other than Newgate with the mask on.'

59 *C.-G.J.*, No. 14, 18 February 1752, Jensen I, 221.

60 Yeats, 'September 1913', *Collected Poems* (London, 1952), p. 120.

61 Compare Yeats's reminiscence, in the Epilogue to *Per Amica Silentia Lunae* (London, 1918), p. 93 ('everywhere in Paris and in London young men boasted of the garret, and claimed to have no need of what the crowd values') with the contemptible figure of the Augustan garreteer as he appears in *A Tale of a Tub* or the *Dunciad*. A whole chapter of literary and social history is contained in the difference.

62 On Yeats's 'ludicrous attempts to ally himself with the aristocracy' and his efforts to prove a noble lineage for himself, see Richard Ellmann, *Yeats, The Man and the Masks* (London, 1961), p. 180.

63 On Yeats's dislike of Pope, see Donald T. Torchiana, *W. B. Yeats and Georgian Ireland* (Evanston, 1966), pp. 20–1, 114.

64 The fullest study of this rich and complicated question is Torchiana's admirable book.

65 Yeats, 'The Seven Sages', *Collected Poems*, pp. 272–3.

66 *T.J.*, IX, i.

67 The level, for example, of Henry Brooke's *Fool of Quality* (1766–70),

2nd edn, II (1767), 152, where it is asserted that 'a beggar's brat . . . may have talents and capacity above the son of an emperor'. But if Fielding hardly gives the issue a Yeatsian gloss, there are moments of proud celebration of 'poetry and poverty': thus Luckless, the hero of *The Author's Farce* (1730), I, v, like Mr Wilson an impecunious poet up against a money-minded world, proclaims himself a favourer of 'the women and the Muses—the high roads to beggary' (ed. Charles B. Woods (London, 1967), p. 15). The theme recurs throughout the play.

68 *Letters*, III, 1145–6, 10 May 1748; see also IV, 1746, 6 June 1751, and the letter to his godson 'to be delivered after his own death', VI, 2944.

69 Yeats, *Autobiographies* (London, 1955), pp. 101–2.

70 The paradox would not surprise Yeats, who spoke vividly of mixing 'Courtesy and passion into one' ('The People', *Collected Poems*, p. 169). See also his beautiful evocation of Guidobaldo's court at Urbino (where Castiglione's *Courtier* is set) as:

> That grammar school of courtesies
> Where wit and beauty learned their trade
> Upon Urbino's windy hill.

('To a Wealthy Man who Promised a Second Subscription to the Dublin Municipal Gallery . . .', *Collected Poems*, p. 120). Contrast Chesterfield's more low-pitched view, which can be refreshing after unduly highfalutin talk but which mainly lacks warmth, that manners are just a mechanical accomplishment (*Letters*, V, 1967–9, 11 November 1752).

71 *The World*, No. 148, *British Essayists*, XXVIII, 228, 231. The essay is said to have been written straight off, without revision. Part of it rewords an earlier letter, and in general it is consistent enough with much of Chesterfield's thinking. The graces are a matter of education, and Chesterfield, who does not believe in innate distinctions or in pride of birth (on this point he is emphatic), says that a ploughman may *acquire* them (*Letters*, IV, 1730–1, 16 May 1751). But it is a poor look out for him if he does not. The unlovability of people who lack good-breeding is a recurrent theme of the letters to his son and godson.

72 *Letters*, IV, 1433, 14 November 1749. Brauer, *op. cit.*, pp. 27–8, quite correctly relates the passage to Chesterfield's view, common to most contemporary courtesy-writers, that the general norms of good-breeding were uniform among all men, whilst local conventions varied. My argument concerns the particular feeling or atmosphere of Chesterfield's discussion as a whole, and I do not dispute Brauer's point.

73 *The World*, No. 148, and *Letters*, passim.

74 *J.A.*, III, iii.

75 Yeats, 'A Prayer for My Daughter', *Collected Poems*, pp. 211–14. J. B. Yeats praised Fielding repeatedly and with great eloquence in his *Letters to his Son W. B. Yeats*, ed. Joseph Hone (London, 1944), pp. 179, 281,

282. Fielding is there seen as Christ-like, 'kinglike', and, in various ways, Yeats-like: 'attended by visions', saint-sinner, and so on; and in some things an example for W. B. Yeats to follow.

76 *Works*, XIV, 263.

77 *Works*, XIV, 265–6.

78 In the sense that real gentility is a thing which involves virtue, and carries the marks of it. Or does Fielding just mean that My Lady is an upstart? and if so, does it come to the same thing?

79 *Works*, XIV, 265–6.

80 *Works*, XIV, 254.

81 *Works*, XIV, 258.

82 *T.J.*, IX, i.

83 *Letters*, IV, 1330–1, 19 April 1749: 'If you love music, hear it; . . . pay fiddlers to play to you; but I insist upon your neither piping nor fiddling yourself. . . .' Chesterfield admitted, however, that music was 'commonly reckoned one of the liberal arts', and it did continue to form part of many 'genteel educations'. For some examples of its inferior status, see John E. Mason, *Gentlefolk in the Making* (Philadelphia, 1935), pp. 70, 177, 298.

84 The main point, of course, is that gentlemen should do most things well, yet not like professionals in those things.

85 *The Dancing-Master: or, The Art of Dancing Explained . . . Done from the French of Monsieur Rameau, By J. Essex, Dancing-Master* (1728), Essex's Preface, p. xi.

86 *Essay on Conversation, Works*, XIV, 248–9.

87 *T.J.*, XIV, i.

88 *T.J.*, IX, v. For an earlier instance of this claim of dancing-masters, see *Love in Several Masques*, III, vii; *Works*, VIII, 50.

89 *Voyage to Liston*, p. 45. See above, p. 18ff.

90 Chesterfield, *Letters*, VI, 2692, 12 December 1765 (to his godson). Pope, see epigraph and opening of ch. II, below.

CHAPTER II

NATURE AND
THE MASTERIES OF STYLE
IN FIELDING, SWIFT AND POPE

✻

Dauncing (bright Lady) then began to bee,
When the first seeds whereof the World did spring,
The fire, ayre, earth, and water—did agree,
By Loues perswasion,—Nature's mighty King,—
To leaue their first disordred combating;
   And in a daunce such measure to obserue,
   As all the world their motion should preserue.

Since when, they still are carried in a round,
And changing, come one in another's place;
Yet doe they neither mingle nor confound,
But euery one doth keepe the bounded space
Wherein the Daunce doth bid it turne or trace.
          (Sir John Davies, *Orchestra*, XVII–XVIII)

True Ease in Writing comes from Art, not Chance,
As those move easiest who have learn'd to dance.
          (Pope, *Essay on Criticism*, 362–3, and
          Imitation of Horace, *Epistle* II, ii, 178–9)

The woods of Arcady are dead,
And over is their antique joy;
Of old the world on dreaming fed;
Grey Truth is now her painted toy; . . .
Of all the many changing things
In dreary dancing past us whirled,
To the cracked tune that Chronos sings,
Words alone are certain good.
          (Yeats, 'The Song of the Happy Shepherd')

Song and dance are, perhaps, only a little less old than man himself. It is with his music and dance, the recreation through art of the rhythms suggested by and implicit in the tempo of his life and cultural environment, that man purges his soul of the tensions of daily strife and maintains his harmony in the universe. In the increasingly mechanized, automated, cybernated environment of the modern world—a cold, bodiless world of wheels, smooth plastic surfaces, tubes, pushbuttons, transistors, computers, jet propulsion, rockets to the moon, atomic energy—man's need for affirmation of his biology has become that much more intense. . . . It is in this connection that the blacks, personifying the Body and thereby in closer communion with their biological roots than other Americans, provide the saving link, the bridge between man's biology and man's machines . . . jazz is the only true international medium of communication current in the world today. . . .

(Eldridge Cleaver, *Soul on Ice*, 'Convalescence')

Pope's famous couplet about 'True Ease in Writing', which stands as an epigraph to this chapter, is neither the first nor the last of a distinguished series of pronouncements through the ages in which the dance appears as an emblem in literary theory. It differs radically from those to which we have become accustomed in modern poetics. In Yeats or Valéry, the dance is autonomous, often solitary, disciplined not to external rules but to its own inner compulsions, trance-like, and, notably, open-ended: 'elle ne possède pas de quoi finir. Elle cesse comme un rêve cesse, lequel pourrait indéfiniment se poursuivre.'[1] As a dream ends because one wakes and not because it has fulfilled itself, the 'danse pure' contains nothing from within that enables one to foresee that it has 'un terme': what brings it to an end are extrinsic factors, the 'convenances d'un spectacle', fatigue, loss of interest. The dance exists only in the act, and is inseparable from the performer: 'How can we know the dancer from the dance?' Similarly, the poem exists only 'au moment de sa diction: il est alors *en acte*':

Cet acte, comme la danse, n'a pour fin que de créer un état; cet acte se donne ses lois propres; il crée, lui aussi, un temps et une mesure du temps qui lui conviennent et qui lui sont essentiels: on ne peut le distinguer de sa forme de durée. Commencer de dire des vers, c'est entrer dans une danse verbale (Valéry, I, 1400).

For many great artists, Valéry concludes, a work of art is never finished.

What Pope means is on the contrary a dance that is patterned, completing itself with an established finality ('une direction et une coordination extérieures, et ensuite une conclusion nette et certaine' [I, 1398], as Valéry described the antithesis of his own ideal), social rather than solitary, a minuet, say, rather than Valéry's dissociated and 'open' ballet. If Valéry's dance is one in which the body is 'détaché de ses équilibres ordinaires' (I, 1397), Pope's dance purports to preserve its earthbound relation to these equilibria, stylizing and ordering rather than abandoning the 'ordinary' graceful movements of everyday life. These movements were normally assumed to have a direct connection with dancing skill, the dance being a formal, decorative patterning of the normal: 'the greatest advantage of dancing well is, that it necessarily teaches you to present yourself, to sit, stand, and walk genteely', Chesterfield wrote to his son (27 September 1748).[2] The dance stood in something like the same relationship to gentlemanly deportment as did those patterns of 'True Ease in Writing', the couplet and the harmoniously rounded period, to ordinary polite speech. Dryden's Neander compared dramatic repartee in good rhymed verse to 'a dance which is well contrived',[3] and there was a common readiness to relate, whether by analogy or something more, the graces of the mind and the body: 'the former', Chesterfield told his godson, 'give an easy engaging turn to the thoughts and the expressions, the latter to the motions, attitude and address' (*Letters*, VI, 2693). These graces are ornamental and social. There is no trace either of Valéry's notion of the pure autonomy of the dance nor of his definition of it as a 'poésie générale de l'action des êtres vivants' in a sense which transcends, and sometimes divorces itself from, the practicalities of ordinary social living (Valéry, I, 1402–3). And Valéry's high conception of verse-speaking as a 'danse verbale' is worlds away from Chesterfield's low-pitched and literal-minded recommendations: verses 'must be recited in my favourite minuet time at the quickest and with all the graces of proper emphases, and just cadences' (1767; *Letters*, VI, 2800).

As one might expect, Chesterfield's formulations stay somewhat glibly on the surface, though doing things 'in minuet time' was for him not only a matter of verse-speaking pace or of elegant physical movement, but of moral poise (e.g., 12 December 1765; *Letters*, VI, 2692). Analogies and interactions between physically harmonious movement or demeanour, and virtue or moral grace, are an ancient commonplace going back at least as far as Plato (e.g., *Republic*, III, xi–xiii), and most eloquently celebrated in English, perhaps, in Sir John Davies's *Orchestra* (1596). Chesterfield's shallowness is clearly not the only possible level of discourse, and Pope's couplet about 'True Ease in Writing' is alive with an imaginative conviction well beyond the courtesy-writer's reach. Nevertheless, Pope shares with Chesterfield, as against Valéry, both a social conception of the dance and an assumption that both arts are, to a substantial degree, teachable by means of recognized rules. If literature is for Pope much more than a question of dancing-steps, some of its excellences are no less specifiable as devices, and Pope shows a marked readiness to go into some prescriptive, technical implications of his image. There must not only be 'no Harshness', but 'The *Sound* must seem an *Eccho* to the *Sense*', and certain basic and specified harmonies must be observed: '*Soft* is the Strain when *Zephyr* gently blows', but where the subject is tempestuous, 'The *hoarse, rough Verse* shou'd like the *Torrent* roar', etc. (*Essay on Criticism*, ll. 364ff.). A flat and vulgar eulogy of the dance like Soame Jenyns's 'Art of Dancing' could therefore easily reverse Pope's lines, point by point, not only asserting that 'True dancing, like true wit, is best exprest/By nature only to advantage drest', but working its leering way through 'nameless graces', Camilla skimming 'o'er the plain', and the like.[4]

Valéry is not indifferent to technique, but he would not have found it easy to formulate general prescriptions with Pope's degree of binding particularity. It is rare for a modern writer in the Symbolist tradition to discuss points of technique with such prescriptive confidence in their general applicability, both because 'organicist' conceptions of the work of art discourage it, and because there no longer exists the sense of shared values that would make such normative statements possible. Exceptions like the following well-known passage from 'Little Gidding' about successful poetic expression,[5]

> where every word is at home,
> Taking its place to support the others,
> The word neither diffident nor ostentatious,
> An easy commerce of the old and the new,
> The common word exact without vulgarity,
> The formal word precise but not pedantic,
> The complete consort dancing together,

are only apparent. The resemblance to a familiar type of neo-classic and classical formulation seems close. But the congruences which Eliot is referring to cannot be illustrated by specific examples which, as in Pope's *Essay*, would be claimed as generally applicable to all poems. Even if Eliot's wording suggests that he is indulging some private image of himself as classicist in literature, he is mainly saying in a general way that *any* poetic 'rightness' entails verbal tact and an overall harmony between the poem's elements. The impersonality of art meant for Eliot not an escape from the self into public forms, but, as C. K. Stead has put it, a further reaching into the self.[6] The poetic exactitude celebrated in 'Little Gidding' is not thought of as a stable and enduring monument, but as a moment wrested from the flux: 'Every phrase and every sentence is an end and a beginning', and the search for it, in the words from 'East Coker', is a lonely, *unceasing* 'intolerable wrestle/With words and meanings' (*Four Quartets*, p. 17). There are no finalities except those of moments 'for a moment final'.[7] Eliot's 'complete consort dancing together' has less to do with a rounded and ceremonious social harmony than with inner fulfilments, epiphanies, focused on a single 'still point of the turning world': 'there', Eliot said in 'Burnt Norton', 'the dance is' (*Four Quartets*, p. 9), and we may compare Valéry's image of the dancer as a top, spinning on a single point of delicate self-contained balance (Valéry, I, 1397), and the vision of the dancer in Yeats's 'Double Vision of Michael Robartes', 'Mind moved yet seemed to stop/As 'twere a spinning-top'.[8]

'At the still point of the turning world', however, private epiphany also transcends the self and glimpses the universal order. The two have always tended to merge, at the highest imaginative reaches. Shelley's *Defence of Poetry* sees poetry as 'the echo of the eternal music', but captured in 'evanescent visitations' and 'vanishing apparitions'.[9] The seventeenth-century poet Thomas Jordan, for whom (as for many others) the dance and the poem were emblems of one another and of the cosmic harmony, not only stated the bald general analogy, 'the Whole Creation is a Dance', but also celebrated the fragmentary glimpse, when he called the dance[10]

> a fit of order, where our eyes,
> have glimpses of the spheres' rotundities.

Jordan's 'Apology for Dancing' also speaks of the dance as fulfilling a time-honoured function of art, to restore 'nature' to its ideal form, perfecting

> the Limbs
> in Gracious Postures; such as nature wou'd
> her self have brought to pass, if that she cou'd

Jordan's formulation combines neo-Platonic aesthetics with the drawing-room concerns of courtesy-writers like Chesterfield, who recommended dancing-lessons to improve the posture! Valéry's description of the dance as a 'poésie générale de l'action des êtres vivants' also calls to mind much neo-platonizing, ancient and modern. But his emphasis, unlike Jordan's, is away from the social and the communal. He speaks very differently of the relation between the 'poésie générale' and the ordinary movements which it restores to an ideal form, preferring to stress a disengagement from, rather than a direct transcendence of, ordinary equilibria. Nor shall we find in him the literal-minded readiness to particularize the universal analogy of all creation to a dance in the detail of Jordan's 'Apology', let alone that of Sir John Davies's *Orchestra*. Romantic and symbolist doctrines of 'correspondences' place much more emphasis on momentary and precarious recovery of total vision by the poet, than on the stable existence of the system as such. It seems fair to say that in our own time, in Western civilization at least, any notions of an all-embracing cosmic harmony, stable and confident enough to be elaborated in extended detail, will seem exceptional other than on the cultural fringe: in more or less eccentric mysticisms, or in neo-primitive fantasy (for an amusing example of the latter, see Henderson's jazzifying of the cosmic dance in Ch. XXII of Saul Bellow's *Henderson the Rain King*), or, perhaps increasingly, in the neo-primitivist glosses to some kinds of revolutionary ideology (as in my epigraph from Eldridge Cleaver). Even in these cases, the emphasis is still usually on the efforts, personal or cultural, which are needed to recover the harmony, or to preserve or restore one's place in it, rather than on the harmony's confident all-embracing existence as an unshakable fact of the universe.

An attractive illustration is provided by Theodore Roethke's sequence, 'Four for Sir John Davies'. It opens with a wittily sceptical rephrasing of the universal harmony as a mere belief (rage for order, so to speak, rather than order itself), and now on the wane at that:

> Is that dance slowing in the mind of man
> That made him think the universe could hum?

Dancing still has its compulsions (it remains the means to 'undo chaos', though now as a private achievement rather than a communal activity), and the poet will 'sing and whistle romping with the bears'. The dancing-bears in Davies are the two constellations (*Orchestra*, LXIV), but they turn in Roethke's poem into literal animals, with a comic gaucheness and desperate gaiety which are also the poet's. This dance is a live, passionate thing, not learned from dancing-masters, performed all alone, its cadence (and more particularly that of the poem) taken 'from a man named Yeats', then given 'back again': 'Yes, I was dancing-mad, and how/That came to be the bears and Yeats would know'. Thus closes the first section, entitled 'The Dance'. (Roethke later qualified the debt to Yeats, saying that the verse rhythms came partly from Raleigh and Davies himself; see Karl Malkoff's *Theodore Roethke* (New York, 1966), pp. 116–17.)

In the sequence's second and third sections, entitled 'The Partner' and 'The Wraith', epiphany is won by the union of lovers, its highest moment rendered by a beautiful couplet,

> In the deep middle of ourselves we lay;
> When glory failed, we danced upon a pin,

a witty, tender evocation of that still point, mind like a spinning-top, which replaces the old, spent grandeurs. In the fourth and final section, 'The Vigil', the experience is seen, quizzically, as a brief encroachment on chaos:

> The links were soft between us; still, we kissed;
> We undid chaos to a curious sound . . .
>
> We danced to shining; mocked before the black
> And shapeless night that made no answer back.

The poem ends with an affirmation which reads, oddly, like the close of the *Dunciad* in reverse: 'The word outleaps the world, and light is all'.[11]

In Pope, the 'Universal Darkness buries all'. But the *Dunciad*'s whole atmosphere implies a coherent frame of values, even though the poem laments their defilement, whereas the reclaimed light in the modern poem is briefly vouchsafed and won only by a private experience of great intensity. The dance, in Pope, is in its deepest nature (as an image of his style) relaxed as Roethke's is not, alive with a 'True Ease' that is not facility. It is probably a less inclusive concept, however, than it had been for Sir John Davies, to whom Roethke's poem is addressed. The cosmological and metaphysical aspects of the universal harmony, as celebrated in parts of the *Orchestra*, had little immediacy for Pope as matters of any active faith. I suspect that even the excitements of the *Essay on Man* (whose 'system', though not identical with Davies's, has a similar inclusiveness) reside less in the poet's secure belief in the 'system' than in the poetic delight, so to speak, of re-inventing it. The coherences which remain vivid for Pope are cultural and social, not metaphysical. They consist first of those moral, intellectual and aesthetic values of the classical heritage ('Still green with Bays each *ancient* Altar stands', *Essay on Criticism*, l. 181), modified and enriched by Christianity, which are still vitally appealed to even in the negative world of the *Dunciad*. Secondly (but not separately), they consist of a social ideal, equally under anarchic pressure, yet retaining, as an animating ideal, much of its loveliness and wholeness. The social and courtly extensions of Davies's cosmic dance,

> Many an incomparable louely payre,
> With hand in hand were interlinkèd scene,
> Making faire honour to their soueraigne Queene;
> Forward they pac'd, and did their pace apply
> To a most sweet and solemne melody—
>
> (*Orchestra*, CXXVIII)

are still real to Pope, though flecked with the ironies of the *Rape of the Lock*, and, later, darkened with a sense of the Hanoverians' disfiguring boorishness. No mere *actual* court impairs, for Pope, the significance of this ideal, and its extension to literary style in the couplet about 'True Ease' is transferred without strain from the early, pre-Hanoverian *Essay on Criticism* to a Horatian imitation of 1737. The direct product of this, in the fabric of the writing, is all that we mean when we talk of the assured urbanity of Pope: the wit and ironic distance, the combination of urgency and grace, the 'easy commerce' (in Eliot's phrase) between the natural rhythms of the spoken language, and the balances, interchanges and finality of social ceremony in the finest sense.

Pope is not the only author, nor the first, whose writings have these qualities, and for whom the analogy between literature and the dance (in its specifically social guise) is a live and beautiful thing. When Dryden's Neander compared well-managed verse-repartee in a play to a well-contrived dance, he explained:

> You see there the united design of many persons to make up one figure: after they have separated themselves in many petty divisions, they rejoin one by one into a gross: the confederacy is plain amongst them, for chance could never produce any thing so beautiful; and yet there is nothing in it that shocks your sight
> (*Of Dramatic Poesy*, I, 89).

The description illustrates well the high valuation of what Valéry repudiates as 'conclusion nette et certaine'. It shows also the sense of gentlemanly ease as a matter not of spontaneous flowering, but of mastery over a skill, and the consequent readiness to put one's real trust in 'Art, not Chance'. Above all it shows the live nature of the social analogy, the social orientation of the literary ideal, the delight in ceremony and cohesion.

The patterned forms of 'couplet-rhetoric', in verse and prose, are probably the most frequent and appropriate expression of these ideals, as we should expect. The apparent restrictions of couplet-styles (though some complained of the fetters of rhyme) do not inhibit the vitality of the best Augustan writings, because they are the natural literary expression of proprieties and restraints inherent in a living civilization. The satisfactions of a disciplined and graceful completeness, the interplay of social responsibility and individual poise, were matters of live and widespread aspiration; and they naturally dictated standards of emotional balance, a witty and rational grasp of unruly circumstance, an easy formality, in literary expression as in social manner. That the ideals and aspirations were often felt to be under threat might well intensify rather than diminish their potency, and poems like the *Dunciad* and the *Vanity of Human Wishes* show that the Augustan couplet could meaningfully carry a massive charge of anguished insecurity and a passionate defensive fervour.

Not all of Pope's contemporaries share these ideals. Many authors outside the Augustan gentlemanly tradition, such as Defoe or Richardson, show little interest in them, and Johnson (whom I discuss elsewhere) is a problematical case. Swift, though close to Pope in his official or declared social and political outlook, and in personal sympathy, is not easily identified with graceful urbanities of style, nor with any real feeling for social cohesion, let alone with any imaginative delight or faith in larger inclusive systems. He could never have written an *Essay on Man*, and as for Thomas Jordan's 'the Whole Creation is a Dance', Swift more than once (most famously in the *Tale of a Tub*'s Clothes Philosophy) showed his shattering contempt for such cosmic analogizing. Swift also lashed the opposite 'modern' *dis*orders of open-endedness, and the mad 'author' of his *Tale* is, after all, a Shandean romantic, connoisseur of epiphanies and vanishing moments, and a non-finisher of books: the squalid underside, so to speak, of Valéry's dancer-artist! But Swift is radically self-implicated in his own anti-'modern' satire and correspondingly insecure in his most assertive allegiances to older and stabler values. His own styles, in both verse and prose, are often open-ended, and even his stricter exercises in couplet-rhetoric (I shall argue) lack the Popeian delight in patterned self-completion. If any dance-emblem describes Swift's writings, it is not that of 'True Ease', but the *Dunciad*'s 'Madness of the mazy dance' with its wild 'Mob of Metaphors' (I, 67–8), which Pope and Swift derided, but which Swift *mimicked*—or, more profoundly still, the internalized spiralling of Beckett's *Molloy*: 'the within, all that inner space one never sees, the brain and heart and other caverns where thought and feeling dance their sabbath'.[12]

My concern in this study, however, is not primarily with styles which depart radically from the forms of couplet-rhetoric, but with styles (including some examples from Swift) which show these forms existing under strain, real or potential: the strains of disorderly or 'unnatural' fact, of powerful or unbalancing emotions, and finally of a painful scepticism of order. My principal example will be Fielding's prose. (I do not imply that Fielding only wrote in 'couplet'-prose; but only that such prose is a characteristic idiom of his, whose study seems to me to yield useful insights.)

The dance-like decorum of neat stylistic interchange, the ceremonious finality of elegant, symmetrical pairings, do not invariably celebrate serenities of cohesion and benevolent harmony. They may, instead, voice or describe certain vicious entrapments of the mind, suffering states of impasse (unhappiness *either way*, as in Johnson's verse), or opposite pairs of contrasting nastiness (the satirist saying 'a plague on both your houses'). Some of the most buoyant patternings of Fielding's prose (or of Pope's verse, notably in the character-portraits of the *Moral Essays*) are 'anti-celebrations' of this sort:

> Master Blifil fell very short of his companion [Tom] in the amiable quality of mercy; but he as greatly exceeded him in one of a much higher kind, namely, in justice: in which he followed both the precepts and example of Thwackum and Square; for tho' they would both make frequent use of the word *mercy*, yet it was plain, that in reality Square held it to be inconsistent with the rule of right; and Thwackum was for doing justice, and leaving mercy to Heaven. The two gentlemen did indeed somewhat differ in opinion concerning the objects of this sublime virtue; by which Thwackum would probably have destroyed one half of mankind, and Square the other half (*T.J.*, III, x).

This passage may be compared with the following, from Swift's *Sentiments of a Church-of-England Man* (probably written in 1704), in which the extremism of both Whigs and Tories is exposed:

> there is a very good Word, which hath of late suffered much by both Parties; I mean MODERATION; which the one Side very justly disowns, and the other as unjustly pretends to. Beside what passeth

every Day in Conversation; any Man who reads the Papers published by Mr. *Lesly*, and others of his Stamp, must needs conclude, that if this Author could make the Nation see his Adversaries, under the Colours he paints them in; we had nothing else to do, but rise as one Man, and destroy such Wretches from the Face of the Earth. On the other Side, how shall we excuse the Advocates for *Moderation*; among whom, I could appeal to an Hundred Papers of universal Approbation, by the Cause they were writ for, which lay such Principles to the whole Body of the *Tories*, as, if they were true, and believed; our next Business should, in Prudence, be to erect Gibbets in every Parish, and hang them out of the Way. But, I suppose it is presumed, the common People understand *Raillery*, or at least *Rhetorick*; and will not take *Hyperboles* in too literal a Sense; which, however, in some Junctures might prove a desperate Experiment. And this is *Moderation*, in the *modern* Sense of the Word; to which, speaking impartially, the Bigots of both Parties are *equally* entituled (Swift, *Works*, II, 13).

In each case, the author makes an ironic attribution of some judicial attitude ('justice', 'moderation') to each of the paired opposites (Thwackum and Square, Tories and Whigs) and shows both up as potential exterminators, between them, of the whole of mankind. Anyone familiar with Swift's writings as a whole will recognize that he is here castigating attitudes and postures which, in some ways and with varying degrees of indirection, he himself mirrors elsewhere. For every Whig or Tory exterminator and every modest proposer that Swift invents and exposes, there is counterbalancing evidence of a primary Swiftian feeling which is unsettlingly similar, a Kurtz-like underside (more ironically elusive, but also more clairvoyant and self-aware than in Conrad's hero) wishing extermination, now of 'all the brutes',[13] now of selected types: 'the Nation's Representers' (*Poems*, II, 635), or 'bullies, sharpers, and rakes' (*Works*, IV, 214), or plump Irish girls wearing foreign fineries (*Works*, XII, 114). Similarly, the Whiggish 'moderation', overtolerant of Dissent and given to a misguided ecumenism of Protestant Unity (*Works*, IX, 175–9; XII, 44), bears in some respects a teasing resemblance to the good 'moderation' and the sensible ecumenism which Swift advocates through Martin in *A Tale of a Tub* (Section VI). Moreover, Swift's reduction of the bad 'moderation' to a form of vicious extremism is mirrored by the passionate extremism with which Swift advocated the good 'moderation' of middle ways and

classical balance, of common forms and received opinion, of accommodations to reason, tradition, law and the religion of the state.

Even so, this passage from the *Sentiments* shows Swift in an unusual
degree of self-exclusion from the vices he attacks. The work in which
it occurs is one of his most straightforwardly unironic pieces, and one
of his most literally 'moderate' in both style and content. The dazzling
interpenetrations of satirist and butt which take place, at white heat, in
the fierce ironic melting-pot of *A Tale of a Tub*, get no chance to
establish themselves vividly in the sober discourse of the *Sentiments*; and
the connections I have been making are inferred externally, from the
rest of Swift's works. One might therefore expect to find here something of Fielding's easy detachment from the turpitudes which he
ascribes to Thwackum and Square, something of the triumphant excitement with which the patness of Fielding's definitions is charged. But in
fact, despite the vivid epigrammatic finality of its punch-line, Swift's
passage has a kind of unpredictable and unsettling fluidity absent from
Fielding's. Instead of the simplifying purity of a pointed couplet-rhetoric
(Fielding's prose counterpart to Pope's verse portraits), Swift's passage
has strange bulging asymmetries, of explanatory elaboration or of
additional and wrily unassimilated sarcasm ('But, I suppose ... a
desperate Experiment'); and where Fielding's syntax weaves and inter-
weaves with shapely assurance, Swift's tends to a garrulous untidiness
which seems at times ready, almost, to dissolve into anacoluthon.

Swift's passage, in a sense, expresses a stylistic refusal to concede that
matters can be as neatly disposed of as Fielding's writing in *Tom Jones*
persistently suggests. Swift is not incapable of the finalities of a patterned
couplet-rhetoric, as when he makes Gulliver list the causes of war:[14]

Sometimes one Prince quarrelleth with another, for fear the other
should quarrel with him. Sometimes a War is entered upon,
because the Enemy is too *strong*, and sometimes because he is too
weak. Sometimes our Neighbours *want* the *Things* which we *have*,
or *have* the Things which we want (*Gulliver's Travels*, IV, v).

But such a passage exists more as an exposure of vacuous, self-enclosed
absurdity, than as a satisfying *explanation*. At times, even the *pretence* of
explanation is dropped, as when we are told that a prime minister 'never
tells a *Truth*, but with an Intent that you should take it for a *Lye*; nor a
Lye, but with a Design that you should take it for a *Truth*' (*Gulliver's
Travels*, IV, vi). To make a vicious folly seem so self-sustaining that it
must be spoken of as outside the domain of rational comprehension is a
familiar satiric procedure, practised by Fielding as well as Swift. But

what Fielding might have presented with an air of confident knowing-
ness, or an arch mock-bewilderment (see, for example, the 'dissertation
concerning high people and low people' in *Joseph Andrews*, II, xiii), Swift
flattens to an astringently naked constatation. The tartness of Swift's use
of a patterned couplet-style suggests none of Fielding's delight in
summation as such, and none of Fielding's sense of the amenability of
life to coherent explanations.

The couplet-style tends towards the epigram, towards a mode of
statement which pretends to truths of unhesitating completeness, but of
somewhat externalized quality, whose clear outlines are unblurred by
doubts and by the loose ends of an introspective self-implication.
Johnson's style, in both verse and prose, is a major exception to this,
his heavy epigrammatic propositions carrying an unusual strong sad
weight of self-questioning and self-examination. But the exuberance of
Pope or Fielding in their feats of epigrammatic summation is accompanied by a masterful detachment, while Swift's flat astringency in the
epigrams about the causes of war and about prime ministers conveys a
clear sense that the nastiness is kept at a distance by the author's dry,
uncompromising distaste. Swift is like Johnson in that his writing
hardly becomes exuberant when it is engaged in ordering chaos into
well-fashioned definitions. But he is unlike Johnson not only because
his definitions are themselves cleanly external rather than self-involving,
but also because he has *other* styles which do kindle into exuberance,
whereas Johnson is seldom exuberant at all. These other styles are open-
ended, unpredictable, unruly. Swift (as I have argued elsewhere) exhibits
his most excited mastery not, like Pope or Fielding, when he subdues
chaos by formal ordering, but when he mimics it: when, for example,
we sense the satirist's own anarchic proclivities energizing the wild
'author' of the *Tale*, or the less sober moments of Gulliver.

The passage about moderation from the *Sentiments of a Church-of-
England Man* is, of course, far removed from these strange self-impli-
cating vitalities. But it differs also from the faultlessly neat ordering of
the tart epigrams I cited from *Gulliver's Travels*, in so far as its leanings
towards epigrammatic summation are, as we have seen, subverted by a
stylistic indecision, or at least untidiness. It may be excessive to infer
from this a certain scepticism over the neat exactitude of his generalization, and over the clarity of his own self-exclusion from it. But Swift's
powerfully ambiguous feelings about moderation (the emphatic readiness to despise other people's pretensions to it, super-imposed on a
similarly emphatic and often over-declaratory allegiance to its official
Augustan guises) would seem at least consistent with the passage's

47

tendency to a strong, almost explosive, finality of epigrammatic definition, as well as with the counter-tendency to slacken into wordy,
obfuscating qualifications.

Swiftian irony is seldom so clear-cut or so simply upside-down that
fixed and simple positives can easily be inferred from it. The moral
extremes which it sometimes polarizes into equal and opposite forms of
viciousness (here Whig and Tory fanaticisms) are seldom powerfully
countered by some moderate compromise or golden mean. Even the
Church-of-England Man, an unusually sustained portrait of virtuous
moderation (Martin, in *A Tale of a Tub*, is neither a sustained, nor an
unsubverted, portrait), becomes, at moments which are kindled by a
real Swiftian intensity, a faintly unreal figure. And Swift's most powerfully realized moderates are not virtuous, but calm upholders of the
world's wickedness, modestly proposing a nominal Christianity, or
mass murder. Behind them stands a Swift whose more absolute moral
denunciations (like his championship of simplifying rules and disciplines)
turn indistinct under strange pressures of self-implication and self-
concealment: 'Drown the World', 'I would hang them if I cou'd'
(*Correspondence*, III, 117; *Poems*, II, 635) are ironic phrases and mean less
than they say literally, but not the opposite of what they say, so that
what remains is a floating, indefinable but inescapably real commitment
to the Kurtz-like curse.

This kind of ironic discourse opens up damaging possibilities without
defining their limits. It is a stylistic manner in direct correspondence with
Swift's feeling that 'the Species of Folly and Vice are infinite' (*Works*, I,
232), and consequently not amenable to orderly and conclusive diag-
nosis. Consider Swift's exposition of man's moral status in relation to
the bestial Yahoos. Book IV of *Gulliver's Travels* concedes, as a whole,
that man is superior to the Yahoos but contains also repeated and
powerful insinuations that (both physically and morally) he is at the
same time inferior. The self-evident point that man has more reason
than the Yahoos is undercut by affirmations that his reason makes him
worse, not better, than they are, and by the occasional ghastly suggestion that this 'reason' (the faculty that traditionally distinguishes men
from beasts) leads to such vicious courses that it is perhaps not reason at
all. The bleak effect of these underminings is to deny all possibility of
clear definition, even of the most damaging kind (which would at least
permit us to know where we stand). The schematized and comforting
notion of man as a golden mean between Yahoo and Houyhnhnm,
which critics sometimes entertain, seems ruled out *a fortiori*.

The traditional satiric formula about the unmendability of man acquires a particular edge in Swift's hands. The rhetorical hopelessness ceases to be a simple matter of sheer recalcitrant vice. The viciousness cannot be fully confronted, because it cannot be fully pinned down: this is the opposite face of Swift's insecurely aggressive insistence on moral truths which are plain and obvious. Moreover, beyond every attempt to define or to cure lie further depths of complication, as well as the crucially disturbing elusiveness of definition itself. The damaging haze of elusive and many-sided accusation with which Swift envelops his presentation of the nature of man (refusing to press his charges on a single and well-defined front), is reinforced by a curious emphasis on man's limitlessly 'unnatural' perversity. Book IV of *Gulliver's Travels* plays heavily on the word Nature, using the term's high or ideal sense (the sense in which Houyhnhnms are *'the Perfection of Nature'* in IV, iii) as a standard by which the 'nature' of man is shown in a disreputable light. The 'Reason' through which men are distinguished from Yahoos serves only 'to aggravate our *natural* Corruptions, and to acquire new ones which Nature had not given us' (IV, vii). Swift is exploiting both ideal and more low-pitched senses of the word 'nature', and when men or Yahoos are under discussion, Nature is imagined as capable of 'giving' or 'allotting' vices (also IV, x). Wickedness is by definition 'unnatural' in the high sense, but it is 'natural' to man. However, whatever depravities are thus 'natural' tend to be subverted by deeper depravities which are 'unnatural' to this 'nature'. Thus it is natural for judges to accept bribes, but still more natural for them to be unjust, so that 'I have known some of them to have refused a large Bribe from the side where Justice lay, rather than injure the *Faculty*, by doing any thing unbecoming their Nature or their office' (IV, v). One becomes unnatural to one's lesser natural iniquities when a greater iniquity competes. This vicious spiral hardly has a rock-bottom. In *Gulliver's Travels*, things grind to a halt as Gulliver says that although he can accept most human depravities as 'all according to the due Course of Things', there is one ultimate unnaturalness which he cannot bear, namely that such a depraved creature as man should have the effrontery to be *proud*. Pride has a special place in the hierarchy of vices, but one feels that it is used here to provide a rock-bottom only because the book (and with it the vicious spiral) must end somewhere. Pride, 'this absurd Vice' and final self-complicating perversion of man, is itself, Gulliver reminds us at the end of IV, xii, part of 'Human Nature' ('for so they have still the Confidence to stile it', says Gulliver in his letter to Sympson), and leaves open the idea of further perversities to be revealed, if the volume had continued. In that sense, with its moral onslaught stopping only because the book, like any human thing, must have an end, *Gulliver's Travels* is an open-ended work, very different from *Tom Jones* and its clear conclusiveness and rounded moral certainty.

This open-ended quality in *Gulliver's Travels*, and still more in *A Tale of a Tub* (which literally purports to be, at various points, incomplete, and leaves its 'author', at the end, waiting 'to resume my Pen') is mirrored in the headlong, anarchic quality of much of Swift's most vital prose: those unending lists, that extravagantly digressive syntax, which come into unruly collocations with the more austere astringencies of patterned epigram. Equally, the overall shapeliness and the large-scale ease and confidence of *Tom Jones* is mirrored by such unSwiftian buoyancies of stylistic ordering as the paragraph about Thwackum and Square quoted earlier: as Robert Alter, among others, has said, Fielding's 'periods, ironically eloquent and eloquently ironic, are often small replicas of the architectural form of the whole novel'.[15] The orderings of the couplet-style, in verse and prose, bear an important relation to that belief in an ordered universe which is so often appealed to by Augustan writers in their use of the word Nature, in its ideal or its normative senses. The relation is surely complex, rather than easily schematic, and many ironies in the major authors (in Pope and Fielding as in Swift) emphasize that the belief in order has been disappointed or frustrated by fact. Moreover, this belief did not always assume the dimensions of an ideology, and Nature was not often too literally thought of as a live organizing deity. On the other hand, Nature held its place as an animating ideal, a live fiction (perhaps) which embodied real and important aspirations. Its prominence in the fourth book of *Gulliver's Travels* as an assertion of positive values is uncompromising, and Swift's despair of the viability of these values in a fallen world is played off against an insistent sense of their rightness. If Swift, like many of his contemporaries, is often ready to make witty or playful capital out of any suggestion of a break in the natural order, his painful scepticism runs deeper than that of Pope or Fielding and has a unique urgency. Neither Pope nor Fielding could match the bitter and shocking eloquence of the sentence in *A Short View of the State of Ireland* (1728) which comes after Swift has listed the conditions which make a country flourish and has tested them against the state of Ireland: 'If we do flourish, it must be against every Law of Nature and Reason; like the Thorn at *Glassenbury*, that blossoms in the Midst of Winter' (Swift, *Works*, XII, 10).

It is not merely that (as critics often say) Swift's imagination kindles at the negative. Pope too can reach a very high pitch of imaginative vitality in repudiating the 'anti-natural' (Pope's own phrase, in *Peri Bathous*, v), as when he transforms parody of bad poets into lines so surrealistically lovely that they suggest a real temporary surrender to the beauty of anti-nature itself:

> In cold December fragrant chaplets blow,
> And heavy harvests nod beneath the snow.
>
> (*Dunciad*, I, 77–8)

The 'anti-natural' winter-blossoming in Swift's *Short View* is not only poignantly beautiful, but full of pain (the vivid cruelty of circumstance which it expresses is further intensified by the fact that the simile occurs in a tract relatively bare of imagery). In Pope, the pain happens to be lacking, but that is not the most important difference. If Pope's lines transcend parody into a vivid imaginative sympathy with the parodied disorder, they fail to transcend the parody's somewhat trivializing aesthetic dimension. The urgent importance which the *Dunciad* attaches to the connection between literary disorder and a larger disarray of social and moral standards, is not validated here. The poetic excitement, real and brilliant, fails to surmount a preoccupation with that rudimentary externalized decorum for which the wittily energetic opening lines of Horace's *Ars Poetica* are the most famous plea, and which finds its proper (that is, crudely didactic) level in the low-pressure mock-fatuities reviewed in the prose of chapter v of *Peri Bathous*. I suspect that Pope's more brilliantly witty mock-disorders are sometimes made by critics to carry a weight of concern which is not really there. Thus the dazzling phantasmagoria of the Cave of Spleen ('Men prove with Child, as pow'rful Fancy works,/And Maids turn'd Bottels, call aloud for Corks', *Rape of the Lock*, IV, 53–4) seems over-interpreted—rather than misinterpreted, however—when Martin Price speaks of the whole passage as: 'an erotic nightmare of exploding libidinous drives. . . . The Cave of Spleen is one of the strongest pictures of disorder in the age: it gives us the measure of order, a sense of the strength of the forces that social decorum controls and of the savage distortion of feeling that it prevents.'[16] The 'order' remains pretty safe. Pope's intuition of the distorting forces, and his self-implication in their subversive splendours and miseries, remain checked by an overall confidence which is, finally, a little stultifying. The assurance and verve of his couplets and his wit are too great a match for his delight in the grotesque or his imaginative understanding of disorder (and of its relevance to himself). When the threat of disorder is most urgently rendered, as in much of the *Dunciad*, this is achieved mainly through 'borrowed' heroic effects (e.g. of grim Miltonic weight), rather than because Pope has transmuted his characteristic couplet-style, as Johnson did, into an idiom of true uncertainty. In the excited *tour de force* about winter flowers and snow-bound harvests, the live patness of the form and the deadening certainty of Pope's allegiance to a crude decorum combine to prevent him from catching up with the potential reach of his 'anti-natural' vision. It is not only because the element of Johnsonian or of Swiftian pain is lacking that we sometimes find Pope's appeals to '*Unerring Nature*, still divinely bright' (*Essay on Criticism*, l. 70) a little trivial. Swift's assertions of Nature's just standard, most real and urgent when the standard is most painfully or bewilderingly violated, are, as we have seen, unlike Pope's in being sceptical (not to say desperate) assertions. But another instructive difference from Pope is to be found in Fielding. For Fielding, though closer to Pope than to Swift in his exuberant couplet-rhetoric, his confident finality, his passionate but poised urbanity, avoids the trivializing risks of Pope's celebrations of Nature in another way.

I noted earlier that Nature, among the writers we are discussing, should be thought of as an animating ideal or live fiction, rather than as a precisely apprehended deity or the embodiment of a coherently formulated ideology. In many major works of Swift and Pope (*Gulliver's Travels*, the *Essay on Criticism* and *Essay on Man*, and the *Dunciad*) the term's ideal and normative senses are given prominence, either through sheer verbal repetition on a large scale (usually with some pointed semantic variation), or through some special charge of feeling, or both. If it is true, as I believe, that these usages in both authors, and in many of their contemporaries, reflect a fascination with simulacra of order, with an idea of order rather than with any strongly sensed normative facts, Pope's error is to over-literalize Nature until the idea almost asks to be seen as a fact. The buoyancies of positive celebration are so insistent that Pope is sometimes betrayed into thinking or seeming to think that there really is such a goddess, thus trivializing a live aspiration by allowing it to over-reach itself. Too much weight comes to be placed on usages which are so frequent in Augustan language that they cannot in fact escape a flavour of the merely commonplace or idiomatic (although that fact itself testifies to a general readiness of the age to think in terms of a notional order or unseen ideal standard). Swift, whose usages have an intensity at least as great as Pope's, escapes the trivializing tendency because Nature, seldom allowed to win in *his* writings, can claim no other reality for itself than that of the passionate disappointments (themselves undoubtedly real) which Swift is expressing. Fielding, on the other hand, escapes trivializing by keeping the usage at its fairly low idiomatic level, without giving up the sense of order which the usage could genuinely embody for him.

A good example of this are the set-pieces of character-portraiture in *Joseph Andrews* and *Tom Jones* (the writings after *Tom Jones* present a different picture). The word 'nature' is used sparingly, with a certain jokey archness supported by a wittily obsessive play with harmony and disharmony, symmetry and asymmetry, in both the syntax and the things described: see the descriptions of Mrs Tow-wouse or Mrs Western (*Joseph Andrews*, I, xiv; *Tom Jones*, VI, ii), or, without the word 'nature', of Mrs Slipslop or Beau Didapper (*Joseph Andrews*, I, vi; IV, ix). Nature in such passages is comically seen (whether or not the word is used) to exercise a certain ordering role, regulating life into surprising shapelinesses of style or appearance, compensating for a defect or pointedly failing to do so, adapting a voice to its speaker's appearance or character, and generally functioning as a rich source of grotesque playfulness and moral irony. Compare part of the portrait of Mrs Slipslop: 'Her nose was likewise rather too large, and her eyes too little; nor did she resemble a cow so much in her breath, as in two brown globes which she carried before her; one of her legs was a little shorter than the other' (*J.A.*, I, vi), with part of Richardson's portrait of her prototype, Mrs Jewkes: 'Her nose is flat and crooked, and her brows grow down over her eyes; a dead, spiteful, grey, goggling eye, to be sure she has; and her face flat and broad.'[17] Or compare the heavy 'unnaturalness' of Mrs Western: 'her masculine person, which was near six foot high, added to her manner and learning, possibly prevented the other sex from regarding her, notwithstanding her petticoats, in the light of a woman' (*T.J.*, VI, ii), with the corresponding part of Smollett's portrait of the rather similar old maid, Tabitha Bramble: 'she is tall, raw-boned, aukward, flat-chested, and stooping; her complexion is sallow and freckled'.[18]

There is no allowance in Fielding's usual style of narration for a description which follows the emotional movements of the narrator's mind (with its spasms of spite, hesitation, or self-reassurance), as in Pamela's account of Mrs Jewkes; nor any submission to the sheer particularity of fact, as in young Melford's account of Tabitha Bramble. Unlike Mrs Jewkes, Mrs Slipslop is described in terms of the harmonies of shape which she grotesquely fulfils or violates; while Mrs Western's tallness and awkwardness, unlike Tabitha's, are pointedly played on as unwomanly, an amusing piece of anti-nature. Of course, the passages from Richardson and Smollett are narrated by characters rather than, as in Fielding, by a semi-authorial narrator. But that difference is itself significant, since Fielding (who seldom narrates through any other voice) invests that narrator with powers of control which are analogous with his idea of Nature's own ordering functions. When Fielding's descriptions note those physical characteristics in a person that naturally go in symmetrical pairs, Mrs Slipslop's 'two brown globes which she carried before her' or Mrs Tow-wouse's 'two bones, that almost hid a pair of small red eyes' (*Joseph Andrews*, I, xiv), the details have the status not of mere facts but of elements in a 'composition'. The composition is simultaneously that of Fielding's set-piece and of Nature's organization of reality itself: it celebrates, as it were, the process of life imitating art. Contrast Smollett, even when (as in the second of the ensuing examples) he is speaking through an authorial narrator and at his most stylized and periphrastic, in descriptions of similar natural pairings of feature:

> The apothecary, who was a little old withered man, with a forehead about an inch high, a nose turned up at the end, large cheek-bones that helped to form a pit for his little grey eyes, a great bag of loose skin hanging down on each side in wrinkles like the alforjas of a baboon; and a mouth so accustomed to that contraction which produces grinning, that he could not pronounce a syllable without discovering the remains of his teeth, which consisted of four yellow fangs, not improperly, by anatomists, called *canine* (*Roderick Random*, ch. xviii).

> [Crabshaw's] forehead was remarkably convex, and so very low, that his black bushy hair descended within an inch of his nose; but this did not conceal the wrinkles of his front, which were manifold. His small glimmering eyes resembled those of the Hampshire porker, that turns up the soil with his projecting snout. His cheeks were shrivelled and puckered at the corners, like the seams of a regimental coat as it comes from the hands of the contractor. His nose bore a strong analogy in shape to a tennis-ball, and in colour to a mulberry; for all the water of the river had not been able to quench the natural fire of that feature. His upper jaw was furnished with two long white sharp-pointed teeth or fangs, such as the reader may have observed in the chaps of a wolf, or full-grown mastiff, and an anatomist would describe as a preternatural elongation of the *dentes canini*. His chin was so long, so peaked, and incurvated, as to form in profile, with his impending forehead,

the exact resemblance of a moon in the first quarter (*Sir Launcelot Greaves*, ch. II).

Details which Fielding might have presented as an ironic challenge to a sense of fitness, Smollett presents for their own, abundant and chaotic sakes. The apothecary's 'great bag of loose skin hanging down on each side in wrinkles' exists less as a travesty of colonnaded pairing than as sheer fact, though admittedly in a grotesque, fantasticated world. The suggestion of pictorial symmetry ends on a pattern-subverting note of delighted, explosive concreteness: 'like the alforjas of a baboon'. All real concern with pattern, even while symmetry is itself preserved, gives way before the vitality of animal life, or the solidity of objects. In Fielding's Mrs Slipslop, eyes that are 'too little' balance a nose that is 'too large': against this balanced and somewhat abstract notation, Smollett's Crabshaw has eyes like a Hampshire porker's and a nose like a tennis-ball. Smollett's abstract language (geometric notation of convex foreheads and incurvated chins) is always close to hard fact as such, a matter of concreteness rearranged or refocused to a fresh precision, in a momentarily new-novelish way (but the device is old in comic narrative). Even when Smollett goes archly periphrastic in a manner comparable to Fielding's, the writing still retains a characteristically brisk efficiency, enjoying the present detail but anxious to pass on to the next, because round the corner of every observation lies the possibility of sudden coruscating enrichments, noses like tennis-balls, chins like the 'moon in the first quarter'. The whole atmosphere of these passages annihilates all suggestion of order and fitness, rather than, as in Fielding, emphasizing betrayal of expectation by elaborate descriptions of mock-fitness and a stylistic mimicry of patterned coherence.

If these ironic appeals to Nature's ordering role are a frequent and essential part of Fielding's styles up to *Tom Jones*, and if they convey a confidence that things hang coherently together even when an expected fitness has been betrayed, a certain change occurs in the later writings. There, a play on the concept of Nature and its harmony is if anything intensified, but the sense of pained betrayal is more radical. Instead of the earlier feeling that betrayals and disappointments (disarmed by Fielding's comic mastery, and subdued by his gentlemanly and righteous voice) themselves confirm the sense of order against which they are viewed, we now have an altogether less confident note. I start with Fielding's last major work, the *Journal of a Voyage to Lisbon*, the first paragraphs of whose opening entry, for 26 June 1754, are:

On this day, the most melancholy sun I had ever beheld arose, and
found me awake at my house at Fordhook. By the light of this
sun, I was, in my own opinion, last to behold and take leave of
some of those creatures on whom I doated with a mother-like
fondness, guided by nature and passion, and uncured and
unhardened by all the doctrine of that philosophical school where
I had learned to bear pains and to despise death.

In this situation, as I could not conquer nature, I submitted
entirely to her, and she made as great a fool of me as she had ever
done of any woman whatsoever: under pretence of giving me
leave to enjoy, she drew me in to suffer the company of my little
ones, during eight hours; and I doubt not whether, in that time,
I did not undergo more than in all my distemper (*Voyage to
Lisbon*, p. 43).

Various oppressive overtones exist here. Nature is a grim agency, whose
force Fielding cannot 'conquer'; 'natural' and virtuous parental feelings
are painful to endure; Nature 'makes a fool' of Fielding, and what we
can recognize as a perfectly commonplace psychological process is
presented through Fielding's phrasing as Nature's betrayal of his
'submission' by a cruel unnatural trick. These usages of the term do not
transcend the idiomatic, any more than in the earlier writings, but they
charge it with a new and anxious intensity. The once confident predisposition to assume that events are referrable to orderly and compre-
hensible laws is now bending under a new weight of sarcasm; and at the
same time there seems to be, throughout the *Voyage*, an increased
frequency of (often cantakerous) verbal harping on notions of natural
order and on the now familiar ironies which surround them. There may
be a connection (at least in some writers, not, however, including Pope)
between a frequency of verbal insistence on natural order, and a loss or
a lack of temperamental ability to believe in the coherence of things:
in this respect, Fielding's later style invites a limited comparison with
Gulliver's Travels, although Swift is there systematically exploring the
viability of an ideal Nature in human things, whereas in Fielding the
usages are almost always kept, so to speak, on a sub-thematic plane.

Consider the following real-life portrait, in the *Voyage*, of the Ryde
landlady, Mrs Francis. Fielding opens, semi-facetiously, by citing
William Derham, the physico-theologian, on how:

in venomous insects, as in the sting or saw of a wasp, [Nature] is
sometimes wonderfully industrious. Now, when she hath thus
completely armed her hero, to carry on a war with man, she never

fails of furnishing that innocent lambkin with some means of knowing his enemy, and foreseeing his designs. Thus she hath been observed to act in the case of a rattlesnake, which never meditates a human prey without giving warning of his approach.

This observation will, I am convinced, hold most true, if applied to the most venomous individuals of human insects. A tyrant, a trickster, and a bully, generally wear the marks of their several dispositions in their countenances; so do the vixen, the shrew, the scold, and all other females of the like kind. But, perhaps, nature had never afforded a stronger example of all this, than in the case of Mrs. Francis. She was a short, squat woman; her head was closely joined to her shoulders, where it was fixed somewhat awry; every feature of her countenance was sharp and pointed; her face was furrowed with the smallpox; and her complexion, which seemed to be able to turn milk to curds, not a little resembled in colour such milk as had already undergone that operation. She appeared indeed to have many symptoms of a deep jaundice in her look; but the strength and firmness of her voice overbalanced them all; the tone of this was a sharp treble at a distance, for I seldom heard it on the same floor; but was usually waked with it in the morning, and entertained with it almost continually through the whole day.

Though vocal be usually put in opposition to instrumental music; I question whether this might not be thought to partake of the nature of both; for she played on two instruments, which she seemed to keep for no other use from morning till night; these were two maids, or rather scolding-stocks, who, I suppose, by some means or other, earned their board, and she gave them their lodging gratis, or for no other service than to keep her lungs in constant exercise.

She differed, as I have said, in every particular from her husband; but very remarkably in this, that as it was impossible to displease him, so it was impossible to please her; and as no art could remove a smile from his countenance, so could no art carry it into hers. If her bills were remonstrated against, she was offended with the tacit censure of her fair-dealing; if they were not, she seemed to regard it as a tacit sarcasm on her folly, which might have set down larger prices with the same success. On this latter hint she did indeed improve; for she daily raised some of her articles. A pennyworth of fire was today rated at a shilling, tomorrow at eighteen-pence; and if she drest us two dishes for two shillings on the Saturday, we paid half a crown for the cookery of one on the Sunday; and wherever she was paid, she never left the room without lamenting the small amount of her bill; saying, she knew not how it was that others got their money by gentlefolks, but for her part she had not the art of it. When she was asked, why she complained, when she was paid all she demanded, she answered, she could not deny that, nor did she know she omitted any thing, but that it was but a poor bill for gentlefolks to pay (*Voyage to Lisbon*, [14] July 1754).

How far, in this late style, Fielding has taken his obsessional emphasis on the theme of order and harmony gone sour may be judged from a glance at earlier prototypes of this portrait. Mrs Joan Vinegar, the scold portrayed in the *Champion* of 5 February 1740,[19] is also, besides other similarities, described in images of musical harmony, and with joking periphrastic allusions to Nature's arrangements, as noted by scientists ('It hath been remarked by some naturalists, that Nature hath given all creatures some arms for their defence; some are armed with horns, . . . and the tongue may, I think, be properly said to be the arms which Nature has bestowed on a woman'). But these elements are relatively sporadic and diffuse; the joking (even if its effect happens to be rather heavy in this case) is meant to seem lightly-carried; and there is no unusually strong syntactical or descriptive pointing of balances or antitheses. In Mrs Slipslop and Mrs Tow-wouse (*Joseph Andrews*, I, vi and xiv), where, as we have seen, syntactical and descriptive symmetries *are* emphasized, the set-pieces of portraiture are very much briefer and less elaborate than the description of Mrs Francis, and wholly lack the note of protracted harping. Since Fielding is sometimes said to have moved, in the later writings, to a less stylized, more Richardsonian form of 'humble prose' (*Voyage*, Preface), and since more informal styles were in any case regarded as appropriate to journals, travel-diaries, and the like, it is instructive to compare the portrait of Mrs Francis with Pamela's portrait of Mrs Jewkes (the original of Mrs Slipslop, we may recall):

Now I will give you a picture of this wretch. She is a broad, squat, pursy, *fat thing*, quite ugly, if any thing human can be so called; about forty years old. She has a huge hand, and an arm as thick as my waist, I believe. Her nose is flat and crooked, and her brows grow down over her eyes; a dead, spiteful, grey, goggling eye, to be sure she has; and her face flat and broad: and as to colour, looks as if it had been pickled a month in saltpetre: I dare say she drinks. She has a hoarse man-like voice, and is as thick as she's long: and yet looks so deadly strong, that I am afraid she would dash me at her foot in an instant, if I was to vex her. So that with a heart more ugly than her face, she frightens me sadly; and I am undone, to be sure, if God does not protect me; for she is very, very wicked—indeed she is.

This is poor helpless spite in me:—but the picture is too near the truth, notwithstanding. She sends me a message, just now, that I shall have my shoes again, if I will accept of her company to walk with me in the garden—To *waddle* with me rather, thought I (*Pamela*, I, 97).

The portraits of Mrs Jewkes and Mrs Francis bring out the dissimilarities between Richardson and Fielding all the more significantly because the two passages not only describe similar persons but share characteristics of context and form which help to minimise contingent differences. Fielding is purporting to describe real-life facts in a journal, which might be expected to reduce his tendency to modify or fantasticate bare narrative by pointed feats of style. He is also, on the face of it, writing almost literally 'to the Moment', the portrait being part of a dated journal-entry. Pamela's account also occurs in a journal-entry. It further happens to signpost itself as a set-piece of portraiture ('Now I will give you a picture of this wretch . . .'), which might seem like the sort of externalizing we more readily associate with the Fielding who, in chapter-headings and in the text of the novels, is notoriously given to labelling his character-portraits explicitly as 'characters', or his dialogues as 'dialogues'. Pamela even hints at certain grotesque symmetries in Mrs Jewkes's size, and (compare Fielding's Mrs Western) gives her an 'unnatural' *man-like* quality. Add to this the obvious similarities of subject-matter: both Mrs Jewkes and Mrs Francis are nasty, shrewish women; they both have an ugly, sinister, misshapen appearance, an unhealthy and disreputable complexion (illustrated in both cases by vividly unpleasant kitchen-analogies), and unnaturally disagreeable voices. It seems probable that Mrs Jewkes was, indeed, an ultimate literary model for Fielding's composition of the real Mrs Francis's portrait, as she was a more immediate model for the earlier Slipslop. The point is significant, for it is the real Mrs Francis, rather than the fictional Mrs Jewkes, who is projected as an artefact, a literary creation.

The two passages differ most remarkably, perhaps, in their shared feeling of catty pungency. Fielding's cattiness springs, after all, from the natural personally experienced feelings of the moment, whereas

Pamela's is merely fictional creation. Yet the only thing which 'modifies' the sheer factuality of the account of Mrs Jewkes is the direct impact of Pamela's strong feelings: the naked words carry a powerful emotional charge, and remain unclothed by any marked stylistic business. The opening list, 'She is a broad, squat, pursy, *fat thing*, quite ugly, if any thing human can be so called; about forty years old', renders exactly the tremors of quickening annoyance, checked by the momentarily smug cosiness of 'if any thing human . . .', and by the unartful temporary return (brilliantly engineered by Richardson) to mere information in the closing phrase. The wonderfully precise word 'pursy' suggests not so much a studied literary effort on Pamela's part, as the almost loving vividness of exacerbated spite. Fielding begins ('She was a short, squat woman; her head was closely joined to her shoulders . . .') on a note which, by comparison, is almost one of impartial and dispassionate scientific factuality. Before long, however, what takes over from this factuality are not the natural modulations of immediate feeling, but a determined pursuit of pattern. The sour quip, in the preliminaries, about Nature's way of harmonizing appearance and character, now comes to be supported by a whole series of pointed balances and counterweights in the list itself. The complexion, 'able to turn milk to curds', is patterned against the fact that it 'not a little resembled in colour such milk as had already undergone that operation'. (Pamela, after stating her kitchen-analogy for Mrs Jewkes's complexion, does not balance it with shapely periphrastic fuss, but merely comments, with commanding economy and explosive emotional truth: 'I dare say she drinks.') The strong voice 'overbalances' the jaundiced look; she is seldom heard by Fielding 'on the same floor', but is loud from a distance; vocal and instrumental music combine in her; her husband is brought in for some crisp antitheses to her; and the portrait concludes with an exposition of her own neatly self-contradictory illogicalities. Pamela's discourse is never like this, even when she does hint at 'anti-nature' or at some mad symmetry. Mrs Jewkes's 'man-like voice' belongs with a Lesbianism of which, in context, Pamela is made hotly and pressingly aware, whereas, for example, Mrs Western's masculinity (*Tom Jones*, VI, ii) is a somewhat more abstract matter of comic redefinition, part of the extended pleasure of standing Nature on its head. Mrs Jewkes's physical proportions, 'as thick as she's long', may similarly be compared with those of blear-eyed Moll in *Amelia* (I, iii), who 'measured full as much round the middle as from head to foot': again, Fielding's emphatically and somewhat abstractly mathematical notation, as well as the entire pattern-conscious context (we shall return to Moll's portrait), highlight the difference from Richardson's passage, where the grotesque symmetry is merely glimpsed for an instant, as an ugly fact among others.

If Richardson makes his novel look like life, Fielding is making life look like one of his novels. Raw facts are not allowed, any more than in the novels, to take their own course, unframed by authorial arrangements. The piece of sour natural history about wasps and rattle-snakes, which serves as a preamble, is an old trick of his, going back at least as far as the *Champion*: it is also a sort of low-pitched variant of such introductory mock-heroic similes as that which ushers in Mrs Wilkins in *Tom Jones*, I, vi, different in being a piece of pseudo-science rather than a burlesque of epic style, and in being somewhat less animated, but serving an essentially similar purpose as a deliberate and conspicuous piece of staging for the factual material. The learned preamble to the portrait of Mrs Francis elaborates a general 'observation', of which it will be the portrait's function to provide an 'example', namely, that evil people usually *look* evil and thus unwittingly announce themselves as evil. The 'observation' runs against one of Fielding's most persistent moral themes (that it is necessary to guard most vigilantly against the snares of wicked men), and is, moreover, so coyly elaborated and so intrinsically feeble, that it is hard to think of it as a reflection which naturally imposed itself in the circumstances, rather than as a rhetorical framework for the portrait. This reluctance to record facts merely because they are facts might, in one of the earlier novels, take the more archly exuberant form and the more 'self-conscious' explicitness of a chapter heading like, 'Consisting partly of Facts, and partly of Observations upon them' (*Tom Jones*, xv, x). A journal is more prone to 'facts' than most genres, and the Preface to the *Voyage* actually warns that 'if any merely common incident should appear in this journal . . . it is not introduced for its own sake, but for some observations and reflections naturally resulting from it.' The perfectly historical Mrs Francis therefore becomes a pointedly illustrative 'character' rather than a fact of life, the more remarkably because the energies of the portrait itself are more dominant than the tired precept it exemplifies.[20]

Contrast Richardson's for once more explicit signposting of a set-piece or 'character', as Pamela says: 'Now I will give you a picture of this wretch.' This is hardly the 'self-consciousness' of a novelist playing with a narrative convention which draws attention to authorial practices. The phrase reads not like a generalizing or externalizing intervention from Richardson, but like Pamela's straightforward attempt, from within the situation she is describing, to put her material together and to make it clear. If Pamela herself shows a slight literary self-awareness, this would seem natural in someone forced by circumstances to think constantly about the problems (including physical obstacles) of writing her story down. Her self-awareness is anyway always close to a more primary introspection, as we see when she checks herself to note that she is being spiteful, and then reassures herself that 'the picture is too near the truth, notwithstanding'. For an instant, however, she lets us glimpse a real partiality which makes the portrait seem a little less, possibly, than the whole truth. The 'self-consciousness' is 'to the Moment', provisional, unsure. When Fielding raises questions of truth and credibility, on the other hand, the effect is totally different. The character of Mr and Mrs Francis is followed by these words:

> The foregoing is a very imperfect sketch of this extraordinary
> couple; for every thing is here lowered instead of being
> heightened. Those who would see them set forth in more lively
> colours, and with the proper ornaments, may read the descriptions
> of the furies in some of the classical poets, or of the stoic
> philosophers in the works of Lucian.

The disclaimer ('imperfect sketch') is merely rhetorical, saying that the account is less than the truth only in the sense which emphasizes how true it really is, unless truth itself were even stranger. Fielding's phrase claims, then, a kind of certainty. Formally at least, the passage as a whole maintains a note of finality. Pamela's portrait, though virtually labelled as a set-piece, is part of the flow of narrative, subject to immediate interruption by events, and to sustained modification or deepening as facts accumulate; Fielding's *is* a set-piece, and stands out from the flow, an enduring typification unlikely to be revised. Pamela 'writes in the present tense', as Fielding jeered in *Shamela* (Letter VI), with the close immediacy of direct speech, reporting what Mrs Jewkes said on particular occasions. Fielding (as so often) uses a past tense which suggests that the facts have been disposed of and hold no unpredictable threats; and he distances dialogue by a hint of *oratio obliqua*, flecked with ironic and generalizing overtones, reporting Mrs Francis's various statements as if they were not particular but habitual.

Yet all the tones of certainty and the air of overall grasp leave the impression, somehow, of being no longer real but a mere habit of mind, the relic of a style. Compared with the portrait of Slipslop, that earlier stylization by Fielding of Richardson's Mrs Jewkes, the account of Mrs Francis seems flat and tired, without buoyancy. If its witty pointedness is greater, one feels that the style has become over-emphatic, has stiffened rather than relaxed, as though Fielding were tightening his stylistic defences in proportion as his raw material imposed itself on him as harsh uncontrollable fact. The resolute notation of Mrs Francis's 'character' seems merely a counterpart to the unpredictable particularity of Fielding's impressions of Captain Veale, who appears in the journal now as boorish and inconsiderate, now as good-natured and brave and kind to his men, now as grossly self-interested; or again as both an incompetent sailor incapable of judging winds correctly, and as a shrewd and experienced captain, and so on (*Voyage to Lisbon*, pp. 50–2, 63, 65, 93, 96, 99, 103, 115–16, 121–2, etc.). It is not that the references to Captain Veale are free of generalizing reflection (far from it), or (e.g., p. 51) of patterned summing-up. This, if anything, makes it seem all the more remarkable that Veale resists ending up as a rounded portrait. Allowance has no doubt to be made for the fact that Mrs Francis was only encountered at a fixed stage of the voyage, as it were in the single role of bad landlady, while Veale was an everyday presence throughout. Even so, it is interesting to see Fielding's organizing impulse giving way to untidy fact. It gives rise to the speculation that even Mrs Francis's 'character', which seems quite definitive from within itself, might have been very different if she had continued to appear: might have been open, that is, to cumulative revision, development or indeed confusion, rather than to those inventive amplifications and confirmations which are all that happen, in the course of the novels, to the 'characters' of Slipslop and her like.

Inconsistency and uncharacteristic behaviour do exist in the earlier work, but they are usually reclassified (at least implicitly) under some more inclusive notion of 'conservation of character', rapidly perceptible beyond the apparently misleading immediate evidence. Apropos of 'Black George running away with the 500 *l*. from his friend and benefactor' (and of a few other similar cases), Fielding will note that 'a single bad act no more constitutes a villain in life, than a single bad part on the stage' (*Tom Jones*, VII, i), reassuring us that any likely inconsistency is in fact under the regulation of a rudimentary moral psychology, and of the rules of art, which life so conveniently imitates in the novels. If the psychology or the rules are ever made to seem not easy but difficult, as when in *Tom Jones*, VIII, i, 'conservation of character' is said to require from an author 'a very extraordinary degree of judgment, and a most exact knowledge of human nature', Fielding's whole implication is that he fully possesses the knowledge and the judgment. Sometimes, with a character like Partridge, Fielding surrenders a little further than usual to the unpredictable variousness of human nature: thus in *Tom Jones*, II, iii, Partridge is a good-natured, convivial man who is then suddenly glimpsed as hating Jenny Jones 'with no small inveteracy'; in VIII, vi and vii, we see his real generosity and loyalty to Tom, and then learn that it is also self-interested; and elsewhere again we know him as a pedantic incompetent grammarian, as an amiable compulsive liar, and many other things. Even here, although Fielding does not spell out a full 'character' which would include all these traits, he makes it clear in VIII, iv, as John S. Coolidge pointed out, that he is 'nonetheless ... working from one': Partridge 'had a great many other particularities in his character, which I shall not mention, as the reader will himself very easily perceive them, on his farther acquaintance with this extra-ordinary person'.[21] We may add that some of the 'particularities' belong largely to a traditional fictional typology (Partridge is, for example, an identifiably Cervantic character), and that whatever variety they have is really a stylization of variety, as though Fielding were playing with the rich fact of abundance itself, holding it in the palm of his hand. In a similar way, many other effects of abundance exist in *Tom Jones* in that kind of heaving festive amalgam which seems to indicate not bewilderment but the gay inclusiveness of the author's grasp: a striking example might be the mixture of tones in IV, ii, where genuine devotion to Sophia, and a delicate realism of description, mingle with blowsy mock-heroic, a near-pedantry of historical and literary reference, a polished urbanity, and an element of rude, not to say obscene, allusion.

Norman Mailer once described how a reading of E. M. Forster's *The Longest Journey* disabused him of the conventional idea 'that when you wrote a novel you tried to build a character who could be handled and walked around like a piece of sculpture'. He learned instead 'that personality was more fluid, more dramatic and startling, more inexact than I had thought'. He goes on to describe how a character in *The Deer Park* 'is a being rather than a character. If you study her closely you will see that she is a different person in every scene. Just a little different.'[22] Captain Veale is presented with less than Mailerian fluidity, but he has a complexity which is more 'untidy' than the oddly sharp and stylized surprises about Partridge, or the patterned discontinuities (to be discussed in the next chapter) of *Amelia*'s blear-eyed Moll. Veale's unpredictabilities would not have seemed to Fielding a valued achievement of his own narrative artistry, so much as a measure of the degree to which life's surprises now defied his sense of fitness. Anything tending to mere constatation meant for Fielding a kind of surrender. He was, however, honest enough as a man and an artist to know intuitively when his true feelings needed to come to terms with harsh fact, either accepting it in all its disorder or registering pained protest in tense reminders of order, but not overwhelming it with buoyancies that belonged to earlier moods.

NOTES

1 Paul Valéry, 'Philosophie de la Danse' (1936), in *Oeuvres*, ed. Jean Hytier, Pléiade (Paris, 1965), I, 1399. In my discussion of the dance as a central symbol of imaginative activity, I am naturally indebted to the stimulus and insights of Frank Kermode's *Romantic Image* (London, 1957). For an exploration, in Fielding's own time, of the relationship between poetry, the dance and the other arts, in terms which bear on the concerns of this chapter, see Charles Batteux, *Les Beaux Arts Réduits à un Même Principe*, 1746.

2 Chesterfield, *Letters*, IV, 1234–5.

3 *Of Dramatic Poesy and Other Critical Essays*, ed. George Watson (London and New York, 1962), I, 89.

4 Jenyns, *Works*, 2nd edn (1793), I, 20–1.

5 *Four Quartets* (London, 1950), pp. 42–3.

6 *The New Poetic* (Harmondsworth, 1967), pp. 127, 131, 143.

7 Wallace Stevens, 'The Man with the Blue Guitar', section VI.

8 Yeats, *Collected Poems* (1952), p. 193.

9 *Literary and Philosophical Criticism*, ed. John Shawcross (London, 1909), pp. 127, 154–5.

10 Reprinted from Jordan's *Wit in a Wilderness* (?1665), in *The Bee, Select Poems from Books and Manuscripts* (1715), III, 12–15.

11 Roethke, *Collected Poems* (London, 1968), pp. 105–7. For some pertinent comments involving the dance in Pope, Davies and a modern poet (in this case Auden), see Fern Farnham, 'Achilles' Shield: Some observations on Pope's *Iliad*', *Publications of the Modern Language Association of America*, lxxxiv (1969), 1580.

12 *Three Novels* (London, 1959), p. 10; Beckett's novels have a fierce and brilliant air of being *Tales of a Tub*, rewritten straight.

13 E.g. 'Drown the World', *Correspondence*, ed. H. Williams (Oxford, 1963–5), III, 117. The following remark by Leslie Stephen, in a letter of 25 December 1874 to Charles Eliot Norton, is amusingly relevant, and should be compared with the passage I quoted from the *Sentiments of a Church-of-England Man*: 'There is [in Swift] a charming sermon on brotherly love, which he inculcates by saying that papists, dissenters,

deists, and all moderate members of the Church of England are a set of hateful and contemptible beings, who will be damned for not loving him and his friends.' (F. W. Maitland, *The Life and Letters of Leslie Stephen* (London, 1906), p. 248).

14 In ensuing paragraphs, I draw upon (and I hope in places add to or modify) material in my two related discussions: 'Gulliver and the Gentle Reader', *Imagined Worlds. Essays . . . in honour of John Butt*, ed. Maynard Mack and Ian Gregor (London, 1968), pp. 51–90, and 'Order and Cruelty: A Reading of Swift, with some Comments on Pope and Johnson', *Essays in Criticism*, XX (1970), 24–56. I apologize for certain verbatim repetitions and the use of some of the same quotations, which seem necessary to the present argument.

15 *Fielding and the Nature of the Novel* (Cambridge, Mass., 1968), p. 53.

16 *To the Palace of Wisdom* (Garden City, N.Y., 1965), p. 153.

17 *Pamela*, Everyman's Library (London and New York, 1955), I, 97.

18 *Humphry Clinker*, Oxford English Novels (London, 1966), p. 60.

19 *Works*, ed. Henley, XV, 181–4.

20 For a very moving description of Mrs Francis in 1755, which argues that Fielding was cruelly unfair to her, and that he was a very troublesome guest, see *Henry Fielding. The Critical Heritage*, ed. Ronald Paulson and Thomas Lockwood (Routledge & Kegan Paul, 1969), pp. 391–2.

21 'Fielding and "Conservation of Character"', *Modern Philology*, lvii (1960), 246 n. 12.

22 *Paris Review* interview, in *Cannibals and Christians* (New York, 1967), pp. 209, 212.

CHAPTER III

NATURE, CRUEL CIRCUMSTANCE AND THE RAGE FOR ORDER: *AMELIA*, WITH REFLECTIONS ON DEFOE, SMOLLETT AND ORWELL

Her eye (for she had but one) . . . had two remarkable qualities;
for first, as if Nature had been careful to provide for her own
defect, it constantly looked towards her blind side; and secondly,
the ball consisted almost entirely of white, or rather yellow, with
a little grey spot in the corner, so small that it was scarce
discernible. Nose she had none; for Venus, envious perhaps at
her former charms, had carried off the gristly part; and some
earthly damsel, perhaps, from the same envy, had levelled the bone
with the rest of her face: . . . About half a dozen ebony teeth
fortified that large and long canal which nature had cut from ear
to ear, at the bottom of which was a chin preposterously short,
nature having turned up the bottom, instead of suffering it to
grow to its due length.

(Amelia, I, iii)

> Le soleil rayonnait sur cette pourriture,
> Comme afin de la cuire à point,
> Et de rendre au centuple à la grande Nature
> Tout ce qu'ensemble elle avait joint . . .
>
> (Baudelaire, 'Une Charogne')

HAMM: Nature has forgotten us.
CLOV: There's no more nature.
HAMM: No more nature! You exaggerate.
CLOV: In the vicinity.
HAMM: But we breathe, we change! We lose our hair, our teeth!
    Our bloom! Our ideals!
CLOV: Then she hasn't forgotten us.   (Beckett, *Endgame*)

At the end of the previous chapter, I noted an unusual fluidity (a lack of rounded conclusiveness and of tidy consistency) in the characterization of Captain Veale in Fielding's last work, the *Voyage to Lisbon*. The *Voyage* is a journal (and one whose Preface celebrates the value of 'true history... in humble prose'), where an unstylized particularity of notation might seem likelier to occur than in carefully planned novels. I argued also, however, that the *Voyage* shows Fielding still tending to forms of artistry which look back to the novels, and that in its account of Mrs Francis the older habits of rounded characterization and of conclusive epigrammatic summing-up are intensified and stiffened rather than relaxed. Even allowing for the difference (relevant to both journals and novels) between major protagonists whose roles are extended and varied, and lesser characters more readily encapsulated in a set character-sketch, there is in the *Voyage* a fluctuating tendency on Fielding's part both to loosen and to over-tighten his authorial grip on the raw material of life. I believe this is equally true of Fielding's last novel, *Amelia* (which precedes the *Voyage* by three years).

Several recent critics have demonstrated that *Amelia* differs from the earlier novels in that some of its characters, as John S. Coolidge has said, 'come into the story in the same way that people come into our lives. ... Our knowledge of a person's character is always provisory, pending further discovery.'[1] I shall not repeat the evidence, which has been fully studied (although I shall have more to say about the reverse side of this in some short conclusive set-pieces on minor characters). The best discussions agree in noting that Fielding seems to waver between the new fluidity and a hankering after his older method, and that some of the weaknesses of *Amelia* spring from the fact that the new way opened up 'complexities and ambiguities which Fielding himself was not quite ready to confront or follow out'[2] or achieved something which in a sense 'he neither desired at the outset nor welcomed when it came'.[3] I shall argue that such uncertainties are radical to *Amelia*, a (partly deliberate) rendering of a larger struggle between Fielding's rage for order and the senseless brutality of fact; and that they produce major and somewhat unique strengths, as well as weaknesses, in the novel.

This fundamental ambiguity exists outside the domain of characterization, as well as within it, in certain general themes which underlie the action, and (once again, but with startling force) in some stylistic forms. Very significant is the novel's insistent preoccupation with Fortune, so insistent that, uniquely among Fielding's major writings, it becomes the focus of a serious thematic interest. In Fielding's earlier writings, Fortune was little more than a notional disguise for the instrumentalities of comic or dramatic plots (coincidences, discoveries, surprises, unravellings and happy endings). We are always reminded, as Martin Price says, 'that the malignant Fortune that hounds [the] characters and the comic providence that extricates them are only two aspects of the author himself, as they are of a benevolent deity'.[4] Alternatively, Fortune's power might be the subject of relatively commonplace asseveration, as in Fielding's *Champion* essay of 6 December 1739. There need be no doubt that Fielding meant what he said in that essay, but one hardly feels the full weight of his deepest emotional conviction when he makes Hercules Vinegar declare that 'human life appears to me to resemble the game of hazard, much more than that of chess'.[5] William B. Coley contrasts this chess metaphor with the moralistic warning in *Amelia* (I, i) that men are responsible for their own distresses and that they blame Fortune 'with no less absurdity . . . than a bad player complains of ill luck at a game of chess'.[6] I wish to suggest that this contrast means something more paradoxical than appears at first sight: namely, not that Fortune finally became insignificant in Fielding's outlook, but that (in the guise of life's cruel unpredictabilities) it acquired on the contrary a more pressing reality than Fielding had earlier been prepared to acknowledge. What seems notable in the passage from the opening of *Amelia*, in other words, is not the fact that it denies the overriding agency of Fortune, but that it speaks on the subject with a new weight of seriousness and urgency.

This increased concern is more evident than any consistent or systematic working out of the ideas in question. After Fielding's admonition that we should usually blame not Fortune but ourselves and our 'predominant passions' for our troubles, we read that Booth also is a believer in the primacy of the 'predominant passion', and we see him contesting the deist Robinson's extreme fatalism on these grounds. At the same time, we learn that Booth and Robinson have little faith in Providence (I, iii). The irreligious quality of Booth's doctrine of predominant passions (as distinct from Fielding's own) is gradually exposed, until Booth penitently defines it himself (XII, v) as part of his final conversion. The distinction between Fortune and Providence is traditional, and we may I suppose take it (if we insist that Fielding is sustaining the statements about Fortune which he made at the beginning) that it is Providence rather than Fortune who finally made things turn out well at the end. But it is also a fact that Fortune is said finally to 'smile' upon the Booths, and to make them 'large amends for the tricks she had played them in their youth' (XII, ix). Similarly, in earlier passages, Fortune is spoken of as unfriendly to Booth and as the cause of his misfortunes (IX, vii; X, v; on Fortune's 'malice', see also VIII, viii); and in a strongly written passage in VIII, iii we read that although Fortune's power to depress a truly virtuous person like Amelia is not absolute, Fortune can nevertheless exercise 'the highest degree of ... malice' upon her, and give her the 'most exquisite distress'. These usages are partly just idiomatic, but Fielding harps on Fortune from the start as a topic of central moral concern, and the attention we pay to the word becomes accordingly rather more than perfunctory. If the various accounts of Fortune need not be taken absolutely literally, nor thought of as radically inconsistent, the oscillations of feeling and emphasis are no longer merely informal. The force of these oscillations transcends not only the normal flexibilities of linguistic usage, but also the conventional patternings of romance. William B. Coley is right in a sense to say that the novel describes the victory of Prudence over Fortune,[7] although I think that even in the special case of *Amelia*, where prudence is especially important, critics often overrate the role of this virtue, which Fielding did not find it easy to admire unreservedly. But equally, it seems hard not to agree with Sheridan Baker that the novel's happy ending is also largely a matter of romance-convention.[8]

At the same time, I would suggest (in opposition to Coley) that the real significance of the moralistic emphasis in the opening chapter and elsewhere is that Fortune is somewhat strenuously played down because its unpredictabilities seemed to Fielding more, and not less, threatening; and (in partial disagreement with Baker) that the romance patternings hardly iron out the unpredictabilities, or restore much active faith in the power of good persons to triumph in a wicked world. There is more pressing conviction in those recurrent exclamations of Amelia, that 'there are more bad people in the world [than good people], and they will hate you for your goodness', that 'there is an end of all goodness in the world', that 'we have no comfort, no hope, no friend left' (IV, iii; VII, x; VIII, ix), than in any ultimate resolution of her troubles. This is true even though Amelia's statements are either qualified in context, or known by the reader to rest partly on an inaccurate analysis of the situation, because the grinding actuality of the Booths' predicament overwhelms finer discriminations. Moreover, none of the good protagonists have the intrinsic energy of their counterparts in the earlier fiction, nor the transferred qualities of stability and vigour which Fielding himself projected into them as inhabitants of his comic world: Amelia is more passive than Sophia, Dr Harrison is infinitely duller than Parson Adams and slightly duller even than Allworthy, Atkinson is

unrelieved by the energizing comicality of Joseph, and Booth, an older
Tom Jones, is also, as Martin Price says,[9] 'shabbier', lacking most of
Tom's romantic appeal. Fortune's unpredictabilities and men's wickedness are not any longer outfaced by the old comic assurances, although
they continue to be challenged by a weaker, willed insistence of
authorial intervention: 'The speaker in *Amelia* does claim a competent
knowledge of the ways of the world in which the story takes place, but
it is a world he never made'.[10]

The unpredictabilities and the wickedness are brought into sharp focus
from the start, in the famous Newgate chapters. The squalor and suffering depicted there flow mostly from the iniquitous magistrate Mr
Thrasher, whose 'character' is this:

> Mr. Thrasher . . . had some few imperfections in his magistratical
> capacity. I own, I have been sometimes inclined to think that this
> office of a justice of peace requires some knowledge of the law:
> for this simple reason; because, in every case which comes before
> him, he is to judge and act according to law. Again, as these laws
> are contained in a great variety of books, the statutes which relate
> to the office of a justice of peace making themselves at least two
> large volumes in folio; and that part of his jursidiction which is
> founded on the common law being dispersed in above a hundred
> volumes, I cannot conceive how this knowledge could be acquired
> without reading; and yet certain it is, Mr. Thrasher never read one
> syllable of the matter.
>
> This, perhaps, was a defect; but this was not all: for where
> mere ignorance is to decide a point between two litigants, it will
> always be an even chance whether it decides right or wrong: but
> sorry am I to say, right was often in a much worse situation than
> this, and wrong hath often had five hundred to one on his side
> before that magistrate; who, if he was ignorant of the laws of
> England, was yet well versed in the laws of nature. He perfectly
> well understood that fundamental principle so strongly laid down
> in the institutes of the learned Rochefoucault, by which the duty
> of self-love is so strongly enforced, and every man is taught to
> consider himself as the centre of gravity, and to attract all things
> thither. To speak the truth plainly, the justice was never
> indifferent in a cause but when he could get nothing on either
> side (I, ii).

This 'character' is unlike others (both early and late) which we have
been examining, in that the personal details about Thrasher which we

might expect to find in a descriptive set-piece constantly give way to elaborations of Fielding's anger. The expected list of 'imperfections', for example, dissolves before it is even begun into the strenuous self-orientated irony of 'I own, I have been sometimes . . .'. We know that judicial misbehaviour would at this time (when Fielding was himself a hard-worked magistrate, and not only sensitive on the score of professional ethics but also a close personal witness of the misery of prison life) seem particularly painful to Fielding. His self-involvement is no longer of the formal, detached sort, but utterly and autobiographically real, without detachment. Much of the old stylistic manner remains: the cutting understatement ('some few imperfections'), the ironic antitheses ('right' and 'wrong', 'laws of England' and 'laws of nature'), the sharp, quasi-paradoxical punch-line at the end ('the justice was never indifferent in a cause but when he could get nothing on either side'). But these are the stiffened forms of an urbanity that no longer really suffuses the argument, or eases the tone. Understatement has become ponderous, and serves as an uncomfortable rhetorical softening-up for the mounting sarcasms. The rhythms lack the old sweeping masterfulness, and waver as ironic discipline slackens to a tense garrulity. The elaboration in the second paragraph of the irony about Thrasher's perverse injustice ('wrong' always having a better chance than 'right'), is in total contrast with Swift's tart economy when he speaks of judges so unjust by nature that they even refuse 'a large Bribe from the side where Justice lay, rather than injure the *Faculty*, by doing any thing unbecoming their Nature or their Office' (*Gulliver's Travels*, IV, v).

Fielding is not uniformly at home in a Swiftian mood, as one might expect. But if the passage lacks the Swiftian astringency of negation, as well as some of Fielding's usual polished command, it remains impressive for the rough, almost awkward painfulness which smoulders through the old framework of stylistic assurance. With it goes an oddly intensified sense of the disconnection of types like Thrasher from ordinary values and purposes. Many of Fielding's earlier professional types—Mr Barnabas in *Joseph Andrews*, I, xiii, the surgeon in *Tom Jones* VII, xiii, and several other clergymen, doctors and lawyers—are trapped in self-absorbed professional postures which combine jargon, laxity and self-interest in pedantic amalgam, and which cut them off from the human needs which their professions are actually intended to serve. But they are often given a comic humanity by that fact itself, as when Barnabas's mechanical treatment of Joseph's spiritual interests completes itself in a Pickwickian hurry to get back to the inn's parlour to squeeze the oranges for punch. In Thrasher, self-centredness also tends to the systematic. The resulting pedantry, however, is no merely comic matter of jargon and forms disguising or supporting egoism, but a systematizing of the egoism itself, which becomes a matter of 'fundamental principle', backed by 'institutes' and 'learned' authority. He reflects social institutions which are in effect radically divorced from humane function, like Swift's judges (though these seem even farther gone in ghoulish abstraction, foregoing even personal interest for the sake of injustice). A variant example, in *Amelia*, is the bailiff who cheerfully causes hardship to Booth without any ill-will, or wish to harm him, or regret:

> notwithstanding the earnest desire which the bailiff had declared to see Booth out of his troubles, he had ordered the porter, who was his follower, to call upon two or three other bailiffs, and as many attorneys, to try to load his prisoner with as many actions as possible.
>
> Here the reader may be apt to conclude that the bailiff, instead of being a friend, was really an enemy to poor Booth; but, in fact, he was not so. His desire was no more than to accumulate bail-bonds; for the bailiff was reckoned an honest and good sort of man in his way, and had no more malice against the bodies in his custody than a butcher hath to those in his: and as the latter, when he takes his knife in hand, hath no idea but of the joints into which he is to cut the carcase; so the former, when he handles his writ, hath no other design but to cut the body into as many bail-bonds as possible. As to the life of the animal, or the liberty of the man, they are thoughts which never obtrude themselves on either (VIII, i).

The same bailiff, in a later conversation with Booth (XII, v), insists on the distinction between legally permitted and all other forms of killing, in a manner which again shows him to be totally and impenetrably unaware of the human or personal aspect of *any* act of homicide. He differs, of course, from Thrasher, who is more consciously self-regarding and cruel, more determinedly 'indifferent in a cause [only] when he could get nothing on either side'. But they are part of the same feeling, pervasive in *Amelia*, of a cruel divorce between social institutions and the human purposes which they theoretically serve; and they have a quality of absurd abstraction which Fielding finds incomprehensible, not in the old confident eyebrow-raising way, but genuinely, and under protest.

The Newgate scenes which follow the portrait of Thrasher, and show the effects of his magistracy, illustrate this incomprehensibility, as well as Fielding's pained determination to maintain some form of organizing grasp over it through pointed orderings of style. The tendency to neat ironic summation reasserts itself very strikingly in a series of brief vignettes in which Fielding seems largely to have shed the garrulous uneasiness of parts of the set-piece on Thrasher himself. This is evident, for example, in the 'pathetic' tableau of the 'young woman in rags . . . supporting the head of an old man in her lap, who appeared to be giving up the ghost': 'These, Mr. Robinson informed [Booth], were father and daughter; that the latter was committed for stealing a loaf, in order to support the former, and the former for receiving it, knowing it to be stolen' (I, iv). The stylistic surface is unscathed (but, in a sense, only just) by very heavy burdens of feeling. The organizing discipline of a deep stylistic habit does not, as in the Thrasher portrait, waver or relax, but is instead in full and open confrontation with ironies of circumstance which no urbanity of tone can tame, and no verbal summation comfortably account for. Out of this deadlock, a new style is created, in which the commentator is not in command through his witty insights, but helpless before a cruel absurdity.

The Newgate vignettes of *Amelia* must be distinguished from those brief moral set-pieces of similar shape which Fielding had produced from time to time in the past (for example, in the Lucianic judgment-pieces in the *Champion* and the *Journey from this World to the Next*, I, vii),[11] which are likewise capped by some sharp reversal or ironic shock. For one thing, the earlier pieces are fairly straightforward nutshell-moralities, noting a preposterous foible (e.g., girls affecting what turns out to be a false pregnancy), or giving a surprising but positive turn to a moral principle (e.g., a lady of self-proclaiming virtue being refused entrance into Elysium, which has no room for prudes):

The next who advanced was a beautiful young creature of about fifteen, so young that we were surprised to see her appear big with child; but more so when we found she had pulled off her clothes and her big belly together. Some body spoke to her on this occasion, and she answered, that it was the fashion for all young ladies to appear with child in the world she came from (*Champion*, 24 May 1740).[12]

There now advanced a very beautiful spirit indeed. She began to ogle Minos the moment she saw him. She said, she hoped there were some merit in refusing a great number of lovers, and dying a maid, though she had had the choice of a hundred. Minos told her, she had not refused enow yet, and turned her back (*Journey from this World*, I, vii).[13]

These underworld glimpses of the grotesque or the morally unexpected may be contrasted with the episode of the 'very pretty girl' in the gruesome metaphorical (or neo-epic) Underworld of *Amelia*:

A very pretty girl then advanced towards them, whose beauty Mr. Booth could not help admiring the moment he saw her; declaring at the same time, he thought she had great innocence in her countenance. Robinson said she was committed thither as an idle and disorderly person, and a common street-walker. As she passed by Mr. Booth, she damned his eyes, and discharged a volley of words, every one of which was too indecent to be repeated (I, iv).

That this girl (she may be related in Fielding's mind to the real-life and almost exactly contemporary girl, 'one of the prettiest . . . I had ever seen', also seen in painfully squalid surroundings, in the *Enquiry into the Causes of the Late Increase of Robbers*, 1751)[14] belongs to a different order of painfulness from the earlier two need not be laboured. It is presumably not the abusive language as such which shocks Fielding, who is fairly ready, here and elsewhere, to record at least such moderate vulgarities as 'damn', 'fart', 'arse', 'bitch', and the like, often with a surrounding periphrastic archness, of course, and a coy use (his or his printer's) of partial blanks. Even his coy refusals to repeat bad language, as when Mrs Western 'uttered phrases improper to be here related' in *Tom Jones*, VII, iii, are in the earlier novels archly knowing rather than evasive, and wholly lack the pained recoil we sense in the 'too indecent to be repeated' of the passage from *Amelia*. The shock resides instead in a quality of cruel surprise, which Fielding has deliberately staged or heightened by his otherwise gratuitous emphasis on the girl's beauty and innocent countenance. That a very similar staging was more than once put to other and milder uses in the earlier work confirms how pointedly the girl is being used here as a (highly formalized) sign of violated faith in the fitnesses of an ordered world.

But it is not only the lighter examples of moral reversal or shock in the earlier writings which differ so radically from the cruel irrational unpredictability of these thumbnail scenes in *Amelia*. One or two of the earlier ironies are themselves rather harsher than the rest, and anticipate specific judicial harshnesses of these Newgate chapters. The poor man, 'a very tender husband and a kind father', who appears before Minos after having been hanged for the 'robbery of eighteen pence' (*Journey from this World*, I, vii),[15] or the famous postilion of *Joseph Andrews*, I, xii, who was 'transported for robbing a hen-roost', may be compared with the distracted prisoner whom Booth and Robinson see prostrate and groaning in *Amelia*: 'This person was, it seems, committed for a small felony; and his wife, who then lay-in, upon hearing the news, had thrown herself from a window two pair of stairs high, by which means he had, in all probability, lost both her and his child' (I, iv). The purpose of the two earlier examples is to highlight the cruelty of a technical legalism which fails to take personal qualities into account. Fielding is not complacent, but he does have the situation emotionally in hand. The treatment is briefly dismissive: a social evil is angrily placed, and its consequences, though painful, are (given the system) predictable. There is no attempt to particularize the after-effects, and the brevity partly suggests confidence that other men of sense and feeling will take the point as self-evident. Moreover, the irony remains on a level of generalization or abstraction: however passionate the author's feelings, they are not focused too disturbingly on the individual case, which exemplifies a relatively constant application of known laws (the severity of which, be it said, Fielding supported in principle, notably in his later thinking, which makes the later passage from *Amelia* even more remarkable). In *Amelia*, by contrast with the two earlier instances, Fielding pauses over the case beyond his immediate point about insensitive judicial severity. The treatment is still 'exemplary', but it passes on to some excruciating and gratuitous hardships of circumstance which are not (whatever the system and whoever the magistrate) simply predictable.

But the most remarkable staging, by Fielding, of an unpredictability so radical that it transcends all explanation (however surprising) which might account for it in terms of a bad society, wicked magistrates, or whatever, is the portrait of Blear-eyed Moll:

> The first person who accosted him was called Blear-eyed Moll, a
> woman of no very comely appearance. Her eye (for she had but
> one), whence she derived her nickname, was such as that
> nickname bespoke; besides which it had two remarkable qualities;
> for first, as if Nature had been careful to provide for her own
> defect, it constantly looked towards her blind side; and secondly,
> the ball consisted almost entirely of white, or rather yellow, with
> a little grey spot in the corner, so small that it was scarce

discernible. Nose she had none; for Venus, envious perhaps at her former charms, had carried off the gristly part; and some earthly damsel, perhaps, from the same envy, had levelled the bone with the rest of her face: indeed it was far beneath the bones of her cheeks, which rose proportionally higher than is usual. About half a dozen ebony teeth fortified that large and long canal which nature had cut from ear to ear, at the bottom of which was a chin preposterously short, nature having turned up the bottom, instead of suffering it to grow to its due length.

Her body was well adapted to her face; she measured full as much round the middle as from head to foot; for, besides the extreme breadth of her back, her vast breasts had long since forsaken their native home, and had settled themselves a little below the girdle.

I wish certain actresses on the stage, when they are to perform characters of no amiable cast, would study to dress themselves with the propriety with which Blear-eyed Moll was now arrayed. For the sake of our squeamish reader, we shall not descend to particulars; let it suffice to say, nothing more ragged or more dirty was ever emptied out of the round-house at St. Giles's.

We have taken the more pains to describe this person, for two remarkable reasons; the one is, that this unlovely creature was taken in the fact with a very pretty young fellow; the other, which is more productive of moral lesson, is, that however wretched her fortune may appear to the reader, she was one of the merriest persons in the whole prison (I, iii).

The 'two remarkable reasons' are almost more shocking because they are not, like the conclusions of the other vignettes, intrinsically painful. The other examples, for all their gratuitous surprises, are still part of a graspable moral theme, concerned with injustice, unforeseeable suffering and the topsy-turviness of prison life: because the surprises are painful, we at least know *why* we are shocked. The conclusion of Moll's 'character', on the other hand, has a startling inconsequence whose very element of gaiety contains a touch of the hysterical. Nor are we able to set much store by the remark that the second 'remarkable reason' is 'productive of moral lesson', although the paradoxical gaiety of prison life has already been noted just before the 'character' began and certain pieties might suggest themselves from this. For no such pieties are in fact entered into (the flat astringency of the suggestion hardly encourages much positive speculation either), and this 'merriest person' is next seen, immediately after, abusing Booth with 'dreadful oaths', and, a little later (I, iv), taking part in the gruesome baiting of a homosexual inmate.

When, by contrast, Defoe's Moll Flanders encounters the same phenomenon of cheerfulness at Newgate, the matter is not treated as a violation of the order of things, but as a fact like any other. Moll questions a woman under sentence of death about her cheerfulness, and receives an entirely mundane explanation, which Moll moralizes without mystery or pointed refusals to explain:[16]

> Well says I, and are you thus easy? ay, *says she*, I can't help myself, what signifyes being sad? If I am hang'd there's an End of me, and away she turn'd Dancing, and Sings as she goes, the following Piece of *Newgate* Wit,
>
> > *If I swing by the String,*
> > *I shall hear the Bell ring,*
> > *And then there's an End of poor* Jenny.
>
> I mention this, because it would be worth the Observation of any Prisoner, who shall hereafter fall into the same Misfortune and come to that dreadful Place of *Newgate*; how Time, Necessity, and Conversing with the Wretches that are there Familiarizes the Place to them; how at last they become reconcil'd to that which at first was the greatest Dread upon their Spirits in the World, and are as impudently Chearful and Merry in their Misery, as they were when out of it.

Defoe surrenders his scene to the ordinary unhighfalutin consciousness of Moll, who takes events as they come, and whose explanations are at an unquestioning level of everyday psychology. By internalizing the event through Moll's reactions, Defoe removes the element of shock from a startling external fact. What passes for mere factual recording in Defoe probably often depends on the kind of consciousness through which his factuality is normally filtered: a consciousness active and individual, yet sufficiently taken for granted as commonplace or 'normal' for its reactions (Moll's moral gloss on the prisoner's explanation, as well as the explanation itself) to seem an inevitable part of the whole factual picture. It is not in Fielding's temperament to record or to iron out life's startling incongruities as normal, and his account, in an odd sense much more externally factual than Defoe's, dramatizes rather than plays down the shock. This refusal to internalize his account, though deeply a matter of neoclassic and gentlemanly conditioning, may in a special sense also be complementary to his often-noted surrender, in other parts of the novel, to the fluidity of character of at least some protagonists. The apparent formal distance from which he describes Moll, and the violent schematism of the portrait itself, seem to contain something of that special stylized externality which certain absurdist authors of our own time have cultivated as a response to life's senselessness and complexity.[17]

The portrayal of Blear-eyed Moll is not, in any event, easily assimilated to that flowing particularity of realistic fiction which is sometimes claimed for *Amelia*. How far the passage is from this may be judged by contrasting it with an episode from George Orwell's *Nineteen Eighty-Four*, which has certain striking similarities of detail with it:[18]

There was a constant come-and-go of prisoners of every description: drug-peddlers, thieves, bandits, black-marketeers, drunks, prostitutes. Some of the drunks were so violent that the other prisoners had to combine to suppress them. An enormous wreck of a woman, aged about sixty, with great tumbling breasts and thick coils of white hair which had come down in her struggles, was carried in, kicking and shouting, by four guards, who had hold of her one at each corner. They wrenched off the boots with which she had been trying to kick them, and dumped her down across Winston's lap, almost breaking his thigh-bones. The woman hoisted herself upright and followed them out with a yell of 'F——bastards!' Then, noticing that she was sitting on something uneven, she slid off Winston's knees on to the bench.

'Beg pardon, dearie,' she said. 'I wouldn't 'a sat on you, only the buggers put me there. They dono 'ow to treat a lady, do they?' She paused, patted her breast, and belched. 'Pardon,' she said, 'I ain't meself, quite'.

She leant forward and vomited copiously on the floor.

'Thass better', she said, leaning back with closed eyes. 'Never keep it down, thass what I say. Get it up while it's fresh on your stomach, like.'

She revived, turned to have another look at Winston, and seemed immediately to take a fancy to him. She put a vast arm round his shoulder and drew him towards her, breathing beer and vomit into his face.

'Wass your name, dearie?' she said.

'Smith,' said Winston.

'Smith?' said the woman. 'Thass funny. My name's Smith too. Why,' she added sentimentally, 'I might be your mother!'

She might, thought Winston, be his mother. She was about the right age and physique, and it was probable that people changed somewhat after twenty years in a forced labour camp.

The detailed parallels with Blear-eyed Moll are so many (the setting in the 'constant come-and-go' of a prison, the dirtiness, age and 'great tumbling breasts' of the two women, the erotic glimpse we have of both with a young man, the quality of high spirits or merriment) that one might suppose that Orwell actually drew on Fielding's passage: Orwell said that Fielding was one of the writers 'I care most about and never grow tired of', and praised *Amelia* for its 'psychological realism'.[19]

But the two passages could hardly be more different in their overall nature. Orwell's character merges naturally into the novel's flow of events, is involved in a naturalistic dialogue reported without obvious authorial interference, never seems self-contained or stylized. Even the hint of romance-coincidence (that Mrs Smith might be Winston's mother, who had disappeared suddenly in a mysterious totalitarian abduction long ago), a grim touch of parody which is left undeveloped but which carries an eloquent momentary irony, deepens the episode's natural absorption within the narrative, rather than distancing it or making it stand out. Mrs Smith's colloquial quip poignantly connects with an old worry of Winston's, and the fact that (unlike in novels) we never learn whether she is his mother or not adds an intimate resonance to the general painfulness (contrast the conventional and stylized crisis, melodramatically highlighted and decisively resolved, over Mrs Waters near the end of *Tom Jones*). It would be hard to guess from this passage that Orwell's novel was a nightmare fantasy of the future, rather than a 'history of his own times in humble prose'.

The portrait of Blear-eyed Moll, on the other hand, stands out in all its schematic boldness, self-contained, stylized even in its cruel surprises. Whether or not Moll was Orwell's source for Mrs Smith (I believe she probably was), the difference is radical while the similarities of detail are to some extent commonplace. The type of grotesque portrait is an old one, looking back to many hags and bawds in Martial and Juvenal, in medieval allegorists and in Ben Jonson, in Overbury and other authors of 'characters', in Swift's 'Beautiful Young Nymph' and its many analogues. Nevertheless, Fielding's passage differs from all others known to me not so much in the fact of grotesquerie, but in its charged formulaic interplay between startling incongruity and the order it subverts. It differs from an equally formulaic piece of shock-writing like Swift's 'Beautiful Young Nymph' in the fierce laconic inconsequence of its surprises, as distinct from Swift's powerful but for once essentially predictable and protracted unravelling of a simple moral irony, in some ways a conventional exercise in probing under fair surfaces. It differs from other grotesques, like Overbury's 'Maquerela, in plaine English a Bawde', transcending descriptive resemblances, however close, and all mere squalor of physical detail, in its unyielding obsessional insistence on fitness and propriety.

In this, it strikes a new note in Fielding, and perhaps in eighteenth-century literature. The stylistic properties of the description are, super-ficially, familiar enough, the balanced assurance in the prose rhythms, the firmness of notation, the 'witty' exploitation of notions of grotesque decorum: nickname matching appearance, Moll's body 'well adapted' to her face, the 'propriety' with which she is 'arrayed'. Nature, that goddess of ordered universes, is painfully ubiquitous, here grimly providing 'for her own defect', there preventing the 'due' growth of Moll's chin. The venereal noselessness becomes a literal matter of Venus, so to speak, getting her own back; and Venus's depredation is balanced and completed by the 'earthly damsel's'. Part of the uniqueness of the passage resides in the intensified emphasis, in the combination of *extreme* grotesquerie with *so many* reminders of order.

But this is not all. Let us compare it with a final and nearly contem-porary example, much concerned with both grotesquerie and order, and in these respects perhaps the closest-resembling of all, Smollett's description of the bawd in *Ferdinand Count Fathom*:

> the rest of the society adjourned in two coaches to the temple of love, where they were received by the venerable priestess, a personage turned of seventy, who seemed to exercise the functions of her calling, in despite of the most cruel ravages of time; for age had bent her into the form of a Turkish bow. Her head was agitated by the palsy, like the leaf of the poplar tree; her hair fell down in scanty parcels, as white as the driven snow; her face was not simply wrinkled, but ploughed into innumerable furrows; her jaws could not boast of one remaining tooth; one eye distilled a large quantity of rheum, by virtue of the fiery edge that surrounded it; the other was altogether extinguished, and she had lost her nose in the course of her ministration. The Delphic sibyl was but a type of this hoary matron, who, by her figure, might have been mistaken for the consort of Chaos, or mother of Time. Yet there

was something meritorious in her appearance, as it denoted her an indefatigable minister to the pleasure of mankind, and as it formed an agreeable contrast with the beauty and youth of the fair damsels that wantoned in her train. It resembled those discords in music, which, properly disposed, contribute to the harmony of the whole piece; or those horrible giants, who, in the world of romance, used to guard the gates of the castle in which the enchanted damsel was confined (ch. XXIII).

The two women are both elderly bawds, one-eyed, noseless, and 'meritorious' in some queer sense. The passages share a tendency (less marked in Smollett) towards paired arrangements, a similarly tart firmness of notation modulating occasionally to periphrastic mock-pompousness, an insistence on 'harmony' and the kind of 'discord' which gives an ironic colouring (or 'contributes') to harmony (Smollett's more explicit elaboration of the musical sense of 'harmony' recalls those other Fielding portraits I have discussed, of Mrs Joan Vinegar and Mrs Francis). It is possible that Smollett's passage, published a year or so after *Amelia*, owes something (like Orwell's Mrs Smith) to Blear-eyed Moll. The differences, however, are once again crucial. Smollett's account, though belonging to a harsh and scabrous context in his novel, is oddly festive, full of vigorous enjoyment of ugliness, and with none of the flat painfulness of Fielding's piece. The paradoxical nature-similes sometimes call beautiful things to mind, poplar-leaves and the driven snow, whose freshness (in a way which partly recalls Pope's December flowers and snow-buried harvests) somehow stays uncancelled by the fact that they depict a palsied shake, or 'parcels' of aged hair. The language, though ironic, evokes festive things positively. The reference to 'fair damsels that wantoned in her train' preposterously hints of epithalamia and similar celebrations. Where Fielding shows neoclassic symmetries cruelly violated, Smollett's 'order' is a 'gothick' one, where ugliness not only violates but also actually accompanies or promises beauty, like 'those horrible giants, who, in the world of romance, used to guard the gates of the castle in which the enchanted damsel was confined' (Smollett's well-known penchant for the thrills of Gothic horror in another sense, which makes certain passages of this novel, and of the earlier *Roderick Random*, precursors of the Gothic novel proper, is not unrelated). To this incongruous fairty-tale harmony belongs the bawd's odd 'meritoriousness', ironic to be sure, yet linked with the cheerful uplift of the passage as a whole, as well as with the simple fact of brothel-pleasures. Fielding's Moll may be much more literally meritorious, for her cheerfulness implies wholesome lessons about gaiety in misfortune, but Fielding renders it as a shocking surprise, almost hysterical in its 'absurd' inconsequence.

This note of 'absurdity', in the technical sense which has become current in our time, is what distinguishes Fielding's passage from Smollett's. The account of Blear-eyed Moll gives a vivid and unexpected glimpse, from the opposite end, of the truth of Martin Esslin's statement that a certain kind of modern absurdist, like Camus, writes in the 'style of an eighteenth-century moralist'.[20] If the harsh surprises of life cannot be submitted to and celebrated, in Smollett's way, they can no longer, as Fielding's earlier style claimed, be brought under control. The early chapters of *Amelia* record these surprising 'unnatural' things with a pretence of bare factuality, of uncommented but desperate constatation. But this factuality is not one which eschews explanations, so much as pointedly refusing them. If fact defies explanation, its outrageousness is highlighted in such a way that the betrayed expectation remains as a helpless norm, the absence of gloss itself a gloss. The style's outward pretences to certainty are if anything stepped up. Despite occasional falterings of cadence or lapses into garrulous pique (as in the portrait of Thrasher), there is a hardening of witty incisiveness and of the old syntactical symmetries. The more unpredictable or untidy things become, the more highly patterned the account: the irony of Blear-eyed Moll and the other prison scenes is stiffened by a grim patness, as though the unexplainable could only be harnessed by a laconic but *pointed* factuality. Fact cannot be left to tell its own tale in any bare, unmannered narration like Defoe's, but needs to be harnessed, if only to the ghost of a system. And so, organized into pointedly inconclusive parables, the brutal forces of an absurd universe meet the Augustan rage for order face to face. The collision produces some of the greatest moments in Augustan literature outside Swift, and if sustained might have altered the history of the novel. The combination, in the paragraphs about Moll, of desperate bewilderment with hard finish and almost unflinching assurance of style, suggests that 'True Ease in Writing', and the 'universal harmony', are not so much losing their rhythm, as performing their dance of death.

'True Ease' was always too close to its own opposite to be anything but a somewhat precarious quality. One 'learn'd to dance' in order to seem to walk naturally, acquiring spontaneous graces of born gentility from the schooling of an ungenteel pedagogue. Percival Stockdale was to complain that Edward Young 'is sometimes, in poetry, what a dancing-master is in manners'.[21] Bewilderment is no gentlemanly state (ideally speaking), yet Fielding's earlier style, where the gentlemanly posture is most prominent and apparently most effortless, is full of gestures of bewilderment. One thinks of his puzzlement over Jenny Jones's 'bitterness' at a reflection on her beauty, after she had patiently borne all 'affronts to her chastity'; or over Mrs Western's litigious fury against Mrs Honour for merely calling her ugly, whereas she had refused to prosecute a highwayman who had stolen her money and earrings, 'at the same time d——ning her, and saying "such handsome b——s as you, don't want jewels to set them off"' (*Tom Jones*, I, vi; VII, ix). These 'bewilderments' are, of course, the ironic instruments of sharp certainty, a device over which Fielding had full command, rather than (as in the case of the prison incidents of *Amelia*) a primary feeling he must come to terms with. They are frequently laced with an amplitude of blowsy or garrulous elaboration. The puzzlement over Mrs Western's temper spreads over a whole paragraph of above a dozen lines, savouring its arch rotundities: 'But now, so uncertain are our tempers, and so much do we at different times differ from ourselves...'. Whether such intellectual clowning, such a protracted emphasis of point-making mimicry are themselves gentlemanly, is doubtless open to question. But the awkward questions are readily waived in the reading, the narrator's ease surviving unchallenged because all the fuss, if not a gentlemanly manner as such, becomes a kind of literary equivalent or substitute, giving an air of ironic wisdom and gentlemanly control to comic fun and earnest moralizing alike. This relaxed over-stated puzzlement is in reality closely akin to an effect of dazzling ironic economy. I refer to those characteristic, and apparently diffident, parenthetic afterthoughts, which turn out to contain the acutest sting of the discourse, as when Laetitia Snap inveighs against her erring sister Theodosia, 'being resolved never to set her foot within the same threshold with the trollop, whom she detested so much the more because (which was perhaps true) she was her own sister' (*Jonathan Wild*, III, xiii). That brilliant 'perhaps' draws sharp attention to what is implied to be a common but shocking 'unnaturalness', which the narrator has, in the same breath, fully sized up. The understated brevity, in context, modulates without discomfort into and out of blowsy mimicries, and insistent rotundities of elaboration, even greater than one often finds in *Tom Jones*. The parenthesis shows 'True Ease' reaching (as Pope's couplet of course meant it to) well beyond gentlemanly overtones to the most consummate literary excellence: but its easy firm mastery is part of what guarantees the gentlemanliness of the rest, silencing possible suspicions that the urbanity of the writing is a good deal more strained than ideals of polite conversation allow for.

A theoretical element of strain (or overstrenuousness) is built-in, a possible source of problems or irritations in all Augustan writers of the urbane sort, and certainly in Fielding, at all periods. Ford Madox Ford fastened on a particularly minor example, in the opening words of *Amelia*, I, ii: 'On the first of April, in the year ——, the watchmen of a certain parish (I know not particularly which) . . .'. Ford's point is that Fielding the novelist had no business not to know the name of the parish, and that his parenthesis is meant to show that he is 'too much of a great gentleman to bother about details'.[22] Ford makes Fielding's rather automatic mannerism sound like a heavy piece of point-making, but his main observation is roughly right. Fielding's usage seems different from that of, say, Defoe's narrators when they utter the same kind of phrase: 'The young Woman, her Mother, and the Maid, had been abroad for some Occasion, I do not Remember what, for the House was not shut up';[23] and 'so we lodg'd at an Inn not far from the Cathedral, I forgot what Sign it was at'.[24] Such details are precisely what a person telling a story informally might well forget, especially when, like both Defoe's narrators, he has his mind on more pressing things. Fielding, unlike Defoe, is his own narrator, frankly omniscient, uninvolved as a character, and making no pretence at artless reminiscence. His mannerism belongs not with the authenticating disclaimers or colloquial realism of Defoe, but with the urbane quasi-witty postures of Augustan verse: 'This Phoebus promis'd (I forget the year) . . .'; 'In days of yore, (no matter where or when . . .)'.[25] A certain signposting of gentlemanly credentials (formalized urbanities, assertions of uprightness and good taste, a withholding of undue intimacy, a note of *nil admirari* and other postures of neo-Horatian rhetoric, as well as minor reticences like the one noted by Ford) would have seemed called for by established literary practice. It seems truer to accept the mannerism as a natural part of a received style, than as the leering self-advertisement that Ford (who read Fielding through the wordy mists of his own dislike of Thackeray) accused Fielding of.

But if Ford read Fielding with a certain wilful refusal of historical sympathy, his complaint touches on at least two points of substance. One is that urbanity seems breached the moment it is asserted, and the familiar Augustan analogies between writing and 'conversation' (including several of Fielding's own) tend to pass over the fact that the literary styles could not simply be retranslated to the drawing-room. Reminders of gentlemanliness are, beyond a certain point, themselves ungentlemanly; Horatian pretensions pressed too explicitly would seem a pedantry of upstart affectation; witty pointed styles and a continuously sustained irony are too pointed for protracted conversation; the modern journalistic tag, 'easy reading, hard writing', extends to the special sense of 'True Ease' and its paradox, celebrated by Pope, of being a hard-won and much-laboured thing. This means that the *literary* urbanities demand of the reader a suspension of scepticism or resistance, even though habits induced by widespread literary convention and (for later readers) a rudimentary exercise of the historical imagination make such a suspension fairly natural and effortless for most. Secondly, there is the special problem of *Amelia*, where the urbanities often seem devoid of their usual functions. If the mannerism about not 'particularly' knowing the name of the parish is not a self-effacing colloquialism as in Defoe, but belongs rather to a convention of quasi-witty *hauteurs* in urbane poems, it is yet neither in itself witty nor very *purposefully* uppish. It is part of a gentlemanly guard, though less crude than Ford's comment ('too much of a great gentleman to bother') allows, against a fussy meticulousness on small points of fact: too great a submission to small details, to the mere course of events and the *factuality* of fact, is alien to the gentlemanly manner, which persistently implies a mastery over circumstance. Yet *Amelia* is special among Fielding's novels precisely in that it records irresistible factualities which cannot be mastered by displays of authorial understanding. Similarly, the portrait of Moll leaves us painfully startled despite all the emphatic pointedness of style, and all the brisk efficiency with which the 'two remarkable reasons' are given (but not explained). But it is not the fact that urbane pointedness is intensified beyond anything in the earlier styles which makes it harder for the reader to waive the awkward questions about urbanity: conventions or habits of mind which can accept the stylistic performance of *Tom Jones* as urbane will probably stretch to accommodate *Amelia* too. The intensification of formal emphases, which gives the style its strange desperate tang, does not put its gentlemanliness in doubt, but implies that the gentlemanliness (and its best properties of confidence and civilized righteousness) are no longer any help. The style's strengths and weaknesses in *Amelia* reside partly in the fact that the urbane accoutrements (like the firm notations which yet withhold explanatory *substance*) now confront a kind of void: powerfully registering Fielding's heightened sense of his non-mastery and incomprehension in great passages like the portrait of Moll, but worn to a painful tic, meaning nothing, in the phrase about not knowing the parish.

As the urbanity is thus transformed, Fielding's relations with the

reader suffer a deadening. When, in *Tom Jones*, VI, i ('Of Love'),
Fielding tells the reader that if he does not believe in love, he should put
down the book, since 'you have . . . already read more than you have
understood', the warning comes charged with the moral passion, and
the bravura, of the preceding eloquent statement on love. The aggressive buoyancy is supremely confident, and the challenge total. Any
reader who even thinks of taking it up is put badly in the wrong. If
there is a touch of Fielding's habitual superiority, it is sustained by a
great warmth of uncanting righteousness, so that the reader who instead
aligns himself with Fielding by reading on not only gets a friendly
welcome, but is made consciously and positively committed to a
generous moral outlook by his very decision. Moreover, the *élan* of the
whole argument is such that, although Fielding stands by every word
of his challenge, he does not seem really to expect any reader to stop.
Thus, despite his explicit references throughout the chapter to bad people
who disbelieve in love, there is an unstated feeling in the air that most
normal people are potentially capable of the goodness and decency he
requires. In this way, the gentlemanly confidence (in the very best sense)
remains validated even when the factual evidence seems to contradict it.

A similar challenge to the loveless reader occurs in *Amelia*, III, i, with
a totally different feeling. Booth is reluctant to describe to Miss
Matthews a 'tender scene' which passed between him and his wife. Miss
Matthews presses to hear it, because 'nothing delights me more than
scenes of tenderness'. Fielding means us to dislike Miss Matthews's
shallowness (her vulgarly sentimental voyeurism is noted more than
once), but there is an odd nastiness which Fielding does not have entirely
under control in the fact that she is an ex-mistress preparing to enjoy
the account of a loving and painful scene between her former lover and
his wife. For Fielding, the tender scene itself, as subsequently described
by Booth, stands independently of Miss Matthews's curiosity, as a
'pathetic' set-piece, claiming its full, straightforward emotional value,
and the reader who has no tenderness is told to pass it over:

> [Booth] then proceeded as Miss Matthews desired; but, lest all our
> readers should not be of her opinion, we will, according to our
> usual custom, endeavour to accommodate ourselves to every taste,
> and shall, therefore, place this scene in a chapter by itself, which
> we desire all our readers who do not love, or who, perhaps, do
> not know the pleasure of tenderness, to pass over; since they may
> do this without any prejudice to the thread of the narrative.

Here, the 'accommodating ourselves to every taste', and the 'chapter by itself', are strained and harsh, quite different from the easy defiance with which, in *Tom Jones*, he tells unsuitable readers to stop reading altogether. It is not just that here, by merely asking him to skip the chapter, Fielding foregoes a grand gesture, resignedly and somewhat naggingly accepting that the reader will go on, and yet not change into a better man. The irony throbs and wavers, as if poised between a strident, aggressive shoulder-shrugging, and something like an exasperated sob. Relations with the reader become sour, but messily, without the controlled dismissiveness of Swift. The tender scene itself is duly narrated in the next chapter, at the end of which Fielding makes Booth weakly conclude, 'This I am convinced of, that no one is capable of tasting such a scene who hath not a heart full of tenderness, and perhaps not even then, unless he hath been in the same situation' (III, ii). This has, among other things, the accidental effect of sentimentalizing Fielding's own earlier statement about untender readers out of much of its original bite. The reader is partly let off by Booth's last remark, so that the earlier hostility now hangs in the air, even more undirected—rather than being partially neutralized, as in *Tom Jones*, VI, i, by a friendly and firm, if incomplete, optimism. The awkward gap between anger and a tearful sentimentality is widened by the fact that we are meant to take Booth's remarks straight, and feelingly. The sarcasm (easily seen through, and meant to be) with which, in the passage quoted from III, i, tender readers are momentarily equated with the falsely tender Miss Matthews as against *un*tender readers, disappears in III, ii, where Booth, and not Fielding, is speaking. Fielding in his own person is more capable, through irony, of seeing round high language, without undermining warm or generous feelings as such, and his control is always at risk when he surrenders the narrative to a character. It may, of course, be felt that the language of III, ii as a whole, though perhaps too crudely emotional by our standards, needs no ironic distancing, because it is fairly common novelistic rhetoric in an age when the self-conscious relishing of the emotions was more normal and more open than it is today. Even so, for Booth to talk of 'tasting such a scene' is unwittingly (and without Fielding's earlier implied discrimination) to put the whole thing on Miss Matthews's level.

It is often noted that *Amelia* contains many Richardsonian elements, possibly conditioned by Fielding's admiration for *Clarissa*. This admiration, though intense, was also ambiguous, as the closing words of the Preface to the *Voyage to Lisbon* imply. Perhaps the main Richardsonian elements in *Amelia* are a new dogged literalism about details of feeling and emotion, and an intensified readiness to give full (sometimes exclamatory) expression to emotional moments, often without under-cutting them with ironic defences. The ambiguity of Fielding's attitude extends to these two things (as also to the related question of the respective merits of unadorned 'humble prose' and pointed stylization). The valuing of tender scenes as a test and an indulgence of the reader's heart is undermined not only by Miss Matthews's cheap emotional epicurism, but by Booth's and Fielding's reluctance to go into such scenes at all, in III, i and elsewhere. Thus, 'Nothing worth notice passed in this miserable company from this time till the return of Mrs. Ellison from the bailiff's house; and to draw out scenes of wretchedness to too great a length is a task very uneasy to a writer, and for which none but readers of a most gloomy complexion will think themselves ever obliged to his labours' (VIII, iii).

But it can hardly be said that the scenes of exquisite distress (any more than those of ecstatic reunion, or the tender tableaux of children at play) are invariably abbreviated or soft-pedalled. The ambiguity gives a special edge in *Amelia* to the otherwise commonplace 'sentimental' amalgam of detailed specifying of the emotional and emotive, and of contrary assertions that the emotion is too painful or intense to be mentioned.[26] Declarations of ineffability are themselves highly emotive, of course, and highly characteristic of novels of sensibility. But Fielding differs, perhaps, from other novelists of sensibility in being somewhat readier (not, as I said, invariably, but occasionally) to stop *in fact*, once the ineffability, or (as in the present instance from VIII, iii) the undue painfulness, have been noted. That there is a genuinely uneasy oscillation, and not merely a mutual reinforcing, between the indulgence of emotional particularities and their silencing as ineffable, is further suggested by the co-presence here, and the general frequency in the novel, of another and much less emotive kind of signposted reticence: 'Nothing worth notice passed.'

This formula is familiar in the earlier Fielding, where it is relatively lighthearted and expansive, and where its purpose is often to help establish the author as one who knows the difference between what is important and what is not. In *Amelia*, chatty announcements of reticence are often replaced by a businesslike severity, and the focus is less on the author's personality than on the immediate matter in hand. Instead of lengthy references to what will be left out and why, such as occur in *Tom Jones*, III, i or XI, ix, *Amelia* tends to have such flat statements as: 'Nothing happened between the Monday and the Wednesday worthy a place in this history', or 'From this time to the day of the masquerade nothing happened of consequence enough to have a place

in this history' (openings of IV, ix and x, ii). With this goes an increased
tendency to such tart summarizing notation as: 'Booth made a modest
answer to the compliment which Miss Matthews had paid him. This
drew more civilities from the lady, and these again more acknowledgments; all which we shall pass by, and proceed with our history' (III, v,
ending). It is not difficult to imagine how the earlier Fielding would
have elaborated the vacuous ceremony, suffusing it with humane
comedy while preserving the full measure of appropriate disapproval.
Now, instead of mock-puzzled rotundities and inventive fantastication,
there is a sarcasm of bare factuality.

This bare factuality is generalized and unspecific, and its relation to
the reticent refusal to note trivial details is straightforward and unpara-
doxical. But there is a paradox in that the increased businesslike brevity
of the announced reticences in this novel go with an increased tendency
to record the kind of trivial details which Fielding would normally feel
to be beneath serious notice. The cold chicken collation and the 'two
pound of cold beef' consumed by three protagonists in VIII, iv, the
'hashed mutton' which Amelia prepared for Booth's supper in x, v, the
frequent tea-drinking which goes on throughout, seem precisely the
kind of Richardsonian 'meanness' which Fielding had derided through
Shamela: 'And Mrs. Jewkes and I supped together upon a hot buttered
apple-pie; and about ten o'clock we went to bed' (Letter x). Such a
particularity offends against the gentlemanly code. Chesterfield noted
that 'a laborious attention to little objects . . . lower[s] a man; . . .
Cardinal de Retz, very sagaciously, marked out Cardinal Chigi for a
little mind, from the moment that he told him he had wrote three years
with the same pen, and that it was an excellent good one still'.[27]

Fielding also retold the Cardinal's words, a little less tartly, in an
essay on trivial employments, pedantry, butterfly-collecting, and the
like, only a few weeks after *Amelia* was published.[28] Such hauteurs are
closely, if indirectly, related to the neoclassic dislike of 'minuteness', and
Fielding gave voice to a less overtly class-conscious (but in context
hardly unclass-conscious) literary extension in the Preface to the *Voyage*:
'if any merely common incident should appear in this journal, which
will seldom . . . be the case, the candid reader will easily perceive it is
not introduced for its own sake, but for some observations and reflections naturally resulting from it'. Arguably, the 'trivial' details and
'common incidents' in *Amelia* are not introduced for their own sakes.
As Mrs Barbauld was later to say, in a famous essay on 'those Kinds of
Distress which Excite Agreeable Sensations', 'They are little circumstances that work most sensibly upon the tender feelings'.[29] Amelia's

cooking of 'hashed mutton' for Booth's supper (x, v) has calculated emotive effects. The dish is frugal, supper is Booth's favourite meal, and sadly Booth (who is trying to regain a gambling loss which, in their desperate poverty, he can ill afford) does not turn up. Their conjugal tenderness, the simplicity of their taste, the pathos of their distress are Fielding's point. But this emotive strategy is far from what, in a more Augustan mood, Fielding meant by 'observations and reflections'; and the 'sentimental' exploitation of small details (soon to be carried to greater lengths by Sterne, Mackenzie and others) would by normal Augustan standards seem closer to the offence of trivial minuteness than to those rational functions which, as Fielding grants in the *Voyage*, might justify it in special cases.

Not surprisingly, therefore, Fielding continually betrays his uneasiness, on the one hand piling on further 'pathetic' details as Amelia waits for Booth to come home, on the other protesting that he 'cannot help relating a little incident, however trivial it may appear to some'. A thoroughgoing novelist of sensibility would go beyond the mere defensive gesture, to say that a sensitive heart would understand and value such things as the most truly 'interesting' of all. Fielding is often shy of saying this straight. When we read in vii, i that 'in stories of distress, especially where love is concerned, many little incidents may appear trivial to those who have never felt the passion, which, to delicate minds, are the most interesting part of the whole', it is not Fielding who is speaking, but the faintly comic (fallen as well as learned) Mrs Bennet. Amelia impatiently cries 'this is all preface', and Fielding makes excuses for the prolixity. At the same time, Mrs Bennet is legitimately overwrought; Amelia knows that important things directly affecting herself are about to be revealed; and there is no doubt that Mrs Bennet's story, when it comes, is meant to be taken as genuinely distressing and has a poignant bearing on Amelia's troubles. The ensuing chapters, which give the narrative, are full of the routines of exquisite pathos, sensibilitous exclamation, and a Richardsonian particularity very like that which we have seen in parts narrated by Fielding himself ('He [admittedly a deceitful villain] took [the child] out of my arms, placed it upon his own knee, and fed it with some fruit from the dessert' etc., vii, vi). There seems to be more imitation than parody of Richardson in the fact that the wicked peer seduces Mrs Bennet with the aid of a drug (vii, vii), and there is an almost Richardsonian humourlessness in the information, as given in vii, ii, that Mrs Bennet's mother died by falling into a well with a tea-kettle in her hand.

The absurdity of this last example (whether or not Fielding is conscious of it) is difficult to assimilate into the atmosphere of Mrs Bennet's narrative as a whole. The comic abundance with which the serious and the preposterous amalgamate without strain in *Tom Jones* is entirely lacking. It is not true that the serious, in these chapters from *Amelia*, lacks all ironic perspective. The sporadic undercutting which is found in almost all Fielding's writings occurs here also (though mostly in uneasy little sarcasms at the end of chapters, as though Fielding were reminding himself of a duty to maintain a knowing distance). Amelia, moreover, predictably faints during Mrs Bennet's narration, and the brisk automatism with which she is revived ('At these words Amelia . . . fell back in her chair. Mrs. Bennet, with proper applications, brought her back to life', VII, vii) makes a familiar point, plentifully present in the earlier writings. When it is Mrs Bennet who faints, in VII, viii, the derision is still more open: 'The reader, if he hath been acquainted with scenes of this kind, very well knows that Mrs. Bennet, in the usual time, returned again to the possession of her voice'.

But such derision strains awkwardly against all the pathos, both of Mrs Bennet's past and of Amelia's present predicament. In *Tom Jones*, by contrast, there seems little strain when, for example, Sophia faints at the (false) news of Tom's death: 'Sophia, . . . having dealt three cards to one, and seven to another, and ten to a third, at last dropt the rest from her hand, and fell back in her chair. The company behaved as usually on these occasions. The usual disturbance ensued, the usual assistance was summoned, and Sophia at last, as it is usual, returned again to life' (*T. J.*, XV, iii). That this gentle and tolerant fuss is free from acerbity is partly due, of course, to the fact that *Tom Jones*, unlike *Amelia*, is a comic novel. But the live coexistence of the mockery with serious respect and affection for the heroine, the absence not only of strain but of any undermining of Sophia, owe still more to the remarkable *inclusiveness* of the irony in *Tom Jones*. This irony, as I suggested earlier in another connection, holds a surprising variety of tones, styles and emotions in mutual relation, giving full value to goodness and tenderness, as here, while maintaining a scepticism of sentimental, naïve or hypocritical effusion, just as elsewhere it exposes bad men passionately, while seeing them within the pattern of a confident world-view which they cannot unbalance. This inclusiveness is closely related to the fact that the novel's style is sustainedly directed towards establishing the character of the narrator as one whose temperament has the relevant breadth of sympathy. In *Amelia*, where there is little emphasis on the character of the authorial narrator as such; where the world-view is not comically confident and where extremes of pathos are too violently out of keeping with ironic play to amalgamate without strain; and where the ironic play (though frequent) is in any case occasional rather than pervasive, the ironic effects do not broaden the feeling as in *Tom Jones*, but flatten it to an alienating sarcasm.

In a certain sense, the ironies of *Amelia*, their urbanity frozen to harshness, are a ghostly version of those of *Tom Jones*, a dance without true ease. The effect is not entirely or at all times unintended. It extends, moreover, to other elements and other stylizations, giving *Amelia* the strange quality of a serious or tragic reembodiment of the earlier comic manner. We have already seen that this is true of its couplet-rhetoric and its moral summations. It applies also to a number of individual episodes. The bedroom-scene in *Amelia*, IX, vi—not without comedy, but fraught with the anxiety over Colonel James's designs on Amelia— would certainly be possible in what the Preface to *Joseph Andrews* calls 'serious romance', but it is also a melodramatic variant of the slapstick bedroom imbroglio exemplified, in its farcical form, in *Joseph Andrews*, IV, xiv. Again, the 'Scene of the Tragic Kind' between Amelia and Atkinson, XI, vi, is, as Sheridan Baker has suggested, a reversal, probably inadvertent, of the scene between Lady Booby and Joseph in *Joseph Andrews*, I, v.[30]

This 'serious' reconstitution of the comic is especially noticeable in some of *Amelia*'s treatment (local, and also, to some extent, structural) of the grand style and other heroic or epic elements. In II, i, Booth descants on Amelia's fortitude after the fateful breaking of her nose (this is *not* meant to be funny, but like Mrs Bennet's mother's tea-kettle, teeters perilously on the edge of it):

'what a magnanimity of mind did her behaviour demonstrate! if the world have extolled the firmness of soul in a man who can support the loss of fortune; of a general who can be composed after the loss of a victory; or of a king who can be contented with the loss of a crown; with what astonishment ought we to behold, with what praises to honour, a young lady, who can with patience and resignation submit to the loss of exquisite beauty, in other words to the loss of fortune, power, glory, everything which human nature is apt to court and rejoice in! what must be the mind which can bear to be deprived of all these in a moment, and by an unfortunate trifling accident; which could support all this, together with the most exquisite torments of body, and with dignity, with resignation, without complaining, almost without a tear, undergo the most painful and dreadful operations of surgery in such a situation!' Here he stopped, and a torrent of tears gushed from his eyes; such tears are apt to flow from a truly noble heart at the hearing of anything surprisingly great and glorious.

The passage as a whole has a mixed ancestry, in which heroic poems and plays, romances and more recent 'sentimental' fiction, combine: Booth shedding tears, for example, is a momentary amalgam of Homeric and 'sentimental' hero. His speech, however, insofar as the 'heroic' aspects of its grandiloquence may be isolated, recalls nothing so much as some of the blowsy mock-heroic speechifying of *Jonathan Wild*, or the famous opening of Canto IV of the *Rape of the Lock*:

> But anxious Cares the pensive Nymph opprest,
> And secret Passions labour'd in her Breast.
> Not youthful Kings in Battel seiz'd alive,
> Not scornful Virgins who their Charms survive,
> Not ardent Lovers robb'd of all their Bliss,
> Not ancient Ladies when refus'd a Kiss,
> Not Tyrants fierce that unrepenting die,
> Not *Cynthia* when her *Manteau's* pinn'd awry,
> E'er felt such Rage, Resentment and Despair,
> As Thou, sad Virgin! for thy ravish'd Hair.

The speech from *Amelia* reads not like a primary example of the grand manner, but as though mock-heroic were being retranslated into a secondary seriousness, and even as though, in a way, the serious were ghoulishly parodying the mock-serious.

The impression is here unintended, and an aspect of the radical unsureness of tone sometimes found in the novel. But it is related to a new kind of mock-heroic, which is deliberately 'straight' insofar as deflation or self-deflation by way of parody are no longer the main point, and in which the old concern to protect urbanity by stylized distancing is transcended. Fielding's declared use, in this novel, of the 'noble model' of the *Aeneid*[31] largely departs from the old satiric formula, in which lapses from the heroic norm are automatically assumed to be (literally or by some metaphorical extension) culpable, or at least ridiculous. The Virgilian parallel is less than uniformly vivid, but, where it does make itself felt, seems closer to Eliot and Joyce in suggesting not simply a modern lapse from ancient grandeurs, so much as a wry universalizing sense of continuity. A particularly fine Joycean touch, which George Sherburn noted, is the parallel between the amours of

Booth and Miss Matthews in prison and of Aeneas and Dido in the cave.[32] It is a parallel which in the most profound and underisive irony converts the 'noble model' from exemplary grandeur to universalizing myth. It extends a step, already evident in certain actively anti-heroic elements in *Jonathan Wild*, in which the heroic, even in its more reputable forms, is, perhaps not always consciously, abandoned as a standard of self-evident good. That such an abandonment is related to a more radical unsureness of values will surprise no one. The heroic ideal, and its embodiment in the ancient epics, were, for conservative Augustans like Fielding or Pope, part of the certainty, an essential element of the sense of order: '*Nature* and *Homer* were, [they] found, the *same*' (*Essay on Criticism*, l.135). That the ideal was no longer viable, was increasingly sensed. For decades, the most vital tributes to it had been taking an ironic, mock-heroic (not anti-heroic) form. The last great mock-heroic of the old sort, which proceeds from an active loyalty to the spirit of the great epics, and whose values rest solidly and conspicuously on its violated grandeurs, is the *Dunciad* (1728–43), a formal lament for the demise of these values. Meanwhile (the story is well-known) came a genre virtually independent of these values, the novels of Defoe and Richardson. As independent as they, Fielding could, and would, not be, and his works are shot through with epic allusion and epic transformation from beginning to end. But his last, posthumous statement on the subject, in the Preface to the *Voyage to Lisbon*, leans, with eloquently mixed feelings, towards this independence and perhaps towards new novels whose nature we shall never guess: 'I must confess I should have honoured and loved Homer more had he written a true history of his own times in humble prose, than those noble poems that have so justly collected the praise of all ages'.

Whether 'humble' means a particular kind of prose, or merely distinguishes prose from verse as a lowlier medium, the remark strikes a new note, and not only in being alien to the old valuation of epic: in *Joseph Andrews*, III, i, for example, Fielding's attitude to history had been more or less Aristotelian, noting the inferiority of mere recorded fact to the universal truths of imaginative literature. It is legitimate to think of *Amelia* as marking a stage in this change of outlook, remote as this novel's combination of sentimentalizing minuteness and emotional overstatement may seem from the sober accents of plain history. Particularity and an emotional rhetoric have in common not only the tendency of minute details to arouse sentiment and foster an intimacy with the reader. In an author like Fielding, they argue a new and deliberate, if ambiguous, self-submission, both to fact and to feeling.

Fielding's admiration for *Clarissa* doubtless helped him to see that a great masterpiece could be created from materials for which official literary theory, and his own gentlemanly and temperamental predilections, made no allowance: a minute rendering of fact and emotion unmediated by protective ironies and stylizations, an assumption of the human importance and interest of the smallest sensation, a total and intimate involvement of both narrator and reader in the drama. *Amelia* still shows much guardedness in these things, however. Gesture of stylization are still interposed, though often uncertainly, frozen to harshness or stiffly overemphasized. Even when this is not so, *Clarissa* seems to have been an unfortunate model for Fielding. His 'minuteness' throbs with triviality, and the emotional rhetoric (without Richardson's exploration of delicate nuances and fluctuations of feeling, and the whole *internalized* quality of Richardson's narrative) comes strident and unearned.

Richardson's importance must not be exaggerated. But it is part of a larger process in *Amelia*, in which (as many contradictory elements merge) potential sources of strength turn to weaknesses, and vice-versa. 'By *Amelia*', says F. R. Leavis, 'Fielding has gone soft',[33] and the sub-Richardsonian elements seem to confirm it. One might equally say that he had gone hard, which is, perhaps, the same thing. The routine didacticism and the indulgence of tearful pathos partly overcompensate for a disaffection which is, at other times, merely cantankerous. The later writings as a whole (*Amelia*, the *Late Increase of Robbers* and the *Effectual Provision for the Poor*, the *Voyage to Lisbon*) exhibit an intensified see-sawing between apparently contradictory elements in his social outlook: between his faith in benevolence and an increasing, at times obsessional, sense of the natural depravity of man; or between his belief that men may be virtuous in every social class, including notably the poorer classes (e.g., *Amelia*, III, vii), and his notions that the poor are more depraved because they have not had the education which helps to erase natural malignity in others (e.g., *Voyage to Lisbon*, 26 June 1754). These various moods exist in the earlier Fielding also, although it is generally agreed that his outlook darkened in later years. In addition to the darkening, however, should be noted an increased intensity of *oscillation* among these attitudes, which are no longer held together by the old poise and inclusiveness of view. It is no mere question of an elderly flagging of talent, for there are things of a fierce vitality in all the later writings. It seems instead to be that Fielding's world has ceased to make total sense, so that his reactions have become fragmentary. The phenomenon of Blear-eyed Moll and that of Amelia simply cannot connect: both are noted, and strongly reacted to, but a world in which both exist can only be acknowledged, not 'explained'. If Fielding's illness and the cares of magistracy account for the wastes of tired flatness and devitalized overstatement, they contributed also that closeness to suffering, that vivid pessimism and that desperate sense of disconnection without which the great and revolutionary early chapters would not have been written. Nor could those unpredictable intensities have been achieved without that active struggle, dramatized in every sentence of the portrait of Blear-eyed Moll, between helpless constatation and the compulsive interference of 'style', between fact and those forms of 'ease' which, with such vivid expressiveness, fail to dance it out of its cruelty.

❁

NOTES

1 'Fielding and "Conservation of Character" ', *Modern Philology*, lvii (1960), 250.
2 Robert Alter, *Fielding and the Nature of the Novel* (Cambridge, Mass., 1968), p. 157; see also Morris Golden, *Fielding's Moral Psychology* (Amherst, 1966), pp. 70–1.
3 Coolidge, 'Fielding and "Conservation of Character" ', p. 258.
4 *To the Palace of Wisdom* (Garden City, N.Y., 1965), p. 305.
5 *Works*, xv, 88.
6 'The Background of Fielding's Laughter', *ELH. A Journal of English Literary History*, xxvi (1959), 250.
7 Ibid., pp. 250–1.
8 'Fielding's *Amelia* and the Materials of Romance', *Philological Quarterly*, xli (1962), 448–9.
9 *To the Palace of Wisdom*, p. 309.
10 Coolidge, 'Fielding and "Conservation of Character" ', p. 249.
11 *Works*, xv, 316–21 and ii, 240–5.
12 *Works*, xv, 317.
13 *Works*, ii, 241.
14 *Works*, xiii, 96–7.
15 *Works*, ii, 243.
16 *Moll Flanders*, Shakespeare Head edn (Oxford, 1927), ii, 100–1.
17 See Martin Esslin's remarks about Adamov's *La Parodie* in *The Theatre of the Absurd*, rev. edn (Harmondsworth, 1968), p. 96. See also Richard N. Coe, *Ionesco* (Edinburgh and London, 1961), p. 31.
18 *Nineteen Eighty-Four*, III, i (Harmondsworth, 1954), pp. 182–3.
19 *Collected Essays, Journalism and Letters* (London, 1968), ii, 24 and iii, 269.

20 *The Theatre of the Absurd*, p. 24.
21 Cited by Howard Weinbrot, *The Formal Strain. Studies in Augustan Imitation and Satire* (Chicago, 1969), p. 128.
22 *The March of Literature* (London, 1947), p. 535.
23 *Journal of the Plague Year*, Shakespeare Head edn (Oxford, 1928), p. 68.
24 *Moll Flanders*, Shakespeare Head edn, i, 153.
25 Pope, *Epistle to a Lady*, l. 283; Thomas Parnell, 'Hesiod, Or the Rise of Woman', *Poems on Several Occasions*, ed. Alexander Pope (London, 1722), p. 2.
26 For a discussion of such assertions, see Alter, *Fielding and the Nature of the Novel*, pp. 167 ff.
27 Letter to his son, 10 August 1749, *Letters*, ed. Bonamy Dobrée (London, 1932), iv, 1380–1.
28 *C.-G.J.*, No. 24, 24 March 1752, Jensen, I, 277.
29 A. L. Barbauld, *Works* (London, 1825), ii, 218.
30 'Fielding's *Amelia* and the Materials of Romance', p. 444, n. 21.
31 *C.-G.J.*, No. 8, 28 January 1752, Jensen, i, 186.
32 'Fielding's *Amelia*: An Interpretation', *ELH. A Journal of English Literary History*, iii (1936), 3.
33 *The Great Tradition* (London, 1948), p. 4.

❋

HEROES, CLOWNS AND SCHOOLBOYS: MUTATIONS IN MOCK-HEROIC

CHAPTER IV

THE HERO AS CLOWN: JONATHAN WILD, FELIX KRULL AND OTHERS

. . . lofty Lines in *Smithfield* Drols . . .

(Swift, *On Poetry: A Rhapsody*, l. 300)

Processions that lack high stilts have nothing that catches the eye.
What if my great-granddad had a pair that were twenty foot high,
And mine were but fifteen foot, no modern stalks upon higher,
Some rogue of the world stole them to patch up a fence or a fire.
Because piebald ponies, led bears, caged lions, make but poor
shows,
Because children demand Daddy-long-legs upon his timber toes,
Because women in the upper storeys demand a face at the pane,
That patching old heels they may shriek, I take to chisel and plane.

Malachi Stilt-Jack am I . . .

(Yeats, 'High Talk')

Two related assumptions about *Jonathan Wild* have seldom been questioned: that the tone of the novel is 'acrid, incisive, mordant, implacably severe'[1] and that its 'hero' is a figure of unrelieved and unsoftened villainy. These assumptions are shared by Coleridge and by Scott, who differ substantially from one another in their valuation of the work.[2] They have held firm among all the other interpretative reappraisals and disagreements of more recent critics. Even when the conventional view of the novel's moral formula, as a simple opposition of 'good' and 'great', has been challenged as incomplete, it is Heartfree and not Wild who has been felt to need reinterpretation.[3] This is understandable because the figure of Heartfree lacks vitality, and because the Preface to the *Miscellanies* offers a third category, 'the great and good' by which we may measure the insufficiencies of mere 'goodness'.[4] Conversely, there seems to be no external invitation to revise the official notion of Wild as a diabolically sinister villain, and Fielding's formulaic harping, within the novel, on Wild's wicked 'greatness' is very insistent. These indications seem conclusive, but they point in fact to a central uncertainty of the novel.

For it is partly because of Fielding's failure to embody his mock-heroic in a live, coherent and self-sustaining fable (like, say, the *Dunciad*'s) that the ostensible schematic certainties hold sway.[5] The mock-heroic has to be activated largely by verbal insistence, so that its moral implications are continually being abstracted into formulaic ironies of linguistic usage, and a tendency to the simplifications of 'moral allegory' inevitably results. Because the formulaic ironies about 'greatness' are pressed with almost obsessional emphasis and consistency, it is easy for the reader to become mesmerized by this dimension of the work, and to attend more to the ironic commentary on Wild than to what the action reveals about him. There are, however, two sides to this verbal abstraction of the mock-heroic element. If the verbal mock-heroics are unsustained (or very imperfectly sustained) by a live core of mock-heroic fiction, they do on the other hand co-exist, as it were in parallel, with another fiction which *is* live, but whose main energies are outside the domain of heroic pretensions. This fiction might be called comic in something like the sense intended by Fielding in the Preface to *Joseph Andrews*, when he distinguished 'comic epic' from mock-heroic, as embodying a humbler and more 'realistic' conception of the 'ludicrous', to which the mock-heroic adds marginal, not radical, ingredients of stylized fun. The comparison requires caution, for the overt conception of Wild obviously resembles that burlesque of 'sentiments and characters' (rather than of mere 'diction'), that 'exhibition of what is monstrous and unnatural', which Fielding describes as the antithesis of anything we shall find in *Joseph Andrews*; and it is even possible that Fielding had *Jonathan Wild* partly in mind when he made the distinction.[6] There is, however, a paradoxical sense in which mock-heroic is more integral to *Joseph Andrews* or *Tom Jones* than to *Jonathan Wild*, because, being less indiscriminately pervasive, it more easily finds its proper place, blending naturally and expressively into Fielding's *own* ironic manner, rather than sustaining an inflexibly schematic pseudo-speaker: to this extent *Jonathan Wild* appropriates the Preface to *Joseph Andrews* to itself, standing it on its head.

Nor, in speaking of the unofficial 'comic' fiction in *Jonathan Wild*, would it be right to insist unduly on the 'realistic' overtones of the term 'comic', and I shall be drawing attention to stylizations which systematically modify any tendency to naked factuality, notably the stylizations of drollic farce. But such stylizations are also, after all, prominent in *Joseph Andrews* and *Tom Jones*, and are a crucial if sometimes unacknowledged part of Fielding's novelistic manner. In some ways, the vitality of Wild as a fictional creation proceeds almost more actively from the budding comic novelist in Fielding, than from the experienced practitioner of mock-heroic. It was Fielding's undoubted purpose to transform burlesque into serious moral satire, in the approved manner. Pope turned his dunces into a menace of epic gravity, and Fielding tried to do as much for Wild. One of the unexpected charms of the novel is that he failed to take the villain as seriously as the mock-heroic commentary purports, and that Wild comes alive less as a diabolical Machiavel, than as a not unengaging comic figure, drawn on a smaller and more human scale.[7]

In the Preface to the *Miscellanies*, Fielding draws attention to the unsuccess of Wild's villainy. He tells us in general of the 'bitter anxiety' which attends 'the purchases of guilt', and that villains seldom prosper:[8]

> And though perhaps it sometimes happens, contrary to the
> instances I have given, that the villain succeeds in his pursuit, and
> acquires some transitory imperfect honour or pleasure to himself
> for his iniquity; yet I believe he oftener shares the fate of my
> hero, and suffers the punishment, without obtaining the reward.

The passage is often overlooked by critics, because their emphasis tends to be on Wild's energy and cunning, not on his failure. One might argue that the passage's main points seem too obvious to need special mention. The moral that crime does not pay is covered by the poetic justice of Wild's execution, and we should anyway expect Fielding to draw prefatory attention to 'the doctrine which I have endeavoured to inculcate in this history', even if the didactic statement turns out to be somewhat reductive. If the novel's ironic scheme ensures a more frequent and declaratory emphasis on the exploits of 'greatness' than seems compatible with an unproblematic prefatory insistence on the victory of good over evil, the fact can be put down to the formal exigencies of the ironic scheme. On the other hand, the confidence expressed in the Preface might not seem altogether appropriate to the presumed earnestness of the novel's political satire. The fact that Walpole had fallen by the time the novel was published, and that Fielding may have gone through a pro-Walpole phase after he had drafted the anti-Walpole part of the novel but before he prepared the whole novel for publication,[9] does not resolve the inconsistency (although it might help to prepare us for certain ambiguities of feeling): the more generalized attack on abuses in high places, and on the corrupting 'doublethink' of social attitudes and political language,[10] must be presumed to remain firm and urgent, and is so taken by the critics. Nor does Fielding's tentativeness in asserting that the wicked sometimes flourish in real life ('though perhaps it sometimes happens') ring true to our notion of his real thinking, or conform with the bitter severity which Fielding seems to have intended for the novel, and which the critics conventionally assume. We may feel surprised at the Preface's implication that Wild, unlike other villains 'perhaps', never 'succeeds in his pursuit' or gains any 'transitory imperfect honour or pleasure to himself for his iniquity'. Are we to take 'transitory' in a large sense, to mean 'of this life' rather than eternity, the other villains being punished only after death, whereas Wild comes to a bad end in his own lifetime? Partly, no doubt: but Fielding also insists on the temporal miseries of wicked 'greatness', the 'difficulty and danger, and real infamy', the 'bitter anxiety'. If the Preface is ambiguous, so, here as elsewhere,[11] is its relation to the novel. It is true that Wild suffers the insecurity and restlessness which prover- bially afflict the 'great', but does he not gain considerable 'transitory imperfect honour or pleasure', leadership (while it lasts) of his gang, the satisfaction of getting his own way in this or that piece of trickery or bullying?

The orthodox answer would be yes, in spite of the Preface, although the most recent orthodoxy tends in other matters (the issue of 'good- ness' *vs.* 'greatness', and the character of Heartfree) to trust the Preface rather than the tale. The answer yes conforms with the accepted notion of Wild as a highly accomplished Machiavel. But the fact is that in the novel Wild continually displays a comic self-imprisonment, and almost invariable failure in crime and in love. He is repeatedly outwitted by his partners and accomplices, and robbed, betrayed, or cuckolded by his women.[12] On this point, the Preface spoke more truly, perhaps, than Fielding meant. If the Preface seems out of phase, it is not in noting Wild's unsuccess, but in solemnifying the moral lesson. The 'bitter anxiety' and insecurity attributed by the Preface to the 'great' is readily transformed into a genial comedy of self-entrapment, as when Wild (tricked by La Ruse, robbed by Molly, and variously humiliated by Laetitia) complains, in his soliloquy on the vanity of human greatness: 'In this a *prig* is more unhappy than any other: a cautious man may, in a crowd, preserve his own pockets by keeping his own hands in them; but while the *prig* employs his hands in another's pocket, how shall he be able to defend his own?' (II, iv). This compulsiveness has its bearings on Fielding's official themes, notably his analysis of Hobbesian insatiability and restlessness.[13] But its real nature belongs with an undercurrent of almost affectionate comicality which flows right through the work, culminating in the final glimpse of Wild, on the gallows, stealing the parson's 'bottle-screw, which he carried out of the world in his hand' (IV, xiv). The examples reveal an exquisite effrontery of self-realization. They also show Wild made absurdly defenceless by his compulsion to pick pockets. Self-entrapment is not necessarily endearing, and the great conqueror's 'abject slave[ry] to his own greatness' leads the narrator to reflect on the bitter unreason, the cruel gaping folly, of 'great' doings:

> when I behold one great man starving with hunger and freezing with cold, in the midst of fifty thousand who are suffering the same evils for his diversion; when I see another, whose own mind is a more abject slave to his own greatness, and is more tortured and racked by it than those of all his vassals; lastly, when I consider whole nations rooted out only to bring tears into the eyes of a great man, not, indeed, because he hath extirpated so many, but because he had no more nations to extirpate, then truly I am almost inclined to wish that nature had spared us this her MASTERPIECE, and that no GREAT MAN had ever been born into the world (I, xiv).

The vast vacuity of this (to adapt Milton's phrase)[14] is a vacuity of infernal vileness, in which an absurd emptiness and a motiveless automatism are paradoxically charged with the most viscerally solid horrors. But the passage only emphasizes how far Wild, as an imaginative creation, is removed from the 'heroic' analogies of the abstract 'moral allegory'. Self-imprisonment in motiveless vice in his case also readily turns to a vacuous automatism, but one which Fielding fantasticates into a charming comic routine:

> the two friends [Wild and La Ruse] sat down to cards, a circumstance which I should not have mentioned but for the sake of observing the prodigious force of habit; for though the count knew if he won ever so much of Mr. Wild, he should not receive a shilling, yet could he not refrain from packing the cards; nor could Wild keep his hands out of his friend's pockets, though he knew there was nothing in them (I, vi).

The disparity is not merely between Wild and those 'great men' in higher places to whom the ironic formula compares him, and whose mischief is on an international rather than a merely private scale. If that were the only disparity, one might see it as a simple mock-heroic diminution of Wild, even though, given an intention to make Wild seem very sinister, such a diminution might feel oddly counterproductive. But the disparity (between grim satiric exposure, and a more genial comedy) also exists within the presentation of Wild himself, and creates some revealing uncertainties, as well as unexpected enrichments.

The end of II, v, for example, is very bitter. Thomas Fierce has been sentenced to death for a crime he did not commit, as a result of machinations by Wild, who outwardly befriended him: 'His only hopes were now in the assistances which our hero had promised him. These unhappily failed him: so that, the evidence being plain against him, and he making no defense, the jury convicted him, the court condemned him, and Mr. Ketch executed him.' This summarizing brevity is very shocking, especially at the end of a chapter in which the narrative has been conducted with a certain particularizing amplitude. Fielding's narrator rounds things off by saying that the event shows Wild to have been 'the most eminent master' of 'policy, or politicks, or rather pollitricks'.[15]

But running against this official view of Wild is the long build-up of this and immediately preceding chapters, where the 'eminent master' is outwitted at every turn with mechanical inevitability and a comic frenzy of plot and counterplot. Wild had set out, in II, ii, 'to impose on Heartfree by means of the count, and then to cheat the count of the booty'. In II, iii, he takes from the count (by arrangement) a casket of jewellery bought on credit from Heartfree, and then arranges for Heartfree to be robbed of money paid by the count (as part of the plot) in down-payment. Wild then meets Molly Straddle, who robs him of this money in the course of 'amorous caresses'. He then goes on to his true love, Letty Snap, who is busy playing him false with a preferred lover, Bagshot. She condescends to see him when she is told by her sister that Wild has some jewels for her, and hides her lover. Meanwhile, Wild discovers the theft of the money, and when Laetitia appears, it turns out that the jewels had been extracted by the count and replaced with counterfeits. Laetitia, who knows a real jewel from a false, vociferously taunts and berates Wild. He leaves in rage and multiple humiliation, while she returns to her lover. Wild rushes to the count's house: 'Not the highest-fed footman of the highest-bred woman of quality knocks with more impetuosity than Wild did at the count's door, which was immediately opened by a well-dressed liveryman, who answered that his master was not at home.' This mock-heroic simile opens II, iv. It gives a deflating glimpse of Wild, as though in the role of a footman, and then has him *actually* rebuffed by a *real* footman. The latter's 'polite' formality makes Wild's oafish fury look even sillier, and comically compounds his humiliation. Wild nevertheless bursts into the house, but fails to find the count or the jewels. After a fruitless pursuit of the count, he retires to a night-cellar, takes 'a sneaker of punch', and delivers his soliloquy on the vanity of human greatness, including the passage about the defencelessness of pickpockets, whose hands are, occupationally, prevented from guarding their own pockets. He endures one or two further subsidiary frustrations, and, 'cocking his hat fiercely', struts out.

The next chapter, II, v, which is to end with Wild's grim plot against Fierce, begins with Laetitia eagerly returning to Bagshot (who has, however, absconded!). It then returns to Wild, who has spent the night in 'successless search for Miss Straddle' and the money, and who now, 'with wonderful greatness of mind and steadiness of countenance went early in the morning to visit his friend Heartfree'.

The 'steady countenance' is continually emphasized (see I, xiv; II, ii; II, iii; a further example in II, v; and III, xi). It supposedly denotes an undeviating brazenness in villainy, and a highly efficient subordination of feelings to expediency. But by this time, the comic diminutions of Wild (his bustling oafishness, the preposterous dandy-ferocity of his cocked hat, the almost charming and definitely subheroic detail of the 'sneaker of punch') incline us to think not so much of a Machiavellian self-command, as of the deadpan expression of a stage-comic. A stage-comparison had already been made explicitly in II, iii, when Wild discovers in Laetitia's house that his money had been stolen by Molly: 'as he had that perfect mastery of his temper, or rather of his muscles, which is as necessary to the forming a great character as to the person-ating it on the stage, he soon conveyed a smile into his countenance'. Several other comparisons draw our attention to the world of the farce and the puppet-show (II, iii; III, xi). And the relentless sequence of snubs and defeats, after which Wild so quickly and automatically presses on undeterred, suggest not mainly a 'heroic' singleness of pur-pose, but the stylized resilience of a clown, who rises instantly to his feet each time he has been knocked down.

These overtones of stylized farce are essential to the novel, and are often drawn attention to overtly. In II, v, their presence is powerful but not entirely overt, and their relationship to the very harsh passage about

Fierce's death is possibly awkward and problematical. But their existence is inescapable. The somewhat frenetic ups and downs of Wild's fortunes and doings in the preceding chapters, for example, lend to the plot itself an air of somewhat extravagant automatism. This is continued and elaborated in II, v. The framing of Fierce, planned in Heartfree's house by Wild and Molly Straddle, for what was actually Molly's theft from Wild of money which Wild had stolen from Heartfree, has, as sheer narrative arrangement, a zaniness which fantasticates the cruelty of the deed itself out of some of its horror.

This zaniness of plot combines with a certain comic speeding-up of narrative tempo, and a slightly routinized presentation of Wild's motions. And such narrative stylization is inseparable from the 'character' of the hero, whose touch of absurd compulsiveness nourishes and gives point to the narrator's manner, as well as feeding upon it. Consider the operations of the 'wonderful . . . steadiness of countenance' as Wild goes to Heartfree's house, knowing Heartfree to have been robbed and wounded by Wild's men. Wild enters 'with a cheerful air', which he immediately 'changed into surprise' on seeing Heartfree's wounded state. As he listens to Heartfree's account of the robbery, he evinces 'great sorrow', and 'violent agonies of rage' against the thieves. This results in a preposterous reversal, in which Heartfree is grieved by Wild's sorrow and tries to cheer him up. He does so partly by assuring Wild that he managed to save La Ruse's (fraudulent!) note from the robbery (by Wild!), upon which Wild 'felicitated' him, and also 'inveigh[ed] against the barbarity of people of fashion' who failed to pay their debts to the poor tradesman. All the while, he is also 'meditating within himself whether he should borrow or steal from his friend, or indeed whether he could not effect both': at such a moment he appears as a kind of twin-engined mechanism, outwardly producing all the appropriate words and appearances, inwardly ticking away at possible further schemes, both equally compulsively.

At this point, Heartfree's apprentice comes in from the shop with 'a banknote of 500*l.*' which a lady 'who had been looking at some jewels, desired him to exchange'. Heartfree recognizes the note as 'one of those he had been robbed of', which makes it clear to Wild (and to the reader) that the lady must be Molly Straddle, who had stolen the money from Wild, and for whom Wild had been searching everywhere. Wild ought by rights to be astonished, delighted, and also confused, for Molly's appearance at Heartfree's house could create obvious embarrassments and difficulties. Instead of any hint of these warring feelings, let alone any such blowsy elaboration of the presumed perplexity as

Fielding sometimes provides in other contexts (an example might be Lady Booby's 'opposite passions distracting and tearing her mind different ways' in *Joseph Andrews*, I, ix), there is a flat resolution of the whole crisis in, once again, Wild's absolute control of his facial muscles: Wild instantly, 'with the notable presence of mind and unchanged complexion so essential to a great character, advised [Heartfree] to proceed cautiously'. Wild offers to see the lady privately, puts on a 'great ferocity in his looks' and addresses an indignant, threatening and moralizing speech to her, which Fielding however 'omits', coming quickly to Wild's proposal to Molly that they should frame poor Fierce (this, Wild makes plain, is her only way of escaping conviction herself). The novel's first edition flattens her reaction to a pure and laconic automatism: 'The lady readily consented; and Mr. *Wild* and she embraced and kissed each other in a very tender and passionate manner'. The revised edition expands the passage, cutting out the passionate embrace and adding a conversation in which Wild asks Molly for the rest of the stolen money, and she confesses that she gave half of it to 'Jack Swagger, a great favourite of the ladies', and spent the rest on 'brocaded silks and Flanders lace'. If the terse cut-and-dried automatism of the first edition is abandoned at this point, the revised edition shows us Wild even more thoroughly deceived by one of his women. He takes this without fuss, and the machinations against Fierce take their course. The outcome is, as we have seen, very sinister, but it is not easy to be sure whether the grimness is altogether successfully given intensity and point by the contrast with what goes before, or whether the earlier overtones of comedy or farce have softened the whole chapter pervasively. Nor are we certain at all times of the extent to which these overtones are themselves fully under Fielding's control: to what extent, for example, they purposefully modify the bleakness, preserving urbanity, proportion, and a sense of authorial control, and to what extent they are subversive of the serious intentions.

In *Joseph Andrews* and *Tom Jones*, Fielding found a tone capable of holding moral urgency and comic modifiers in a coexistence enriching to both and subversive of neither. What prevents this in *Jonathan Wild* is the stridency of the ironic framework. The stiff acerbities of the commentary on 'greatness' exist in a schematic separation from the action, and sometimes fail to blend with it. The action, on its own, tends against odds towards the more integrated amplitude of Fielding's novelistic manner, with fitful success. At times, the collision is untidy, fragmenting. The gap between what is said about Wild and what we see in the action is too great. At others, the wholeness and vitality of a scene or episode are strong enough for the action to assert its independent force, and even to bend the commentary to itself, as though the comic novelist had for the time found his true voice within an alien genre of prose satire and a foreign idiom of 'Swiftian' ironic negation.

One area of genuine uncertainty is that of the scale or magnitude of Wild's operations. In the affair of Heartfree's jewels, despite the undercurrent of comic deflation, the scale is undoubtedly large. Thomas Fierce loses his life, Heartfree is temporarily ruined, and eventually the liberty and indeed survival of Heartfree and his family come to be in grave jeopardy, as a more or less immediate consequence of the affair. The sums of money involved in the initial series of frauds and thefts are, as it happens, relatively large (by the standards of the novel), running into many hundreds of pounds. Against this runs a certain unreality. Since Fierce never appears in the novel, except to be briefly disposed of off-stage in II, v, his fate has a somewhat disembodied air: his oddly chosen name adds to this, since no ferocity ever emanates from him and since the only impression he is allowed to make on us is that of a somewhat distant pathos. The Heartfrees are much more central, and their distresses are undoubtedly particularized, but their schematic role is to be suffering victims whose troubles will be resolved by a happy ending once the 'moral allegory' has had its say.

As to the more technical question of sums of money, it should be said that while the sums involved on this occasion are large enough to ruin a defenceless tradesman like Heartfree (and need, for reasons of plot, to do this), many of the other incidents in the novel involve sums which are pointedly, and sometimes ludicrously, small. The settlements for the marriage between Wild and Laetitia Snap involve fussy parental machinations over 'a pint silver caudle-cup' and conclude thus: 'At length, everything being agreed between the parents, settlements made, and the lady's fortune (to wit, seventeen pounds and nine shillings in money and goods) paid down, the day for their nuptials was fixed, and they were celebrated accordingly' (III, vii). The parenthesis, as so often in Fielding, is the most pointed part of the sentence, masquerading as an afterthought only for added emphasis, and its whole implication is of the small-scale shabbiness of the business.

On an earlier occasion, Wild loses money at play, takes on a henchman to rob the most prosperous-looking gamester, and finds that the total takings amount to two shillings. Fielding highlights this episode strongly. He not only (in a manner which was to become characteristic of his novelistic style) closes a Book on it: 'This was so cruel a disappointment to Wild, and so sensibly affects us, as no doubt it will the reader, that, as it must disqualify us both from proceeding any farther at present, we will now take a little breath, and therefore we shall here close this book' (I, xiv), but returns to it, with a pointed elaboration, at the start of the new Book. Despite the smallness of the sum, Wild has troubled to bully his accomplice out of the largest share, and the second paragraph of II, i opens thus: 'But to proceed with our history: Wild, having shared the booty in much the same manner as before, *i.e.*, taken three fourths of it, amounting to eighteen-pence, was now retiring to rest, in no very happy mood, when by accident he met with a young fellow'. Again, the deflating details of the petty-cash appear in a syntactically subordinate place, and again we may feel that the offhand manner of the disclosure is deceptive, a function of the pointedness itself. But if the detail kindles the subordinate clause with its spark of comic significance, the main clause in this case also commands weighty attention. For the 'young fellow' whom Wild meets is, of course, Heartfree, and the meeting initiates the most crucial part of the entire action. It is, moreover, made clear beforehand that the newly introduced character (and his wife) will have a momentous role. The *first* paragraph of II, i, which immediately precedes the passage about the 'eighteen-pence', gives us Fielding's other and perhaps more sober reason for starting a new Book just here:

> One reason why we chose to end our first book, as we did, with
> the last chapter, was, that we are now obliged to produce two
> characters of a stamp entirely different from what we have
> hitherto dealt in. These persons are of that pitiful order of mortals
> who are in contempt called good-natured; being indeed sent into
> the world by nature with the same design with which men put
> little fish into a pike-pond in order to be devoured by that
> voracious water-hero.

The two tendencies of the very self-conscious transition from Book I to Book II (the comic reduction of Wild's operations, and the signposting of major and sinister new developments) are aspects of an ambiguity which seems, at this moment, not fully in Fielding's control.

There seems little doubt, for example, that the sarcasm about 'the voracious water-hero' is intended to be harsh. Its actual effect, however, is more uncertain, as a comparison with parallel examples helps to confirm. The image of big fish devouring little fish is commonplace in works which satirize various kinds of wicked exploitation, and occurs in specifically related works like the *Beggar's Opera* (Airs XLIII and XLV) and Brecht's *Threepenny Opera* and *Threepenny Novel* (e.g. the songs about Mackie the Knife in both), as well as elsewhere in Fielding (*Jonathan Wild*, I, xi; *Amelia*, XI, v).[16] The image's earlier occurrence in *Jonathan Wild*, though not undercut by the matter of eighteen-pence, is comically softened by being part of a long mock-simile, whose wordy elaboration has a playful dimension (I, xi, *ad fin.*). By contrast, Air XLIII of the *Beggar's Opera* (in other ways often a more gracefully genial work) makes the point with an eloquent bareness:

> Like pikes, lank with hunger, who miss of their ends,
> They bite their companions, and prey on their friends.

So too does Fielding's later and more unequivocally bitter novel, *Amelia*, when, in XI, v, poor Booth is reduced to bribing a 'great man': 'The great man received the money, not as a gudgeon doth a bait, but as a pike receives a poor gudgeon into his maw. To say the truth, such fellows as these may well be likened to that voracious fish, who fattens himself by devouring all the little inhabitants of the river'. The passage from *Jonathan Wild*, II, i, lacks both the blowsy expansiveness of the earlier example from the same novel, and the controlled laconic force of those from the *Beggar's Opera* and *Amelia*. Instead, it rattles with a kind of detached cantankerousness (the sarcasm about 'that pitiful order of mortals who are in contempt called good-natured' seems top-heavy and—oddly—disembodied, since we have not met the Heartfrees yet, and do not know how to apply it), before leading to the let-down of the eighteen-pence.

The smallness of the booty, then, makes Wild appear at this moment to be, as pikes go, not too impressively frightening. It adds in some ways to Wild's discredit, of course, contributing to our sense of his meanness, and of that restlessness 'in inventing means to make himself master of the smallest pittance reserved by [his coadjutors]' which the concluding chapter describes, in no genial way (IV, xv). Yet that restlessness, as we have seen, is not only a Hobbesian insatiability, but also a comic mechanical self-entrapment, compulsive in a Bergsonian, as much as in a Hobbesian, sense. When Wild browbeats his victims or accomplices into surrendering even the little which he originally promised or allowed them, the shameless combination of threats and of openly dishonest lies has a bullying effrontery to which we respond more as a feat of style than as a revelation of character, so that Wild becomes as much a comic turn as a dangerous villain.

It is not always clear how much Fielding is in control over this effect. Some degree of assimilation of Wild's villainy to the domain of clowning and farce is not only intentional but explicit. Whether it is always meant to disarm the harsher ironies is more uncertain. An extended and elaborate series of theatrical and literary analogies in III, xi compares Wild to a puppet-master who makes his puppets do his bidding whilst himself remaining unseen. It goes on to take up the now familiar image of the actor's 'solemnity of countenance' in order to compare the doings of the great world with those of village farces:

> It would be to suppose thee, gentle reader, one of very little knowledge in the world, to imagine thou hast never seen some of these puppet-shows which are so frequently acted on the great stage; but though thou shouldst have resided all thy days in those remote parts of this island which great men seldom visit, yet if thou hast any penetration, thou must have had some occasions to admire both the solemnity of countenance in the actor and the gravity in the spectator, while some of those farces are carried on which are acted almost daily in every village in the kingdom.

Arguably, the allusion to farce does not attenuate the acerbity here. The comparison of the world, and of government, to a farce is only a familiar kind of cynical commonplace, not a humorous stylization. The address to the reader has a tart and somewhat nagging quality, and the passage goes on to make a wry reflection on mankind's positive willingness to be deceived, like 'the readers of romances' (the passage, like other reminders of farce, belongs with a larger network of analogies, in this novel, between life and art—serious plays, farces, puppet-shows, romances—to which I shall return).

If there is little geniality, and little affectionate diminution of the 'hero' in this instance, what are we to make of the information in I, iii that Wild, as a schoolboy, not only admired some disreputable exploits of epic heroes, but that 'the Spanish Rogue was his favourite book, and the Cheats of Scapin his favourite play'? Or of the sustained drollic allusion when, in II, iii, Wild opens the casket of jewels for Laetitia, and finds that counterfeits have replaced the real thing:

> He then offered her the casket, but she gently rejected it; and on a second offer, with a modest countenance and voice, desired to know what it contained. Wild opened it, and took forth (with sorrow I write it, and with sorrow will it be read) one of those beautiful necklaces with which, at the fair of Bartholomew, they deck the well-bewhitened neck of Thalestris, queen of Amazons, Anna Bullen, Queen Elizabeth, or some other high princess in Drollic story?

Besides being in themselves disarmingly funny, these two instances explicitly link Wild with a not unamiable tradition of clowning roguery, in fiction and on the stage. The substitution of counterfeit jewels, or of mere stones, for the genuine contents of a casket or other container, is a stock situation in the 'literature of roguery', occurring, notably, in Alemán's *Guzmán de Alfarache*[17] ('the Spanish Rogue': Part II, Bk II, ch. ix),[18] and recurring in Smollett's *Ferdinand Count Fathom*, 1753 (ch. xx), the novel which Scott, in a well-known passage, preferred to *Jonathan Wild*.[19] The Spanish rogue Guzmán is also, like Wild, robbed by a woman during amorous caresses (II, III, i),[20] and in general Wild's career in the novel has many resemblances to that of the picaresque hero of his 'favourite book' (cuckoldry, spells in prison, a proneness to comic discomfitures, etc.). Moreover, the picaresque hero, from Guzmán to Thomas Mann's Felix Krull, has had a close traditional relation to the stage comic or clown. Guzmán and other characters in Alemán's long work are repeatedly involved in a variety of clownish pranks and in some scenes of scatological slapstick of a sort which one might associate with 'the fair of Bartholomew', and Guzman serves for a time as a professional fool or jester (II, I, i ff.).[21] The connection between rogue and clown, in the specific case of Fielding's novel as well as in the picaresque tradition at large, is reinforced by such a figure as Scapin, hero of Wild's 'favourite play' (Otway's adaptation of Molière).[22] The more recent type of picaro, in fiction or farce, was usually not a detestable villain, but a combination of mischief-maker and social outcast who arouses admiration, or at least a degree of affectionate tolerance and complicity, in the reader. Scapin in particular is a prankster whose mischief is beneficently devoted to the service of the young lovers in the play.

To the extent that Wild, unlike Guzmán or Scapin, *is* a detestable villain, he has to be thought of as outside the more amiable forms of the picaresque tradition.[23] But it is specifically to Guzmán and to Scapin that Fielding alludes, and the allusion actively defies the novel's official insistence on Wild's villainy. Fielding seems to admit this when he says that these particular literary tastes, unlike Wild's predilection for heroic writings, were a 'blemish' to his 'true greatness' (I, iii). The force, and the functions, of this defiance will need further definition, but some of its limits should be stated at once. The official insistence against which it tends is by no means totally overcome, and this is natural and right: all Fielding's purposes would be deeply violated if it were otherwise. In particular, the analogy between rogue and clown stops well short of any transfiguration of the hero into an exalted symbolic role, of wise fool, or existentialist outsider, or (as in the case of Mann's Felix Krull, who offers himself for instructive comparisons) of the artist as immoralist, above the crowd and its common rules. Such transfigurations would be unlikely not only in a profoundly conformist author like Fielding, but at a stage in the cultural history of Europe when a basic consensus of moral values was, or could be felt to be, solid and secure enough at least to discourage radical reversals of this kind. Various adumbrations of reversal were, of course, already well-established in several literary conventions: not only in the figure of the amiable picaresque outcast, but in wise fools and 'praises of folly', and in the ancient poetic persona of the proud, defiantly lonely satirist. But these reversals seldom became radical. 'Praises of folly' came nearest to doing so, but their insistence on a wisdom opposed to the wordly remains deeply rooted in traditional Christian and humanist values.[24] Where they seem more fundamentally subversive than this, as in Swift's *Tale of a Tub*, the effect is not only largely unintended, but also exceptionally 'modern'. The rogue outcast, when he is a sympathetic rather than a mainly reprehensible figure, is normally a wily and more or less charming scamp, set in a stylized world (inverted Arcadia, or 'Newgate pastoral'),[25] in which his exploits score against the pompous and the wicked of the social establishment: a sanctioned challenge to existing society (part disaffection and part holiday), but from within and, basically, in the name of traditional moral values. As to the outsider as artist, and especially as satirist, he is an outsider precisely because he upholds traditional values, not because he defies them. This artist, moreover, is almost invariably a poet, not an actor (whose status would be much lower), and least of all a clown. Swift wrote to Pope on 20 April 1731 that 'The common saying of life being a Farce is true in every sense but the most important one, for it is a ridiculous tragedy, which is the worst kind of composition'.[26] The constatation about life is bitterly felt, but the rule of theatrical decorum against which life offends remains, for Swift, firm and unbending. The order of art must be preserved, in the teeth of life's unruliness (a notion relevant, as we shall see, to Fielding's interest in the analogy of theatre and life in *Jonathan Wild*), and 'ridiculous tragedies', mixtures of the tragic and comic modes, are for Swift impermissible.[27] Those of Swift's contemporaries and those later eighteenth-century authors who theorized in favour of, or actually attempted, the celebrated mixture of genres, did so at a level, precisely, of *mixture* rather than fusion, and sentimentality was the normal result. In later writers, like Mann or, say, Ionesco with his 'tragic farces', the fact that life is a 'ridiculous tragedy' entails a radical intermerging of comic and tragic, not (as for Swift) a defiant categorization, and this intermerging is often achieved at the highest imaginative pressure. The kind of seriousness (not sublimity, for that belongs to another, though related, mode, of Shakespearian fools and Dostoievskian saints, where 'wisdom' and 'folly' are fused together at an exceptionally high emotional pitch)[28] with which the clownesque protagonists are treated in Beckett's *Waiting for Godot*, even as we laugh at zany dialogue and music-hall routine, would seem unthinkable to Swift or Fielding.[29] They would react to the clown on a single level, as mainly or 'merely' funny, and the clown would seem to them an 'outsider' only in the sense that he was entirely beneath notice except as someone to be amused by for a few pence[30] (Fielding was, however, interested in 'low' farce, and was for a time involved in puppet-theatre).[31] Thus, when Wild is equated with the clown we seem simply invited, for the moment, to laugh, more or less genially, *at* him and from above. In the case of Felix Krull, we laugh *with*, not *at*, and his splendid arrogance and ease makes us feel inferior rather than superior.

If it is easy for Fielding and his contemporaries to equate the rogue with the clown, it is not easy for them to equate either with the artist in any high or serious sense, as does Mann, inheriting Nietzsche's view of the artist as joker, illusionist and swindler.[32] Robert Alter remarks that this equation, in the positive or mainly non-pejorative form in which it is found notably in *Felix Krull*, is 'distinctively modern', resting on 'the tension between the artist and society' characteristic of our own time.[33] Alter also notes suggestively that there is an old form of this equation which works in the reverse direction: 'at least as far back as Boccaccio's Bruno and Buffalmacco, writers on occasion have chosen to present the artist as a rogue or trickster.'[34] But even the positive equation can be found, in an unformed or potential state, early in the picaresque tradition. Unlike the 'ordinary man', to whom 'things happen', the picaro, 'in his aspect of master-of-his-fate, actually handles experience much the way an artist handles the materials of his art', and, as Alter further notes, he has from the start been a master of illusionism and disguise.[35] It is the extension of the disguise-analogy, beyond the clown or the mountebank, and even beyond the actor, to the figure of the creative artist, and the high valuation placed on the artist as 'illusionist' and impersonator, which we cannot, I think, expect to find in Fielding. Conceptions of the artist as merging his personality in his creations, so that the two are not simply separable, have an old ancestry; but they probably do not reach their greatest maturity and completeness, or achieve their highest importance and estimation, until Romantic and post-Romantic times, in Keats's account of the 'camelion Poet' (letter to Woodhouse, 27 October 1818) and its many contemporary and future analogues.[36] Ben Jonson, in verses 'On the Author, Worke, and Translator' prefixed to Mabbe's translation of *Guzmán*, speaks warmly of 'this Spanish Proteus'.[37] But the description, though applied to Guzmán, is not primarily a celebration of his Protean talents (and still less of his 'immoralism'), but a compliment to the literary work of which he is the hero, and which captures his vices so truthfully. Contrast Hazlitt's praise of Shakespeare as 'the Proteus of human intellect', or Thomas Mann's exploration of the positive connection between genius and a Protean immoralism, in *Lotte in Weimar* and elsewhere.[38]

This account should prepare us to expect certain precise distinctions between Mann's confidence man and Fielding's. But some analogies, which make the juxtaposition instructive, may be noted first.[39] Like Wild, Krull is repeatedly spoken of as an exceptional or pre-eminent figure, above common mortals, and reserved or 'born' for a special fate (for Wild this means hanging, for Krull a high success in his progress through the world, a difference obvious and piquant, but which, I shall argue, is in some ways much less than it seems). Krull used to play, as a boy, at being emperor and hero,[40] and Wild, in his schooldays (and after) 'was a passionate admirer of heroes, particularly of Alexander the Great' (I, iii). A further amusing coincidence is that Krull's sister, Olympia, bears a name very close to that of Alexander's notorious mother, Olympias! In the important episode of Krull's visit to the circus, the confidence man's relation to clowns and other circus artists is explored, more concentratedly than in *Jonathan Wild*, but clearly within the same time-honoured tradition.[41] It is at this point, where analogy and difference are elaborately intertwined, that the most meaningful distinctions (from our present point of view) may be felt to crystallize.

Krull, 'with a thoughtful fellow-feeling', thinks of the circus artists, 'these ageless, half-grown sons of absurdity', painted and masked and grotesque, as outside the 'human' world of 'every-day daily life'. He does not, of course, think of himself literally as a circus performer, but he embraces his shared identity with them 'as a member of a more general profession, as an entertainer and illusionist'. The acrobats and others also evoke notions of the deep impersonality of art, and its separateness from and superiority to the 'unheroic, gaping crowd', which, as in Jonathan Wild's final 'apotheosis' (IV, xiv), wildly applauds. Amusingly, many of them have names of mock-epic or mock-imperial resonance: 'the star of the circus' is a trapeze artist called Andromache, and the lion tamer Mustafa rules over lions with names like Achille and Nero, a touch of slipshod grandeur not unlike that evoked by Fielding when he lists the 'high princess[es] in Drollic story' who are enacted in Bartholomew Fair farces (II, iii), or when he otherwise links the heroic with low farce.

These relations between confidence trickster and circus artist are, in Mann's novel, self-consciously explored by the confidence trickster himself. Or rather, there is a fluid interplay between the relations which occur in the consciousness of Krull, and those which are authorially given. For example, the mock-heroic names of the performers are not presumed to have been invented by Krull, but they convey the ironic poignancy, the sense of shabby splendour, of Mann's identification not only of roguery with art, but of both with such gaudy tinsel.[42] It is not only because Krull is his own first-person narrator that his activities and reflections seem much more internalized than those of Wild. Mann's own self-involvement with Krull, which has led one critic to describe the novel as 'A Portrait of the Artist as a Young Swindler', is felt vividly and at a high creative pressure.[43] Krull's disguises, like Wild's poker-faced deceptions, are usually in pursuit of some technically criminal end: however, not only does Krull enjoy them *per se*, as artistic achievement and as ever-renewable modes of self-realization, but Mann himself (as the novel's tone unmistakably reminds us throughout) casts a festive and triumphant verve over, and into, all Krull's operations. Where the multiplicity of Krull's deceptions and disguises is a proclamation of plasticity, of the fluidity of boundaries, of the inappropriateness to a fully human life of simplified or static postures, Wild's deceptions are frozen into a sharply-defined criminal-cum-comic role. Of course, the underlying comedy of Wild (like much of Fielding's comedy elsewhere) rests also on an ideal of spontaneous and vital plasticity, and on a corresponding proto-Bergsonian view of the rigid and the mechanically self-entrapped. But for Fielding, the ideal of vital plasticity is different from that celebrated in Mann's novel, partly because for Fielding plasticity meant carrying one's full humanity within one's appointed social role, whereas for Mann plasticity is a transcendence or even a denial of any given role. Moreover, Fielding's notion of an ideal plasticity was at the same time contained within a securely held and strongly manifested moral outlook. It is always clear that Wild is doing wrong, but never conceded that Krull is, a distinction not unconnected with the fact that, by roughly similar misdemeanours, Wild reduces life into routine (thus losing his plasticity), while Krull frees himself from the routines of common life.

Fielding's well-known externality, here as elsewhere, is an aloofness which not only asserts the author's moral and social superiority, but suggests the poise of one who is sufficiently sure of his standards not to need to involve himself in the unduly intimate scrutiny of a nasty situation. Or, for that matter, of any other situation: if character is determined by its relation to a moral code, it will seem correspondingly natural to feel that a personality can be confidently defined. Where Krull is endlessly various and elusive (truly Protean beyond the reach of Guzmán's or any other mere picaro's skills), Wild shows to the end a notable 'conservation of character' (IV, xiv). Fielding's uses of this and related phrases suggest that the notions of 'self-consistency' and of the referability of character to a fixed moral standard are interwoven in his mind with a profound intimacy. The topic exercises his irony throughout *Jonathan Wild*, and makes its first appearance in I, i, when Fielding sarcastically rebukes the historians who 'destroy the great perfection called uniformity of character' by attributing to 'great' personages like Alexander and Caesar certain alien touches of 'goodness'. This ironically overstated postulate of an unmixed purity of good or evil should not, in itself, be exaggerated. It has a fictive or rhetorical role that belongs naturally among the work's formulaic contrasts of 'greatness' and 'goodness', and it is moreover undercut in the same chapter and elsewhere by reminders that no man is perfect and that even a 'great' man like Wild has a few 'weaknesses' (I, i; IV, iv; IV, xv).[44] Furthermore, in the Preface to the *Miscellanies* Fielding tried to rectify what in sober truth, as opposed to the novel's ironic extravagance, would seem an over-simple division, by adding a third category of the 'great and good'.[45] On the other hand, the concessions in the novel over Wild's 'weaknesses' are themselves mainly rhetorical (the weaknesses are, in the words of the closing paragraph of I, i, 'only enough to make him partaker of the imperfection of humanity, instead of the perfection of diabolism'), and the mixed category of the 'great and good' in the Preface seems to extend only to a very few rare persons. In any event, even this mixed category hardly weakens the connection between the notion of character as a fixed and coherent thing, and the very straightforward moral norms against which it is tested.

But a more interesting convergence between a categorizable self-consistency of character, and the domain of stable and predictable moral judgments (notably the domain of those merited rewards and punishments which constitute 'poetic justice'), occurs in the two closing chapters. First, in the important and memorably comic paragraph in IV, xiv in which Wild swings 'out of the world' with the ordinary's bottle-screw in his hand, we read of the 'admirable conservation of character in our hero' which makes him maintain his pickpocketing habits 'to the last moment'. It is not clear, and does not need to be clear, whether it is Wild who is 'admirable' for having retained his self-hood unflinchingly, or whether 'nature' is to be congratulated for creating such a consummately self-consistent personality, or whether the author of the novel has achieved a triumph of artistic coherence. The three notions closely intersect, without blurring each other's sharp and witty clarity (just as the genial humour of Wild's mortal exit does not blur the firmness with which it is brought home to us that Wild deserved his fate). The parallels and reciprocities between 'art' and 'nature' exercised Fielding as much and as buoyantly as they did Mann, differently though the two novelists interpret them. In IV, xv Fielding returns, in a slightly modified form, to the point first raised in I, i, that Wild's 'greatness' was unflawed by those uncharacteristic ingredients of 'goodness' which 'weak writers' have commended in Alexander and Caesar, and 'which nature had so grossly erred in giving them, as a painter would who should dress a peasant in the robes of state, or give the nose or any other feature of a Venus to a satyr'. A few lines later, as part of the 'finishing' (a pun) of Wild's 'character', we are reminded of 'the conformity above mentioned of his death to his life'. This 'conformity' is a reference to the moral logic of events: he was hanged, as any 'hero' should be, hanging being not only the end for which he was born, but also the properest end for 'great' men, though 'so few GREAT men can accomplish' it.

The ideal congruence between Wild's moral character and the judgment of fate upon him, which makes hanging a 'finishing' of 'character', establishes itself as very close to 'conservation of character' in the other senses. An elaborate assimilation occurs at the beginning of IV, xiv, the hanging-chapter, where the operations of life are, with grandiloquent fuss, judged by standards derived from stage drama:

> The day now drew nigh when our great man was to exemplify the last and noblest act of greatness by which any hero can signalize himself. This was the day of execution, or consummation, or apotheosis (for it is called by different names), which was to give our hero an opportunity of facing death and damnation, without any fear in his heart, or, at least, without betraying any symptoms of it in his countenance. A completion of greatness which is heartily to be wished to every great man; nothing being more worthy of lamentation than when Fortune, like a lazy poet,

winds up her catastrophe awkwardly, and bestowing too little care on her fifth act, dismisses the hero with a sneaking and private exit, who had in the former part of the drama performed such notable exploits as must promise to every good judge among the spectators a noble, public, and exalted end.

But she was resolved to commit no such error in this instance. Our hero was too much and too deservedly her favourite to be neglected by her in his last moments; accordingly all efforts for a reprieve were vain, and the name of Wild stood at the head of those who were ordered for execution.

The reference to a hoped-for reprieve may, as we shall see, be a playful glance at the *Beggar's Opera*, where Macheath is saved at the last minute because 'an opera must end happily'.[46] It is as though, in the opera, the rules of art have exerted their domination upon the action in a way that prevents, instead of furthering, the 'completion of greatness' in a fit catastrophe. This 'completion', like the next chapter's 'finishing of . . . character', means simultaneously due punishment, a satisfying end, and self-fulfilment for the hero. For this intermerging of moral propriety (or poetic justice) and true coherence of character in some kind of *actual* sense, Fielding at least once attempted an explanation in terms of psychological truth or 'probability'. The explanation, in *Tom Jones*, viii, i, is particularly relevant here, because it explicitly links 'conservation of character' (which requires of authors 'a very extraordinary degree of judgment, and a most exact knowledge of human nature') with the kind of poetic justice that sends or ought to send villains of plays to the gallows. After noting a type of unnatural characterization ('Should the best parts of the story of M. Antoninus be ascribed to Nero, or should the worst incidents of Nero's life be imputed to Antoninus, what would be more shocking to belief'), Fielding goes on to say:

> Our modern authors of comedy have fallen almost universally into the error here hinted at: their heroes generally are notorious rogues, and their heroines abandoned jades, during the first four acts; but in the fifth, the former become very worthy gentlemen, and the latter, women of virtue and discretion: nor is the writer often so kind as to give himself the least trouble, to reconcile or account for this monstrous change and incongruity. There is, indeed, no other reason to be assigned for it, than because the play is drawing to a conclusion; as if it was no less natural in a rogue to repent in the last act of a play, than in the last of his life; which

we perceive to be generally the case at Tyburn, a place which might, indeed, close the scene of some comedies with much propriety, as the heroes in these are most commonly eminent for those very talents which not only bring men to the gallows, but enable them to make an heroic figure when they are there.

This assertion of a link between propriety and probability is not, of course, to be taken as a bald and literal truth. Here, as in *Jonathan Wild*, Fielding is exploring ironic connections, imaginative meeting-points, with a cautious indirection which guards him against imputations of undue facility, and in a context which guarantees that he is fully aware of the actual turpitudes and disorders of real life. But he is also assuming, in this passage as in the overall shape of *Tom Jones*, a greater notional congruence between the patterned ideal and the actual shape of things than we find in, say, Swift, when, in the *Project for the Advancement of Religion*, Swift similarly complains of the perverse kinds of 'distributive Justice' in modern playwrights.[47] Probability, realism and the rest do not enter, and their absence is attributable almost as much to Swift's temperamental resistance to any feeling that actuality can in itself be orderly, as to the overriding didactic preoccupation of his *Project*. The order of art is conceived by Swift as *holding down* the subversive unruliness of the actual, not as shaping that unruliness into its potential coherence, nor as exploring any live and meaningful mutualities or adaptabilities between energy and rule. Appropriately, the *Project*'s solutions are external and reductive: for example, let a censor be appointed 'to strike out every offensive, or unbecoming Passage from Plays already written, as well as those that may be offered to the Stage for the future'.[48]

For Swift, a fifth-act reprieve is simply an offence against moral order, an official sanctioning by art of the all too evidently existing gap, in life, between what is and what ought to be. Fielding is by contrast hanging on to the notion that the actual is not wholly disconnected from the ideal. Last minute reprieves, and other artificially imposed happy endings, are objected to not merely because they violate an absolute standard of moral decorum, but because they are an extension of untrue notions of character: it is no less 'natural in a rogue to repent in the last act of a play, than in the last of his life'. Nature is seen as at least *sometimes* behaving in such a way that the actual, the 'characteristic' and the morally appropriate coincide. Hence a feeling (playfully elaborated throughout *Jonathan Wild*) that nature and art are engaged, no doubt imperfectly, in a parallel *and* collaborative enterprise. This means partly the familiar notion that art must correct nature where the latter is deficient, even doing (Fielding says at the end of IV, xiv) 'a violence to truth' in cases where the factual arrangements of fortune are imperfectly shaped. Thus, in the novel, not only Wild but 'all the other persons mentioned in this history in the light of greatness' suffer 'the fate adapted to it' (i.e. hanging), except two: Theodosia Snap, for whom Fielding had a soft spot because her main lapse was sexual and because she was reviled by the canting Laetitia for giving birth to a bastard (III, xiii; at the end of the novel, Theodosia 'was transported to America, where she was pretty well married, reformed, and made a good wife'), and Count La Ruse, who was 'broke on the wheel' (an elegant variation, morally equivalent to hanging) (IV, xv, *ad fin.*).

But if Fortune sometimes behaves like a lazy poet, and needs real poets to put her right, she committed 'no such error' in the case of Wild, whose real-life end happened (happily!) to be morally deserved, and appropriately grand. Fielding almost festively celebrates this convergence of the real with the due order of things. Wild's failure to get a reprieve is a triumphant instance of life imitating art, a point which emerges all the more sharply if a tacit contrast with Macheath's reprieve is intended. The pattern had already appeared in reverse in IV, vi, when Heartfree's reprieve, which *does* come (unlike Wild's) but which is also and this time *explicitly* contrasted with Macheath's, is cheekily presented as an example of art imitating life:

> lest our reprieve should seem to resemble that in the Beggar's Opera, I shall endeavor to show [the reader] that this incident, which is undoubtedly true, is at least as natural as delightful; for we assure him we would rather have suffered half mankind to be hanged than have saved one contrary to the strictest rules of writing and probability.

This sense of the reciprocity of life and art is very buoyant in *Jonathan Wild*. That it is at the same time playful need not be laboured. But the playfulness and the sense of reciprocity differ greatly from Gay's (Fielding admired Gay, of course, and imitated him in his plays).[49] Gay's playfulness, though it has a very sharp tang, expresses itself with a lightly-carried panache, while Fielding's in this novel is a heavier exfoliation of oafish grotesquerie. Gay's preoccupation with 'strict poetical justice' in the matter of Macheath's hanging is aired by the Beggar, before the Player overrides it with his reference to the operatic proprieties, which demand a reprieve (*Beggar's Opera*, III, xvi). But in the 'Introduction' to *Polly*, he makes the Poet, who now replaces the

Beggar, say that he had been 'unjustly accused of having given up my moral for a joke, like a fine gentleman in conversation', but that this time he 'will not so much as seem to give up my moral'. Macheath is accordingly hanged in this sequel, the last Air proclaiming that 'Justice long forbearing . . . Hunts the villain's pace'.

In *Polly*, Macheath is less charming than in the *Beggar's Opera*, shadier, more ponderous, somewhat trapped in his own sexuality, rather than a gay easy-going and successful rogue. His character in these respects is (like his ending) closer to that of Wild, and closer also to that of his own Brechtian reincarnations, in the *Threepenny Opera* and also the *Threepenny Novel*. Brecht's *Opera*, however, like the *Beggar's Opera* and unlike *Polly*, ends with a reprieve, but a grotesque reprieve to which are added (while Macheath is standing at the gallows) elevation to the peerage, a castle, and 'a pension of ten thousand pounds a year', all by order of the Queen.[50] Brecht not only does not provide the kind of 'poetical justice' on which *Polly* had closed, but also converts the reprieve in Gay's earlier opera from merry inconsequence to an absurdly apt and pregnant social criticism in its own right. In one sense, its heaving grotesquerie may be felt to resemble the hanging-chapter of *Jonathan Wild*, despite its contrary outcome, because both share an element of deliberately ponderous fantastication, in service of a similar satiric irony. In such a style, Gay is not at home. An approximation to the later Macheath may be sensed in *Polly*, but *Polly* is an unsuccessful work. In the less alien idiom of the *Beggar's Opera*, the hero is an attractive and charming rogue for whom a bad end might seem out of place. When he is saved by the rules of opera, we know that some mockery of operas is taking place, but Macheath's attractiveness throughout the work has been such that the ending has a primary and not mainly a parodic aptness.

This is not to say that the *Beggar's Opera* ends by giving up its 'moral for a joke'. After the Beggar and the Player have agreed on the reprieve 'to comply with the taste of the town', the Beggar gets his moral in. He says that 'through the whole piece' the 'similitude of manners in high and low life' is such that 'it is difficult to determine whether . . . the fine gentlemen imitate the gentlemen of the road, or the gentlemen of the road the fine gentlemen'. More important, he adds to these often-quoted words a further biting irony: 'Had the play remain'd, as I at first intended, it would have carried a most excellent moral. 'Twould have shown that the lower sort of people have their vices in a degree as well as the rich: And that they are punish'd for them.' This closes the dialogue, and the scene in which it occurs (III, xvi). The Beggar is not only allowed the last word, but uses it to give a bitter final countertwist to his moral. It might be felt that Gay is thus enabled to get all the moral effect of that stricter 'poetical justice' which the Beggar 'at first intended', merely by stating the intention; and that he does so with even greater point for this sharp rhetorical underplaying. After all, *Polly*, where Macheath is finally executed, ends unmemorably, with deadening commonplaces about how truth and justice must always prevail.

The ending of the *Beggar's Opera* differs chiefly from that of *Jonathan Wild*, however, because it lacks that sense of the reciprocity of art and life which is characteristic of Fielding's work. Gay's ending, like Fielding's, is festive as well as bitter, but the two notes are kept separate and not, as in Fielding, in a grotesque unison. 'Art' is given its head, and a sharp moral follows, separately. Nor is it a simple case of bad art being mocked in Macheath's reprieve. Such mockery exists also in Fielding's contrary ending, and Gay's joke at the expense of operas, as I suggested, also gives primary satisfaction, because Macheath is so likable. This effect is so far from being cancelled by the Beggar's closing words, that it is reaffirmed in a further scene and a final song. For the Beggar's last words occur in the penultimate, not the last, scene. In the last, Macheath celebrates the reprieve by starting a dance of the assembled company, pairing off all present and himself taking Polly 'for life'. The final Air is on the theme that 'The wretch of to-day, may be happy to-morrow'. It is this separation of the realm of aesthetic order and aesthetic satisfaction from both actuality and the relevant moral comments made within the work that we do not find in Fielding. It is not that Fielding insists that his work exactly reproduces what actually happened (he specifically denies this in the Preface, asserting his more 'general' satiric concerns and refusing to compete with 'authentic' biographical accounts of Wild),[51] although Wild did, of course, actually die on the gallows in real life. Still less does Fielding say that life always fulfils those universal or ideal patterns of moral coherence for which art properly speaks. Wild differs from his own historical original in not offering a final gesture of repentance, in the style of those real-life criminals mentioned in *Tom Jones*, VIII, i, who complete their lives like a bad play. Fielding's insistence that 'poetical justice' and 'conservation of character' have been not only scrupulously observed but shown to be interrelated, in the construction of his book as in the career of his fictionalized hero, asserts a reciprocal interplay rather than any identity between art and life. Fielding's joke that his book is well constructed, and ends as such books should, means also that the course of events described there (unlike the facts on which the story is based) has the superior truth of art. Gay's joke about opera-endings, on the other hand, insists only on the greater fun of art, and stays distinct from the graver and harsher truths which his opera also proclaims.

The fitness of Wild's finishing, and the care bestowed by Fortune on the 'fifth act' of his drama, are no merely local or isolated quips. They are prepared for throughout the novel by a whole series of allusions to the fact that Wild was born to be hanged, and that Fortune and Nature (though not always to be relied on to govern the lives of men with a proper consistency) jealously reserved Wild for this due end. In II, xii, Wild is alone at sea and in mortal danger, but he is saved from drowning in fulfilment of the proverb that he who was born to be hanged shall never be drowned. The point is elaborated in a facetious and wordy application of Horace's *Nec Deus intersit*: Wild's astonishing survival was due not to 'supernatural' but to 'natural' causes, because it was Nature's intention to hang him! When Wild is stabbed by Blueskin in IV, i, Fortune, like an Iliadic goddess, 'carefully placed his guts out of the way' of the knife, so that the wound is not mortal and Fortune's 'purpose' to hang Wild is safeguarded.[52] In IV, xii, when Wild is sentenced, the familiar sarcastic comparison is made between this 'proper end' and Fortune's remissness in not finishing off some other great men in the same way. And in IV, xiv, some paragraphs after the elaborate stage-metaphor about the fit 'fifth act', Wild's eleventh-hour attempt to kill himself with laudanum to avoid hanging is again foiled by Fortune.

In all these passages, the play of literary (and especially theatrical) allusion is very pointed. It is part of a larger network, which includes not only the references to clowns and Bartholomew Fair farces, but also a host of other references to the 'stage of life' (I, iii; II, xii), to Nature as a 'dramatic poet' (I, iii), to epic and historiographic parallels *passim*. The cumulative effect of these is to reinforce the playful sense of cosmic tidy-mindedness which comes, notably, from the fulfilment of Nature's and Fortune's purposes in the matter of Wild's hanging. A certain sense of life as a well-made play survives, even when the analogies are negative (when certain kinds of art are seen to falsify actuality or to violate moral standards, or when real life is said to be less orderly than art). This is even true when 'the stage of the world differs from that in Drury Lane' in a way that is unflattering to both:

> the stage of the world differs from that in Drury-lane principally
> in this—that whereas, on the latter, the hero or chief figure is
> almost continually before your eyes, whilst the under-actors are

not seen above once in an evening; now, on the former, the hero or great man is always behind the curtain, and seldom or never appears or doth anything in his own person. He doth indeed, in this grand drama, rather perform the part of the prompter, and doth instruct the well-dressed figures, who are strutting in public on the stage, what to say and do. To say the truth, a puppet-show will illustrate our meaning better, where it is the master of the show (the great man) who dances and moves everything, whether it be the king of Muscovy or whatever other potentate *alias* puppet which we behold on the stage; but he himself keeps wisely out of sight, for, should he once appear, the whole motion would be at an end. Not that anyone is ignorant of his being there, or supposes that the puppets are not mere sticks of wood, and he himself the sole mover; but as this (though every one knows it) doth not appear visibly, *i.e.* to their eyes, no one is ashamed of consenting to be imposed upon (III, xi).

This is one of the more acrid of the novel's theatrical comparisons, and hardly implies sympathy for Wild's behind-the-scenes manipulation of his accomplices, or for the willingness of mankind to be taken in by such perfunctory concealments.[53] The image, of course, points particularly to Walpole, who was commonly presented by satirists as a theatrical manager or an actor, and specifically as a Colley Cibber, patentee of Drury Lane.[54] The anti-Walpole, anti-Cibber allusion, with its attendant implication that Walpole's government is a farce, links the passage with several of Fielding's plays, as well as with the *Dunciad*.[55] It also provides a specific satiric charge within the more general and continuous theatrical metaphor in the novel as a whole. Such specific implications, against Walpole and Cibber, might not seem calculated to soften the passage very much. On the other hand, the characteristic glint of uppish humour at Cibber's expense, and the patronizing chatter about puppet-shows, do introduce a note of comicality sufficient to suggest that the viciousness of Wild and Walpole stop short of destroying the narrator's emotional poise.[56] The puppet 'king of Muscovy', like the roll-call of 'high princess[es] in Drollic story' in II, iii, and the circus figures with the heroic or imperial nicknames in *Felix Krull*, is lit by the fun which is inherent to such hobbling stylizations in the lower theatrical arts, and by the added fun of stylized allusion to these stylizations in a sophisticated and highly articulate ironic fiction. References to the order of art, the setting up of stylized frames to surround the action or the moral commentary, are, with Fielding, in themselves signs that the author is in control. The naked rawness of circumstance and any undue immediacy of authorial feeling are distanced into a world where artifice and moral irony combine to reassure us of certain essential stabilities. The fact that differences between art and life are noted as often as analogies is less significant than the fact that relations as such, whether positive or negative, are insistently explored. It is the meaningful existence of relations, and the positive turn which is almost always sensed as a potential in Fielding's irony (but seldom in Swift's), which matter.

Behind these relations lies the notion, tentative and exploratory but also (for Fielding) vitally active, of life imitating art. The agent of this process is often called Nature, that ordering principle which was for Fielding and others part metaphor of an ideal, part object of aspiration, seldom totally an actuality but always a potential to which actuality tends or against which it can be measured. When life imitates art, Fielding is always (except in his last works) able to seem buoyantly in control, partly because this imitation makes life seem amenable to that wisdom of the artist-gentleman-moralist which he likes to project as his own. This is true even when the imitation is incomplete, for a degree of comparability is presupposed, and there is also a sense (again absent in Swift) that a vital interaction between the two domains is at every moment possible. Hence the positive quality in Fielding's ironic negations, even in the formulaically negative *Jonathan Wild*, and especially in a context of continuous parody, that is of continuous awareness of the domain of art as a measure (this effect of the systematic parody in *Jonathan Wild* may be contrasted with the much more radically destructive quality of the parody in Swift's *Tale of a Tub*). When 'greatness' is played off against heroic ideals of which it is part imitation and part travesty, when these ideals as celebrated by epic poets and imperial biographers are played off against a humbler 'goodness', when the events of the story are discussed in terms of what does or does not happen on the stage or in novels, or when these events are asserted to be unlike everyday life but better, or unlike fiction but truer, the result is a buoyant cumulative proclamation of the living relevance of the confrontation between life and art.

In III, vii, after the marriage of Wild and Laetitia, Fielding says that, unlike 'most private histories [i.e. novels], as well as comedies', his story does not end with the wedding of the principals and its happy-ever-after implications. Apart from the obvious fact that there is more of the story to come, the marriage was not happy:

Now there was all the probability imaginable that this contract

would have proved of such happy note, both from the great
accomplishments of the young lady, who was thought to be
possessed of every qualification necessary to make the marriage
state happy, and from the truly ardent passion of Mr. Wild; but,
whether it was that nature and fortune had great designs for him
to execute, and would not suffer his vast abilities to be lost and
sunk in the arms of a wife, or whether neither nature nor fortune
had any hand in the matter, is a point I will not determine.

The uncertainty whether Nature and Fortune had 'great designs' or no
'hand in the matter' is playful, and can afford to be. There are no real
or pressing doubts, no ambiguous valuations. We know what the 'great
designs' are, and how Wild is destined to end anyway. 'I will not determine' really means 'I (and you, reader) know very well': the marriage
will not be happy because Laetitia is a mercenary wanton, and Wild a
dupable, boorish and foul-tempered lecher. Moreover, Fortune, truer
than any novel or play, but in this novel also morally truer than in
everyday life (yet also literally true to the career of the historical Wild),
is reserving Wild for hanging. When Fortune is noted elsewhere (e.g.
in IV, xii) as failing to reward other great men with a similar fate, the
fact appears as a lapse in the cosmic plan, deplorable indeed but also
incapable of seriously undermining one's faith in the ideals which the
plan embodies: contrast the very cruel sense of the violation of Nature's
laws in a late work like *Amelia*. In the present passage, the irony is so
confidently in control of itself as to be self-enjoying, without smugness,
containing rather than denying an evil whose fetid energies are made
very clear. The two personified terms, 'nature' and 'fortune', are so
lightly carried as to be little more than idiomatic usages. Any additional
resonance which they have is derived from the fact that they occur a
good deal in the novel as a whole, in mutually echoing contexts, and
that they are at all times, as here, brought into relation with great and
disorderly forces of character and circumstance. When Fielding shows
us life imitating art in a work of art imitating life, he makes us feel (not
least because the imitations, in both directions, are incomplete) that the
process, though not flawlessly circular, is vitally and genuinely reciprocal,
loose ends and all.

These reciprocities are, paradoxically, most vividly felt when Fielding
can be playfully ironic about them, as normally happens in his fiction
before *Amelia*. It is a measure of the 'positive' quality of his irony
that this should be so. In *Amelia*, where a note of bald literalness
governs some of the main assertions of the art-life relationship, the

matter is rigidified to something more like mere analogy than live interplay:

> Life may as properly be called an art as any other; and the great incidents in it are no more to be considered as mere accidents than the several members of a fine statue or a noble poem. The critics in all these are not content with seeing anything to be great without knowing why and how it came to be so. By examining carefully the several gradations which conduce to bring every model to perfection, we learn truly to know that science in which the model is formed: as histories of this kind, therefore, may properly be called models of HUMAN LIFE, so, by observing minutely the several incidents which tend to the catastrophe or completion of the whole, and the minute causes whence those incidents are produced, we shall best be instructed in this most useful of all arts, which I call the ART of LIFE (*Amelia*, 1, i).

Such a passage is more literal and more emphatic, and there is no doubt that it is deeply felt. But it has none of that sense of continuous and variegated interaction which we find in *Jonathan Wild*, as also in *Joseph Andrews* and especially in *Tom Jones*. It makes its points in a rather compartmentalized way. First, a good life is a fine and elaborate achievement, comparable to a great work of art. Secondly, since novels are in a special sense 'models of HUMAN LIFE' (special presumably because they trace the careers of private persons, because they are more detailed and more 'realistic' than other genres, etc.), they can provide particularly detailed instructions for the Art of Life. Thus not only are the buoyant reciprocities of the earlier fiction levelled to a somewhat commonplace analogy, but there is also a deadening conception of the work as in some oversimple sense a handbook on how to live.

Again, a phrase like 'the catastrophe or completion of the whole' ostensibly has the same force as the reference to Wild's 'finishing', linking the notion of aesthetic roundedness with that of moral responsibility. Fielding had just been arguing that men too readily ascribe to Fortune events which in fact proceed from their moral character, and especially their 'predominant passion'. It is absurd to attribute to Fortune not only 'the success of knaves, the calamities of fools' and 'the miseries in which men of sense sometimes involve themselves', but also any happiness which the righteous may succeed in achieving, despite certain flaws of character. He is presumably alluding in advance to the happy ending which finally rewards the imprudent and much-suffering Booth, when he says:

> To retrieve the ill consequences of a foolish conduct, and by
> struggling manfully with distress to subdue it, is one of the noblest
> efforts of wisdom and virtue. Whoever, therefore, calls such a
> man fortunate, is guilty of no less impropriety in speech than he
> would be who should call the statuary or the poet fortunate who
> carved a Venus or who writ an Iliad (*Amelia*, I, i).

Paradoxically, however, the unpredictabilities of Fortune, as I argued
in chapter III, are felt particularly pressingly and painfully in this novel,
despite (and perhaps partly because of) these assertions. And when we
come to the actual ending, and its 'poetical justice' to the Booths, we
read that 'Fortune seems to have made them large amends' (*Amelia*,
XII, ix), in the form of the customary providential 'discovery' of a
legacy. The conventional romance conclusion, the rounding-off of the
artefact, seems in the event at least as closely associated with Fortune as
with the consequences of the hero's character; and this impression is all
the starker for the fact that the novel has hitherto been exhibiting with
considerable emphasis the cruel unpredictabilities of life. The fact that
from then on the Booths 'enjoyed an uninterrupted course of health and
happiness' gives its proper satisfaction, but it does little to bridge that
gap between art and life which Fielding's initial statements might lead
us to expect would be bridged. The sober, earthbound phrasing
(mentioning health, as well as happiness, ever after!) does not help,
because it keeps things flatly within the realm of the *literal*, where the
art-life connection is hardest to establish. In the 'poetical justice' of
Jonathan Wild, the logical gap may be almost as wide, but it is bridged
by the blowsy fantasy of the style, with its special blend of saving irony
and moral certitude playfully rendered.

In *Amelia*, the 'art of life' is assumed to be practised by the characters,
whereas in *Jonathan Wild* (and the other novels) it is visibly shaped and
dominated by the author. For the characters in *Amelia* this is hard,
uphill work, often unsupported by displays of authorial confidence.
The author is now a subdued presence, making a few passionate bids
(out of eloquent but also harsh survivals of his earlier style) to create
order out of the chaos of cruel circumstance, but often lapsing into
cantankerous sentimentality. In *Jonathan Wild*, the author is master of
circumstance, like Felix Krull but *unlike* Wild. Fielding's distinct
separation from his character means first that in his novel the figure of
the artist is exclusively authorial, and secondly, since Wild is sometimes
seen in the role of a clown, that the artist and the clown are very
distinct beings. In Mann, there is instead a deep interpenetration: Mann

himself, Krull the confidence man, and the circus artists, are not simply identical, but their interinvolvement is close and the boundaries between them fluid.

The fact that Krull has no 'single identity to preserve'[57] is itself his triumph as an artist. It is a kind of 'triumph' which Swift foresaw long ago as 'modern', and mockingly pre-enacted in the *Tale of a Tub*. The *Tale's* 'author' (not without his own associations with, among others, the mountebank of the *Stage-Itinerant*), represents, however, a *deplorable* fluidity, the engulfing vitality of moral and intellectual chaos. In some ways, Swift's 'author', in his characterless and subterranean energy, even more resembles (or is a negative version of) that 'undifferentiated man' whom Lawrence was to describe as buried beneath all our civic roles, alive in the 'fecund darkness' of our primal being.[58] The closeness (in which mutually opposing valuations are sometimes hard to disentangle from elements of essential agreement) of Swift to his satirized 'author' and of both to Lawrence becomes vivid if we set the *Tale's* Clothes Philosophy beside, say, Ursula's cherished conception of the inner man of every civic puppet as 'a piece of darkness made visible only by his clothes', and her contempt for their daylight manner of assuming 'selves as they assume suits of clothing'.[59] Fielding never gets entangled in his own satirized opposites as Swift does. Where Swift and Lawrence see the retreat from roles as a descent into an undifferentiating inner darkness (whether nasty or vitally creative), Fielding and Mann think in terms of a multiplication or variegation of being: criminal hypocrisies, mendacities of clownish facial expression in Wild, gay adoption of disguises and 'double' identities by Krull. But there is an overriding difference, which is cultural, between the eighteenth-century authors on the one hand, and the twentieth-century ones on the other. For both Swift and Fielding, our civic roles, our appointed functions in society, though subject to uppish ridicule for their tendency to self-entrapment or professional rigidity, are nevertheless essential to the order on which society rests. For Lawrence and Mann, that order is so far from being sacrosanct, and its categorizations so untrue or irrelevant, that they need to be destroyed or at least transcended, in an overriding plasticity of being, and a correspondingly fluid system of values. 'Conservation of character' and 'poetical justice' not only cease to have the importance which they had for Fielding, but also lose their reciprocal tendency to merge the concepts of character-consistency and moral-propriety into one another. It is by emphasizing this convergence in the 'finishing' of Wild that Fielding makes the artist (i.e. himself) triumph over life, whereas Krull triumphs over life by remaining unpunished, and striding from success to success.[60] It is as right for the earlier confidence man to be hanged, as for the later one to flourish. Both are victories for the artist, and proud consummations for the confidence man, but in Fielding the two are different persons, the artist having kept Nature in order (or corrected her unruly tendency to the fortuitous) by ensuring that the confidence man is eliminated. If both authors say that life is a confidence game, Fielding wants the artist to expose the confidence game by appeal to a truer morality, while Mann wants him to play the system by being the supremest confidence trickster of all. Mann belongs to a century which can think, scientifically and without necessary attribution of blame, of human behaviour as an interplay of fictive roles, a puppet show or a circus act, and which can likewise present the analogy between society and a confidence game as a sober sociological fact rather than as a moral scandal.[61] The sociologist might, for example, note the 'sincerity' of Nazi murderers who subsequently describe themselves as having been merely 'bureaucrats faced with certain unpleasant exigencies':[62]

> Their human remorse is probably just as sincere as their erstwhile cruelty. As the Austrian novelist Robert Musil has put it, in every murderer's heart there is a spot in which he is eternally innocent. The seasons of life follow one another, and one must change one's face as one changes one's clothes. At the moment we are not concerned with the psychological difficulties or the ethical import of such 'lack of character'. We only want to stress that it is the customary procedure.

Mann's thinking on such questions has not the scientific objectivity of the sociologist, nor is it necessarily true that his thinking was shaped by developments in scientific psychology and sociology. Like Yeats and some other twentieth-century authors who have been preoccupied with the problems of role and mask, Mann is not concerned merely with the sociological fact of role-playing, nor even with the practical exploitation of the sociologist's understanding of human trickery, but with the artist's high and special function in relation to these. In a world of relative deceptions and delusive appearances, the *radical* trickery of art becomes the only reality or truest fiction, the most authentic assertion of selfhood.[63]

It is not a simple question of immoralism. The sociologist I have quoted certainly does not condone Nazis (neither, to put it mildly, did Mann). But Swift and Fielding would not have been able thus to separate 'ethical import' from mere psychological fact. For them, 'changes of clothes' in this sense are overridingly culpable, and not only when the gravest moral or political issues (such as tyranny or mass murder) are involved. The traditional image of hollowness and un-reality which occurs in satirical Clothes Philosophies ('Is not Religion a Cloak . . .'),[64] and in their most reductive exemplar, the Beau (as when in Jonathan Wild, I, x, Fielding says of Tom Smirk that 'As we take dress to be the characteristic or efficient quality of a beau, we shall . . . content ourselves with describing his dress only'), makes a simple moral judg-ment about hypocrisy, or about culpable triviality. When Lawrence talks of the hollowness of the 'dressed-up creatures', it is more in terms of an inauthenticity in respect of their most vital selves, than in respect of any simply definable moral code.[65] The insufficiency of the handsome and elegant Skrebensky (very deeply and sympathetically explored in a manner unthinkable not only in Swift or Fielding, but perhaps even in the Richardson of Clarissa) is in particular seen as a matter of 'unreality' rather than 'immorality', although some critics would feel that such redefinitions have, in Lawrence, a rewritten Puritanism, a new morality as binding as the old.

What Lawrence's 'puritanism' could not be expected to emphasize is that element of *deception* in serious art which Mann constantly asserted.[66] A festively conceived exhibition of the artist as swindler was outside the range of his sympathies, as it would (for other but not unrelated reasons) be outside the range of Swift's or Richardson's, but perhaps not Fielding's. The figure of the author in Jonathan Wild gets away with a great deal of sleight-of-hand when talking about the relation of his art to truth, and about the identity of real-life truths themselves. This sleight-of-hand, moreover, is at times cheekily trans-parent, and the cheek is not entirely unlike Krull's. Something of Krull's 'life's task of making the world respond gladly to the reality his own imaginative powers can create'[67] is sensed in Fielding's signposted projection of events through the ordering and distorting rearrange-ments of art. But Fielding holds back from any full commitment to the artist as swindler. The parts of Fielding which resemble Krull are different from the parts of Wild which resemble Krull, even when Wild is seen, in his small way, as himself an artist (i.e. a clown). Where Krull the artist appropriates to himself the picaro's mastery over his own fate, Fielding claims mastery only over his characters' fate, and Wild ends up with no mastery at all. Wild's hanging and Krull's successful survival are both triumphs of art over the apparent disorders of life, but the triumph in Fielding is not only a victory and not a defeat for traditional moral values, but also the triumph of Fielding alone. If Wild also triumphs in a sense, in that he proudly maintains his loutish selfhood to the end, the triumph is of a different nature from that of his author, although it is part of the author's triumph to have brought about that of the character. In the case of Krull's continuing brilliant success, Mann the artist is inextricably interwoven with Krull the artist. Mann confers some of his own authorial superiority on Krull, Fielding keeps his authorial superiority to himself. Krull as clown differs from Wild as clown. Krull has the clown's freedom from the conventional restrictions of common life, Wild the clown's entrapment in stock situations and the clown's mechanical limitation of response. This means that Fielding can patronize him and that, where Krull's arrogance charms and slightly awes the reader, Wild's arrogance has an oafish helplessness of which we can take a genial view.

This happens in spite of Wild's moral disrepute, and in spite also of the fact that for Fielding the 'art of life' is a moral more than an aesthetic matter. A reason for this may be that, as in *Joseph Andrews* and *Tom Jones*, he is able to establish himself visibly as master of the unruly turpitudes which he describes, to project that feeling, so familiar to readers of both these novels, of a sense of order, a power of containment and of wise definition, strong enough to outclass *without denying* the energies of evil. The stylizations of art were for Fielding live symbols of this order, except in the very last works. Even there, in *Amelia* and the *Voyage to Lisbon*, they figure prominently, as the pointedly and painfully visible shell of an ideal which has been shattered by cruel fact. They retain, in the much earlier *Jonathan Wild*, all their force, and make this work, despite the asperity of the ironic formula, very different from the bitter writings of the last years. The formulaic schematism has often disguised this, by competing, in its often wooden insistence, with the real fictional life, and by directing the attention of critics to more prominent but more inessential things: the pseudo-Swiftian irony, the 'moral allegory'. In terms of these, Wild is bound to seem what Robert Alter, and so many before and after him, have called 'an absolutely unmitigated scoundrel'.[68] Critics, and among them some of the best, also remind us that *Jonathan Wild* is in some sense not a novel, but 'prose satire', 'formal satire', or the like.[69] This is true in a strictly formal sense, and it is in some contexts important to say so. But there is another sense in which *Jonathan Wild* comes nearer to Fielding's novelistic manner than is often acknowledged. In the Preface to *Joseph Andrews*, Fielding dismissed 'blackest villainies' from the realm of the 'ridiculous', and this and other remarks in the Preface may seem partly intended to distinguish in his own mind between the mock-heroic *Jonathan Wild* (unpublished but probably substantially completed when the Preface to *Joseph Andrews* was written) and the 'comic epic' *Joseph Andrews*. But it is precisely the containment of Wild by the comic spirit as we know it in the next two novels that takes some of the sting out of Wild's viciousness. If this containment is sometimes unintended, and too intermittent to ensure a total artistic success, it is strong enough to release that blend of moral confidence and rich ironic understanding in which Fielding found his truest voice as a writer. The energies of the author of *Joseph Andrews* and *Tom Jones* are continually encroaching on the 'formal satirist', and it is this, more than the strenuous schematics, that it seems proper to take note of now.

There is, however, a further dimension to *Jonathan Wild*, which transcends both 'satire' and its 'novelistic' transformations. It is a dimension of 'black humour', in which the 'hero', though in one sense diminished, yet acquires unexpected grandeurs of a special kind. If mock-heroic has partly been scaled-down to the humbler proportions of a stylized comic novel, it also acquires, or tends towards, certain bloated freedoms which have their own 'heroic' stature. The next two chapters are concerned with this topic.

NOTES

1 Dudden, I, 485.
2 Coleridge, *Literary Remains* (London, 1836–9), II, 376–7; Scott, 'Henry Fielding', *Lives of Eminent Novelists and Dramatists* (London, Chandos Classics, n.d.), p. 428, and also 'Tobias Smollett', p. 465.
3 Allan Wendt, 'The Moral Allegory of *Jonathan Wild*', *ELH. A Journal of English Literary History*, xxiv (1957), 306–20. See ch. VII, below.
4 *Works*, XII, 245–6.
5 See ch. V below.
6 This would presuppose that *Jonathan Wild* was sufficiently advanced in composition when the Preface to *Joseph Andrews* was written. On the dating, see ch. V, n. 1 and ch. VII, n. 16. Fielding would also be concerned to make it clear that *Joseph Andrews* was not in the same mode as his theatrical burlesques, nor just 'another anti-*Pamela*' (see Homer Goldberg, 'Comic Prose Epic or Comic Romance: the Argument of the Preface to *Joseph Andrews*', *Philological Quarterly*, xliii (1964), 202–3).

7 The real-life Wild was considered as a Machiavel or worse, and an early biographer says that Wild's doings show 'a System of Politicks unknown to *Machiavel*' (*The Life of Jonathan Wild from his Birth to his Death*, by H. D. [possibly by Daniel Defoe, see below, ch. VI, n. 18], (1725), p. v; cited in Gerald Howson, *Thief-Taker General. The Rise and Fall of Jonathan Wild* (London, 1970), p. xiv). This is one of the many ways in which Fielding's Wild differs from his historical original, as well as from the assertions of Fielding's own commentary. An attempt to suggest that Fielding's work is modelled on writings by Machiavelli himself seems to be baseless (Bernard Shea, 'Machiavelli and Fielding's *Jonathan Wild*', *Publications of the Modern Language Association of America*, lxxii (1957), 55–73; see R. S. Crane's comments in *Philological Quarterly*, xxxvii (1958), 328–33).

8 *Works*, XII, 244.

9 On this possibility, see below, p. 225 n. 92.

10 See Glenn W. Hatfield, *Henry Fielding and the Language of Irony* (Chicago and London, 1968), esp. pp. 89–108, 157–8.

11 A better known example is its discussion of 'goodness' and 'greatness', studied below, ch. VII.

12 In this too he differs from the historical Wild portrayed in the contemporary documents, whose 'personal magnetism is attested by the awe in which the criminals held him, and by the number of women who were his mistresses and, in some cases, remained loyal to him to the end' (Howson, *Thief-Taker General*, p. 245). The *Life of Jonathan Wild* by 'H.D.' says '*Jonathan* was always a great Man amongst the Ladies' (p. 13). See also the work which Fielding most probably consulted, Defoe's *True and Genuine Account . . . of the late Jonathan Wild* (1725), pp. 5, 18–19. On Fielding's acquaintance with contemporary accounts of Wild, see ch. VI, n. 18. In III, iv, Fielding says Wild 'had that weakness of suffering himself to be enslaved by women, so naturally incident to men of heroic disposition', a passage which combines exposure of Wild's 'slavery to his own appetite', with a travesty of the epic theme of the hero tempted, sidetracked or brought down by sensual lures.

13 W. R. Irwin, *The Making of Jonathan Wild* (New York, 1941), pp. 59–60. See also ch. V, n. 24. Fielding's point on this matter is that Wild exemplifies a psychology which Hobbesian authors apply to all men, not just 'heroes'. More generally, in his Preface to the *Miscellanies* (*Works*, XII, 243), in *Tom Jones*, VI, i, and elsewhere, Fielding says that those authors who accuse human nature of being depraved only reveal their own bad minds (Martin C. Battestin, *The Moral Basis of Fielding's Art* (Middletown, 1959), pp. 55–6 and 169nn.). In this, Wild is like the philosophers: 'Mr. Wild, not being able . . . to find in a certain spot of human nature called his own heart the least grain of . . . honesty, had resolved, perhaps a little too generally, that there was no such thing' (III, x).

14 *Paradise Lost*, II, 932.

15 The spellings with 'k' are Fielding's, and make an obvious point. They occur in the first edition (1743) but not in the revised version (1754) nor in the Henley edition, which is based on 1754 and from which I normally quote. I have incorporated the first edition spellings in this case to preserve the full force of the original irony. (The World's Classics edition of the novel (1932) usefully gives the text of 1743, collating with 1754.)

16 See also the extended analogy between politics and fishing in *Champion*, 15 December 1739, *Works*, XV, 103–6; Swift's *Poems*, I, 253 and III, 824; and an example from *Guzmán de Alfarache*, cited by Irwin, *The Making of Jonathan Wild*, p. 88.

17 I have used throughout the translation by James Mabbe, *The Rogue* (1622), Tudor Translations (London and New York, 1924), 4 vols. This is described by Alexander A. Parker, *Literature and the Delinquent* (Edinburgh, 1967), p. 100, as 'despite certain freedoms, fundamentally faithful to the tone and to the plot of the original'. Fielding's title, 'The Spanish Rogue', suggests, however, that he was probably referring either to *The Spanish Rogue, Or, The Life of Guzman de Alfarache*, Printed for Tho. Smith, in Corn-hill, n.d. (British Museum copy, 12490 aa 20, is certainly early eighteenth century, and not 1790, as tentatively suggested in catalogue), a greatly abridged version; or to *The Life of Guzman d'Alfarache, or the Spanish Rogue* (1707), translated from Sébastien Brémond's French translation of 1695. This, and Lesage's very free translation (1732), both play down the serious moral and theological elements of the Spanish original, and Brémond expands the comic elements (Parker, pp. 115 ff.). Parker argues that the more genial novel of roguery, the more good-humoured conception of the picaresque, which we associate with Lesage's *Gil Blas* (1715–35), is really a phenomenon of the eighteenth century (Parker, pp. 120 ff., 136–7). These facts are of crucial relevance to our understanding of the picaresque overtones of *Jonathan Wild*. Parker's important book seems nevertheless to exaggerate the lack of comedy or lightheartedness in the earlier, Spanish forms of picaresque, of which *Guzmán* is a prototype (see the review of Parker by C. A. Jones, *Modern Language Review*, lxiii (1968), 726, and Vivienne Mylne's view that 'the comparison of the *pícaro* with the delinquent occasionally seems rather forced', *French Studies*, xxii (1968), 246). The English term 'rogue' could of course carry both more and less severe senses.

The relationship of *Guzmán* to *Jonathan Wild* is touched on by A. Digeon, *The Novels of Fielding* (London, 1925), pp. 99, 108 n. 2, who cities Lesage's version; and Irwin, *The Making of Jonathan Wild*, pp. 94 and 131 nn. 45–7. Irwin plays down the picaresque element against Digeon. F. W. Chandler, *The Literature of Roguery* (London, Boston and New York, 1907), II, 302–7, devotes several pages to *Jonathan Wild* but notes that it is in some ways outside the Spanish picaresque tradition (II, 306).

The fondness of Fielding's Wild for 'the Spanish Rogue' may be an amusingly modified echo of a passage in *Mist's Weekly Journal*, 12 June 1725, about the real Wild: 'the Authors which he study'd most were *Machiavel, The English Rogue, The Lives of the High Way Men, Cook upon Littleton, Echard's History of England, a Collection of Sessions Papers,* and *Cornelius Tacitus*' (see A. F. Robbins ' "Jonathan Wild the Great". Its Germ', *Notes and Queries*, Series XI, ii (1910), 262). See below, ch. V, n. 17.

18 *The Rogue*, vol. IV, pp. 19 ff.

19 Scott, 'Tobias Smollett', *Lives of Eminent Novelists*, p. 465. I discuss Scott's comparison, in relation to these episodes of jewel-substitution, in 'Fielding and Smollett', *Dryden to Johnson*, ed. Roger Lonsdale (Sphere History of Literature in the English Language, IV, London, 1971), pp. 292–3. The most recent comparison between the two novels is in Paul-Gabriel Boucé, *Les Romans de Smollett. Etude Critique* (Paris, Brussels and Montreal, 1971), pp. 200 ff. Smollett is usually thought to have been influenced by *Jonathan Wild*: see Chandler, op. cit., II, 313–4, Boucé, pp. 202, 212.

20 *The Rogue*, vol. IV, pp. 93–4.

21 *The Rogue*, vol. III, pp. 41 ff. For a discussion of archetypal relationships between trickster, jester, and clown, see Paul Radin, *The Trickster. A Study in American Indian Mythology* (London, 1956: With Commentaries by Karl Kerényi and C. G. Jung).

22 A ballad-opera based on this play, *A Cure for Covetousness or the Cheats of Scapin* and other versions or adaptations of the play were performed in Bartholomew Fair and Southwark Fair in the 1730s and early 1740s (Sybil Rosenfeld, *The Theatre of the London Fairs in the 18th Century* (Cambridge, 1960), pp. 38–9, 42, 47, 50, 94, 148). Otway's play was frequently performed on the more orthodox stage throughout the first half of the eighteenth century. There were also a number of pantomimes, farces and operas about well-known criminals performed at the London theatres and fairs. Jack Sheppard was a particular favourite, and was the hero not only of Thurmond's *Harlequin Sheppard* (1724), but of *The Prison Breaker* (1725) and *The Quaker's Opera* (1728). Wild came over the years to be a stock pantomime figure, well-known on the popular stage in the nineteenth century as the 'standard pantomime villain' to Sheppard's 'standard pantomime hero' (Howson, *Thief-Taker General*, p. 226).

23 Robert Alter, *Rogue's Progress. Studies in the Picaresque Novel* (Cambridge, Mass., 1964), p. 26, finds Wild 'an absolutely unmitigated scoundrel', and for that reason somewhat too grim to belong comfortably to the picaresque genre. On the other hand, Parker, op. cit., pp. 131–3, seems to find the work insufficiently grim by authentic and original picaresque standards, which are in his view properly represented in writings much

less genial and light-hearted than Fielding's (who is also disqualified on other grounds). It is refreshing to find a critic playing down the grimness of *Jonathan Wild*, even though Parker's brief discussion of the work is in other respects on the crude side, and not well-informed.

24 See Barbara Swain, *Fools and Folly during the Middle Ages and the Renaissance* (New York, 1932), esp. chs. III and VIII; and Walter Kaiser, *Praisers of Folly* (London, 1964), especially the fine discussion of Erasmus in Part I, with its exploration of Erasmus's 'transvaluation of values', and of the limits of that transvaluation (pp. 51 ff.); its emphasis on Socrates and Christ as ideals of wise folly (pp. 53, 58 ff., 81 ff., 84 ff.); and its analysis of the radical ambiguities in Erasmus's presentation of Folly as both good and bad (pp. 27 ff., 35 ff. *et passim*). Ambiguity is an essential feature not only of the whole world of Erasmian paradox, but of that of 'wise fools' in society. One aspect of this ambiguity is very well put by William Willeford, *The Fool and his Sceptre* (London, 1969), pp. 155–6, when he speaks of the jester's 'ritualised rebellion' as a challenge to authority, but also as its support: 'The fact that the rebellion is allowed and even encouraged implies that the social institutions and the persons in power are strong enough to tolerate it; thus it serves the interests of authority and of social cohesion'. Willeford is here making an anthropological point of extensive application, but its aptness to the Renaissance fool is particularly strong. Moreover, the licensed jester of Renaissance courts and households often combined his relative freedom to speak unwelcome truths with a low and somewhat despised position in society (Swain, ch. IV, pp. 53 ff.). Swain has some comments also on the Fool and the Dance of Death (chs III–IV, pp. 44 ff., 65 ff.).

  For some very vivid explorations of fool paradoxes in Erasmus, Shakespeare and others, see William Empson, *The Structure of Complex Words* (London, 1951), chs V and VI.

25 Swift to Pope, 30 August 1716, suggested that Gay might write 'a Newgate pastoral, among the whores and thieves there', a suggestion which later bore fruit as the *Beggar's Opera* (Swift, *Correspondence*, ed. Harold Williams (Oxford, 1963–5), II, 215).

26 Swift, *Correspondence*, III, 456; see below, p. 194.

27 Fielding probably felt much the same, at least in his overt or conscious thinking on the question. The Preface to *Tom Thumb. A Tragedy* (1730) mocks 'Modern Tragedy' for arousing laughter, but it is not certain whether Fielding means that it mixes the tragic and the comic or that it is unintentionally ridiculous (see *The Tragedy of Tragedies*, ed. James T. Hillhouse (New Haven and London, 1918), pp. 51 and 147n.). The Prologue to *The Author's Farce* (1730) says mockingly, 'Beneath the tragic or the comic name, /Farces and puppet shows ne'er miss of fame' (ed. Charles B. Woods (London, 1967), p. 4). But see below, pp. 191 ff.

28 The kind of sublimity we associate with the Fool in *Lear* is, I assume,

almost unique. Lear's Fool owes this sublimity as much to the exceptional nature of the play and of the centrality and poignancy of his role in it, as to any traditional qualities he has in common with other fools. To the extent that he 'transcends' other Shakespearian fools 'in the quality of his wisdom', moreover, it is so as to become 'a wise fool in the Erasmian or Pauline sense' (Robert H. Goldsmith, *Wise Fools in Shakespeare* (Liverpool, 1958), pp. 67, 66) rather than to achieve what Kaiser would call a more 'drastically revolutionary' or Nietzschean 'transvaluation' (*Praisers of Folly*, pp. 52–3). Robert H. Goldsmith's discussion seems right both in cautioning against overromantic readings of the Fool, and in drawing attention nevertheless to the challenge he poses to those stricter neoclassic objections to the mingling of comic and tragic, and of clowns and kings, of which the chief Elizabethan spokesman was Sidney (Goldsmith, pp. 60–7, 95–9). In any case, Lear's Fool was impossible on the eighteenth-century stage. He was omitted in Tate's version (1681) and was not restored until 1838 (D. Nichol Smith, *Shakespeare in the Eighteenth Century* (Oxford, 1928), pp. 20–5); Tate also gave the play a happy ending, and the play had a happy ending on the stage until 1823, a fact which has its bearing on the discussion of poetic justice later in this chapter. It is significant in this connection that, according to Enid Welsford, the 'court-jester came to an end, as a significant institution, with the death of Charles I', despite stray survivals of household fools, and that in eighteenth-century Europe 'the court-fool was rapidly becoming an anachronism' (*The Fool. His Social and Literary History* (London, 1968), p. 192; see also pp. 182, 247—quotation from Shadwell—248).

The Dostoievskian holy fool also partly derives from traditional Christian conceptions of 'simplicity and purity of heart' (Willeford, op. cit., p. 232), and, like the Fool in *Lear*, derives some of his sublimity from literary contexts of exceptional greatness and intensity. For a tradition of holy fools in Russia, see Welsford, pp. 77–8; doubtless like other similar traditions, it was open to faddish quackery and even nastiness (Norman Cohn, *Warrant for Genocide* (Harmondsworth, 1970), pp. 96 ff., 103–5). But it may be that Dostoievski's 'transvaluations', which belong to a post-Romantic and more radically questioning world, are more profoundly subversive than their Shakespearian and other Renaissance counterparts.

29 The clownish or music hall element of Beckett's Vladimir and Estragon needs no illustration. But it is interesting that a potentially clownish act like Pozzo's fart in Act II of *Waiting for Godot* is fraught with the pathos of Pozzo's loneliness and blindness more than with any comical or farce element. This occurs in the French text, *En Attendant Godot* (Paris, 1952), p. 137. The fart was changed to a belch in the English version (London, 1959), p. 81, but was restored to the English text later (London, 1965).

In Swift's and Fielding's writing, farts (and belches) belong either to a satire of humiliation and exposure, as in the *Tale of a Tub* or the *Mechanical Operation of the Spirit*, or are presented as comic routines belonging simply to the world of farce, or both. See Swift, *Poems*, III, 777, where 'Punch . . . lets a F—t', and my discussion of petomanic episodes in Fielding, in 'Some Considerations on Authorial Intrusion and Dialogue in Fielding's Novels and Plays', *Durham University Journal*, lxiv (1971), 42–3.

30 See some contemptuous remarks in Swift's 'Hints towards an Essay on Conversation' (Swift, *Works*, IV, 91). Cf. Nichol Smith's comment on Tate's omission of the Fool in Lear: 'Tate appears to have regarded the Fool as a senseless jester whose only function was to amuse the theatre-goers of an unrefined age' (*Shakespeare in the Eighteenth Century*, p. 21; see also Garrick's attitude, cited p. 22).

31 See below, pp. 192 and 220 n. 42.

32 If Swift identifies any artist with the mountebanks of the stage-itinerant, it is only the Grubstreet authors of such works as '*Six-peny-worth of Wit*, Westminster *Drolleries, Delightful Tales, Compleat Jesters*, and the like' (*Tale of a Tub*, I, *Works*, I, 38). Contrast Mann's celebration of 'the primitive origin of all art, the inclination to ape, the jester's desire and talent to entertain' in his essay on 'Chekhov', *Last Essays*, trs. R. and C. Winston and T. and J. Stern (London, 1959), p. 182. For the view of the artist as clown, joker, illusionist, swindler etc., and its Nietzschean elements, see R. Hinton Thomas, *Thomas Mann. The Mediation of Art* (Oxford, 1963), pp. 9, 60–1, 63, 121, 124, 151, 172, 176; H. P. Pütz, *Kunst und Künstlerexistenz bei Nietzsche und Thomas Mann* (Bonn, 1963), esp. pp. 39–40. A certain ambiguity enters into Mann's feelings over this, and its corresponding tendency to assert the artist's immoralism; and indeed into Mann's whole attitude to Nietzsche, which finally became fraught with deep misgivings (*Thomas Mann. The Mediation of Art*, pp. 138 ff.; *Last Essays*, pp. 141 ff.). For an example of Nietzsche's equation of artist and swindler, see *Human, All Too Human*, II, Part i, No. 188. Cf. Baudelaire's view, in his Preface to his translation of Poe's *Raven*, that a little charlatanism is proper to genius (*Baudelaire on Poe*, trs. and ed. L. and F. E. Hyslop (State College, Pa., 1952), p. 156).

A related phenomenon is the nineteenth-century figure of the Pierrot as a persona of certain poets like Laforgue. Enid Welsford gives a glimpse of Pierrot turning 'into a Bohemian artist' at the hands of Adolphe Willette, 'an habitué of the *Moulin Rouge*' (*The Fool*, pp. 307–8). See A. G. Lehmann, 'Pierrot and Fin de Siècle', *Romantic Mythologies*, ed. Ian Fletcher (London, 1967), pp. 209–23.

Sterne is perhaps a transitional figure here, as in so many ways. His jester-like posturings are an important exploration of the connections between artist and clown, and look forward to more modern treatments.

But his coyness and self-undercutting contain a shrinking from the full implications of the connection, a kind of refusal to take the clowning, and his claims for it, as boldly and with such serious gaiety in paradox as does Mann in his *Felix Krull* mood. But there is an affinity between the two, and Mann praised Sterne (Herman Meyer, *The Poetics of Quotation in the European Novel*, trs. Theodore and Yetta Ziolkowski (Princeton, 1968), pp. 233–4, a context in which Fielding is also mentioned; see also Oskar Seidlin, 'Laurence Sterne's *Tristram Shandy* and Thomas Mann's *Joseph the Provider*', *Modern Language Quarterly*, viii (1947), 101–18.

33 *Rogue's Progress*, p. 129.
34 *Rogue's Progress*, p. 129.
35 *Rogue's Progress*, p. 128.
36 For some romantic examples, see M. H. Abrams, *The Mirror and the Lamp: Romantic Theory and the Critical Tradition* (London, 1960), pp. 245 ff. and notes on pp. 375 ff.
37 *The Rogue*, vol. I, p. 31.
38 Hazlitt, *Complete Works*, ed. P. P. Howe (London and Toronto, 1930–34), VIII, 42, cited Abrams, op. cit., p. 245; Andrew White, *Thomas Mann* (Edinburgh and London, 1965), p. 51; Mann, *Lotte in Weimar*, ch. III, trs. H. T. Lowe-Porter (Harmondsworth, 1968), pp. 73–4.
39 A brief comparison occurs in R. B. Heilman, 'Variations on Picaresque (*Felix Krull*)', *Sewanee Review*, lxvi (1958), 559.
40 *Confessions of Felix Krull, Confidence Man*, I, ii; trs. Denver Lindley (Harmondsworth, 1958), pp. 10–11. A parallel exploration of the relation of artist and prince occurs in Mann's early novel, *Royal Highness* (1909), finished just before Mann started *Felix Krull* (see Ignace Feuerlicht, *Thomas Mann* (New York, 1968), pp. 22 ff., 92). Mann never finished *Felix Krull*. Part of the work was published in 1937, and the novel as we have it now in 1954.
41 *Felix Krull*, III, i, pp. 166 ff.
42 Mann's identification may be contrasted with Swift's total refusal to see grandeur in tinsel, in the famous passage of the Digression on Madness about 'Artificial *Mediums*, false Lights, refracted Angles, Varnish, and Tinsel', a passage which starkly repudiates every superficial 'Vehicle of *Delusion*', and which, like both *Jonathan Wild* and *Felix Krull*, is partly concerned with the relations between 'the *World* [and] the *Play-House*' (Swift, *Works*, I, 109).
43 Feuerlicht, *Thomas Mann*, p. 92 (title of ch. VIII). On Mann's feeling that *Felix Krull*, with its 'new twist [partly inspired by the memoirs of the Rumanian swindler Manolescu] to the theme of art-and-the artist, to the psychology of the unreal, the illusionary form of existence', was perhaps his 'most personal' work, see *A Sketch of My Life*, trs. H. T. Lowe-Porter (London, 1961), pp. 41–2.
44 See the discussion below, pp. 149–50.

45 *Works*, XII, 245. See below, ch. VII.

46 *Beggar's Opera*, III, xvi.

47 *Project for the Advancement of Religion* (1709), Swift, *Works*, II, 55–6. It is true, however, that many years later, in praising the *Beggar's Opera* in *Intelligencer*, No. 3 (1728), Swift did not complain of the opera's happy ending. But he describes the work in a way which implies that it nevertheless has all the poetic justice that the strictest morality requires: 'It shews the miserable Lives and the constant Fate of those abandoned Wretches: For how little they sell their Lives and Souls; betrayed by their *Whores*, their *Comrades*, and the *Receivers* and *Purchasers* of those Thefts and Robberies' (Swift, *Works*, XII, 36).

48 Swift, *Works*, II, 56.

49 See Dudden, I, 67, 89; Martin Price, *To the Palace of Wisdom* (Garden City, 1965), p. 256. An early poem 'Written on the first Appearance of the Beggar's Opera' was attributed to Fielding and published posthumously (Howard P. Vincent, 'Early Poems by Henry Fielding', *Notes and Queries*, clxxxiv (1943), 159–60).

50 *Threepenny Opera*, trs. Desmond I. Vesey and Eric Bentley, in *Three German Plays*, ed. Martin Esslin (Harmondsworth, 1963), p. 225.

51 Preface to *Miscellanies*, *Works*, XII, 242. On Fielding's relationship to the real-life sources, see further pp. 137 n. 12, 166 n. 2, 179 ff, 218–19 n. 18, 219 n. 21.

52 Horace, *Ars Poetica*, l. 191. The notion that Fate had arranged for Wild to die otherwise than by Blueskin's dagger is contained in the phrasing of some real-life accounts, though without Fielding's pointed elaboration (e.g. Defoe, *True and Genuine Account*, p. 75; Defoe also passingly speaks, in theatrical terms, 'of the last scene of his Life at the Gallows', p. 38).

53 This may be seen as a specifically political form of that '*Possession of being well deceived*; The Serene Peaceful State of being a Fool among Knaves' which Swift exposed in the Digression on Madness (Swift, *Works*, I, 110), and which it is Felix Krull's life work buoyantly to exploit.

54 See John Loftis, *The Politics of Drama in Augustan England* (Oxford, 1963), pp. 134–5; Maynard Mack, *The Garden and the City. Retirement and Politics in the Later Poetry of Pope, 1731–1743* (Toronto, 1969), pp. 158 ff.; Malcolm G. Largmann, 'Stage References as Satiric Weapon: Sir Robert Walpole as Victim', *Restoration and 18th Century Theatre Research*, ix (1970), 35–43, where Walpole appears as rogue, clown, strolling-player, as well as puppet-master. Largmann gives several Fielding references. See further *Champion*, 22 April 1740 (*Works*, XV, 289), and *Tom Jones*, VII, i, which also contains one of Fielding's larger discussions of the traditional analogy of world and stage.

55 For some relations between the *Dunciad* and some of Fielding's plays, see George Sherburn, 'The *Dunciad*, Book IV', *University of Texas Studies in English*, xxiv (1944), 174–90.

THE HERO AS CLOWN

56 On the tone of Fielding's attacks on Walpole and theatrical managers, this comment by William B. Coley is also pertinent: 'Towards Walpole, as towards Rich, Fielding displayed a revealing ambivalence: in theory both were impermissibly "low" subjects for neoclassical art; in practice they were among the means of its liberation' ('The Background of Fielding's Laughter', *ELH. A Journal of English Literary History*, xxvii (1959), 247).

57 Susan Meikle, 'Clownesque Elements in Works of Four Modern German Writers' (Unpublished M. A. dissertation, University of Birmingham, 1969), p. 186. On Krull's non-identity, see also Andrew White, *Thomas Mann* (Edinburgh and London, 1965), p. 56.

58 D. H. Lawrence, *The Rainbow* (Harmondsworth, 1950), ch. XV, pp. 453–7.

59 *The Rainbow*, p. 453. For Lawrence's puppet imagery, see p. 454.

60 Krull's story is unfinished, though in its existing form it ends on a triumphant climax. In the novel's opening paragraph, moreover, we see Krull sitting down to write his memoirs 'at leisure and in complete retirement—furthermore, in good health, though tired', a beginning which seems to show us Krull in a happy and prosperous retirement after a successful career (see Feuerlicht, *Thomas Mann*, p. 93), although he was in the course of this career to have temporary spells in prison. R. B. Heilman says, however, that 'The story was to end conventionally: the picaresque hero exposed and jailed' ('Variations on Picaresque', op. cit., p. 573). I have not been able to find the evidence for this.

61 See for example Peter Berger's excellent discussion, *Invitation to Sociology. A Humanistic Perspective* (Harmondsworth, 1967), pp. 159–60, 187 *et passim*.

62 *Invitation to Sociology*, pp. 127–8.

63 I speak here of Mann's more buoyant, art-asserting mood, which seems to me dominant in *Felix Krull*. That there are ambiguities in his view of the artist as swindler, and moral reservations about the value of art, is an important part of Mann's outlook. See above, n. 32, and R. Hinton Thomas, *Thomas Mann. The Mediation of Art*, *passim*.

64 Swift, *Works*, I, 47.

65 *The Rainbow*, p. 453. In 'Art and Morality', Lawrence rejected 'the common claptrap that "art is immoral" ', and said that art 'substitutes a finer morality for a grosser'. He elaborates on this in 'Morality and the Novel', saying that 'morality is that delicate, for ever trembling and changing *balance* between me and my circumambient universe'. It is not a 'stable equilibrium'. 'Everything is true in its own time, place, circumstance, and untrue outside of its own place, time, circumstance'. A crude moralizing in art is as immoral as licentious freedom. In the closing paragraph of 'Why the Novel Matters' occurs the clearest statement of the opposition between a deadeningly fixed morality, and the 'finer morality' which the novel can most fully express, by giving

'*all* things . . . full play', realizing their true vitality. 'In life, there is right and wrong, good and bad, all the time. But what is right in one case is wrong in another. . . . And only in the novel are *all* things given full play, or at least, they may be given full play, when we realize that life itself, and not inert safety, is the reason for living. For out of the full play of all things emerges the only thing that is anything, the wholeness of a man, the wholeness of a woman, man alive, and live woman' (*Phoenix. The Posthumous Papers of D. H. Lawrence* (London, 1936), pp. 521, 525, 528–9, 538).

66 Lawrence in general recoiled from Mann. See his review in 1913 of *Death in Venice*, in which he sees in Mann a corrupt and deadening Flaubertianism *Phoenix*, pp. 308–13). Mann also did not much like Lawrence, 'who is no doubt a significant phenomenon and characteristic of our times, but whose fevered sensuality has little appeal for me' (*Letters of Thomas Mann*, trs. Richard and Clara Winston (London, 1970), I, 213).

67 Meikle, 'Clownesque Elements', p. 32.

68 *Rogue's Progress*, p. 26.

69 Robert H. Hopkins, 'Language and Comic Play in Fielding's *Jonathan Wild*', *Criticism*, viii (1966), 214–5; Alter, *Fielding and the Nature of the Novel*, p. 149.

CHAPTER V

EPIC *vs.* HISTORY:
JONATHAN WILD AND
AUGUSTAN MOCK-HEROIC

❈

A heroic poem, truly such, is undoubtedly the greatest work which
the soul of man is capable to perform.
(Dryden, Dedication to the Aeneis)

I should have honoured and loved Homer more had he written
a true history of his own times in humble prose, than those noble
poems that have so justly collected the praise of all ages.
(Voyage to Lisbon, Preface)

He was brought then gradually back to his old ideas. Greek-like
struggles would be no more. Men were better, or more timid.
Secular and religious education had effaced the throat-grappling
instinct, or else firm finance held in check the passions.
(Stephen Crane, The Red Badge of Courage, ch. I)

The [First World] War . . . was too vast for its meaning, like a
giant with the brain of a midge. Its epic proportions were
grotesquely out of scale, seeing what it was fought to settle. It was
far too indecisive. It settled nothing, as it meant nothing. Indeed,
it was impossible to escape the feeling that it was not *meant* to
settle anything—that could have any meaning, or be of any
advantage, to the general run of men.
(Wyndham Lewis, Blasting and Bombardiering, IV, i)

He could not forgive the astronauts [of Apollo 11] their resolute
avoidance of an heroic posture. It was somehow improper for a
hero to be without flamboyance as if such modesty deprived his
supporters of any large pleasure in his victories. What joy might
be found in a world which would have no hope of a Hemingway?
Or nearest matters first, of a Joe Namath, or Cassius Clay,

147

Jimmy Dean, Dominguin?—it was as if the astronauts were
there to demonstrate that heroism's previous relation to romance
had been highly improper—it was technology and the absence
of emotion which were the only fit mates for the brave.

(Norman Mailer, *A Fire on the Moon*, I, iv, 2)

The main *mock-heroic* scheme of *Jonathan Wild* was Fielding's first great
fictional conception.[1] It is also his most thoroughgoingly formulaic
exercise in mock-heroic, pre-dating the disclaimers of a radically mock-
heroic form in the Preface to *Joseph Andrews*, and partly contravening
the spirit of these disclaimers. It is not, in spite of analogies noted in the ,
previous chapter, outwardly and formally a 'comic epic' in the sense in
which the phrase applies to *Joseph Andrews* and *Tom Jones*, where the
emphasis falls on the word 'comic' with its connotations of 'truth to
nature' as against burlesque exaggeration. Fielding's distinction, in
defining 'comic epic', between a 'burlesque of diction' which leaves
comic realism of character intact, and a more radical burlesque of
'sentiments and characters', has a special application to *Jonathan Wild*.
But it is not applicable in the first, obvious sense: mock-heroic in this
work could hardly be claimed as a marginal stylistic embellishment for
the entertainment of the classical reader, but is the sustaining element of
the entire fiction.

This does not mean that its style consistently parallels or parodies that
of ancient epic poems, as in the mock-heroic poems of Pope. Nor does
its overall shape have the sort of rudimentary epic analogy which makes
it possible to think of *Joseph Andrews* and *Tom Jones* as *Odysseys* of the
road. Nor again, despite some ironies which equate Wild's career with
the shape of a well-made play, is there any significant feeling that
Jonathan Wild is a burlesque of heroic plays, developing from Fielding's
earlier dramatic burlesques. The immediate formal sources are rogue-
biographies, including at least one of the non-fictional biographies of
Wild himself, and straight biographies of illustrious men on the
Plutarchian model.[2] The front line of the parody largely refers to these:
blowsy accounts of rogue exploits, adulatory celebrations of eminent
historical figures, the stylistic routines of biographers (genealogies,
accounts of omens at the hero's birth, the grandiose speeches in which
'the historian adheres faithfully to the matter, though he embellishes
the diction with some flourishes of his own eloquence').[3]

On the other hand, it would be hard to feel in the reading that such
parody amounts to a serious attack on historical writings as such, or that
their stylistic features are a dominant preoccupation in *Jonathan Wild*.[4]

The central and most damaging aspect of this parody, namely the suggestion that historians glorify 'great' men who in reality are no better than thieves and murderers, is focused less on the historians than on a prevailing moral topsy-turvidom for which they happen to provide a convenient framework of literary expression. We think less about 'Plutarch, Nepos, Suetonius, and other biographers' (I, i), than about Alexander, Caesar, Wild (and Walpole), about the ironic link between gangsters and emperors or prime ministers, and about the world's habitual failure to acknowledge the identity between the reputable and the disreputable forms of 'greatness'.[5] It is doubtful whether specific historical works which Fielding mentions are meant to suffer very much from his treatment, or whether the particular moral momentum which is built up in the novel leaves room for much active attention to these superficial objects of the parody. This seems true even at the start, in the preamble in which Fielding explicitly discusses the practice of historical writers:

> But before we enter on this great work we must endeavour to
> remove some errors of opinion which mankind have, by the
> disingenuity of writers, contracted; for these, from their fear of
> contradicting the obsolete and absurd doctrines of a set of simple
> fellows, called, in derision, sages or philosophers, have
> endeavoured, as much as possible, to confound the ideas of
> greatness and goodness; whereas no two things can possibly be
> more distinct from each other, for greatness consists in bringing
> all manner of mischief on mankind, and goodness in removing
> it from them. It seems therefore very unlikely that the same
> person should possess them both; and yet nothing is more usual
> with writers, who find many instances of greatness in their
> favourite hero, than to make him a compliment of goodness into
> the bargain; and this, without considering that by such means
> they destroy the great perfection called uniformity of character.
> In the histories of Alexander and Caesar we are frequently, and
> indeed impertinently, reminded of their benevolence and
> generosity, of their clemency and kindness. When the former had
> with fire and sword overrun a vast empire, had destroyed the
> lives of an immense number of innocent wretches, had scattered
> ruin and desolation like a whirlwind, we are told, as an example
> of his clemency, that he did not cut the throat of an old woman,
> and ravish her daughters, but was content with only undoing them.
> And when the mighty Caesar, with wonderful greatness of mind,
> had destroyed etc . . . (I, i).

Clearly the chief emphasis in this paragraph is not on the historians, but on such historical personages as Alexander and Caesar and the point they illustrate about the viciousness of the great. In the economy of the chapter as a whole, these emphases are in turn subservient to the purpose of introducing Wild, and of establishing his 'greatness' in the appropriate moral perspective. Much of the content of this paragraph strikes one more as a diffuse exfoliation of angry sarcasm against the 'great', than as a logically disciplined and relevant contribution to the ostensible argument about the practice of writers. The remark about the incompatibility of 'greatness' and 'goodness' highlights Fielding's exasperated distaste for 'great men' at a rhetorically appropriate moment, but as a general proposition it tends not only against the assertions of the Preface to the *Miscellanies*,[6] but also against the concession in the same chapter of *Jonathan Wild* that no human character is absolutely unmixed, and that even Wild has some faint traces of that imperfection called goodness. If the ironist can claim to have kept his categories clear, unlike the historians, by indicating that any spark of goodness is an imperfection unworthy of greatness, his acknowledgment that Wild had such small weaknesses is presumably itself a breach of 'uniformity of character', differing from the historians' lapses only in degree. The playful literary joke about 'uniformity of character' (taken up again in the reference to Wild's 'conservation of character' in the final hanging-scene) has important functions which we have already studied, but it hardly strikes us as a serious indictment of the malpractices of historians. If, as seems probable, the mention of 'the histories of Alexander and Caesar' refers mainly to Plutarch, it runs against Fielding's known admiration for that author,[7] and indeed against the quite different tone of the reference to him earlier in the same chapter. The slightly fantasticating patter about historians is a piece of literary 'business', staged not for its own sake but for that of the main moral irony.[8]

This is true *a fortiori* where, in the body of the novel, the anti-historical element is a matter of oblique formal parody, rather than, as here, of explicit statement. The mock-genealogy, the account of the omens, the 'embellished' speechifying have many effects, playful as well as harsh. But the main and effective impact of such parody of historical method is hardly felt to be to the discredit of historians, though an element of residual mockery may sometimes rub off on them. To this extent, the mock-history resembles the familiar mock-*epic* procedures of Pope and other Augustan poets, where the parody of heroic poems attacks not the heroic poems themselves, but something else. The parallel is incomplete, as we shall see. But it co-exists with certain further relationships between *Jonathan Wild* and the mock-*epic* writings which should be noted first.

For although the main structural formula of *Jonathan Wild* is mock-historical rather than mock-epic, its style is in fact shot through with reminders of ancient epic. There are, first of all, the many individual mock-epic routines, of a kind so frequent elsewhere in Fielding and in other Augustan writers, the elaborate or grandiose similes, for example, and a fairly wide range of specific local allusions. These are partly a matter of mock-learned fun, for the 'entertainment' of the 'classical reader', as the Preface to *Joseph Andrews* says, though they tend to be less expansive than is often the case in *Joseph Andrews* or *Tom Jones*, more narrowly integrated with the main harsh feeling of the narrative. Consider one of the more playful examples:

> Mr. Wild, on his arrival at Mr. Snap's, found only Miss Doshy at home, that young lady being employed alone, in imitation of Penelope, with her thread or worsted, only with this difference, that whereas Penelope unravelled by night what she had knit or wove or spun by day, so what our heroine unravelled by day she knit again by night. In short, she was mending a pair of blue stockings with red clocks; a circumstance which perhaps we might have omitted, had it not served to show that there are still some ladies of this age who imitate the simplicity of the ancients (II, iii).

The pleasant outrageousness of the analogy between Doshy and the chaste Penelope, the wittily managed reversal of the Homeric pattern, the skittish delight in the particularization of 'a pair of blue stockings with red clocks', make the joke playfully gratuitous, a piece of extra fun. But unlike some of the exuberant mock-heroic performances in the later novels, this freezes to the tart brevity of the closing comment, one of a series of ambiguous sarcasms which, throughout the work, review the ancients in terms of Wildian values; and we are briskly brought back to the sarcastically businesslike narrative which had been momentarily interrupted.

A parallel epic joke concerns Doshy's still more disreputable sister:

> How must our reader, who perhaps has wisely accounted for the resistance which the chaste Laetitia had made to the violent addresses of the ravished (or rather ravishing) Wild from that lady's impregnable virtue—how must he blush, I say, to perceive her quit the strictness of her carriage, and abandon herself to those loose freedoms which she indulged to Smirk! But alas! when we

discover all, as to preserve the fidelity of our history we must, when we relate that every familiarity had passed between them, and that the FAIR Laetitia (for we must, in this single instance, imitate Virgil when he drops the *pius* and the *pater*, and drop our favourite epithet of *chaste*), the FAIR Laetitia had, I say, made Smirk as happy as Wild desired to be, what must then be our reader's confusion! We will, therefore, draw a curtain over this scene, from that philogyny which is in us, and proceed to matters which, instead of dishonouring the human species, will greatly raise and ennoble it (I, x).

The epic reminder, as in the previous example, is an isolated allusion rather than part of a protracted context of epic parody, a joke which erupts with some of the gratuitous flavour of super-added 'entertainment'. When, after the signposted abandonment of the epithet *chaste* 'in this single instance', Fielding with gay casual insolence takes himself so literally as to revert to it in the very next sentence (which opens a new chapter): 'Wild no sooner parted from the chaste Laetitia than . . .', we recognize the kind of high-spirited *acte de presence* familiar in the next two novels. But this expansiveness is held in check by the metallic, cheerless quality of the comment which the entire passage makes about Laetitia.

Fielding exploits this joke once again, after her sister Doshy has disgraced herself by giving birth to an illegitimate child. Laetitia's fury at the dishonour to the family is, in view of her own vastly greater misconduct, outrageously comic. The whole scene, even before Laetitia's reactions are given, has a blowsy extravagance which almost borders on fun, as the narrator unburdens himself of a cascade of virtuous cant, and as he tells by contrast of Wild's easy oafish tolerance (his interest was not involved, so he merely 'asked with a smile, "Who was the father?" '). But the comic grotesquerie momentarily curdles into plain nastiness as the 'epic' formula is brought back to introduce Laetitia's reaction: 'But the chaste Laetitia, we repeat the chaste, for well did she now deserve that epithet, received it in another manner. She fell into the utmost fury' (III, xiii). The significance of the epithet here rests on the sour joke, common in Augustan satiric writings, according to which a woman, whatever her conduct past or present, is 'chaste' in the eyes of the world provided she is married—and Laetitia by now is married to Wild. The passage soon recovers its comic extravagance as Laetitia's hypocritical nastiness exfoliates in outrageously pious speechifying, and (though there are of course many sour undertones) the entire scene is somehow funnier for the delightfully specified fact that it occurs over breakfast. But the 'epic' reminder, unlike much of the mock-heroic in *Joseph Andrews* and *Tom Jones*, tends to contract the mood, flattening the scene to a recognition of hard reality instead of releasing it into further fantastication.[9]

Epic parody and mock-epic allusion are, by definition, usually grandiloquent, and grandiloquence in Fielding tends to be genial and expansive. Some grandiloquence exists in this last example, in the moralizing rant of the narrator and of Laetitia. This creates a degree of high-spirited fun, however mingled with satiric distaste, but it is not in this case mainly a mock-*epic* grandiloquence. The one genuine epic allusion within the passage has, on the contrary, a somewhat tart and flattening effect. Indeed, the flights of high writing in *Jonathan Wild* as a whole, though they tend in my view towards comic extravagance rather than mere undiluted sarcasm, are often not strictly mock-epic, as distinct from being mock-heroic or mock-grandiloquent in a more general, perhaps vaguer, sense. By contrast, some of the specifically *epic* reminders (Doshy-Penelope; *chaste Laetitia—pius Aeneas*) are joking or sarcastic parallels which emphasize the shabbiness of this novel's world, without conferring upon it any of the usual playful grandeur of mock-heroic. This may partly be because mock-epic in the strict sense is incidental rather than systematic within the novel's mock-heroic scheme, so that individual epic allusions, however frequent, tend to be isolated barbs rather than parts of a sustained epic elaboration. There are, for example, relatively few 'Homerican' set-pieces such as we find in *Joseph Andrews* and *Tom Jones*, which, however adulterated by elements of anti-romance and other impurities, do genuinely sustain some protracted if crude parallels with epic eloquence.[10] Penelope is brought in solely to make a local point about Doshy; and the Virgilian dimensions of Laetitia's unchastity are isolated though recurrent quips. They neither occur in immediate contexts of protracted epic imitation, nor does the novel's overall plot provide any significant role for a modern Penelope or a female Aeneas.

Another, rather more recurrent example of the conventional Virgilian epithet is the frequent labelling of Fireblood as Wild's *fidus Achates*, usually in contexts where he is pointedly *un*faithful to his friend.[11] There is no active sense, beyond the immediate needs of the sarcasm about Fireblood, in which Wild appears as a modern Aeneas; and the Achates-joke is an *ad hoc* irony rather than part of a meaningful mock-epic scheme. Because such allusions to Virgil cannot in themselves be said to form a consistent and developing fantastication, they remain, deliberately, rather flat moral diminutions, unsoftened and undignified by a playful extravagance of epic grandeur. At the first introduction of the Achates-joke, indeed, Fielding takes care to divert the emphasis from epic to history, from Aeneas to Alexander:

> The name of this youth, who will hereafter make some figure in this history, being the Achates of our Aeneas, or rather the Hephaestion of our Alexander, was Fireblood. He had every qualification to make a second-rate GREAT man; or, in other words, he was completely equipped for the tool of a real or first-rate GREAT man (III, iv).

As the second half of the quotation suggests, the passage proceeds not with elaborations of the Virgilian story, nor even with any mock-heroic exploitation of Macedonian history, but with relatively low-pitched moral sarcasms about 'greatness': this is part of the tendency throughout *Jonathan Wild*, away from the 'fictional' energies of mock-heroic *narrative* to a more starkly conceptual moralizing. But one effect of the initial, momentary emphasis on Alexander rather than Aeneas, is to arrest the flowering of the strictly epic fiction by means of a reminder of distasteful *historical fact*.[12] Alexander was for Fielding the outstanding type of the disreputably brutal gangster-conqueror, and this (in any case conventional and widely-received) view of him has by this time been well-established within the novel.

The irony about Fireblood thus rests on a double mock-heroic allusion. The first, or epic, parallel with Achates exposes him as the antithesis of a hero's faithful friend; the second, or historical, parallel with Hephaestion reduces him (Alexander being what he is in Fielding's eyes) to the level of a gangster-conqueror's favourite henchman, with Fireblood eventually emerging as still more disreputable than Hephaestion because repeatedly faithless to his chief.[13] The basis for these ironies is the Virgilian stock-epithet *fidus*, which is damagingly implicit every time the Fireblood-Achates analogy is repeated. Nevertheless, such fragmentary pieces of Virgilian (or Homeric) background, whilst they interpenetrate with the *historical* mock-heroic, must partly be distinguished from it. The epic figures are on the whole good (Achates, Aeneas, Penelope), while the historical ones are bad (Alexander, Caesar). The action of *Jonathan Wild* is mock-heroic in relation to both epic and history, in that it is a small-time version of both. But its relation to history is one of direct parallel, whereas its relation to epic tends to be inverted. Fireblood is a small-time equivalent of Hephaestion (although, unlike Hephaestion, he is faithless), but he is the *opposite* of

Achates (*because*, unlike Achates, he is faithless). Similarly, Wild is a small-time Alexander, but for brief moments, a small-time opposite of Aeneas.

This distinction between the 'heroic' world of historical wars, and that of the great epic poems, was of some importance to Fielding. Comparing military and poetic fame in an essay of 1739, he quoted approvingly 'Sir William Temple's observation, that the world hath produced a thousand equal to Alexander, but scarce one capable of writing an Iliad'.[14] This is the background to Wild's belief, in the novel, 'that there were not fewer than a thousand in Alexander's troops capable of performing what Alexander himself did' (i, v). And the whole of *Jonathan Wild* is a special ironic illustration of the principle that there are 'a thousand equal to Alexander': one needs only, like Wild, to be sufficiently criminal. And just as the novel's outward form resembles history-books more than epic poems, so it is the historical figures of Alexander and Caesar, rather than the epic personages, who dominate the 'heroic' background of the mock-heroic action. Not only do Alexander and Caesar, in the novel's scheme, *resemble* Wild directly, as distinct from being, like Aeneas, opposites. They also offer a parallelism which is consistent in supporting throughout the major theme that gangsters and 'great' military and political leaders are morally identical; while the epic allusions are less systematic, pointing an irony here and there, often by means of contrast, but sometimes (in the case of Achilles, for example, to which I shall return) by means of amusingly ambiguous parallels.

But if the historical and the literary allusions are broadly to be distinguished from one another, there is no complete separation in practice. For one thing, the epic allusions and parody, though unsystematic and *ad hoc*, are fairly ubiquitous. Epic style was, after all, for Fielding and his contemporaries, the most readily available idiom for mock-heroic aggrandisement. Although, as Fielding says plainly at the outset, Fireblood resembles Hephaestion rather than Achates, all subsequent references in fact allude to Achates. This is not only because the epithet 'faithful' provides a useful irony, but because the regular recurrence of the formula 'faithful Achates' automatically provides a jeering and cumulative Virgilian resonance through sheer verbal association. A minor, illogical result is that Achates becomes faintly contaminated by his association with Fireblood-Hephaestion, as does Aeneas by *his* association with Wild-Alexander.

But the discredit to heroic poems is not always thus limited to accidents of stylistic usage. It was not unusual in Fielding's time for

connections between heroic poems and the more disreputable facts of
ancient history to be made quite explicitly. Richardson's Charlotte
Grandison asks: 'Would Alexander, madman as he was, have been so
much a madman, had it not been for Homer? Of what violences, murders,
depredations, have not the Epic poets been the occasion, by propagating
false honour, false glory, and false Religion?' A contemporary critic
commented: 'These remarks are, I suppose, occasioned by the great
veneration which the Macedonian hero professed for Homer's writings,
and by his famous imitation, or rather improvement, on the cruelty of
Achilles, in dragging round the walls of a conquered city its brave
defender.'[15] Fielding's attitude to Homer was more richly ambiguous,
and included an admiration more intense and enthusiastic than we
should expect to find in Richardson or Defoe. But underlying much of
Jonathan Wild is an uneasy consciousness of the fact that the great heroic
poems do celebrate exploits of war and plunder not always manifestly
different from the actions of bad men like Alexander and Caesar.
Plutarch records, in a passage which Fielding must certainly have noted
with ironic amusement, that Alexander kept the *Iliad* 'lying with his
dagger under his pillow', calling it 'a viaticum of the military art'.
Alexander was a great admirer of Achilles; Caesar a great admirer of
Alexander.[16] The link suggested in Plutarch's parallel lives of Alexander
and Caesar is ironically exploited in *Jonathan Wild*, whose hero admires
all three. Achilles is mentioned in the amusing account of Wild's
classical education (in translation). The reference is playful, but has a
sour tang which makes it more than just good fun:

> He was wonderfully pleased with that passage in the eleventh
> Iliad where Achilles is said to have bound two sons of Priam upon
> a mountain, and afterwards to have released them for a sum of
> money. This was, he said, alone sufficient to refute those who
> affected a contempt for the wisdom of the ancients, and an
> undeniable testimony of the great antiquity of priggism (I, iii).

This discreditable gloss on the passage may not be in Homer's tone, but
Wild describes the episode accurately, and it is not open to us to be
certain in our minds that Wild's cynical appraisal is out of step with the
facts as reported.[17] If the gap between Homer's view and Wild's is so
wide as to tend towards genial amusement, there remains a certain tart
uneasiness because Wild's view is in itself anything but outrageous.

The passage about Achilles is a signal, in this chapter, that mock-
heroic disapproval rubs off, however hesitantly and marginally, on the
epic poems themselves. The figure of Achilles is probably one of the

most morally ambiguous of all the major epic heroes of antiquity, and Alexander's well-known admiration for him provided a focus for some of the revulsion against epic morality among Fielding's contemporaries. After two more epic instances (a heroic exploit of Nestor, recalled in the same book of the *Iliad*, which Wild praises as an act of efficient plunder; and an oafish gloss on the story of Cacus in *Aeneid*, VIII), there is the customary return to historical nastiness, amusingly spiced with some boyish arrogance from Wild:

> He was a passionate admirer of heroes, particularly of Alexander the Great, between whom and the late King of Sweden he would frequently draw parallels. He was much delighted with the accounts of the Czar's retreat from the latter, who carried off the inhabitants of great cities to people his own country. *This*, he said, *was not once thought of by* Alexander; *but* added, *perhaps he did not want them.*

Swift had said, in one of his 'Thoughts on Various Subjects': 'It is *Homer* and *Virgil* we reverence and admire, not *Achilles* or *Aeneas*'. He added that it was different with historians: 'our Thoughts are taken up with the Actions, Persons, and Events we read', rather than with 'the Authors'.[18] Swift's is one of many expressions of a tendency to separate the morality (or immorality) of epic heroes from the imaginative splendour of the poems which celebrate them. An admiration for the epic genre had not necessarily entailed, even in the Renaissance, any wholehearted commitment to heroic *values*, and by 1735 Thomas Blackwell, in his *Enquiry into the Life and Writings of Homer*, could say: 'tho' ... [your *Lordship* may] regret the Silence of the Muses, yet I am persuaded you will join in the Wish, *That we may never be the proper Subject of an* Heroic Poem'.[19]

The flourishing of mock-epic forms in the late seventeenth and early eighteenth centuries is partly a reflection of the growth of such a divided feeling. As Austin Warren says, 'The mock-epic is not mockery of the epic but elegantly affectionate homage, offered by a writer who finds it irrelevant to his age'.[20] Inevitably, as the gap widened, the epic poems themselves came to seem increasingly difficult to separate from an unacceptable heroic morality, and the traditional devotion to ancient epics became fraught with inhibiting reservations. Some mock-heroic writings, and notably *Jonathan Wild*, reflect this difficulty, tending (often uneasily or unintentionally) to subvert revered imaginative achievements along with the bad actions of their protagonists, and the turpitudes of historical villains. Wild's liking for the *Iliad* and *Aeneid* does not mean that Fielding is repudiating them, but only that Wild's perverse reasons are not Fielding's. But despite some light-hearted fun over this, there is also a disturbing sense in which Wild is not altogether wrong in his analysis. Though there is hardly a complete equivalence between the morality of Alexander and that of the *Iliad*, there is an uncomfortable overlap between them. The connection so starkly suggested by Charlotte Grandison was something to which Fielding was more awkwardly sensitive than he might be prepared to admit. This awkwardness is reflected in the mock-epic manner of *Jonathan Wild*, which differs in interesting ways from that of, say, Pope.

The *Dunciad*, in a sense, is concerned with this very change, lamenting the demise of an older world of traditional cultural allegiances. Its massive mock-heroic edifice preserves undiminished the grandeur of the heroic norm, even though modern realities are dislodging this grandeur. In *Jonathan Wild*, the grandeur itself becomes deeply suspect. Fielding, like Pope, plays the heroic off against a shabby modern reality: but he is unable to keep the epic grandeurs entirely separate from the historical evils of the ancient world, or from their modern counterparts. *Jonathan Wild* in this respect marks a step towards a more modern and sceptical kind of mock-heroic, whose positive allegiances are themselves insecure. The force of its mock-heroic attack tends not only one way, as in the *Dunciad*, but both ways, as in the *Waste Land*. The grandeurs of the past are no longer merely a foil to the present, but partake of the present shabbiness also.

Fielding was not the first neoclassic author to be uneasy about epic morality, or to dislike such historical 'heroes' as Alexander and Caesar. Both attitudes were fairly traditional.[21] The martial ethos of epic poetry, abstracted from the poems, would hardly as a *morality* invite the unqualified assent of such older and more loyal masters of mock-heroic as Dryden or Pope. Both made statements, in prose, about the murderous brutality of some aspects of heroic behaviour. Dryden, who was jeered at in the *Rehearsal* for preferring 'that one quality of singly beating of whole Armies, above all your moral vertues put together, I gad',[22] himself spoke of Homer as a poet who 'provokes to murther, and the destruction of God's images; he forms and equips those ungodly man-killers whom we poets, when we flatter them, call heroes; a race of men who can never enjoy quiet in themselves, till they have taken it from all the world'[23] (an irony about 'heroes' on which Fielding improves in *Jonathan Wild*, I, xiv, where 'great men' like Alexander do not even then 'enjoy quiet', but feel distress because they have left 'no more nations to extirpate').[24] Pope, who praised Homer's art in arousing compassion and softening his 'Descriptions of Battels',[25] is nevertheless apologetic about scenes of cruelty in Homer and noted a 'shocking . . . Spirit of Cruelty' in him.[26] Where Pope writes straightforwardly heroic verse, as in the translation of Homer, the moral reservations are naturally kept out of the verse (although Pope often softens or Augustanizes more 'barbarous' elements)[27] but get into the commentary. (It is a fact that the greatest straightforwardly heroic writing of both Dryden and Pope occurred, as it were, by proxy, in the translations of Virgil and Homer, and that neither was able to complete an epic poem of his own.)

Radical criticism of the heroic is likewise firmly kept out of the great Augustan *mock*-heroics. What bites deep into the fabric of *Jonathan Wild* hardly touches *MacFlecknoe*, the *Rape of the Lock*, or the *Dunciad*, where the mock-heroic rests confidently on an admiration for epic poetry as a total literary achievement, rather than on the disconcerting implications of an extrapolated moral aspect.[28] Such mock-epic fragments of martial celebration as these poems might contain exist merely as parts of a general playful rhetoric of mock-grandeur, and are of a sort to neutralize rather than encourage any questioning of epic morality.

Nor do we readily find, in the great Augustan mock-epics, any special tendency to confront epic heroes with the parallel acts of disreputable real-life conquerors, even where the authors are on record as disliking such 'great men' (Pope, for example, in a passage in the *Essay on Man* concerned, like *Jonathan Wild* and other of Fielding's writings, with 'true' and 'false greatness', had listed both 'Macedonia's madman' and Caesar as bad examples).[29] It might be argued that one reason why the positive heroic norms of the *Dunciad* retain most of their splendour is perhaps a merely negative one: the subject of the poem steers clear of those situations of killing and plunder which give rise to moral uneasiness, and which are directly in play in Fielding's work. Pope may also have found it easier to ignore or overlook the awkward moral implications of the epic because he belonged to a generation which held its allegiances to the classical heritage more securely and unquestioningly than did Fielding's. It is significant that the main mock-heroic ironies of *Jonathan Wild* are focused on terms of moral approbation like 'great' and 'admirable' rather than upon episodes or characters of epic story. The stylistic emphasis is on heroic morality, abstracted from the total feeling of a heroic poem.

The separation of mock-heroic diction from 'sentiments and characters' which is affirmed in the Preface to *Joseph Andrews* does not apply to *Jonathan Wild* in so far as Fielding was implying in the Preface that mock-heroic elements in *Joseph Andrews* were incidental and sporadic, superadded and superficial pieces of extra fun. But although mock-heroic in *Jonathan Wild* is pervasive, there is yet a separation of heroic diction from epic re-creation, and it would be possible to argue that the emphasis on 'diction' is here more radically subversive of epic loyalties than the high-spirited mimicries of *Joseph Andrews* or *Tom Jones*. The fact that Fielding emphasized the distinction between 'diction' and 'sentiments and characters' as he did may in itself suggest that for him (as not for Pope) mock-heroic involved a less than complete imaginative engagement with the heroic norm. But 'diction' in *Joseph Andrews* means only the stylistic routines of heroic poems and romances, whereas in *Jonathan Wild* it means abstraction of *moral* implications from the epic fiction. This abstraction, which entails commentary on heroic qualities and which is the essence of the irony of *Jonathan Wild*, is fairly rare in *Joseph Andrews* and *Tom Jones*. Correspondingly, while these later novels are less systematically mock-heroic than *Jonathan Wild*, they contain many lengthy set-pieces which are in themselves more strictly and elaborately mock-*epic*. The several 'Homerican' battles, for example, are comic low-life counterparts of the many man-to-man combats in the *Iliad*. They are closer to Homer than any passage of equal length in *Jonathan Wild*, and yet their tendency to subvert the 'Homerican' original is much less. It is probably true in Fielding that the more complete and self-consistent the epic parody, the less anti-heroic it is. So long as the epic fiction remains 'pure', so long, that is, as Fielding is prepared to surrender a passage wholly to the fictional energies of the parody and does not step outside the parody to moralize about the 'heroic', the epic originals remain undamaged. The famous battle of the churchyard in *Tom Jones*, IV, viii, and Tom's battle with Thwackum and Blifil in V, xi, are set-pieces of this sort. There is, significantly, no pointed exploitation of terms like 'great' and 'admirable', nor even of 'hero', in either. The word 'hero' occurs, of course, but merely in a way which plays in with the fiction that an epic battle is going on: Molly 'overthrew the carcass of many a mighty heroe and heroine', 'Thus, and more terrible, when he perceived the enemy's approach, leaped forth our heroe' (i.e. Tom). The word here receives only its share of the general comic inflation, and does not carry any external charge of moral sarcasm, as throughout *Jonathan Wild*. In such circumstances, the mock-epic pays its traditional Augustan homage to the epic, of parody which (whatever else it mocks) casts no essential slur on the original.

By comparison with Pope's *Dunciad*, Fielding's allusions to, or mimicry of, specific features of epic style, are despite their frequency, local and sporadic, rather than securely and pervasively embodied in a complete and self-sufficient epic fiction. Where the *Dunciad* absorbs its mock-epic style into a total image of grotesque and terrifying coherence, *Jonathan Wild* seems only a series of mock-epic fragments bound together by a moral theme, a formulaic system of anti-heroic abstractions. This fragmentariness of mock-epic allusion may tend towards a modern type of mock-heroic, like that of the *Waste Land*. In Eliot's poem, however the fragmentation is itself a deliberate and essential element of the poem's world. The ancient grandeurs (no longer strictly epic) which Eliot recalls with ironic eclecticism have had to be assembled for the poem, 'A heap of broken images', fragments shored against those ruins, both of the shadowy protagonist and of a whole civilisation, which are the poem's theme. Their imaginative coherence is powerful, but arbitrary and esoteric, self-created rather than resting on a widely-recognized tradition. The ancient norms of the *Dunciad*, on the other hand, were the still widely-shared loyalties of Pope's age: their threatened collapse, as the poem sees it, was the collapse of a great and unified edifice, not the inchoate wreck of many buildings.

By the same token, neither Pope nor Fielding needed, like Joyce, to recreate in massive detail the scheme of any single ancient poem, in order to establish its live ironic relationship to a modern reality. Where both Eliot and Joyce had to create afresh their entire world of allusive reference, Fielding had at least this in common with Pope, that he could assume a Homeric or Virgilian allusion to have a live, as distinct from a merely academic, significance for his reader. Fielding might suggest that his flights of 'Homerican' burlesque were slightly specialized pieces of extra fun for the 'classical reader'. But in a certain sense, most of his readers were 'classical readers'. Many, of course, did not know the classical languages, and some would not have read Homer even in translation. But few would feel that a passage of mock-heroic was entirely lost on them, if only because the live importance and supreme dignity of the great epics were still a matter of ordinary assumption, so that a gesture of friendly irreverence would have some meaning for the most ignorant. Popular 'Homerican' parody would be inconceivable today, but many forms of heroic and mock-heroic style (however crudely debased from their ultimate epic originals) were, in Fielding's time and for many decades earlier, maintained in the romances, in burlesque poems, on the stage, and even in the farces of the London fairs.[30] The manner in which many of Fielding's burlesque flights have a 'drollic' element, easily accommodating verbal horseplay and farce-routines along with the 'learned' classicizing, indicates not only a sophistication which imports popular elements into a more 'literary' idiom, but also one which exploits a blend already existing in some form. A popular awareness of the broad rhetorical habits, and of the chief characters and episodes, of epic story could be relied upon by Fielding.

The result is that even a relatively isolated and 'gratuitous' allusion, like the comparison of Doshy, unravelling 'by day [what] she knit again by night', with Penelope, who did the same in reverse order, makes its point naturally and without fuss even in the absence of any Joycean context of sustained (though at the same time relatively discreet and unobtrusive) reference to the *Odyssey*. It might be argued that this allusion is, in all conscience, obvious enough to any elementarily literate reader. But the question is less one of intelligibility than of naturalness, of the readiness with which allusions of this kind will fall into place in the fabric of Fielding's writing. Fielding's joke was exploiting a well-recognized cliché, which, incidentally, Swift had included in his 'Tritical Essay upon the Faculties of the Mind': 'to weave *Penelope's* Web; unravel in the Night what we spun in the Day'.[31] The figure of Penelope happens also to be a favourite of modern novelists, but her modern appearances have as often as not an uncomfortable air of being merely 'literary', instead of possessing the easy, witty unselfconsciousness of Fielding's passage. A revealing example of the difference is the embarrassing archness of a similarly isolated and playful parallel with Penelope, from a novel by Ford Madox Ford, where, as in *Jonathan Wild* and in contrast with Joyce's *Ulysses*, there is no strong internal relation with the *Odyssey* to draw on. Sylvia Tietjens, the hero's unfaithful wife in *No More Parades*, is being told by the worthy Cowley[32]

> that when he, Sergeant-Major Cowley, went to the wars—seven of them—his missus, Mrs. Cowley, spent the first three days and nights unpicking and re-hemstitching every sheet and pillow-slip in the 'ouse. To keep 'erself f'm thinking. . . . This was apparently meant as a reproof or an exhortation to her, Sylvia Tietjens. . . . Well, he was all right! Of the same class as Father Consett, and with the same sort of wisdom.

Cowley does not know he is comparing his wife to Penelope, but Ford does. This fact by itself (and not Sylvia's snobbery) makes the passage so desperately supercilious, a coy authorial snigger hardly disguised by the author's technical self-effacement. For if Sylvia's uppishness can legitimately be said to be hers rather than Ford's, the decision to put such archly 'significant' words into Cowley's unsuspecting mouth can only be Ford's. But the *factitiousness* would probably not be less if

Cowley knew what he was saying: for, in order not to seem merely the forced whimsy of the author, such an allusion would need, in a twentieth-century novel, to be validated either by a full-scale Joycean context, or by a specialized situation (e.g. a conversation between characters established as literate and facetious enough to be given to such jokes). An analogous falseness is evident in the intermittent flights of classicizing mock-heroic in Richard Aldington's *Death of a Hero*.[33] Admittedly, Fielding's Penelope-joke occurs in a novel whose sustained idiom is mock-heroic (if not always strictly mock-epic) in one form or another, so that epic allusions have there a more natural ambience: but neither a quip of this sort, nor occasional flights of mock-heroic fun, would seem very out of place in any of Fielding's other prose.

But if epic allusions, and a style involving mock-epic ironies, came naturally to Fielding and were unstrenuously acceptable, as a normal literary idiom, to his readers, there is nevertheless a certain lack of substance in *Jonathan Wild*'s relation to the epic poems which form part of its background. It is a relation not only more sporadic, but less intimate and profound, than that of either the *Dunciad*, or of *Ulysses*.[34] Serious mock-heroic depends on a full imaginative engagement in the heroic norms such as both Pope and Joyce, from almost opposite vantage-points, were able to achieve. The true heroic voice was still, for Pope, a real focus of aspiration. Behind the dunces stands a norm of ancient grandeur to which Pope is passionately loyal. Its survival, and that of the whole social and cultural order on which it rests, were, as the poem says, under threat. But there is no doubt in the poem of Pope's total commitment to it, as the highest embodiment of a great cultural ideal; and it is a reflection of this commitment, and of the strength of feeling that went into its expression, that the poem's mock-heroic acquired an epic grandeur of its own. For Joyce, on the other hand, the heroic ideal was no longer viable in the old sense. 'My intention is to transpose the myth *sub specie temporis nostri*'.[35] This had to mean, not so much seeing modern reality as lapsed from epic grandeur, but seeing the heroic world of epic as applicable, in an essentially non-heroic way, to a modern reality which is also unheroic.[36] For Joyce, the viability of the *Odyssey* as a myth for our time rested not on Odysseus's status as hero, but on his being (as clearly emerges from Joyce's account to Frank Budgen) a complete non-heroic man: son, father, husband, war-dodger before the event, jusqu'auboutist in war, and so on.[37]

A measure of the change in the status of the heroic ideal between Pope's time and Joyce's may be seen in the fact that Augustan mock-heroic is invariably satiric, as if the lapse from the ideal were in a sense simply *culpable*; whereas for Joyce or Eliot, the mock-heroic is often non-satiric and never simply satiric, because there is no assured and coherent heroic ideal to lapse from. The difference is partly a matter of the collapse of that 'consensus regarding ends, values and the business of life that produced its great poem in the fourth book of the *Dunciad*' which F. R. Leavis invoked in one of his discussions of Eliot. Leavis says some of Eliot's writings come 'as near to major satiric poetry as anything we are likely to get in our age', but adds that they are not satire, 'because the word "satire" . . . entails the idea of critical animus, and criticism implies standards—positive standards'.[38] This is true *a fortiori* of a satire which, like much of Eliot's, has heroic overtones. A profound link between serious satire and the heroic was sensed by many Augustans, and explored in many tones of angry or witty majesty. Dryden spoke of 'the most beautiful and most noble kind of satire' as containing within it 'the majesty of the heroic'.[39] And a live tradition of heroic writing, in tragedy or epic, doubtless similarly depended, as Sartre pointed out, on a 'société intégrée'. Where values lose their cohesion heroic modes can only subsist 'à titre de survivances et de pastiches'.[40] Sartre rightly saw this loss of cohesion as becoming evident in the eighteenth century. In our time, it has become more radical still.

It would seem to follow from this that serious *satirical* use of mock-heroic is impossible in the twentieth century: the crudities and sham Augustanism of Roy Campbell are perhaps its only likely result, and it takes a Roy Campbell to try. The tragic vision of Eliot, the human comedy of Joyce, unfold themselves not against a background of Augustan reliance on norms of ancient splendour, but against their own personal (that is private as well as highly individual) refashionings of heroic myth. Although some of the fundamental ironies of any mock-heroic form are bound to survive (reality pitted against a grandeur, however qualified or tarnished; the familiar simultaneous diminution and aggrandisement of both), they no longer rest on a steady faith. The notable vitality with which, in Pope and in Joyce, the epic world is realized, proceeds from virtually opposite causes in each case.

Fielding was, in *Amelia*, to make a first step towards the Joycean kind of epic imitation, in which the epic parallels and reverberations are a matter not primarily of satiric point, but of a deepened and enlarged vision of the human comedy. It marks perhaps a first understanding of the possible relation, in a modern sense, of novel to epic: for the 'comic epic' experiments of *Joseph Andrews* and *Tom Jones* did not really involve any large-scale or structural epic resonance, as distinct from using mock-heroic as one of several devices of distancing and stylization. *Jonathan Wild* is different again, because mock-heroic is its main idiom, and mock-*epic* allusions, though more notable for their frequency than for their systematic nature, are an important part of this idiom. The mock-heroic (epic and historical alike) is, as in Pope, satirical. But it is satirical in ways which no longer confidently assume the goodness of the heroic norm, one aspect of this being, as we have seen, Fielding's readiness to allow the epic world to be contaminated by a disreputable historical reality.

Not surprisingly, Fielding's mock-heroic is less secure in tone than Pope's. We have already seen that in *Jonathan Wild* it oscillates nervously between acerbity and fun, thereby achieving some new and unexpected triumphs, in some ways out of line with the work's ideological tendencies, as well as some debilitating uncertainties. The equivalence which it implies between epic heroes and historical villains, past and present, is established from the start, and one of its most notable expressions is in I, iii, where the schoolboy Wild expresses his admiration for the scabrous deeds of epic heroes. It is there, for example, that Achilles and other Homeric and Virgilian personages are spoken of in a way which connects them with 'Alexander . . . and the late King of Sweden'.

But the acerbity of this is complicated by the fact not only that Wild has other and less heroic literary favourites ('the Spanish Rogue was his favourite book, and the Cheats of Scapin his favourite play'), but also that his epic tastes are those of a schoolboy. Fielding is fond of seeing Wild in a schoolboy context. In I, viii, Wild amusingly invokes his schoolboy knowledge of Aristotle and the Bible to justify his bad principles, and in II, i there is a recollection of the schooldays of Wild and Heartfree in which Wild emerges as a schoolboy hero of some physical courage.[41] The chapter which deals at length with his school career and his epic tastes (I, iii) is only the first of several passages in which the gangster-hero is glimpsed as a schoolboy, and in which hints of a peculiar connection between heroic and schoolboy codes are allowed to take shape.

NOTES

1 There have been arguments that the novel was begun as far back as 1737. Cross, on the other hand, believed that the whole novel belongs to 1742 (Cross, I, 409–12). Dudden, whose discussion of the dating (Dudden, I,

470–83) seems to me the most persuasive, concludes that the main Wild
section (i.e. the mock-heroic or 'great man' satire against Walpole), and
Mrs Heartfree's travel-narrative, were first drafted about 1740, and the
rest of the Heartfree section in 1742, the parts being put together into the
complete work in the second half of 1742 and the early weeks of 1743
(Dudden, I, 482–3). But see below, ch. VII, n. 16.

2 For some account of the literature about the real-life Jonathan Wild, and
of the background of rogue-literature in general, see W. R. Irwin, *The
Making of Jonathan Wild* (New York, 1941), pp. 11 ff., 80 ff. On the
relationship of the mock-heroic in *Jonathan Wild* to serious biographical
writing, see W. J. Farrell, 'The Mock-Heroic Form of *Jonathan Wild*',
Modern Philology, lxiii (1966), 216–26.

3 See *J.W.*, I, ii; I, iii; III, vi, etc.

4 In the Preface to the *Voyage to Lisbon*, p. 29, for example, Fielding
upholds the historian's right to make stylistic 'embellishments' of the
'speeches' of his protagonists, citing without disapproval Sallust (among
others), who had been named in the sarcasm about the 'eloquence' of
Jonathan Wild, III, vi, and claiming his own right to adorn his factual
writing with ornaments of style.

5 The role played in this failure by corruptions of political *language* has
been studied by Glenn W. Hatfield (see above, ch. IV, n. 10).

6 *Works*, XII, 245.

7 *T.J.*, XVII, ii, *ad fin.*; *C.-G.J.*, No. 10, 4 February 1752, Jensen, I, 195.

8 It is true, however, that Plutarch records acts of clemency or generosity
by Alexander and Caesar (*Alexander*, XII, 3; XXI; XXX; XXXIX.
Caesar, XV, 3; XXXIV, 4; XLVIII, 2; LV, 2; LVII, 3). All my references
to the two parallel lives by Plutarch cite the Loeb edition of *Plutarch's
Lives*, vol. VII (London and Cambridge, Mass., 1949). Fielding reverts to
'the clemency of Alexander and Caesar' at the end of the work, this time
accusing Nature rather than historians of giving them such unsuitable
qualities (IV, xv), the historians being only to blame for commending
such weaknesses.
   Plutarch's two speeches 'De Alexandri Magni fortuna aut virtute',
which praise Alexander fulsomely, are rhetorical exercises which do not
represent his views exactly (J. R. Hamilton, *Plutarch Alexander. A
Commentary* (Oxford, 1969), p. xxxiii).

9 Contrast also the flavour of the mock-gallant reference to 'that
philogyny which is in us', with the similar but more genial protestation
in *J.A.*, I, viii (*à propos* of Lady Booby), of 'wonderful tenderness for that
beautiful part of the human species called the fair sex'.

10 There are exceptions, e.g. the simile of the bulls and cows in *J.W.*, IV,
x, which is both mock-epic in a moderately sustained way, and
expansively funny.

11 See *J.W.*, III, iv; III, x; III, xiv; IV, ii; IV, vi.

12 The distinction is not strictly speaking as sharp as this, because much of
the material of epic poetry was often thought of as historical. But it is
history transformed by poetic vision, by what Pope, in the Preface to the
Iliad, called Homer's 'amazing Invention', his 'unequal'd Fire and
Rapture' (Pope, *Translations of Homer*, Twickenham Edition, vols VII–X
(London and New Haven, 1967), VII, 4 *et passim*, and Introduction, pp.
xlix–l). The great epics were, needless to say, normally rated more
highly than mere histories. But Fielding came late in life, not to abolish
the distinction, but to make an opposite valuation, in the well-known
passage of the Preface to the *Voyage to Lisbon* (p. 26), cited as an epigraph
to this chapter.

13 The 'Fire' in Fireblood may have a punning association with Hephaestion
(by way of Hephaestus, the god of fire), as well as having a secondary
aptness to Fireblood's amorous exploits with Wild's wife Laetitia.
Hephaestion, on the other hand, may have been a homosexual lover of
Alexander.

14 *Champion*, 27 November 1739, *Works*, XV, 79. Temple's remark, which
Fielding repeated in *True Patriot*, No. 8, 24 December 1745, occurs in his
essay 'Of Poetry', *Works* (London, 1770), III, 404. Temple does not name
Alexander specifically but mentions in general terms 'great generals of
armies, or ministers of state' (see Henry Knight Miller, *Essays on Fielding's
Miscellanies* (Princeton, 1961), p. 401 n. 41).

15 *Sir Charles Grandison*, Shakespeare Head edn (Oxford, 1931), V, 334.
Critical Remarks on Sir Charles Grandison, Clarissa, and Pamela, 1754
(Augustan Reprint Society, No. 21 (Series IV, No. 3), 1950), p. 49.
Charlotte's words closely reflect Richardson's own feelings: see Ian Watt,
The Rise of the Novel (London, 1957), p. 243. For Defoe's and Richardson's
hostility to Homer, see Watt, 'Defoe and Richardson on Homer: A Study
of the Relation of Novel and Epic in the Early Eighteenth Century',
Review of English Studies, N.S. iii (1952), 325–40, and *Rise of the Novel*,
pp. 240 ff.

16 Plutarch, *Alexander*, VIII, 2; XV, 4–5; *Caesar*, XI, 3.

17 Contrast Pope's note to his *Iliad*, XI, 143, on this episode: '*Homer*, says
Eustathius, never lets an Opportunity pass of mentioning the Hero of his
Poem, *Achilles*: He gives here an Instance of his former Resentment, and
at once varies his Poetry, and exalts his Character. Nor does he mention
him cursorily; he seems unwilling to leave him; and when he pursues the
Thread of the Story in a few Lines, takes occasion to speak again of him.
This is a very artful Conduct, by mentioning him so frequently, he takes
care that the Reader should not forget him, and shews the Importance of
that Hero, whose Anger is the Subject of his Poem' (Twickenham
Edition, VIII, 42).

　　Mist's Weekly Journal, 12 June 1725, noted the real Wild's fondness for
extracts from the classics in translation, and his notion, derived from

Tacitus, that Roman times 'were fine Times to get Money' (loc. cit. above, ch. IV, n. 17).

18 Swift, *Works*, I, 242.

19 Thomas Blackwell, *Enquiry into the Life and Writings of Homer* (1735), p. 28.

20 Austin Warren, 'Pope', *Essential Articles for the Study of Alexander Pope*, ed. Maynard Mack (Hamden, Connecticut, 1964), p. 87. See also pp. 91–2 on the 'failure of the post-Miltonic epic', a failure which 'lay . . . in the supposition that the heroic poem could be written in an unheroic age'.

21 See Donald M. Foerster, *Homer in English Criticism. The Historical Approach in the Eighteenth Century* (New Haven, 1947), chs. I–II. For a related sixteenth-century Humanist attack on the heroic and tyrant-glamourizing ethos in medieval romance, see Robert P. Adams, 'Bold Bawdry and Open Manslaughter: The English New Humanist Attack on Medieval Romance', *Huntington Library Quarterly*, xxiii (1959–60), 33–48. On Alexander and Caesar, see Miller, *Essays on Fielding's Miscellanies*, pp. 386–409, and Irwin *The Making of Jonathan Wild*, pp. 48 ff. See also Rabelais, I, xlvi.

22 *Rehearsal*, IV, i; ed. Edward Arber (London, 1919), p. 97, and see the Dryden passage on p. 96, from the Epistle Dedicatory to the *Conquest of Granada*.

23 John Dryden, 'To . . . Lord Radcliffe', prefixed to *Examen Poeticum* (1693), *Of Dramatic Poesy and other Critical Essays*, ed. George Watson (London and New York, 1962), II, 167. But Homer is praised for his power to arouse 'the manly passions' and to 'cause admiration', which 'is, indeed, the proper and adequate design of an epic poem' (II, 166).

24 See below (pp. 194, 221 nn. 53–5). An amusingly sycophantic celebration of the insatiability of 'great men' is Dryden's praise, in the Epistle Dedicatory to the *Conquest of Granada*, of the Duke of York's great conquests, and his 'restless' valour in 'still mediating', in between conquests, ' on new triumphs . . . another navy to overcome, and another admiral to be slain'. Such a passage may well be one of the targets of Fielding's many jibes about the restless insatiability of 'heroes', including perhaps the glimpse of Wild in II, v 'meditating within himself' on possible further trickeries against Heartfree. Dryden's heroic plays, notably the *Conquest of Granada*, had been among the principal targets of Fielding's burlesque *Tragedy of Tragedies; or the Life and Death of Tom Thumb the Great* (1731). This 'restless, amiable disposition, this noble avidity which increases with feeding, is the first principle or constituent quality of these our great men' (*J.W.*, I, xiv; see also , II, ii), and is probably also an allusion to Hobbesian psychology (W. R. Irwin, *The Making of Jonathan Wild*, pp. 59–60).

25 Pope, 'An Essay on Homer's Battels', *Translations of Homer*, Twickenham Edition, VII, 255. See the Twickenham Introduction, VII, li, xc, xcix, clxxiv, for Pope's softening of Homer, and the 'ethical emphasis' of his whole presentation of Homer.

26 Pope's note to his *Iliad*, XIII, 471, Twickenham Edition, VIII, 129. Pope also took issue in his Preface to the *Iliad* with Mme. Dacier's praise of Homer's times, pointing out that in those days 'a Spirit of Revenge and Cruelty, join'd with the practice of Rapine and Robbery, reign'd thro' the World. . . .' (Twickenham Edition, VII, li, 14). These were matters of heated debate. See Twickenham Edition, VII, lxxviii ff. and Donald M. Foerster, *Homer in English Criticism*. But the issue ramifies into the whole Ancients-Moderns controversy.

27 Twickenham Edition, VII, li ff.

28 This is not to imply that, for Dryden or Pope, the 'total literary achievement' of the great epics could be separated from morality. As the Twickenham introduction eloquently says: 'Both saw in the great ancients a grasp of massive human issues that transcended the commitments of credal faith . . . crucial insights about man as a suffering, struggling but creative and significant being. . . . Their insight was inseparable from their artistic grasp' (VII, clxxxiv ff.). It is when separations were made that epic values and epic poems became particularly vulnerable to that 'reduction of the whole matter to a simple moral judgment' which Ian Watt shows in Defoe (*Rise of the Novel*, p. 240).

29 *Essay on Man*, IV, 217 ff. But see also an earlier comparison of Alexander and Caesar, *Temple of Fame*, 151-8. Alexander is also mentioned in Pope's note to his *Iliad*, VI, 88, in connection with the military lessons he learned from Homer; and see Parnell's 'Essay on Homer' prefixed to Pope's *Iliad*, Twickenham Edition, vol. VII, pp. 59-60.

30 For drolls on heroic subjects, including the siege of Troy, see below, pp. 213, 226 nn. 102 ff.

31 Swift, *Works*, I, 250.

32 Ford Madox Ford, *No More Parades* (West Drayton, 1948), II, ii, p. 172. For a not dissimilar, but perhaps slightly less uncomfortable, example, see D. H. Lawrence, *The Rainbow* (Harmondsworth, 1950), I, i, p. 11.

33 Richard Aldington, *Death of a Hero* (London, 1965), II, ii–iv, pp. 134–6, 149, 155–6.

34 For an emphasis on *similarities* between Fielding and Joyce (not, however, involving *Jonathan Wild*), see Frederick W. Hilles, 'Art and Artifice in *Tom Jones*', *Imagined Worlds. Essays on Some English Novels and Novelists in Honour of John Butt*, ed. Maynard Mack and Ian Gregor (London, 1968), pp. 98 ff.

35 Letter to Carlo Linati, 21 September 1921, *Letters of James Joyce*, ed. Stuart Gilbert (London, 1957), pp. 146–7.

36 For a small glimpse, as distinct from Joyce's pervasive vision, of this aspect of the Ulysses myth in a twentieth-century novel, see Saul Bellow *Henderson the Rain King* (Harmondsworth, 1966), ch. III, pp. 24–5. Stephen Crane's *Red Badge of Courage* (1895) had shown a soldier feeling that the old epic aspirations were dead. If modern wars, like the First

World War, have vast or 'epic' proportions, they turn out to be, as
Wyndham Lewis put it, meaningless or absurd (see epigraphs to this
chapter, for the passages from Crane and Wyndham Lewis).

37 Frank Budgen, *James Joyce and the Making of Ulysses*, 2nd edn (London,
1937), pp. 15–18. For untypical or unheroic elements in the Ulysses myth,
which made Ulysses especially suited among ancient heroes for Joyce's
adaptation, see W. B. Stanford, *The Ulysses Theme*, 2nd edn (Oxford,
1963), ch. V, pp. 66–80, 'The Untypical Hero'; see also pp. 82–4, 97,
117, and, for a study of the versions of Joyce and Kazantzakis, ch. XV,
pp. 211–40, 'The Re-Integrated Hero'.

38 F. R. Leavis, 'Why "Four Quartets" Matters in a Technologico-
Benthamite Age', *English Literature in Our Time and the University*
(London, 1969), p. 122.

39 'A Discourse Concerning the Original and Progress of Satire' (1693),
Of Dramatic Poesy and other Critical Essays, II, 149. See also, for example,
the discussion of 'Epic Satire' in Walter Harte's *Essay on Satire,
Particularly on the Dunciad* (1730), *passim* (Augustan Reprint Society,
No. 132, 1968).

40 Jean-Paul Sartre, 'Qu'est-ce que la Littérature?', *Situations II* (Paris, 1948),
p. 150.

41 On this courage, see below, pp. 178 ff., 187 ff., 249 f.

CHAPTER VI

THE WORLD OF WILD
AND UBU

❀

On, on, you madman [Hannibal], drive
Over your savage Alps, to thrill young schoolboys
And supply a theme for speech-day recitations!
   One globe seemed all too small for the youthful Alexander:
Mierably he chafed at this world's narrow confines . . .
                        (Juvenal, x, 166 ff.; trs. Peter Green)

Cornegidouille! nous n'aurons point tout démoli si nous ne
démolissons même les ruines!
                        (Père Ubu in Epigraph to *Ubu Enchaîné*)

I say farce, but with the enfeebled humour of our times the word
is a misnomer; it is the farce of the old English humour, the
terribly serious, even savage comic humour, the humour which
spent its last breath in the decadent genius of Dickens.
            (T. S. Eliot, 'Christopher Marlowe', on the *Jew of Malta*)

. . . satire like Jonson's is great in the end not by hitting off its
object, but by creating it. . . .
                        (T. S. Eliot, 'Ben Jonson')

I go to the first performance of Alfred Jarry's *Ubu Roi*. . . . The
audience shake their fists . . . The players are supposed to be
dolls, toys, marionettes, and now they are all hopping like wooden
frogs, and I can see for myself that the chief personage, who is
some kind of King, carries for sceptre a brush of the kind that we
use to clean a closet. Feeling bound to support the most spirited
party, we have shouted for the play, but that night at the Hôtel
Corneille I am very sad, for comedy, objectivity, has displayed
its growing power once more. I say: 'After Stephane Mallarmé,
after Paul Verlaine, after Gustave Moreau, after Puvis de Chavannes,

after our own verse, after all our subtle colour and nervous rhythm,
after the faint mixed tints of Conder, what more is possible?
After us the Savage God'.

(Yeats, *Autobiographies*, 'The Tragic Generation', *ad fin.*)

When Yeats wrote in 'The Song of the Happy Shepherd':[1]

> Where are now the warring kings?
> An idle word is now their glory,
> By the stammering schoolboy said,
> Reading some entangled story:

the answer contained two elements of interest to the student of Fielding's
mock-heroic and of *Jonathan Wild*. The first (resonantly expressed in
Yeats's refrain: 'Words alone are certain good') speaks of the greater
permanence of poems than of heroic deeds, the point made (with a
somewhat different ironic emphasis) in *Champion*, 27 November 1739:[2]

> Alexander had the immediate honours of his victories, and perhaps
> much more than they deserved; but poor Homer was, during his
> life, reputed little better than a ballad-singer; . . . Yet the poet
> hath some advantage in his turn; for his works . . . will outlive
> the others; to which we may add Sir William Temple's
> observation, that the world hath produced a thousand equal to
> Alexander, but scarce one capable of writing an Iliad.

Like Fielding, Yeats scorns 'the warring kings,/Word be-mockers' (the
poem's first version adds the line: 'They were of no wordy mood'),[3]
although he lacks here Fielding's wry understanding that the ethos of an
Iliad was in some ways not far removed from that which animated the
exploits of Alexander. If the imaginative embodiment of heroic aspirations in poems is valued by both men more highly than the practice of
heroic deeds, Yeats is prepared to be more crudely nostalgic about the
old heroic world, which has become sophisticated into a kind of make-
believe glory which Yeats does not altogether reject, the source of words
and dreams in a prosaic world. Grey truth and dreary science have
shattered the old worlds, Arcadian or heroic. Since these worlds, for
Yeats, are in a sense truer than science ('Of old the world on dreaming
fed'), their survival in 'words', 'some entangled story' (the first version
reads: 'In the verse of Attic story'),[4] is somewhat ambiguously valued
beyond the simple distinction between 'words' and 'deeds': 'words' are
better than 'deeds', but the word-hallowed deeds of old are better than
today's prosaic fact. Fielding admired ancient epics at least as much as

Yeats, but he came, as we saw, to prefer prosaic fact to heroic deception:
'I should have honoured and loved Homer more had he written a true
history of his own times in humble prose, than those noble poems that
have so justly collected the praise of all ages'.[5] The ambivalence here
seems more tough-minded, less sentimental, than Yeats's.

But Yeats is also saying that heroic times have dwindled to the
dimensions of the classroom, an 'entangled story' read by schoolboys.
And this implication is worth juxtaposing with an insight which Yeats
was perhaps at this period too self-important to follow through, but
which lesser figures like Auden and Isherwood have explored, that there
is something in common between the values of a heroic world and
those of a boys' school. The emphasis on daring leadership, on feats of
physical prowess and of cunning, on codes of honour and on gang-
solidarity (complicated by internal resentments and feuds) link the
Homeric epics, or the sagas, to Isherwood's 'Gems of Belgian Architecture'[6] and Auden's *Paid on Both Sides* or *The Orators*. Isherwood
said:[7]

> The saga-world is a schoolboy world, with its feuds, its practical
> jokes, its dark threats conveyed in puns and riddles and
> understatements . . . I once remarked to Auden that the
> atmosphere of *Gisli the Outlaw* very much reminded me of our
> schooldays. He was pleased with the idea: and, soon after this, he
> produced his first play, *Paid on Both Sides*, in which the two worlds
> are so inextricably confused that it is impossible to say whether
> the characters are really epic heroes or only members of a school
> O.T.C.

Isherwood's story, 'Gems of Belgian Architecture', shows some boys
revisiting 'the school where their old saga-life is still being lived, by
another generation; but they themselves can make no contact with it.
They have become anachronisms'.[8] This part of the story was inspired
by his meeting at Cambridge a boy whom he had known at school as
oafish and ruthless, and who had now become 'a charming, amusing,
highly sophisticated young man': 'I planned to show a group of
characters who have not only changed individually in the process of
growing up but have evolved historically, as it were, from the tenth to
the twentieth century'.[9] The Yeatsian vision of a dwindling, through
the ages, of heroic life to class-room re-enactment is restated with a new
and more sceptical ambiguity. A 'charming, amusing, highly sophisticated young man' is better than a ruthless oaf. Yeats's 'warring kings,/
Word be-mockers' were not as good as the 'words' they mocked, but

they went back to a more romantic and whole-hearted time. Isherwood, in a fine passage in *Lions and Shadows*, sees through the whole heroically inviting schoolboy myth as self-indulgent make-believe, a 'homosexual romanticism' with some sinister implications at which it is dangerous simply to sneer: 'the rulers of Fascist states do not sneer—they profoundly understand and make use of just these phantasies and longings'.[10]

Auden's retrospective Foreword to *The Orators* also understands the connection, and the way in which it implicates himself: 'My name on the title-page seems a pseudonym for someone else, someone talented but near the border of sanity, who might well, in a year or two, become a Nazi':[11]

> The central theme of *The Orators* seems to be Hero-worship, and we all know what that can lead to politically. My guess to-day is that my unconscious motive in writing it was therapeutic, to exorcise certain tendencies in myself by allowing them to run riot in phantasy. If to-day I find 'Auden with play-ground whistle', as Wyndham-Lewis [*sic*] called him, a bit shy-making, I realise that it is precisely the schoolboy atmosphere and diction which act as a moral criticism of the rather ugly emotions and ideas they are employed to express. By making the latter juvenile, they make it impossible to take them seriously. In one of the Odes I express all the sentiments with which his followers hailed the advent of Hitler, but these are rendered, I hope, innocuous by the fact that the Führer so hailed is a new-born baby and the son of a friend.

We shall not expect to find, in Fielding, this degree of self-implication. He is too separate from Wild, and too secure in the values which lead him to reject Wild. He was also probably too convinced of the essential dignity of the ancient epics to involve his own feelings too closely in a parallel which so radically reduced their stature. But he certainly sensed that the parallel (between hero and schoolboy) existed, and would have understood Auden's remarks in *Letters from Iceland*: 'The Nazis have a theory that Iceland is the cradle of the Germanic culture. Well, if they want a community like that of the sagas they are welcome to it. I love the sagas, but what a rotten society they describe, a society with only the gangster virtues.'[12] The distinction between the sagas and the 'rotten society they describe' is similar to that which underlies Fielding's ambiguous attitude to the epic. And the link between conquest or tyranny, the gangster-virtues, and the schoolboy world (already hinted at in the lines from Juvenal cited as an epigraph to this chapter) is close to that of *Jonathan Wild*, in which Alexander and Caesar and Walpole, and the real-life Wild, and the fictional Wild with his schoolboy delight in the nefarious deeds of Homeric and Virgilian heroes, unite in a peculiar amalgam.

Another tradition also feeds the schoolboy image, a tradition of punitive satire:[13]

> I have observ'd some Satyrists to use the Publick much at the
> Rate that Pedants do a naughty Boy ready Hors'd for Discipline:
> First expostulate the Case, then plead the Necessity of the Rod,
> from great Provocations, and conclude every Period with a Lash.
> Now, if I know any thing of Mankind, these Gentlemen might
> very well spare their Reproof and Correction: For there is not,
> through all Nature, another so callous and insensible a Member as
> the *World's Posteriors*, whether you apply to it the *Toe* or the *Birch*.

Thus the 'author' of Swift's *Tale of a Tub*. His points about the uselessness of 'general satire' and the incorrigibility of the world are also in a manner Swift's points. At the same time, Swift is himself directly committed to the images of the punishing pedagogue and of the peccant posteriors which call for his attention:[14]

> Let me, tho' the Smell be Noisom,
> Strip their Bums; let CALEB hoyse 'em;
> Then, apply ALECTO's Whip,
> Till they wriggle, howl, and skip.

This ritual combination of schoolboy reduction and scatological exposure exists also in Book II of the *Dunciad*, whose mock-heroic framework (not present in Swift) brings it even closer to the world of *Jonathan Wild*, and where the parody of epic Games transforms itself into a part infant, part schoolboy romp. Emrys Jones has written brilliantly of how the dunces[15]

> run races, have urinating, tickling, shouting, and diving
> competitions, and finally vie with each other in keeping awake
> until 'the soft gifts of Sleep conclude the day' ... 'Here strip, my
> children!' cries their mother Dulness at one point, and they strut
> about naked, play games, quarrel, and shout, as free of inhibition
> and shame as any small infant. Pope evokes the unrestrained glee
> of childhood, its unthinking sensuality (as in the tickling match)
> and the deafening noise made by children at play:
>
> > Now thousand tongues are heard in one loud din;
> > The monkey-mimics rush discordant in;

> 'Twas chatt'ring, grinning, mouthing, jabb'ring all,
> And Noise and Norton, Brangling and Breval . . .

The world of Book Two seems in many ways a version of pre-literate infancy, and to enter it is to experience a primitive sense of liberation.

'Pre-literate infancy' seems to me not quite exact. The last-quoted lines are immediately followed by a chattering competitiveness which suggests schoolboys and undergraduates:[16]

> Dennis and Dissonance, and captious Art,
> And Snip-snap short, and Interruption smart,
> And Demonstration thin, and Theses thick,
> And Major, Minor, and Conclusion quick . . .
>
> (*Dunciad*, II, 239–42);

and the competitions as to who shall run fastest or urinate the highest (*Dunciad*, II, 35 ff., 161 ff.) are schoolboy rather than infant events. But Jones seems to me undoubtedly right about the note of geniality and liberation. He is careful to recognize that 'As a satirist Pope is of course degrading his enemies'. But there is an unofficial level at which 'the poetry is doing something more interesting than a narrowly satirical account would suggest' and where the treatment is almost affectionate. The contemptuous diminution has about it a childish vitality combined with a curious tenderness.

The feeling of tenderness does not occur when Swift treats *his* victims as 'naughty Boy[s] ready Hors'd for Discipline', but it does occur in *Jonathan Wild*. Wild's relationships with women are, as we have seen, one of the most conspicuously recurrent examples of a process in the novel by which his sinister stature is diminished. On one occasion at least the diminishing involves a schoolboy image. In I, ix, Wild is rebuffed by Laetitia (who has just been disporting herself with Tom Smirk) in a manner which reduces him from a 'great hero' to the level of a chastised schoolboy:

> for, though she had not yet learned the art of well clenching her fist, nature had not however left her defenceless, for at the ends of her fingers she wore arms, which she used with such admirable dexterity, that the hot blood of Mr. Wild soon began to appear in several little spots on his face, and his full-blown cheeks to resemble that part which modesty forbids a boy to turn up anywhere but in a public school, after some pedagogue, strong of arm, hath exercised his talents thereon.

The humiliating episode not only makes Wild seem a great deal more vulnerable than all the abstract talk about his diabolical greatness implies, but also, largely through the comically scabrous image of the schoolboy's posterior, gives him a sort of ragged pathos, dissolving sarcasm in a not unfriendly kind of laughter. The special piquancy of the diminution in both Fielding and Pope derives from a mock-heroic scheme which, at another level, insists with urgency that the enemy (Wild or the Dunces) is gravely and massively dangerous—and does so not only because the upside-down formula insists on their greatness to imply the opposite, but because a primary magnitude of evil is shown to be at work. This peculiar interplay is, once again, absent in Swift, who is not given to affectionate impulses towards his butts, nor to swelling his discourse with heroic or mock-heroic pretensions in the first place.

In the *Dunciad* Book II, the diminution takes place through liberations of childish energy, rather than through homely humiliation. But there is an opposite process also, in which childish energy (of an oafish sort) attaches to Fielding's villain more than to some of Pope's dunces. In Book II, a certain Brobdingnagian gigantification goes alongside the childish diminution. Jones cites the passage about Blackmore in the shouting competition:

> But far o'er all, sonorous Blackmore's strain;
> Walls, steeples, skies, bray back to him again.
> In Tot'nam fields, the brethren, with amaze,
> Prick all their ears up, and forget to graze;
> Long Chanc'ry-lane retentive rolls the sound,
> And courts to courts return it round and round;
> Thames wafts it thence to Rufus' roaring hall,
> And Hungerford re-echoes bawl for bawl.
> All hail him victor in both gifts of song,
> Who sings so loudly, and who sings so long.
> *(Dunciad*, II, 259–68)

Jones comments: 'It is as if this dunce has grown to a figure of Brobdingnagian size, or as if the City has shrunk to the dimensions of a toytown with a child standing astride over it ... the image of deafening, gigantesque noise—as of a giant *shouting* over London—is, though comic, a disturbingly powerful one'.[17] This is right. But it is an effect curiously static in its massiveness. Jones uses the passage to show 'an example of a dunce who combines qualities of infantility with the manic energy of a madman'. But 'manic energy' suggests a quality of

177

movement, of hysterical animation, which is not, in my view, there. Unlike some earlier images of infantile play, of the Monkey-mimics and their 'chatt'ring, grinning, mouthing, jabb'ring', this passage gives a sense of huge operatic order, as of a vast chorus playing its proper part, the sounds strong and rolling, echoing in precision, 'bawl for bawl'. And the immediate context maintains the note of amplitude and of a kind of slow dignity, alive with squalor certainly:

> . . . where Fleet-ditch with disemboguing streams
> Rolls the large tribute of dead dogs to Thames
>
> (*Dunciad*, II, 271–2)

but at the same time grand and stately with a heavy charmlessness brilliantly rendered by Pope, and far removed from the tear-away oafishness which suffuses some of the grandeurs of *Jonathan Wild*.

Compare the operatic 'composition' of Blackmore's song, the crowds struck dumb 'with amaze' and admiration, and the disciplined echoes dominating the city in due and orderly rhythm, with Wild's 'heroic' end on the gallows. Having failed in a suicide attempt with laudanum, because he was after all born to be hanged ('the fruit of hemp seed, and not the spirit of poppy seed' was destined to overcome him),

> he exerted that greatest of courage which hath been so much celebrated in other heroes; and, knowing that it was impossible to resist, he gravely declared he would attend [his guards]. He then descended to that room where the fetters of great men are knocked off in a most solemn and ceremonious manner. Then shaking hands with his friends (to wit, those who were conducting him to the tree), and drinking their healths in a bumper of brandy, he ascended the cart, where he was no sooner seated than he received the acclamations of the multitude, who were highly ravished with his GREATNESS.
>
> The cart now moved slowly on, being preceded by a troop of horse-guards bearing javelins in their hands, through streets lined with crowds all admiring the great behaviour of our hero, who rode on, sometimes sighing, sometimes swearing, sometimes singing or whistling, as his humour varied.
>
> When he came to the tree of glory he was welcomed with an universal shout of the people, who were there assembled in prodigious numbers to behold a sight much more rare in populous cities than one would reasonably imagine it should be, viz. the proper catastrophe of a great man.

But though envy was, through fear, obliged to join the general voice in applause on this occasion, there were not wanting some who maligned this completion of glory, which was now about to be fulfilled to our hero, and endeavoured to prevent it by knocking him on the head as he stood under the tree, while the ordinary was performing his last office. They therefore began to batter the cart with stones, brickbats, dirt, and all manner of mischievous weapons (IV, xiv).

This passage is as much of a set-piece as anything in the *Dunciad* (and even involves a procession), and also sustains a powerfully stylized effect of heroic aggrandisement. But this aggrandisement is accompanied by animated activity, rather than held, as in the passage about Blackmore, in a slow and stately massiveness. Where Blackmore's audience is stilled to a vast 'amaze', Wild 'received the acclamations of the multitude', and, later, a ragged and unruly shower of 'stones, brickbats, dirt, and all manner of mischievous weapons'. Blackmore is echoed sonorously by a disciplined landscape, 'Walls, steeples, skies' braying back 'bawl for bawl', Wild answered by a loud and thronging crowd. Where Blackmore, motionless and stentorian, gives forth his loud and single 'strain', Wild 'rode on, sometimes sighing, sometimes swearing, sometimes singing or whistling, as his humour varied'. This variety of mood combines queerly with Wild's boorish unconcern, an unconcern which is part drunken stupor, part clown's deadpan, and which also acquires overtones of heroic indifference to danger. (The suggestion of a cowardly side to this in the suicide attempt, the stiff cordials, etc . . ., is beautifully played down by Fielding, though strongly present in some of the real-life accounts.)[18]

Pope's aggrandisement tends towards massiveness and majesty, even in degradation. The pace is often slowed down almost to the statuesque: 'Slow rose a form, in majesty of Mud' (*Dunciad*, II, 326). And images of 'Monumental Brass' (II, 313), and of the real statues of 'Great Cibber's brazen, brainless brothers' (I, 32), emphasize this. This is part of Pope's way of giving true heroic stature to his mock-epic world. Fielding's aggrandisement is more problematical. Even here, one of the highpoints of heroic realization in *Jonathan Wild*, much of the aggrandisement depends on verbal insistence and authorial commentary, rather than, as in Pope, on the nature of the imagery, on the living shapes of the created fiction. Where Pope gives a Brobdingnagian stage-set and a stentorian Blackmore, Fielding harps on how right it is for 'great' men to be hanged, how 'heroic' it is for Wild to attain this proper end, how appropriate (i.e. 'truly great and admirable') his behaviour was on that occasion, and how like a noble drama is his story's end. In Fielding's *action*, as against the *words* of the ironic commentary, there is not only the disorderly and life-size animation of the crowd scene, but also a peculiar non-heroic geniality, and a kind of stylized realism which turns the hero into a much humbler, comic novelistic figure, with his convivial 'bumper of brandy' and the delightful specifying that among Wild's various reactions ('swearing', 'singing', 'whistling') was included an occasional sigh.

The sigh comes from fear, as does the drinking, and yet it is a curious effect of Fielding's presentation that such details do not diminish Wild's oafish impressiveness. When Fielding says at the beginning of IV, xiv that Wild's 'execution, or consummation, or apotheosis' was a great event, 'which was to give our hero an opportunity of facing death and damnation, without any fear in his heart, or, at least, without betraying any symptoms of it in his countenance', the last words convey a subheroic reality which the pamphlet-biographies emphasized, and which is theoretically in line with Fielding's contemptuous exposure of Wild's 'bombast greatness'. But the actual impression upon us of Wild's drinking the health of his guards 'in a bumper of brandy' as 'he ascended the cart' transcends the tart commentary in a general pageantry of crude triumph. The preservation of a brave front, or unmoved countenance, may be the special property of clowns and of shameless and fraudulent 'heroes' (Pope's friend Warburton said in a piece prefixed to the *Dunciad* in 1743 that the mock hero's 'Courage is all collected into the *Face*'),[19] but in the particular circumstances it acquires overtones of heroic valour in a primary sense.

Fielding achieves this effect not merely by emphasizing feats of brazenness, however. If Wild's drinking, 'that true support of greatness in affliction', enabled him 'to curse, swear and bully and brave his fate' (IV, xii), it is also associated with an engaging conviviality, and even a kind of yokel grace. The scene with the ordinary of Newgate (IV, xiii), which immediately precedes the hanging chapter, is worth examining in detail. The ordinary enters, saying 'I hope you rested well last night'. Wild replies with an unfussy, if oath-ridden, factuality: 'D-n'd ill; sir. I dreamt so confoundedly of hanging, that it disturbed my sleep'. The laconic directness of the answer is in itself more striking than the terrors which it mentions. Wild imposes himself upon the scene as a vividly deadpan personality, curiously separate from the naturalistic fact that he experiences the normal unromantic fears of a condemned prisoner. We learn that he 'fell asleep' the last time the ordinary warned him about 'everlasting fire'. When the ordinary now repeats his hell-fire bombinations and other clerical pedantries, Wild reacts with his usual resilient automatism, emitting a string of asterisked obscenities followed by a more intelligible refusal to accept defeat:

> You *** to frighten me out of my wits. But the good *** is, I doubt not, more merciful than his wicked **. If I should believe all you say, I am sure I should die in inexpressible horror.

Talk then turns to the possibility of a reprieve. Wild asserts:

> I am not without hopes of a reprieve from the cheat yet. I have pretty good interest; but, if I cannot obtain it, you shall not frighten me out of my courage. I will not die like a pimp. D—n me, what is death? It is nothing but to be with Platos and with Caesars, as the poet says, and all the other great heroes of antiquity.

These garbled notions of 'antiquity' look back amusingly to his schoolboy reverence for 'the wisdom of the ancients' (I, iii). They may be based on a passage in some of the pamphlet-biographies, notably that of the Ordinary of Newgate, in which Wild enquires 'how the noble Greeks and famous Romans, who slew themselves, came to be so glorious in History, if self-murder be a Crime'.[20] Wild is told there that suicide is considered a cowardice and a crime not only by Christians but by the wiser heathens, but he attempts it nevertheless. His appeal to ancient history was an attempt to square his proposed action with his conscience, and to allay his fears of the afterlife. Fielding, however, moves Wild's thoughts about the ancients away from any relation with the contemplated suicide. In the next chapter, Fielding does follow the biographers in recording the suicide attempt, but without dwelling on Jonathan's cowardice or the stupefying effects of the laudanum. He steers away from Wild's *feelings*, using the episode (as we saw) to exemplify the proposition that Wild was born to be hanged and that Fortune would not permit any rearrangement of her plan. The stylized fantastication works to divert attention from the character at a point where his grandeur might be reduced.

In Fielding, Wild's reference to the deaths of the 'great heroes of antiquity', the Platos and Caesars, who were not suicides, is meant to stiffen his courage to die. There is no suggestion that Wild is trying to justify a suicidal evasion of hanging. It is the ordinary, not Wild, who now dwells on the fear of death, telling Wild that 'life is sweet', that the ancients were a pack of heathens 'who are, I doubt not, in hell with the devil and his angels', and that Wild will join them if he is not careful. 'You will then be ready to give more for a drop of water than you ever gave for a bottle of wine'.

Wild's immediate response: 'Faith, doctor! well minded. What say you to a bottle of wine?', sparkles with convivial unconcern. The harsh world of the prison turns into a sweetly scabrous never-never land of Pickwickian geniality. Wild's 'courage' acquires a vivid if unexpected dimension. It is the clergyman who has all the gloomy thoughts that Wild ought to be having, while Wild's whole effort is to steer the conversation into a more companionable mood. The ordinary says he won't drink with an atheist. Wild says: 'It is your business to drink with the wicked, in order to amend them', adding that the ordinary must show Wild the way to heaven. The ordinary replies: 'the gates are barred against all revilers of the clergy'. Wild says: 'I revile only the wicked ones' who obtain preferments without merit, and adds that on merit the ordinary would have been a bishop by now. The ordinary rather agrees but coyly starts preaching again. Wild: 'All this is very true; but let us take a bottle of wine'. The ordinary prefers punch, 'as it is nowhere spoken against in scripture', and is healthier anyway. Wild says how careless he was not to have remembered that the ordinary preferred punch. He will drink to his being made a bishop. The ordinary says *he* will drink to Wild's reprieve. If he is not reprieved, the ordinary will give a good account of his soul. He then summarizes the sermon he has in his pocket. Wild, predictably, falls asleep. 'But here the punch by entering waked Mr. Wild . . . and put an end to the sermon; nor could we obtain any farther account of the conversation which passed at this interview.'[21] This, in some degree, is in Fielding's mature novelistic manner. It is of a piece with Joseph's 'death-bed' interview with Parson Barnabas (*Joseph Andrews*, I, xiii), and contains the sort of comedy which dissolves hostility all round.[22] The difference is that in *Joseph Andrews* it is only the parson who needs redeeming by the importation of convivial humour, which is brief and appears only at the end. Here both speakers are disreputable in different ways, and the redeeming is more sustained. But what is really important is that this scene differs from that in *Joseph Andrews* because the comedy proceeds from character rather than plot. It is Wild, not Fielding, who brings in the convivial note. And when we consider that Wild is on the point of death, and that all probability, as well as the historical sources, point to a behaviour both less grand and less charming, Fielding's presentation of Wild becomes very striking. If, at the end of this chapter, we are more inside the genial world of *Joseph Andrews* and *Tom Jones*, a world of the comic rather than of mock-heroic, that fact itself paradoxically prepares us for the rather grander mock-heroic note in the hanging chapter which follows. For Wild's geniality is in the circumstances a kind of greatness.

Although Fielding had earlier briefly conceded the traditional point that Wild drank to keep his courage up, his real emphasis, then, is on the conviviality of Wild's drinking. This conviviality amounts to a positive challenge to the hardness of his fate, not a gloomy and sodden retreat from it. Wild's situation before hanging lacks the glamour of Macheath's, because Wild has not Macheath's easy charm, his success with women, his gaiety (and Macheath is after all reprieved because 'an opera must end happily'). But it is worth recalling that Macheath also drank to keep his courage up ('So I drink off this bumper—And now I can stand the test,/And my comrades shall see, that I die as brave as the best'),[23] and that this fact does not radically diminish the aura of dashing gaiety which surrounds him throughout. Wild by contrast lacks any kind of panache throughout most of the novel, but he comes at this point to acquire an oafish bravura that commands our sympathy as Macheath (with his easier grace) commands it.

The romantic appeal of hanging scenes is a recurrent theme of the *Beggar's Opera*:

> The youth in his cart hath the air of a lord,
> And we cry, there dies an Adonis!

'I hear the crowd extolling his resolution and intrepidity', says Polly in a fond daydream.[24] Fielding remarked in the *Champion*, 3 January 1740 (an essay which noted Macheath's popularity with the ladies):[25]

> Whoever frequents the execution of malefactors, must have observed, that such as die with bravery and intrepidity never fail of meeting pity, and even some degree of esteem among the spectators. Whereas, the contrary behaviour would on those occasions be much more decent and commendable.

This gallows-glamour is a recurrent motif of rogue-literature, as well as a sociological fact. We find it in Quevedo's *El Buscon* (I, vii), and in some Swiftian jokes about the brazenness of malefactors on the cart.[26] Fielding the social thinker was gravely concerned about the effect of these Tyburn triumphs on public morality; in the *Enquiry into the Causes of the Late Increase of Robbers* he was to propose ways of deglamourizing the death-penalty and strengthening its effectiveness as a deterrent to crime.[27] Such deglamourizing was presumably part of his deliberate intention in *Jonathan Wild*. But the difference between Fielding's explicit statement of his attitude in the (much later) *Enquiry* and his particular unfolding of it in the fullness of imaginative creation here, shows a kind of surrender to the attractiveness of his hero which partly pulls the other way. And because the hero (unlike the historical original described by Defoe and others) remains true to himself by a kind of coarse effrontery and weird courage, Fielding seems partly to respond to the human appeal of a situation which in principle he would have deplored. Despite the heavy sarcasms against Wild, and the satirical harping on the theme of gallows greatness, Fielding's treatment operates less on a plane of sociological condemnation, than in the freer atmosphere of a literary tradition which (as in Quevedo and Gay) was partly emancipated, in imagination, from contemplating the social problem as such.

Indeed, the moralist or sociologist is more radically transcended in Fielding's case than in Gay's. In Gay, the gallows-glamour is largely a matter of charm and handsomeness and sex-appeal: the ladies 'think every man handsome who is going to the camp or the gallows',[28] and the glory is gained through positive admiration. In Fielding, on the other hand, a moment of glory is achieved by arousing hate, not love. The public clamour of 'admiration' for Wild cannot *simply* be taken straight, and his proud moment of public limelight partly consists of having 'stones, brickbats, dirt, and all manner of mischievous weapons' thrown at him. There is a kind of amorality in this which recalls the final wish of Camus's Outsider, that, for a proper 'consummation' ('Pour que tout soit consommé'), his execution should be viewed by a large and angry crowd, greeting him with cries of hate: 'Pour que tout soit consommé, pour que je me sente moins seul, il me restait à souhaiter qu'il y ait beaucoup de spectateurs le jour de mon exécution et qu'ils m'accueillent avec des cris de haine.'[29]

Fielding's treatment, unlike this, exists in a comically extravagant key.[30] I shall argue later that it tends, however gingerly and certainly not consciously, towards a peculiarly modern domain of amoral or 'black' humour. What is of interest here is the way Wild is finally accorded an offbeat heroic stature. Naturalistic details about fear and drunkenness and a cheery subheroic companionability become transmuted into a form of 'greatness' not merely because the hero rises to an evil grandeur of defiance, but partly, and paradoxically, because he can preserve much of his humbler, small-scale character intact. Wild's undeviating truthfulness, even at the moment of death, to his sub-heroic character as a compulsive small-time crook achieves its highest manifestation in the closing words of the account of the hanging:

> We must not, however, omit one circumstance, as it serves to show the most admirable conservation of character in our hero to the last moment, which was, that, whilst the ordinary was busy in his ejaculations, Wild, in the midst of the shower of stones, &c., which played upon him, applied his hands to the parson's pocket, and emptied it of his bottle-screw, which he carried out of the world in his hand (IV, xiv).

The abstract verbalizing of the ironic formula is still maintained ('the most admirable conservation of character'), and within five lines occurs a summarizing paragraph which begins: 'Thus fell Jonathan Wild the GREAT, by a death as glorious as his life had been . . .'. But a peculiar triumph of this passage is that the act of petty pickpocketing is not very much out of line with the magniloquence. This congruence is achieved not by grand behaviour, but by an absurd self-consistency, a 'conservation of character' which is 'admirable' not so much in the bad 'heroic' sense as for its roguish integrity.

The satire of the parson calls to mind a passage in the Circe episode of *Ulysses*:[31]

> His Eminence, Simon Stephen Cardinal Dedalus, Primate of all Ireland, appears in the doorway, dressed in red soutane, sandals and socks. Seven dwarf simian acolytes, also in red, cardinal sins, uphold his train, peeping under it. He wears a battered silk hat sideways on his head. His thumbs are stuck in his armpits and his palms outspread. Round his neck hangs a rosary of corks ending on his breast in a corkscrew cross. Releasing his thumbs, he invokes grace from on high with large wave gestures and proclaims with bloated pomp.

In both places, the common element is the ecclesiastic with a corkscrew instead of a cross. Joyce's satire magnifies in one of satire's recognized and familiar ways, achieving a baroque grandeur, 'bloated pomp'. By contrast, Fielding's parson is a shabby and small-scale figure, who had, just before the passage I quoted, been shown to disappear for safety into a hackney-coach while Wild was being pelted with brickbats, and who has none of the grotesque ostentation of the Joycean cardinal. The passage in *Ulysses* is a projection of the mind of Stephen. Fielding's passage is a detail in a sustained and externalized prose satire. And yet it is in Joyce, the novelist of the inner mind, that an exuberantly anticlerical satire dominates at this moment over any competing novelistic effects, whereas in Fielding attention is deflected, with a brilliant precision of effect, from the satirized parson to Wild. The satire becomes subordinated to, indeed put to the service of, a characterological consummation, a sustaining of 'character'.

The 'self' which is thus sustained is, as we have seen, in its way a petty one, just as the whole imagery of the passage, unlike that of Joyce's, lacks the external properties of 'bloated pomp'. And yet the assertion of 'self' becomes, in a way, heroic. The mock-praise and mock-aggrandizement are no longer simply cancelled into their ironic opposites. But if they have a basis in real admiration and aggrandizement, this is not simply the result of that customary mock-heroic process, in which heroic praise, although meant to be taken at an opposite valuation, nevertheless rubs off on its subject, bloating it to a kind of epic grandeur of its own. The heroic potential of mock-heroic here combines paradoxically with a stylized 'realism' of 'comic epic' in such a way that a genial characterology belonging more to the world of *Joseph Andrews* than to that of mock-heroic actually helps to swell, instead of reducing or normalizing, the stature of Wild. Not only is Wild's craven drunkenness transformed to an impressively genial charm in adversity, but his compulsive habits of pilfering, maintained to the end, turn into an 'apotheosis' of roguish courage and resourcefulness. While the parson cravenly hid, Wild withstood the 'shower of stones, &c.' with his customary control of his features, and performed a feat not only of great presence of mind, but of the most witty dexterity at the very moment of death, swinging 'out of this world' with a 'universal applause' which suddenly seems exactly right, a festive operatic finale.

The Wild whom we encounter at such points is a kind of *alter ego* to the helpless clown. The mock-heroic reduction of hero to clown is reversed: the clown has become a hero again. And he is, in a sense, the hero as schoolboy. As he performs his last prank with the parson's corkscrew, we sense the gallantry of the schoolboy hero and schoolboy joker, receiving his punishment unmoved, and showing to his fellows an undiminished and cunning defiance of authority, and a deadpan exhibitionism, even in final adversity. As in Auden and Isherwood, there is a note of admiration for the gallantry of the exploit, as well as moral reservation or satiric reduction. Fielding's presentation may or may not have been deliberate, with this end consciously in view. But it does at least markedly depart from the real-life sources, the pamphlets about the real Wild, which, as we saw, say that Wild died not bravely, but a weak and broken man, in a drunken stupor.

This cocky, defiant Wild appears most grandly in this final 'apotheosis'. But that is not in fact the first time we meet him. The oafish dandy who in the hanging chapter 'cocked his hat in defiance, and cries out greatly —"Zounds who's afraid?" ' (IV, xiv) is very similar to the swaggering bully who, at the end of II, iv, 'cocking his hat fiercely, . . . marched out of the room without making any excuse or any one daring to make the least demand', or who, alone in a 'shattered boat', with 'half-a-dozen biscuits' (II, x) for provision, defies death with a cocky mixture of insecurity, self-parading and real determination:

'who's afraid then, d—n me?' At which words he looked extremely fierce, but, recollecting that no one was present to see him, he relaxed a little the terror of his countenance, and, pausing a while, repeated the word, d—n! 'Suppose I should be d—ned at last,' cries he . . . 'd—n me I will think no longer about it. Let a pack of cowardly rascals be afraid of death, I dare look him in the face. But shall I stay and be starved? No, I will eat up the biscuits the French son of a whore bestowed on me, and then leap into the sea for drink, since the unconscionable dog hath not allowed me a single dram'. Having thus said, he proceeded immediately to put his purpose in execution, and as his resolution never failed him, he had no sooner despatched the small quantity of provision which his enemy had with no vast liberality presented him, than he cast himself headlong into the sea (II, xi).

The whole episode of Wild thrown out to sea in II, x–xiii, keeping himself alive with plucky (though at times frayed) determination, a sound instinct for survival (and a share of good fortune), has distinct overtones of the schoolboy adventure-story of a later age. His situation has, of course, come about in a way far removed from any schoolboy yarn. The French sea captain has thrown him off his ship after hearing of his attempts to rape Mrs Heartfree, and Wild's resentment at the captain for not having allowed him 'a single dram' belongs to maturer years. Even so, his accents carry a strong note of schoolboy bluster. And later readers might feel that some of Wild's drinking generally has overtones of the snifter in the dorm, while the French captain's biscuits might almost as easily have come from the tuck-shop.

Fielding's treatment of Wild's 'courage' is always ambiguous. Just as he failed in fact, perhaps despite his conscious intention, to conform to the conventional accounts of the real-life Wild's cravenly drunken end, showing instead a genuine if boozy defiance, so in other ironic assertions of his 'courage' the *fact* of bravery remains uncancelled by the purportedly upside-down irony. The comparison between Wild and Heartfree in their schooldays may not place either man in quite the light Fielding intended, and we may well feel that its irony becomes somewhat unfocused. But Wild momentarily appears with a certain plucky dash, while Heartfree emerges as the timorous and unadventurous fellow who has to pay another to take the whippings for his scrapes:

> whereas Wild was rapacious and intrepid, the other had always more regard for his skin than his money; Wild therefore had very generously compassionated this defect in his schoolfellow, and had brought him off from many scrapes, into most of which he had first drawn him, by taking the fault and whipping to himself (II, i).

As the irony develops, it soon becomes clear that Heartfree's scrapes, 'into most of which' Wild had in any case 'first drawn him', are part of Wild's carefully planned profiteering operations: 'He had always indeed been well paid on such occasions'. But if Wild's morals are as usual exposed, his 'courage' is not, and when Fielding says that by contrast with Wild, Heartfree 'had always more regard for his skin than his money', the very phrasing captures something of that schoolboy ethos by which Wild can be judged not unfavourably.[32]

This 'courage' is sometimes given a grotesque quality which goes beyond the boyish into a world of black comedy. The episode for which Wild was thrown to sea was an attempt to rape Mrs Heartfree in the middle of what looks like imminent shipwreck. Wild, instead of making for safety, devotes his whole energies to consummating the rape before death overtakes the passengers:

> Mrs. Heartfree, who had no other apprehensions from death but those of leaving her dear husband and children, fell on her knees to beseech the Almighty's favour, when Wild, with a contempt of danger truly great, took a resolution as worthy to be admired perhaps as any recorded of the bravest hero, ancient or modern; a resolution which plainly proved him to have these two qualifications so necessary to a hero, to be superior to all the energies of fear or pity. He saw the tyrant death ready to rescue from him his intended prey, which he had yet devoured only in imagination. He therefore swore he would prevent him, and immediately attacked the poor wretch, who was in the utmost agonies of despair, first with solicitation, and afterwards with force (II, x).

If this display of sexual commitment has its nasty side, there is about it a perversity so singleminded and blinding that it acquires a quality of (ludicrously fantasticated) innocence. Fielding tones down the nastiness by seeing to it that Mrs Heartfree is rescued in the next paragraph, and highlights the preposterousness by registering the captain's reaction[33] with a deadpan automatism: 'the captain rapped out a hearty oath, and asked Wild if he had no more Christianity in him than to ravish a woman in a storm?' Not only Wild's courage, but the headlong pedantry of lust which leads him to seek sexual satisfaction above survival, compel a weird admiration: a true Fielding villain like Blifil has neither courage nor lust, and it is interesting that Wild's prototype Alexander was said by Plutarch to be very moderate in his sexual appetites.[34] When Fielding speaks of 'a contempt of danger truly great ... as worthy to be admired perhaps as any recorded of the bravest hero', the routine sarcasms seem to sustain the mock-heroic onslaught by an emptily formulaic verbal gesture, while the *action* comically defies the irony, and enriches and even validates the literal terms of the mock-praise.

A continuous thread of heavy extravagance runs through the sexual comedy in *Jonathan Wild*. Robert H. Hopkins has recorded some good examples of this.[35] To these may be added more generally the ponderously hot-tempered 'dialogues matrimonial' (and some premarital ones too) between Wild and Laetitia in I, ix; III, viii; IV, xiv; and the outrageousness with which Laetitia continually plays him false. Their last meeting in prison in IV, xiv begins very tenderly, as Wild is about to die. But soon Laetitia is retailing her grievances with a pedantic perfectionism, and Wild, encumbered in his chains, is nevertheless furiously beating her out of the room:

> She then proceeded to a recapitulation of his faults in an exacter
> order, and with more perfect memory, than one would have
> imagined her capable of; and it is probable would have rehearsed
> a complete catalogue had not our hero's patience failed him, so
> that with the utmost fury and violence he caught her by the hair
> and kicked her as heartily as his chains would suffer him out of
> the room.

The ponderously graphic physicality of this recalls an earlier prison scene, where Wild discovers Fireblood in Laetitia's arms, and comes to blows with his rival, 'though with some difficulty, both being encumbered with the chains which they wore between their legs' (IV, x). The thought that Fireblood and Laetitia were also thus encumbered in their amorous caresses presents itself to the imagination.

These grotesqueries bring to mind nothing so much as the world of Jarry's Ubu. In *Ubu Enchaîné*, for example, the chain-encumbered hero fights, dances, quarrels with his wife, lords it over his fellow-convicts. The extravagant and extortionist tyrant of Jarry's zany dramas, who originated in his author's schooldays in a series of satires on one of the masters, and who combines black humour with a freewheeling quality of schoolboy romp, is in many other ways very close to Wild. Both men share a Rabelaisian extravagance which, though more unsettling and sombre than we normally find in Rabelais, is not without a strange, engaging geniality. Both are amalgams of gangsterhood and 'enfant terrible' prankishness, who do their evil with a sort of joyless exuber-ance, exploding into comic furies of abuse, peculating with a compul-sive voraciousness, continually engaging in frenetically quarrelsome dialogues with their wives, and being massively cuckolded and other-wise outwitted and outdone.[36] And even in these lowest humiliations, both achieve a certain preposterous sublimity. The terrible *dégringolade* suffered by Wild in II, iii is an example. After being miscellaneously outwitted and robbed by his partners in crime and in love, he makes his way to the chaste Laetitia to propose marriage to her with the gift of what he thinks are Heartfree's jewels, interrupts what the reader knows to be her faithless wantoning with Bagshot, and is cruelly rebuffed and berated by her when she finds that the jewels are counterfeits (substituted without Wild's knowledge by La Ruse). This has a progressive logic of humiliation so stylishly relentless that a kind of upside-down honour is derived from the sheer outrageousness. The episode is not just a *diminishing* of Wild but a proud climax of zany humour. And similarly, at the end of *Ubu Colonial*, when Mrs Ubu gives birth to a negro child, Ubu's shame at this visible proof of his cuckoldry is undercut by the Irish logic of his wife's explanation: 'Misérable! tu m'as trompé avec une négresse!'[37] In such passages, a certain magnificence of effrontery rubs off on the hero (Wild or Ubu), even though he is the victim of the effrontery rather than its perpetrator. Wild and Ubu become bathed in the poetry of it, all the more easily of course because their wives' bullying cheek is very like their own in other contexts.

Catulle Mendès wrote of *Ubu Roi*: 'un type nous est apparu, créé par l'imagination extravagante et brutale d'un homme presque enfant'.[38] The praise was tempered by distaste for the work's 'lowness', its elements of crude fairground farce: 'un bas guignol et une saleté de funambul-esquerie foraine'. Jarry himself insisted on this folk quality, prescribing fairground music and demanding a style of production deliberately reminiscent of the puppet-show.[39] (From the early days of schoolboy production onwards, some Ubu scripts were also given actual puppet-show productions). Ubu's oafish splendours belong to a mock-heroic universe (*Ubu Roi* is a well-signposted travesty of *Macbeth*, for example) transfigured by farce, like those of Jonathan Wild or, on occasion, of Pope's dunces. Pope and Fielding would feel gingerly about confessing this too openly. 'Farce and Epic get a jumbled race', Pope wrote, in disapproval of the mixture, on the contemporary stage, 'of Tragedy, Comedy, Farce and Epic' (*Dunciad*, I, 70, and note); and some of the farce ingredients in the mock-heroic *Dunciad* may be taken as deliberate mimicry of such scrambled styles.[40] Fielding would have endorsed this disapproval, although his juxtapositions of 'Farce and Epic' in *Jonathan Wild* were not primarily (or indeed to any significant extent) directed at this particular literary abuse. Moreover, even if the intention of his mock-heroic, like Pope's, was partly to aggrandize rather than reduce the enemy, the formulaic degradation which is radical to mock-heroic naturally accommodates farce in a way which straight heroic does not. In any case, Fielding's 'intentions', and his critical positions (notably those expressed in the Preface to *Joseph Andrews*), are often more cautious or more orthodox, and especially more *simple*, than his novelis-tic practice, which is very bold in its mixing of incongruous tones. In the mock-heroic introduction of Sophia in *Tom Jones*, IV, ii, verbal horseplay and coarse humour mingle not only with a highly emotional rhetoric but with a very personal tenderness, and with accents of uppish good-breeding. Fielding's readiness to juxtapose the farcical not only with heroic deflations, but with some of his most serious and some of his most sentimental passages, is not always adequately recognized.

One of Fielding's most insistent orthodoxies was that black villainy could not be the subject of comedy. In the Preface to *Joseph Andrews* he restates an Aristotelian notion that it is not 'villainy' or grave viciousness, but lesser frailties, which are the true domains of the Ridiculous. Only to a very mistaken notion of the Ridiculous, he says, 'can we attribute the many attempts to ridicule the blackest villainies, and, what is yet worse, the most dreadful calamities[.] What could exceed the absurdity of an author, who should write *the Comedy of Nero, with the merry Incident of ripping his Mother's Belly?*' Fielding was fascinated by this last example, and, as Battestin notes, returned to it in the *Jacobite's Journal*, 26 March 1748, when he declared 'his intention to abandon ridicule as a weapon against the Jacobites who were trying to overthrow the government: "To consider such Attempts as these in a ludicrous Light, would be as absurd as the Conceit of a Fellow in *Bartholomew-Fair*, who exhibited the comical Humours of *Nero* ripping up his Mother's

Belly . . ." '.[41] In both places, the example erupts with a queer force, a force and a fascination which convey not only that there is something funny in imagining this sort of thing to be funny, but also that the comedy of Nero ripping up his mother's belly is a tempting (though officially forbidden) area of imaginative exploration. We have already seen that he was exercised, more or less genially, by the notion of Bartholomew Fair farces on heroic, including bloody, subjects, like 'Anna Bullen', that 'high princess in Drollic story' (ii, iii). In *True Patriot*, No. 16, 11–18 February 1746, he praised the use of 'Punchinello in a Puppet-shew' to ridicule Greatness and lamented the recent decline in such entertainments; and he may well at a later time have had a hand at heroic farce in his own puppet theatre in Panton Street.[42] Moreover, again and again, Fielding returned in his critical writings, both early and late, to the more sensational Roman emperors, Caligula, Nero, Domitian, and was often on these occasions concerned with the paradoxes which challenge the tidy-minded divisions of the comic and tragic. Thus, in *Covent-Garden Journal*, No. 55, he wrote:[43]

> By the Manner of exerting itself likewise a Humour becomes ridiculous. By this Means chiefly the Tragic Humour differs from the Comic; it is the same Ambition which raises our Horror in Macbeth, and our Laughter at the drunken Sailors in the Tempest; the same Avarice which causes the dreadful Incidents in the Fatal Curiosity of Lillo, and in the Miser of Moliere; the same Jealousy which forms an Othello, or a Suspicious Husband. No Passion or Humour of the Mind is absolutely either Tragic or Comic in itself. Nero had the Art of making Vanity the Object of Horror, and Domitian, in one Instance, at least, made Cruelty ridiculous.

The reference to Nero is a challenge to the principle of the Preface to *Joseph Andrews* that vanity and hypocrisy, rather than graver villainies like cruelty, are 'the only source of the true Ridiculous'. Here Vanity becomes 'the Object of Horror', not ridicule, while Domitian's cruelty could become ridiculous. The reference is to Domitian's hobby of catching flies and stabbing 'them with a keenly-sharpened stylus',[44] which, in an earlier paper, No. 24, Fielding ridiculed as a virtuoso silliness in the same class as those other forms of duncery, laboriously minute scholarly annotation, abstruse and trivial researches, butterfly-collecting and the rest.[45] There Tiberius is mocked as a pedantic scholiast, and Nero for the obsessive musical hobby which he practised 'with such unwearied Industry on the Stage, that several Persons counterfeited Death, in order to be carried out of the Theatre from hearing him'.[46] If this shows Nero's 'Vanity' back in its merely 'ridiculous' element, the mental association with Nero's most famous musical exploit, recorded a few pages later in Suetonius (from whom Fielding drew many of these examples), is very close. Having set fire to Rome on a mere conversational whim, he viewed 'the conflagration from the tower of Maecenas and exulting, as he said, in "the beauty of the flames", he sang the whole of the "Sack of Ilium", in his regular stage costume'.[47]

This episode is a vivid example of a hideous mock-heroic farce enacted on the stage of history, literally to the tune of the Iliadic story.[48] The extreme wilfulness, the indulgence of cruel whims and bloody practical jokes, which are ascribed to several Roman emperors in the pages of Suetonius not only fascinated Fielding, but led him to explore the connection between the comic mischief of the prankster, and the 'tragical Farces' brought about by these and other emperors, as well as by Alexander the Great. In *Covent-Garden Journal*, No. 19, he discusses 'practical Humour', which is 'produced by doing little jocose Mischiefs to others'. Fielding notes the relation of such jests to that 'tragical Humour' which 'consists in afflicting Men with the greatest and most serious Evils; in a Word, in ruining, destroying, and tormenting Mankind'.[49] The passage continues, in terms very pertinent to the concerns of *Jonathan Wild*:[50]

As the Species of practical Humour, just before spoken of, are produced by doing little jocose Mischiefs to others, this tragical Humour consists in afflicting Men with the greatest and most serious Evils; in a Word, in ruining, destroying, and tormenting Mankind.

Histories abound with Examples of Men who have very eminently possessed this Kind of Humour. There hath scarce existed indeed a single Tyrant or Conqueror upon Earth, who, tho' otherwise perhaps extremely dull, was not a great Master this Way. Alexander the Great was much gifted with this Quality, of which we have many Instances in the Accounts of his Asiatic Expedition. His burning the City of Persepolis in particular, was a Performance of most exquisite Humour.

What were the Reigns of Caligula and Claudius, of Nero and Domitian, of Commodus, Caracalla, Heliogabalus, and all those Imperial Bucks or Bloods of Rome, but great tragical Farces in which one Half of Mankind was with much Humour put to Death and Tortures, for the Diversion of the other half.

'Tragical Farces': Swift, as we saw, called life a 'ridiculous tragedy, which is the worst kind of composition'.[51] In a passage like this, Fielding expresses an almost Swiftian sense of the sheer indecorum of reality, of life's almost hysterical refusal to conform to the tidy arrangements of art and of artistic prescription. And the irony of 'one Half of Mankind' being 'with much Humour put to Death and Tortures, for the Diversion of the other Half' may be compared with Gulliver's account to the Houyhnhnm of human warfare, where huge carnage takes place 'to the great Diversion of all the Spectators'.[52]

This is an area of feeling which Fielding fitfully explores in *Jonathan Wild*, although his irony is there cruder and more awkward, and although he is not often at this earlier stage of his writing career given to expressing the more 'absurd' painfulness characteristic of parts of *Amelia* or of the passage in the *Covent-Garden Journal*. The latter's reference to Alexander and the havoc wrought by the Roman conquerors clearly links up with the rasping irony of this reflection in *Jonathan Wild*, I, xiv, where the narrator says:

> when I behold one great man starving with hunger and freezing with cold, in the midst of fifty thousand who are suffering the same evils for his diversion; when I see another, whose own mind is a more abject slave to his own greatness, and is more tortured and racked by it than those of all his vassals; lastly, when I consider whole nations rooted out only to bring tears into the eyes of a great man, not, indeed, because he hath extirpated so many, but because he had no more nations to extirpate, then truly I am almost inclined to wish that nature had spared us this her MASTERPIECE, and that no GREAT MAN had ever been born into the world.

The anger is partly Swiftian. The great man who wept is Alexander,[53] and Wild later refers to the story again, in a spirit of emulation: 'I ought rather to weep with Alexander that I have ruined no more than to regret the little I have done' (IV, iv).[54] Fielding's irony is here ponderous, lacking the dimension of cruel play, but the episode is one which Swift treated with a tart parodic playfulness in 'A Tritical Essay upon the Faculties of the Mind': 'I have read in a certain Author, that *Alexander* wept because he had no more Worlds to conquer' (Alexander was, incidentally, a named example of the conqueror-madman in the Digression on Madness).[55] And the theme is one which Fielding could manipulate in such a way as to release a degree of sympathy for Alexander. In Fielding's 'Dialogue between Alexander the Great and

Diogenes the Cynic' (published, like *Jonathan Wild*, in the *Miscellanies*), Diogenes taunts Alexander with his bloody conquests and with the doomed insatiability of his desires. Alexander then tricks Diogenes by offering to avenge Diogenes's grievances against Athens and to give him the pleasure of beholding the city in flames. The philosopher gleefully accepts the offer, and even asks that Corinth and Lacedaemon be thrown in for good measure, thus showing his philosophic detachment for what it is.[56] Fielding was no admirer of Alexander, but this reversal, in which he gets the better of Diogenes, is not only a notable moral victory for Alexander in itself, but all the more so for being, as Henry Knight Miller has pointed out, a departure from conventional renderings of the dialogue between the two men.[57]

When Fielding, in *Covent-Garden Journal*, No. 19, discussed the 'tragical Humour' of despots as a species of practical joke, he called Alexander's 'burning the City of Persepolis in particular ... a Performance of most exquisite Humour'. The bitterness of his irony will not be missed. But it is useful also to remember that such deeds, and the whole despotic syndrome of insatiability with which Fielding is so obsessively concerned in *Jonathan Wild*, are a major ingredient of black comedy in the world of Ubu. Again and again, with loutish glee, Ubu projects or perpetrates exterminations, boasts that 'De tous côtés on ne voit que des maisons brûlées et des gens pliant sous le poids de nos phynances', and proclaims: 'Cornegidouille! nous n'aurons point tout démoli si nous ne démolissons même les ruines!'[58] If the ironies about brutal conquest in *Jonathan Wild* do not always become flecked, as in Ubu's case, with the amoral freedoms of black humour, Fielding is not insensitive to the humour which attaches to the smaller cruelties of Wild and his henchmen. When Wild toys with the idea of getting rid of Heartfree by murdering him, he feels that Fireblood would gladly do the job, 'for that youth had, at their last interview, sworn, D—n his eyes, he thought there was no better pastime than blowing a man's brains out' (III, iv). The laughability of this erupts beyond all moral outrage, the loutish sadism being so naïvely spontaneous and so grossly automatic that its sheer self-realization is more vivid to us than its moral implications. The comedy is heightened by Fielding's characteristic manner of reporting Fireblood's speech, giving the full colloquial text in a brisk form of *oratio obliqua* which ostensibly suggests rapid summary rather than circumstantial recording.[59] The explosive and highly piquant little drama of expression thus resolves itself incongruously into a bare statement of essentials, as though we were to take for granted both the idiom and the sentiments as commonplace, typical. For the stylistic procedure also contributes a note of deadpan mechanism, of taking shocking or surprising things as habitual, which resembles the passage in II, x where the sea-captain 'rapped out a hearty oath, and asked Wild if he had no more Christianity in him than to ravish a woman in a storm?'

It may be that part of the comic disengagement from moral sanctions in such passages is due to the fact that, as Wild is aware (IV, iv) and as we are authorially reminded in IV, xv and elsewhere, Wild's operations, and even Walpole's, were on a somewhat smaller scale than those of Alexander and his like. But even the comic passages we have just examined deal with attitudes and situations which, in the cold light of day, are extremely vicious. And Wild's persistent emulation of Alexander, Caesar, and the rest, and the work's continual assertion of *moral* equivalence between him and the conquerors, so that, in the end, differences of scale are said to cease to matter, and 'we may challenge not only the truth of history, but almost the latitude of fiction' to equal the magnitude of Wild's 'glory' (IV, xv), are very emphatic. This type of equivalence, moreover, was commonplace, and would be quickly taken for granted. It is a theme of the *Beggar's Opera* and many lesser works. Macheath, reproved for his crimes in Gay's *Polly*, III, xi, replies '*Alexander* the Great was more successful. That's all', and in *Champion*, 4 March 1740, in a discussion which mentions the historical Jonathan Wild and the fact that he enjoyed a powerful reputation at one time, Fielding himself remarked: 'Had Alexander been entirely defeated in his first battle in Asia, he would have been called only a robber by posterity'.[60]

It is not only in late writings like the *Covent-Garden Journal* that Fielding explored the connection between practical jokes or grotesque play and the large-scale villainy of Alexander, of Roman emperors, and of modern rulers. In the *Champion* for 22 April 1740, close to the time and to the idiom of *Jonathan Wild*, he compared politics to pantomime, instancing as supreme examples of 'political pantomime' some episodes from Suetonius's life of Caligula:[61]

This hero (says my author) having sent a few of his guards over the Rhine, where they were to conceal themselves, ordered an alarm to be brought to him after dinner, of the enemy's approach in vast numbers. Upon which he presently hastened with his chief officers, and a party of the Pretorian horse into the next wood, whence he returned with the sham trophies of a victory, upbraiding the cowardice of those who stayed behind, and crowning the companions and partakers of his victory with chaplets of a new name and species. Another time, having privately sent forth some of his hostages, he arose hastily from his supper and brought them back in chains, boasting of his pantomime adventure in the most extravagant manner, desiring those who told him that all the troops were returned from the expedition, to sit down in their armour, and ridiculously repeating to them a celebrated verse of Virgil; in which Aeneas encourages his followers to persevere in encountering all dangers and toils in hopes of their future happiness; inveighing bitterly at the same time against the Senate, and those Romans who were absent, and enjoyed the pleasures of Rome, whilst Caesar exposed himself to such imminent dangers. Lastly, he drew out his army on the sea-shore, and disposed every thing as for a battle, no one knowing or even guessing what he intended, when suddenly he ordered all the soldiers to fill their helmets with cockles, which he called the spoils of the ocean, worthy of a place in the Roman temples. Here, after he had built a tower as a monument of his victory, the remains of which are still extant, according to Pitiscus, called by the English the Old Man, he rewarded his soldiers with one hundred *denarii* per man; and, not contented yet with all this pageantry, he writ to Rome to demand a triumph.

Caligula's 'political pantomime' bears on *Jonathan Wild* in many ways. In a context of familiar parallels between farce and government, and Cibber and Walpole, it becomes an allegory for Walpole himself, who, Fielding adds a few lines later, 'hath played a very comical part, which, though theatrical, hath been acted on a much larger stage than Drury Lane'. The essay goes on to jeer at Cibber's *Apology*, and its tyrannical, i.e. illiterate, treatment of the English language ('for surely he must be absolute master of that whose laws he can trample under feet, and which he can use as he pleases'),[62] torturing words to meanings which they do not have, or even to contrary meanings. Fielding concludes with an image of schoolboy castigation:[63]

> This spirit of absolute power is generally whipt out of boys at school, and I could heartily wish our adept had been in the way of such castigation. And perhaps it is on this account that one of our poets says 'That he who never felt birch, should never wear bays,' *i.e.* That no man should be trusted with a pen who will take this method to show us his great command of words.

This punning pursuit of the Caligula-Walpole-Cibber analogy into the world of the schoolroom, so that tyrants are like masters of language who have not been whipped out of their illiteracy at school, is very close in atmosphere to *Jonathan Wild*. Cibber the illiterate man of letters becomes a lout very much in the style of the schoolboy Wild, whose illiteracy does not preclude a somewhat specialized taste for heroic poems (in translation), any more than Cibber's disqualifies him for the laureateship. And Caligula the prankster, who garnishes his hoaxes with quotations from Virgil, and who, as we learn a few paragraphs later in Suetonius (ch. LII), is fond of wearing the breastplate of Alexander the Great, has likenesses with Wild the connoisseur of Homeric and Virgilian roguery and admirer of Alexander, as well as with the grimmer Nero, who sings 'The Sack of Troy' while Rome is burning.

Fielding has not in this passage listed any of Caligula's gorier exploits (of which Suetonius offers a wide choice). Caligula's 'pantomimes' here stop well short of *'the Comedy of Nero . . . ripping up his Mother's Belly'*. (Elsewhere, as in *Tom Jones* VIII, i, Caligula and Nero are interchangeable as types of exceptional wickedness.) The 'pantomimes' were also something less than 'practical Jests' in a pure state,[64] in that, like the deceptions of Walpole (or of Wild), they were politically motivated, and they had for Fielding the Opposition pamphleteer a direct bearing on the state of England: 'Ridiculous as this parade now appears, it is probable not a few of the more ignorant Romans were imposed on by it, and looked on Caligula as a real conqueror; a circumstance, which, if we consider the several tricks played since by ministers and statesmen, will not appear so strange and incredible'.[65] But the examples are 'strange and incredible' by any standards. Caligula's 'tricks' are far in excess of any soberly calculated propaganda objectives, and enter a world of extravagant play. The order to his 'soldiers to fill their helmets with cockles, which he called the spoils of the ocean, worthy of a place in the Roman temples' is the sort of episode in Suetonius which, as it implies a grandiose fantasy of battle with the sea itself, looks forward to the Caligula of Camus's play,[66] who wants the moon because to attain the impossible is the only fit challenge to the order of things. Suetonius (ch. XXII) had presented the moon-longings as a crazed mixture of self-deification and sexual fantasy, but they turn in Camus to a pursuit of 'liberté', of an authenticity which would transcend the 'mensonges', the accommodations, the cheap practicalities of ordinary political life.[67]

Camus's *Caligula* shows in a pure, extreme form certain elements to which Fielding's imagination was, tentatively and unconsciously, drawn. Like the *Beggar's Opera* and *Jonathan Wild*, it establishes the analogy between government and robbery: 'Gouverner, c'est voler, tout le monde sait ça. Mais il y a la manière. Pour moi, je volerai franchement' (I, viii). Executions and extortion are the logical consequences of a system in which money, the values of the Treasury, are paramount: 'Si le Trésor a de l'importance, alors la vie humaine n'en a pas' (I, viii). The difference is that Camus's hero, unlike those of Gay or Fielding, plays the system frankly, and for truth rather than gain: 'c'est que tout, autour de moi, est mensonge, et moi, je veux qu'on vive dans la vérité' (I, iv).[68] The analogy between government and puppet-show occurs in Camus, as in Fielding and in Jarry: an important stage-direction in Act II, Scene v suggests that all the actors except Caligula and his wife Caesonia might perform 'comme des marionettes'. But the implication of this in Camus is to highlight the untrammelled and in its way noble freedom of Caligula, whereas Fielding's point in both *Jonathan Wild* and the *Champion* essay is to expose the puppet-master Walpole as a mean back-stage operator, while Jarry's wish that his actors should resemble puppets includes Ubu himself, and he notes that in puppet-shows puppets command armies.[69]

Caligula's 'tragic Farces', in Camus as in Fielding's *Champion* and *Covent-Garden Journal* discussions, show a scrambling of cherished categories, a confusion of the ridiculous and the extravagantly monstrous or horrible. Camus's hero projects this deliberately, as an autocratic aesthete of the arrangements of life: 'Je veux mêler le ciel à la mer, confondre laideur et beauté, faire jaillir le rire de la souffrance' (I, xi). There is a pride in this which his author endorses, to the extent that it is superior to (and also, it is claimed, ultimately less bloody or expensive than) the activities of a conventional despot, or 'tyran raisonnable' (III, ii). His delight in being hated has a cool arrogance whose splendours differ equally from those of Wild's oafish triumph on the scaffold, and from the flat alienation of Meursault in *l'Etranger*, desiring that at *his* execution there should be cries of hate so that he might feel less lonely.

Although there are reservations in the play (Caligula fails to get the moon, and recognises in the end that 'Ma liberté n'est pas la bonne' IV, xiv), Camus's hero is invested with a powerful glamour, a glamour unthinkable in the Caligula-Walpole of the *Champion* as in the gangster Walpole of *Jonathan Wild*. Camus has written that Caligula erred in denying mankind. 'On ne peut tout détruire sans se détruire soi-même'.[70] But this was said much later. Certainly, an association with Nazism may be part of the atmosphere of the play,[71] but this is not allowed to come into the open, and does not, in the play, lead to radical repudiation. There is evidence of a certain self-identification between Camus and Caligula, and even of a tendency on Camus's part to present Caligula more favourably than in Suetonius's portrait.[72] Any anti-Nazi critique which may be buried in the play is likelier to consist not of conscious repudiation of Caligula, but in an unconscious exorcism of romanticized attitudes to power and the absolute in Camus himself,[73] as Auden later claimed that *The Orators* might have been an unconscious attempt to exorcize 'certain tendencies in myself by allowing them to run riot in phantasy'.[74] In the overt drama of the play itself, Caligula emerges as a Promethean rebel, who lives out in his own way his protest at the fact that 'Les hommes meurent et ils ne sont pas heureux' (I, iv); who performs a daring quest for the impossible 'aux limites du monde, aux confins de moi-même' (IV, xiv), a quest to which the notebooks of the time show Camus himself to be drawn;[75] and whose murderous satisfactions are fraught with a magnificent sterility ('un bonheur stérile et magnifique' IV, xiii) which might be envied by many Romantic Agonists.

This sterility gives the play an ice-cold brilliance which is far removed from Fielding, or from Jarry, or, for that matter, from its principal source, Suetonius. The mind-boggling cruelties of Caligula are ironed out not only by the relentlessly precise elegance of Camus's dialectic, but also by their self-conscious *ordering* quality as artistic manipulations. In one place his 'méchanceté désintéressée' is called a 'lyrisme inhumain' (II, ii), and in another his cruelties and blasphemies are described by himself as 'art dramatique': 'L'erreur de tous ces hommes, c'est de ne pas croire assez au théâtre. Ils sauraient sans cela qu'il est permis à tout homme de jouer les tragédies célestes et de devenir dieu. Il suffit de se durcir le coeur' (III, ii). The interpenetration of art and life has none of the buoyancy which we find in Ubu (or, on a more comfortably comic plane, in *Felix Krull*), because life is somehow denied all its ragged edges. This is true in spite of the convulsive enormity of Caligula's doings, and in spite of assertions of his vitality, as when, dying of stab-wounds, he cries 'Je suis encore vivant!' as the curtain drops.[76]

Camus has clearly been excited, as Fielding's imagination was excited, by the immense wilfulness, the monstrous caprice and the power to act upon this caprice, which Suetonius's lives of the Roman emperors record. He has taken this wilfulness to its extreme, systematized it, turned it into a philosophical posture. In doing so, he has paradoxically reduced, rather than heightened, the quality of capriciousness. The essential element has been tamed to a discipline foreign to its nature—a discipline of caprice and negation, but still a discipline. It lacks the oath-ridden, tearaway explosiveness with which Ubu 'déchire les gens parce qu'il lui plaît ainsi et prie les soldats russes de ne point tirer devers lui, parce qu'il ne lui plaît pas'.[77] One might say that Camus's play achieves all the amorality required for 'black humour', but none of the humour. Yet that too would be inexact. Camus's reversal of morality creates an upsidedown morality even more systematic, certainly more tightly elaborated, than anything it replaces. Caligula's gratuitous acts are done, finally, more for the sake of the gratuitousness than for the whim. Ubu is immoral, and our delight in him transcends morality, because he acts not in reverse of morality but beyond it, for gain or self-preservation or 'parce qu'il lui plaît', but never according to an intellectualized conception of himself or the world.

Suetonius, Camus's source and Fielding's, made no bones about disapproving of Caligula's doings. But he recorded the whims and the practical jokes with a factuality which claimed no pattern, and left the messy vitality of the deeds to speak for themselves. In chapter XXVII, for example, we read that Caligula 'had the manager of his gladiatorial shows and beast-baitings beaten with chains in his presence for several successive days, and would not kill him until he was disgusted at the stench of his putrefied brain'. Suetonius leaves the hideous painfulness unimpaired, but the passage erupts with a cruel vitality, a sick exuberance, that we do not find in Camus ('Caligula a horreur du désordre', says Caesonia in the play, II, iv). Although the shockingness of Suetonius's account is pretty joyless, it is closer in some ways to the comedy of Ubu's *décervelages*, where exuberance turns to a kind of joy, beyond moral sanctions, as the mangled brains splash about to a merry tune.[78]

The passage in Suetonius continues with two further examples which have about them a wild schoolmasterly horror: 'He burned a writer of Atellan farces alive in the middle of the arena of the amphitheatre, because of a humorous line of double meaning. When a Roman knight on being thrown to the wild beasts loudly protested his innocence, he took him out, cut out his tongue, and put him back again.' In the first episode, the immoralist capriciously turns puritan. In both, the boyish wilfulness translates itself, as in Ubu, to the punitive whim of the mad, autocratic pedagogue. Camus's Caligula is also conscious of a schoolmasterly role. After he has outlined in I, viii his policy of execution and extortion, and the philosophy behind it, Caesonia asks him in I, ix if 'C'est une plaisanterie', and he replies 'C'est de la pédagogie'. But the reference is more to his performance as an expositor of his system, than to any capricious transition from boyish 'plaisanterie' to schoolmasterly bossiness, and if such transitions, including some very sudden ones, do exist in the play they remain themselves part of the system, of Caligula's rigorous logic of wilfulness. Even their unpredictabilities remain systematic.

Fielding too was, consciously or otherwise, exercised by the relationship between the schoolboy tease and the punishing schoolmaster, and in the sometimes surprising transitions that (as in Suetonius's passage) can take place from one to the other. After listing, in *Covent-Garden Journal*, No. 19, several imperial perpetrators of 'tragical Farces' (Alexander burning Persepolis, Caligula, Claudius, Nero and the other 'Imperial Bucks or Bloods of Rome'), he concludes with the example which of all others pleases him most. It is the well-known story of the tyrant Phalaris, 'a great Lover of the tragical Humour', to please whom Perillus had invented a new entertainment. Persons would be put in the belly of a brazen bull, which would then be heated, so that the cries of the person being roasted within would sound like the roaring of a real bull: 'Phalaris highly approved the Project; but being himself a Man of great Humour, he was willing to add somewhat of his own to the Joke. He therefore chose Perillus, the Inventor, for the Person on whom the Experiment was first to be tried, and accordingly shut him up and roasted him in his own Bull.'[79] It is characteristic of Fielding that a list of grim horrors should settle in the end on one which has the reassuring lineaments of a parable where right triumphs, and the essay ends with some admonitions against the metaphorical 'roasting' of men's characters and reputations. The old story might almost qualify for a place in Swift's School of Political Projectors, except for the well-plotted rightness of the outcome (where right has the upper hand in any project in Swift's Academy, there is a suggestion either of zany fortuitousness, or of the hopeless impracticability of any desirable or deserved outcome in a bad world). If the 'tragical Farces' of emperors are a monstrous version of such schoolboy jests as 'Kicks on the Backside, pulling away your Chair',[80] and if cruel boyish whims turn into a kind of schoolmasterly despotism, Fielding is more concerned finally with endorsing the schoolmaster, rather than (as in Ubu) his schoolboy victim and *alter ego*.[81] In this, he is with Swift. And along with a morality of fitting outcomes (less frequent in Swift only because Swift is more pessimistic), there is a dimension of playful pleasure in the cruel horror with which the fitting outcome is achieved in the anecdote about Phalaris.

It is within some such framework of stern moral disapproval that play is released, and the same may be said of the glimpse we get of the '*merry Incident*' of Nero '*ripping up his Mother's Belly*', or of Fireblood swearing 'D—n his eyes, . . . there was no better pastime than blowing a man's brains out', or of Wild heroically attempting to rape a woman in a storm. We are never in any doubt of Fielding's disapproval, even where this is transcended by comedy, as we are sometimes in doubt of Swift's, when the rightness of flaying whores, dismembering beaux, or cannibalizing Irish girls who buy English luxuries comes up for examination. Swift was a sterner moralist than Fielding, but his capacity for allowing certain extravagant cruelties of imagination to go beyond satire and beyond morality was correspondingly more intense. Such effects in Swift tend to be starkly polarized, the punitive moralist and the black humorist coming together as opposites come together at their extremes, in moments of particular intensity. In Fielding, by contrast, the moralist and the black humourist modulate or shade into one another, disapproval being coloured (as in the case of Wild) by an element of genial tolerance, or of delight in the compulsive doings of the clownish criminal and in the quirkiness of the situations he creates for himself. Hence, as seldom in Swift, geniality is frequently the mode of emancipation from moral blame. This geniality, on a more grotesque and unbuttoned scale, also exists in the world of Ubu. But this differs from both Fielding and Swift in the degree of its emancipation from moral values, in the extent to which ideas of good and evil become irrelevant to its exuberant, anarchic grossness. Ubu's decervelations resemble the mad surgeries which have been a theme in the literature of satire and protest from Swift to Burroughs. The difference is that in Jarry they are not mainly satire or protest.

This is not to say that Jarry's work lacks an understanding of the horror of Ubu's doings. André Breton, including him in his anthology of black humour, notes that Ubu is prophetic of both fascism and Stalinism.[82] Jarry himself had said that Ubu was 'un être ignoble', adding however that in this 'il nous ressemble (par en bas) à tous', and identifying himself with Ubu openly.[83] This sense of a universal community of basic (and base) instincts distinguishes Jarry from Fielding, whose superior detachment from Wild proclaims, among other things, that the author and all decent readers are a fundamentally different kind of human being. Swift, on the other hand, knew that all of us had an 'être ignoble' within us, and would certainly recognize a shared identity, but unlike Jarry would feel obliged to protest and to set up moral defences against it. If Fielding and Jarry share a quality of genial tolerance absent in Swift, it is for opposite reasons: because Fielding lacked, and was therefore untroubled by, any deep sense of the universal or archetypal nature of his gangster-tyrant, while Jarry had this sense, like

Swift, but *accepted it* without Swift's passionate recalcitrance. Jarry's satiric understanding moves 'beyond satire'[84] through a coarse geniality which comes from a sense of community, of participation, of released instincts, whereas Swift, as we saw, has no geniality at all. Ubu is not only an 'être ignoble', but an 'enfant terrible' and (so far as is possible within human limits) 'anarchiste parfait':[85] if Swift had no doubt of the radical human tendency to anarchy, or of the intimate relation between anarchy and tyranny, he felt that the tendency must be unremittingly held back, rather than allowed, even in imagination, to attain its 'perfection' (except through a hostile exposure).

Although Fielding said in the Preface to *Joseph Andrews* that 'blackest villainies' and the 'true Ridiculous' were incompatible, he had written a few years before with an opposite emphasis. A critic in the *Daily Gazetteer* for 7 May 1737, attacking Fielding's political plays, suggested among other things that Fielding's 'Wit and Humour' in *Pasquin* had made light of great evils, a practice comparable with that of the *Beggar's Opera*, 'which exposed with *Wit*, what ought to be punished with *Rigour*', and which, by turning vicious characters 'into *Heroes* and *Heroines*', had had a corrupting effect. Fielding replied in *Common Sense* for 21 May:[86]

> you seem to think, Sir, that to ridicule Vice, is, to serve its Cause.
> And you mention the late ingenious Mr. *Gay*, who, you say, in
> his *Beggars Opera* hath made Heroes and Heroines of Highwaymen
> and Whores. Are then Impudence, Boldness, Robbery, and picking
> Pockets the Characteristicks of a Hero? Indeed, Sir, we do not
> always approve what we laugh at. So far from it, Mr. *Hobbes* will
> tell you that Laughter is a Sign of Contempt. And by raising such
> a Laugh as this against Vice, *Horace* assures us we give a sorer
> Wound, than it receives from all the Abhorrence which can be
> produced by the gravest and bitterest Satire. You will not hardly,
> I believe, persuade us, how much soever you may desire it, that
> it is the Mark of a great Character to be laughed at by a whole
> Kingdom.

The statement antedates *Jonathan Wild*, but the 'great Character' is of course the same: Walpole. And the passage has a further bearing on *Jonathan Wild* by the fact that a few sentences later Fielding says 'nothing can be more Burlesque than Greatness in mean Hands', instancing the actor Penkethman making a 'ridiculous . . . Figure' in a burlesque treatment of Alexander the Great.[87]

The letter to *Common Sense*, however, is a denial of geniality. The special problem, and a richness, of *Jonathan Wild* is that, as we saw, it does make its hero amiable, although not in such a way as to be likely to encourage imitation of his behaviour. In the latter point, it differs from the *Beggar's Opera* in not being open to the kind of charge made in the *Daily Gazetteer*. Fielding's defence of Gay's opera greatly exaggerates its severity. Macheath and his friends *are* glamourized: they have an easy charm and gaiety, success with women, and a genial gangster camaraderie which, with all due reservations, is not without its liberality and sense of honour. They are aristocrats of the underworld, who at a certain level combine the virtues of the noble and the beggarman, as against the Peachums and the Lockits, mean merchant fumblers in a greasy till.

Wild is not charming in this way. He is a brutal oaf, more like Peachum (another incarnation of Walpole). When Fielding asks 'Are then Impudence, Boldness, Robbery, and picking Pockets the Characteristicks of a Hero?', our answer is likely to be, in Macheath's case, yes: the *Daily Gazetteer* was right to the very considerable extent that Macheath is presented favourably, so that if we laugh, it is with him rather than at him. Fielding seems wrong to meet the *Daily Gazetteer* on its own terms on this point. His somewhat rhetorical passage is irrelevant (rather than untrue) to Gay's protagonist, but might seem appropriate in a defence of the later *Jonathan Wild*, where touches of geniality defy a much more ponderous armature of overtly hostile derision. The specific idiom of Fielding's harangue also applies better to a truly mock-heroic world, like that of the *Dunciad* or *Jonathan Wild*, where 'hero' means something more specific than ' "good" protagonist', and where Impudence, Boldness and the rest are systematic inversions of true heroic qualities as found in epic poems. Warburton made Ricardus Aristarchus say that the heroes of mock-heroic poems (or *'little Epics'*) like the *Dunciad* are related by analogy to those of true or 'greater' epics:[88]

> it is not every Knave, nor (let me add) Fool, that is a fit subject
> for a Dunciad. There must still exist some Analogy, if not
> Resemblance of Qualities, between the Heroes of the two Poems;
> and this in order to admit what Neoteric critics call the *Parody*,
> one of the liveliest graces of the little Epic. Thus it being agreed
> that the constituent qualities of the greater Epic Hero, are *Wisdom*,
> *Bravery*, and *Love*, from whence springeth *heroic Virtue*; it followeth
> that those of the lesser Epic Hero, should be *Vanity*, *Impudence*,

and *Debauchery*, from which happy assemblage resulteth *heroic Dulness*, the never-dying subject of this our Poem . . .

. . . as from Wisdom, Bravery, and Love, ariseth *Magnanimity*, the object of *Admiration*, which is the aim of the greater Epic; so from Vanity, Impudence, and Debauchery, springeth *Buffoonry*, the source of *Ridicule*, that 'laughing ornament' . . . of the little Epic.

Wild unites these qualities of the Dunciadic hero with the habits of robbery and pickpocketing ascribed by both Fielding and the *Daily Gazetteer* to the protagonists of Gay's opera. In *Jonathan Wild* Fielding probably carried even further than Pope the formulaic inversion of values called for by the mock-heroic scheme, and, when writing about the work in the Preface to the *Miscellanies*, made an important analogy between burlesque and the *real-life* wickedness of bad 'great' persons, an analogy which goes beyond the simple formulaic procedure of calling the good bad and the bad good or great. After calling 'the great and good . . . the true sublime in human nature . . . the Iliad of Nature' he proceeds to 'that greatness which is totally devoid of goodness', saying that it resembles in the domain of Nature what the 'false sublime' is in the domain of poetry: i.e. *in itself* a kind of *Dunciad* rather than an *Iliad*. He calls it also a 'bombast greatness', which is 'by the ignorant and ill-judging vulgar, often mistaken for solid wit and eloquence'.[89]

Evil 'greatness' itself becomes a kind of farce or (as Ricardus Aristarchus says) '*Buffoonry*', a farce at which one does not laugh in its real-life enactments, but farce nonetheless, and closely related to a mock-heroic which, in art, would readily turn to 'ridiculous' buffoonery. Fielding was not the first to talk of vice as a 'false sublime'. Young, for example, had used the phrase in the last satire of the *Love of Fame* (VII, 174) to describe an ambitiousness devoid of virtue, and the concept is not unconnected with a larger readiness (whether specifically Shaftesburian or not) to blend the order of morality with the order of art. Young's poem, which was written in praise of Walpole and dedicated to him, had not used the word 'bombast', with its comic overtones, or the glimpse of strutting fatuity evoked by the bombast villain's show of 'solid wit and eloquence'. But he also translates the '*false* sublime' (l. 174) into images of grotesque ridicule, showing it in 'ass's ears' (l. 170), for example, and presents Alexander's conquests as the global raving of a mad bully: 'The Grecian chief, the enthusiast of his *pride*,/ With Rage and Terrour stalking by his side,/Raves round the globe' (ll. 35–7). The blend of horror and farce here is not unlike that of *Jonathan Wild*.

If any geniality may emerge from such a mixture, it will clearly be of a different order from that in the *Beggar's Opera*, whose protagonists, in spite of their bad actions, are given qualities of charm and of a virtue in some ways higher than that of the rules against which they offend. Wild's grotesque likeability has to emerge in spite of an unremitting insistence on his meanness and villainy. If we sometimes find him charming, it is usually because of certain procedures of comic manipulation on Fielding's part, rather than, as in the case of Macheath and his friends, because of intrinsic qualities of character attributed to him in the work. His robberies and trickeries are transfigured into a clownish comedy of clockwork automatism, for example, but they are not *morally* revalued by that fact. In this sense, Wild's likability is a property of Fielding's style rather than of Wild's own nature. The only major exceptions to this seem to occur through certain perverse extensions of the mock-heroic scheme, as when heroic courage translates itself not into cowardice, nor into mere impudence, but into that real courage of which Wild's behaviour on the gallows is the supreme example. Here the mock-heroic reversal backfires, and the heroic claim is taken more or less literally, in spite of a massive context of formulaic assertion which purports to pull the other way.

Even here, however, the moral aggrandizement depends partly on Fielding's *staging* of the episode, that is to say on strategies of style. A peculiar collaboration of clownish farce and heroic rant enacts itself. If one of the effects of farce is to diminish the mock-hero into a clown, another is to create (often simultaneously), the grotesque aggrandisements of caricature. Wild stealing the parson's corkscrew in one sense reduces himself to the dimensions of a clownish prankster, but in another sense achieves, if not the baroque gigantism of the Joycean vision of Cardinal Dedalus, at least a strong climactic triumph in the operatic composition of the final 'apotheosis'. The staging of that 'apotheosis' (the procession, the jeering crowds, the elaborate ceremoniousness of the style) are an important factor, without which Wild's 'courage' might have appeared as something more closely resembling the broken weeping ignominy of the historical personage.

But if Wild's 'courage' is only partly a matter of courageous behaviour, and owes part of its impressiveness to staging, there is no doubt that it emerges as a literal endorsement rather than as an upside-down version of Fielding's mock-heroic praise. That is always a potential, as well as a risk, of mock-heroic, as of other kinds of irony. And Fielding himself came later to believe explicitly that mock-heroic villains tended to become 'amiable' thanks to the reversal of values created by the upsidedown irony. In the Preface to *David Simple* (1744) Fielding returned to the subject of 'comic epic', and expressed a conception of the ridiculous as not involving black villainy, which is closer to the Preface to *Joseph Andrews* than to the Preface to the *Miscellanies* or the earlier letter to *Common Sense*. He appears tacitly to depart from the Preface to *Joseph Andrews*, however, in no longer insisting on the distinction between comic epic and mock-heroic, or burlesque, and in including the *Dunciad*, for example, among comic epics. He then proposes that the 'main end or scope' of a comic epic must be 'at once amiable, ridiculous, and natural'. This immediately confronts him with the problem of 'amiability' in some satiric works (presumably like the *Dunciad*) which have been admitted under the definition, and which 'set before us the odious instead of the amiable'. Fielding is uneasy about this, and feels that such works are to some extent faulty. But he nevertheless finds that his argument is partly validated by the upsidedown irony, which preserves at least a surface of praise even when the intention is to blame.[90]

> If it be said that some of the comic performances I have above mentioned differ in the first of these, and set before us the odious instead of the amiable; I answer, that is far from being one of their perfections; and of this the authors themselves seem so sensible, that they endeavour to deceive the reader by false glosses and colours, and by the help of irony at least to represent the aim and design of their heroes in a favourable and agreeable light.

There is about this an element of acrobatic theorizing, which reminds us of the risks of taking Fielding's critical pronouncements too seriously or too literally as parts of a coherently developed aesthetic scheme. Here, as in the Prefaces to *Joseph Andrews* and to the *Miscellanies*, there is an *ad hoc* quality, a tendency to serve the local argument rather than to think the theoretical implications through. This results, often, in a suspicion of ambiguity and fudging, but it could be argued that such things perhaps reveal the nature of his preoccupations, both acknowledged and unacknowledged, rather better than any clearheaded, simplifying and wholly consistent pronouncements might have done. We know from his very inconsistencies, as well as from the frequency with which he returns to the problem, of Fielding's obsessive uneasiness with the question of the farcical scoundrel and of the laughability of the very evil, its potential for farce and burlesque, as well as its place in comedy. The comic actor Penkethman 'In the Burlesque of *Alexander*' seems to have fascinated him, for he reverted several times to this treatment of his favourite political villain in essays in *Common Sense* and the *Champion*.[91] The laughter in question is often derisive or punitive (to Fielding, Penkethman's Alexander equals Walpole, and the point of the joke is that Walpole's 'Government is a *Farce*'), but it also has tendencies to take us beyond the area of moral condemnation into an area of play, where the imaginative contemplation of bad deeds is liberating, where political evil turns into comic strutting and bad men acquire likability of a sort. That these tendencies are not always deliberate, and that they are often engendered by features of style which run against the overt or official attitudes which Fielding expresses, does not make them any less vivid.

The grotesque likability of Jonathan Wild (and perhaps in some measure that of Ubu) is in some ways dependent on the mock-heroic— a mode which Swift, whose villains are never likable, hardly ever practised. The likability of Gay's Macheath is not supported by the accident of an upsidedown irony, but neither does it require such support. Whether mock-heroic *necessarily* provides a tendency to likability, as Fielding came to believe, is not certain. The fact that he had it in him to believe it may have influenced the process in *Jonathan Wild*, even though he had no conscious sense of it *then*: conversely, the formulation in the Preface to *David Simple* may have been partly influenced by an *ex post facto* recognition of the geniality which suffuses *Jonathan Wild*.

A work where mock-heroic hardly induces likability is Brecht's *Resistible Rise of Arturo Ui*, a play which, like *Jonathan Wild*, satirizes a hated political leader (Hitler) in the figure of a gangster and protection racketeer (Ui, who resembles, or is based on, Al Capone). It is also written in a mock-heroic style, though its associations, like those of *Ubu Roi*, are not with epic poems, but Shakespearian plays (especially *Richard III* and *Julius Caesar*). Like Wild, Ui is a mean and loutish bully, whose 'heroic' quality manifests itself in a similar combination of naked cruelty, awkward bombast, and cheap cunning. But he never acquires Wild's peculiar bloated charm. In many ways, he is to Wild what Brecht's Macheath is to Gay's, a deliberately heavy, joyless, flattened version.

There are good extrinsic reasons for the difference. Where the subject is Hitler, likability would be more profoundly out of place than where it is Walpole, and a Walpole whom Fielding perhaps did not at all times oppose.[92] Fielding's work, though first drafted before Walpole's downfall, is able to end with villains duly punished and with poetic justice discharged all round. Brecht was writing in 1941, with no end in sight, and Ui riding high in the final scenes. Even Brecht's epilogue (presumably written near the time of the play's first production in 1958) warns that although Hitler was stopped, there could well be another on the way. Among eighteenth-century English writers, perhaps only Swift, and certainly not Fielding, had this profoundly pessimistic sense of humanity's potentiality for evil. Nor could Alexander and Caesar, or even Louis XIV or Charles XII of Sweden, provide for eighteenth-century authors examples of viciousness so immediate and total as Hitler displayed in our own time. Like Fielding, and Jarry, Brecht is saying to us:[93]

> If we could learn to look instead of gawking,
> We'd see the horror in the heart of farce.

But in this context, the farce no longer has the heart to be very funny.

Formal differences in mock-heroic style must take a very secondary role before substantive differences of such magnitude. But it is a fact (doubtless not unrelated to the larger differences) that Brecht's mock-heroic fails to give its hero the comic aggrandisement achieved by Wild. Brecht was not only writing at a time much less vividly conscious than was Fielding's of the heroic in the old 'epic' sense, but was alluding to a set of 'heroic' conventions which were themselves less formulaically predictable, more complex, more diffuse, and more questioning. The 'heroic' norm behind his travesty is not the relatively straightforward and unified one of ancient epic or Restoration heroic play, but a 'Shakespearian' grand style which already contained in the original a probing critique of political and military viciousness. At the same time, Brecht is here less at home than Fielding in a mock-heroic idiom of *any* sort. Thus, when Ui learns speech and deportment from a dilapidated Shakespearian actor who teaches him to recite set speeches of Shakespeare, the situation loses all relation to the reality of Hitler or the doings of Ui's Chicago gang (Scene vii). Wild merely learns from Count la Ruse and others to walk and talk like an underworld parody of a gentleman (I, vi); and when he comes to feats of 'heroic' speechifying, that is taken for granted as the natural idiom of the novel's ironic scheme (a scheme whose vocabulary of 'greatness' has not had to be invented for the occasion, but was already part of the staple jargon of political, and especially of anti-Walpole, satire). Wild's high talk has not had to be expressly learned at the hands of a specialist in Homer or the ancient historians, whom Wild can anyway be said, like the other schoolboys around him, to have encountered at school (I, iii).

Mock-heroic comes more easily and more naturally to Fielding, for reasons which we have already considered. But it is also true that attitudes to the heroic, and to the great epic poems, were becoming more ambiguous and uncertain in Fielding's time. This has relations with the quality of abstraction in Fielding's heroic fable, the fact that the heroic is largely simplified into a somewhat stiffened verbal formula. But even this contributes paradoxically to the differences between Ui and Wild. For where Ui's 'heroic' identity is diffuse and tends to lack definition, Wild's, for being simplified into certain moral essentials, comes to be all the more heavily defined and extravagantly asserted. And because Wild's 'heroic' quality is so largely a matter of upside-down verbalism, the process described in the Preface to *David Simple*, by which ironic praise is taken literally, is here greatly encouraged, whether or not it is invariably at work in the mock-heroic mode.

Mock-heroic can undoubtedly contribute to 'the horror in the heart of farce'. Alexander and his copy of the *Iliad*, Caligula quoting Virgil, Nero singing the 'Sack of Ilium' and drinking out of cups carved with scenes from Homer's poems, Wild's admiration for epic heroes, Ubu's Macbeth-like career in *Ubu Roi*, Arturo Ui in his heavy world of Shakespearean allusion, all show situations in which monstrous behaviour feeds grotesquely upon heroic literature. Bad deeds, by thus acquiring classic models, become mythologized into a new and hideous magnitude. 'Bombast greatness' is a 'monster', whose 'native deformity' is in real life clothed in a terrifying yet preposterous stylistic dress. Fielding says it is his business to 'expose' this deformity.[94] Oddly this exposure is conducted in a mock-heroic idiom, despite Fielding's contention that he had used burlesque only in the episode of Mrs Heartfree's travels, and that burlesque is in some way the antithesis of 'probability' as well as of what the Preface to *Joseph Andrews* called 'exactest copying'. The Preface to *Joseph Andrews* also spoke of 'burlesque' (specifically a burlesque of the mock-heroic sort) as 'the exhibition of what is monstrous and unnatural', likening it to '*Caricatura* . . . in painting', whose aim is 'to exhibit monsters, not men'. To these modes, Fielding preferred the true 'comic', which consists 'in the exactest copying of nature' (and of a nature which steers clear of 'blackest villainies' and 'dreadful calamities' at that).

As early as 1732, in the Prologue to *The Lottery: A Farce*, Fielding made a similar and indeed commonplace contrast between farce, with its 'magnifying right', its privilege of exaggeration in order to show follies 'in stronger light' on the one hand, and true comedy, whose 'just glass' does not exaggerate, but 'shows you as you are' on the other. Here, however, Fielding defends the more distorting medium, because some follies 'scarce perceptible appear' in a merely realistic presentation. The apparent 'inconsistency' is not great. Part of Fielding's point in the Prologue seems to be to imply that some of his farcical exaggerations are actually true to life. Besides, comedy is in any case rated more highly than farce in the play's Prologue as in the Preface to *Joseph Andrews*, and burlesque and caricature are not totally repudiated even in the Preface.

Despite Fielding's persistent lip-service to an ideal of comic realism or 'exactest copying', however, the stylizations (mock-heroic, farcical and other) in his writings show a traditional Augustan recoil from the merely real, from naked circumstantial recording. He undoubtedly felt in some measure what Hume expressed in his essay 'Of Simplicity and Refinement in Writing', that mere unadorned factuality does not give aesthetic pleasure. Nature needs to be represented 'with all her graces and ornaments, *la belle nature*; or if we copy low life, the strokes must be strong and remarkable, and must convey a lively image to the mind'.[95] The idealizations of *la belle nature* share with the 'strong and remarkable' strokes of portrayals of 'low life' (Sancho Panza is Hume's example) a tendency to transform the bare factualities of life. The notion of style as the 'dress' of thought is not merely concerned with the problem of *appropriate* styles, but has also to do more fundamentally with covering the sheer nakedness of reality. Hume's passage resembles, though it is not in every way identical with, Dryden's view that the heroic and the burlesque are parallel modifiers of reality: 'the one shows nature beautified', and 'the other shows her deformed', as in the picture 'of a lazar, or of a fool with distorted face and antic gestures, at which we cannot forbear to laugh, because it is a deviation from nature'.[96] This comment is in turn directly related to a later judgment on *Bartholomew Fair*, where Dryden says Jonson achieved by a proper kind of 'heightening' what 'he could never have performed, had he only said or done those very things that are daily spoken or practised in the fair: . . . he hath made an excellent lazar of it; the copy is of price, though the original be vile'.[97] 'Heightening' is thus a stylistic operation which refers not only to a heroic raising 'above the life',[98] but also to the stylized grotesqueries of burlesque and farce, which may achieve this by making their subject uglier, more strikingly 'burlesque', perhaps even 'lower' in some ways than real life.

It is partly in connection with this that the somewhat parallel roles of burlesque and farce in Fielding's discussions in the Prologue to *The Lottery* and the Preface to *Joseph Andrews*, however widely separated in time, are of interest. Fielding's protestations of unadorned truth to nature in the Preface need to be set against the transforming roles of both burlesque and farce in many passages even of *Joseph Andrews* and *Tom Jones*. In *Jonathan Wild*, where burlesque is pervasive and where Fielding nevertheless argues that he has confined himself 'within the rules of probability',[99] it could be argued that Fielding is telling us sarcastically that things really are as 'monstrous' and 'deformed' as the portrayal of Wild implies. The Preface to the *Miscellanies* speaks of 'exposing' his 'native deformity', whereas the Preface to *Joseph Andrews* had spoken of avoiding the 'monstrous and unnatural' of burlesque.

The force of such a sarcasm has to be acknowledged, as does the fact that one tendency of mock-heroic is to add urgency to the satire by blowing up the villain to an enhanced, though disreputable, stature. But if there is horror in the heart of farce, so there is farce in the heart of horror. Farce too acts by exaggeration and expansion, as Fielding said, and both modes give their protagonists certain large-scale freedoms of self-realization absent in less stylized forms of writing. Hence perhaps the popularity of 'lofty Lines in *Smithfield* Drols',[100] and of farces on heroic subjects at Bartholomew Fair and other places of popular entertainment, where, as Fielding notes in *Jonathan Wild* itself, one could see drolls and puppet-shows about 'Anna Bullen' and other high princesses (II, iii), or the exploits of 'the king of Muscovy' (III, xi).[101] Some of the topics were not only 'heroic', but extremely bloody. A French fairground droll of 1705 on the fall of Troy is full of scenes of carnage and exhortations to mass destruction.[102] In 1707, Elkanah Settle wrote an immensely popular and spectacular Bartholomew Fair droll on the *Siege of Troy*,[103] the second act of which, for example, opens with a view of Sinon under the feet of the Trojan Horse, 'with a mangled Face all bloody, his Nose cut off, his Eyes out, etc. bound in Irons'.[104] The whole work is full of violence, with carnage and fire, crowds of women shrieking, and Helen leaping into the blaze.

Rant, interludes of low comedy, sometimes (as in the *Siege of Troy*) with extravagant and elaborate scenery, characterized many of the heroic drolls of the London fairs. A liberating and preposterous expansiveness in language, scenery (in the more spectacular shows) and action was the essence of their vulgarity and their fun. The shows were sometimes satiric. Some dealt with political events of the day,[105] and many were drollic adaptations or parodies of serious heroic plays, like Lee's *Rival Queens*, the probable original of Penkethman's burlesque of Alexander. But Sybil Rosenfeld notes that 'The satirical droll on contemporary events was not as popular in the eighteenth century as in the preceding decades',[106] and there seems no doubt that the mock-heroic rant, and the gory bloodshed, were also enjoyed beyond any satiric purport, in that ancient domain of folk art where the ludicrous and the sinister coexist in an extravagant holiday from conventionally partitioned or prescribed responses. The 'deformities' of burlesque, of farce and of caricature are not merely convenient stylizations of raw actuality for sophisticated Augustan writers like Dryden or Fielding. The 'distorted face and antic gestures' that Dryden wrote about are also, as Arthur Murphy was to indicate (in some comments which distinguish, in Fielding's manner, between comedy and farce, caricature and burlesque), licensed violations of 'due proportion': 'the nose may be represented shapeless', and other 'lineaments extended beyond their boundaries'. Murphy speaks of such procedures as means 'to season the ridicule', and, by impressing 'the signatures of ridicule more strongly on the mind', to make the portraiture both more memorable and more laughable, as is seen within certain limits even in not predominantly farcical works like *Joseph Andrews* and *Tom Jones*.[107] To this genial explanation might be added Fielding's comments in 1732 about the moral effectiveness of the exaggerations and distortions of farce.

But there is also a more primitive force in such distortions of 'due proportion', which operates in the less comfortable world of *Jonathan Wild*, and for which we cannot expect the conscious theorizing of Fielding or Murphy to give an adequate account. *Jonathan Wild* possesses a combination of the truly sinister with the genially farcical, of the detestable with the likable, of horror and laughter, which are unsettling as *Joseph Andrews* and *Tom Jones* never are, and for which there is a parallel in the much later world of Ubu. Jarry quite consciously thought of his art as related to certain energies of folk-drama, notably to that world of the 'guignol' which suggests, as Perche notes, a protagonist 'à mi-chemin entre le sinistre et le grotesque, et surtout disposé à faire rire'.[108] He sought in the staging of *Ubu Roi* a grotesque portraiture where vices are 'exaggerated' with the help of the kind of visual caricature which gives villains a bull's horns and a dragon's body.[109] The formula, we may note, is a radical violation of precisely that fundamental kind of Augustan decorum which Horace wittily prescribed in the opening lines of the *Ars Poetica*. Jarry may or may not have known what he was dissociating himself from. But he knew exactly the tradition to which he did aspire: it was 'le comique macabre d'un clown anglais ou d'une danse des morts'.

The English clown, the dance of death, plus a wild anarchic amorality of carnage and bloodshed. The literature of black humour and gratuitous 'cruelty', with its element of paganized emancipation from moral sanctions, has long been known to draw deeply on primitive traditions of folk art and ritual. This was part of what disturbed Yeats on the first night of *Ubu Roi*: 'After us the Savage God'.[110] It seems likely also that the strutting and blowsy fatuity of the murderous Ubu, or of Jonathan Wild, has one of its sources in a folk-literature dedicated to the *Christian* God, in those old plays where Vice and the Devil are figures of fun. For if strutting villains are common enough in most comic writing, the combination of strutting absurdity with Satanism, or with such *extreme viciousness* as Ubu's, Alexander's, and by extension Wild's (a viciousness with national or global consequences), is perhaps a special case.

A hint of such a relationship may be buried in the declaration of Ricardus Aristarchus that the '*Bravery* . . . of the true Hero' turns, in his burlesque counterpart the 'mock Hero', into 'an high courage of blasphemy'.[111] One of Aristarchus's targets is Cibber, whose blasphemies are noted in a grotesque mock-Miltonic passage in *Dunciad*, I, 115 ff. Part of the comedy of Wild is an explosively oath-ridden vocabulary, vulgarly spirited or, at times, almost endearingly silly, as when we are told in II, xiii that, stranded alone at sea, 'He spent his time in contemplation, that is to say, in blaspheming, cursing, and sometimes singing and whistling'. A paradox about blasphemy is that it is on the one hand a direct and grievous insult to the Almighty ('the most *daring* Figure of Speech, that which is taken from the *Name of God*', says Aristarchus),[112] but on the other (partly because it involves rant) one of the principal ways in which the Devil makes himself ridiculous. Addison discussed in *Spectator* No. 303 how it was that Satan's impieties in *Paradise Lost* manage to avoid offending 'a religious reader': 'Amidst those Impieties which this Enraged Spirit utters . . ., the Author has taken care to introduce none that is not big with absurdity, and incapable of shocking a Religious Reader.' Addison resolves the issue in good didactic terms, as well as, quite properly, appealing to a decorum of character: Satan's 'Sentiments are every way answerable to his Character, and suitable to a created Being of the most exalted and most depraved Nature'. Addison's description of the 'absurdity' of Satan has a certain cosiness in its feeling that laughter tames the whole situation. But, as C. S. Lewis said, Milton too, less smugly, 'believed everything detestable to be, in the long run, also ridiculous'. Lewis adds the comment that 'mere Christianity commits every Christian to believing that "the Devil is (in the long run) an ass" '.[113]

But there is a side to this laughter which is in some ways separate from such moral sanctions, and not amenable to rationalizations which see the laughter as simply punitive and seek to reintegrate it with official

codes of value. Both Vice and the Devil of early popular drama have
relations with the fool or jester, through whom we are partly allowed a
holiday from these codes of value, and there is also a relation between
devils and Harlequin.[114] In such instances, however, the treatment is
usually light-hearted, without the 'exalted' element. Milton's Satan, as
viewed by Addison, combines 'absurdity' with an 'exalted' stature, a
mixture of the ludicrous and the heroic which theories of the epic do
not normally allow for,[115] but which is always a subversive potential
of the imagination and may come into its own in mock-heroic. Burns's
affectionate 'Address to the Deil'[116] not only carries for cunning purposes
of comparison a 'sublime' epigraph from Milton ('O Prince! O Chief
of many throned Pow'rs'), but opens with lines which echo the large
friendliness of Pope's address to Swift in *Dunciad*, I, 19–20:[117]

> O Thou! whatever title suit thee!
> Auld Hornie, Satan, Nick, or Clootie . . .

> O Thou! whatever title please thine ear,
> Dean, Drapier, Bickerstaff, or Gulliver!

Burns succeeds in domesticating the sublimities of heroic and mock-
heroic alike, defying the former, and incorporating some of the grandeur of affectionate informality of the latter. He goes further than
Fielding in suffusing his whole treatment with a roguish geniality.
Fielding, like Jarry, preserved in the midst of the humour a particularly
active sense of his hero's extreme villainy. But it may be that once evil
is conceived of as a 'bombast greatness', its cruellest enormities are
potentially capable of arousing illicit sympathies, not only in Wild and
Ubu, but even in its 'straight' or Miltonic as distinct from mock-heroic
manifestations. Nor does the dimension of ridicule prevent the villain
from becoming sublime again, in a revalued way. Milton's Satan turned
heroic rebel in the eyes of some Romantics, and Ubu (whose author,
incidentally, was a *fin de siècle* figure, capable not only of Ubu-esque
humour, but of some of the darker, more solemn postures of the time)
has become the darling of some radical sensibilities of our own time.
Felix Krull was in Mann's eyes a roguish counterpart to that towering
diabolist genius, Doctor Faustus. Wild falls short of these sublimer
achievements, but I have tried to suggest some of the ways in which the
potential is manifest, even in him.

Fielding would not have confessed to such things. He would not have
been aware of them in a way that a later literary experience has enabled
us to be aware of them. We have seen that many aspects of *Jonathan*

Wild seem to be in conflict with his literary theories, but also that his literary theories often conflicted with one another in revealing ways. The 'bombast' in Wild's 'greatness' may well be thought to relate the character to those official sources of the 'true Ridiculous', 'vanity' and 'hypocrisy'.[118] But the 'greatness' consists of many 'blackest villainies' which do not officially belong to the province of the 'true Ridiculous'. *Jonathan Wild* is 'burlesque' rather than 'comic epic' (although Fielding was not consistent in maintaining the distinction between the two), so his 'greatness' may be allowed to be shown as 'monstrous and un-natural'. But at the same time this 'greatness' is scaled down to comically genial proportions which approximate to the manner of the next two novels, and to something like the 'true Ridiculous' envisaged in the Preface to *Joseph Andrews*. And yet this geniality also paradoxically opens up larger-than-life splendours of proud self-realization and a final heroic 'apotheosis'.

Like Ubu, Wild is both arch-villain and childish prankster. As in parts of Book II of Pope's *Dunciad*, and (in Fielding's case but not in Jarry's) in spite of the author, vice and folly have become play, a type of play which in its absurd vigour and integrity emancipates us from the values of virtue and sense which we are officially invited to apply. As in the Ubu plays, there is a complex and sophisticated reliance on popular art forms and folk drama. At times, the relationship involves Fielding in piquant coils of elaboration. His mock-heroic contains stylized evocations of, or allusions to, drollic works about Alexander, or Anne Boleyn, or the Czar of Muscovy, which were themselves sometimes travesties or adaptations of serious plays. Part of Fielding's manner, unlike Jarry's, is to keep a stylized and uppish distance from these things, showing the reader by knowing allusion and other mannerisms that he knows what he is doing, and can manipulate his 'low' sources at will.

But if his conscious and gingerly ways of looking back on folk-drama differ from the zany and unselfconscious immediacy of Jarry, and if his didactic and satiric purposes are strongly proclaimed, there is also a primary gusto, and an element of emancipation from, or transcendence of, satire. There are places where a quality of black fun exists in that 'pure state' desiderated by Breton. If its conscious relations with folk-drama are hedged with urbane ironies and protective cautions, it yet has tentacles which reach towards the future, towards the black humour of Ubu, that 'enfant terrible' and 'anarchiste parfait' whose portrayal (whilst undoubtedly satiric in its way) genuinely goes beyond valuations of good and evil. Fielding the theorist could hardly make even a tenta-tive gesture towards that final step, Breton's celebration of 'humour noir'. But Fielding the maker of fictions explored its periphery, with a buoyant and delighted fascination.[119] And just as in his last novel, *Amelia*, are elements which remain undeveloped until the literature and the drama of cruelty in our time, so in the first major narrative of that ostensibly most conservative of early masters of English fiction are adumbrations of a subversive art of the future, far beyond anything in those official literary revolutionaries, Defoe and Richardson.

NOTES

1 W. B. Yeats, *Collected Poems*, p. 7.
2 *Works*, XV, 78–9. See above, ch. V, n. 14.
3 *Variorum Edition of the Poems of W. B. Yeats*, ed. Peter Allt and Russell K. Alspach (New York, 1957), p. 65.
4 *Variorum Edition*, p. 65.
5 *Voyage to Lisbon*, p. 26.
6 Christopher Isherwood, *Exhumations* (Harmondsworth, 1969), pp. 201–26.
7 *Exhumations*, p. 31, reprinted from *New Verse*, November 1937, pp. 5–6. See also Isherwood's *Lions and Shadows* (London, 1963), p. 119.
8 *Exhumations*, p. 197.
9 Ibid., pp. 196–7.
10 *Lions and Shadows*, p. 48.
11 W. H. Auden, *The Orators*, 3rd edn (London, 1966), pp. 7–8.
12 W. H. Auden and Louis MacNeice, *Letters from Iceland* (London, 1967), p. 117.
13 Swift, *Works*, I, 29.
14 Swift, *Epistle to a Lady*, 177–80 (*Poems*, II, 635).
15 Emrys Jones, 'Pope and Dulness', *Proceedings of the British Academy*, liv (1968), 253–4.
16 See also *Dunciad*, II, 379 ff.: 'Three College Sophs, and three pert Templats came . . .'.
17 Jones, op. cit., pp. 254–5.
18 The accounts in the newspapers and in the pamphlet-biographies of the historical Wild speak of Wild's death as much more simply ignominious. What is stressed is his fear and dejection, physical illness and mental confusion, and the depression and stupor induced by alcohol and by the unsuccessful attempt at suicide by laudanum at the very end. See W. R. Irwin, *The Making of Jonathan Wild* (New York, 1941), pp. 9–10; Gerald Howson, *Thief-Taker General. The Rise and Fall of Jonathan Wild*

(London, 1970), pp. 268 ff. Fielding knew some of the sources. The Preface to the *Miscellanies* (*Works*, XII, 242) speaks of newspapers contemporary with Wild's death, 'the Ordinary of Newgate his account', and an 'excellent historian' presumed to be Defoe, author of *The True and Genuine Account of the Life and Actions of the Late Jonathan Wild* (1725), and possibly of one other biography (see Dudden, I, 452; J. R. Moore, *A Checklist of the Writings of Daniel Defoe* (Bloomington, 1960), Nos. 473, 471). In the Preface to the *Miscellanies*, Fielding plays down his knowledge of the historical facts, and explicitly disclaims any concern with historical veracity. On his relation to the real-life sources, see Irwin, pp. 32 ff.

19 *Dunciad*, 'Ricardus Aristarchus of the Hero of the Poem', Twickenham Edition, vol. V, 3rd edn (London, 1936), p. 257. Aristarchus mockingly impersonates the classical scholar Richard Bentley.

20 Cited Howson, op. cit., p. 273. See also Defoe's *True and Genuine Account* (1725), p. 37; Captain Charles Johnson, *General History of . . . Highwaymen*, etc. (1734), p. 471.

21 The real-life ordinary of Newgate was Thomas Purney, the minor poet. Despite some scurrilous attacks upon him, he is said to have been 'a pious and abstemious' man. Howson says that he was in any case 'away from London' during Wild's last days (Howson, pp. 119 n., 271). See also Irwin, op. cit., pp. 117–18, n. 156, and the introduction by H. O. White to *The Works of Thomas Purney* (Oxford, 1933). Irwin refers to the drunken ordinary in *Moll Flanders*, Shakespeare Head edn (Oxford, 1927), II, 103: Purney became ordinary in 1719 and was ordinary when *Moll Flanders* was published in 1722.

22 I discuss this dialogue more fully, together with that from *Moll Flanders*, in 'Language, Dialogue and "Point of View" in Fielding: Some Considerations', *Quick Springs of Sense. Essays . . . in Honor of Lodwick Hartley*, ed. Larry S. Champion, University of Georgia Press, forthcoming.

23 *Beggar's Opera*, III, xiii.

24 *Beggar's Opera*, I, iv; I, xii.

25 *Works*, XV, 134.

26 Swift, *Poems*, II, 399–400; Swift, *Works*, X, 148–9; XIII, 44–5.

27 Fielding, *Works*, XIII, 121 ff. For a useful account of executions, see Dudden, I, 499–500, n. 2.

28 *Beggar's Opera*, I, iv.

29 Albert Camus, *L'Étranger* (Paris, 1953), p. 172.

30 Camus's passage is not comic nor meant to be. But see the Outsider's feeling that the ridiculous and the criminal are not very different from one another (p. 119), a view which would not *consciously* commend itself to Fielding.

31 James Joyce, *Ulysses* (London, 1955), p. 497.

32 The passage is problematical, and its complexities are more fully considered in ch. VII.

33 I.e. not the French sea captain, but the captain of the boat which Wild and Mrs Heartfree originally embarked on at Harwich.

34 Plutarch, *Alexander*, IV, 4–5; XXI, 3–5; XXII, 1 ff.; XLVII, 4.

35 Robert H. Hopkins, 'Language and Comic Play in Fielding's *Jonathan Wild*', *Criticism*, viii (1966), 213–28, esp. pp. 219 ff.

36 They even share a peculiar comedy of small financial returns. Just as Wild's operations often leave him with tiny profits (see pp. 110 ff, above), so in *Ubu Roi*, III, vii, Mère Ubu points out that Ubu's entire tax on marriage 'n'a encore produit que 11 sous' (*Tout Ubu*, ed. Maurice Saillet (Paris, 1962), p. 83).

37 *Tout Ubu*, p. 431.

38 Cited in Louis Perche, *Alfred Jarry* (Paris, 1965), p. 35.

39 *Tout Ubu*, p. 20. See Yeats's account of the first performance of *Ubu Roi*: 'The players are supposed to be dolls, toys, marionettes, and now they are all hopping like wooden frogs . . .' in *Autobiographies* (London, 1955), p. 348.

40 James Ralph threw Pope's line about farce and epic back at Pope himself, by citing it on the title-page of his *Sawney. An Heroic Poem. Occasion'd by the Dunciad* (1728). See J. V. Guerinot, *Pamphlet Attacks on Alexander Pope 1711–1744* (London, 1969), p. 124.

41 See *Joseph Andrews*, Wesleyan Edition, p. 7, n. 1. Fielding was citing Aristotle, *Poetics*, V, 1–2, for the view that villainy is not the object of comedy. Aristotle's formulation is itself variously ambiguous: see J. W. Draper 'The Theory of the Comic in Eighteenth-Century England', *Journal of English and Germanic Philology*, xxxvii (1938), 210.

42 Martin C. Battestin, 'Fielding and "Master Punch" in Panton Street', *Philological Quarterly*, xlv (1966), 191–208. Among the offerings of that theatre was 'a Comical Puppet-Shew Tragedy, call'd FAIR ROSAMOND. With the Comical Humours of King *Henry* II and his Queen' (p. 201, citing Fielding's advertisement in the *General Advertiser* of 14 April 1748: the phrase 'Comical Humours' is the same as that used on 26 March in the *Jacobite's Journal* of '*Nero* ripping up his Mother's Belly'. It was the customary phrase for the low comic interludes in drollic plays, and appears constantly in advertisements, titles, etc. See Sybil Rosenfeld, *The Theatre of the London Fairs in the 18th Century* (Cambridge, 1960), p. 148 *et passim*). Fielding probably 'designed several new scenes for the satiric parts of *Fair Rosamond*' ('Fielding and "Master Punch" ', p. 208), to which was added a Tyburn scene, satirically representing the execution of the comedian Samuel Foote (pp. 202–3, 205). The story of *Fair Rosamond* was an old favourite on the popular stage.

43 Jensen, II, 63, No. 55, 18 July 1752.

44 Suetonius, *Domitian*, III, 1. All references to Suetonius cite the Loeb edition and its translation, 2 vols. (London and Cambridge, Mass., 1950–51).

45 Jensen, I, 276–7, No. 24, 24 March 1752.

46 See Suetonius, *Nero*, XXIII, 2.

47 *Nero*, XXXVIII, 2. Tacitus, *Annals*, XV, xxxviii–xxxix, does not commit himself as to whether the fire itself was deliberately caused by Nero himself, or merely an accident, but he too reports rumours that Nero sang of the destruction of Troy. The poem may have been Nero's own composition. See Juvenal, VIII, 220–1.

48 Suetonius also records that Nero had possessed 'two favourite drinking cups, which he called "Homeric", because they were carved with scenes from Homer's poems' (*Nero*, XLVII, 1). He dashed them to the ground in a fit of rage, however.

49 For a recent exploration of connections between villainy and the practical joke, see Auden's essay on Iago, 'The Joker in the Pack', *The Dyer's Hand and other Essays* (London, 1963), pp. 246–72.

50 Jensen, I, 251, No. 19, 7 March 1752. For some of Nero's cruel practical jokes, see Suetonius, *Nero*, XXVI. Among Caligula's amusements were gladiatorial shows in which 'worthless and decrepit gladiators' were matched against 'mangy wild beasts' and in which there were fights between respectable citizens 'conspicuous for some bodily infirmity' (Suetonius, *Caligula*, XXVI, 5). Such activities would be particularly offensive to Fielding's sense, expressed in the Preface to *Joseph Andrews*, of the impropriety of making 'natural imperfections the object of derision'.

51 Swift to Pope, 20 April 1731, *Correspondence*, ed. Harold Williams (Oxford, 1963–65), III, 456. See above, p. 115.

52 *Gulliver's Travels*, IV, v.

53 Plutarch tells the story that Alexander wept when he heard from Anaxarchus that there was an infinite number of worlds, explaining that he wept because he had not conquered any yet ('On Tranquillity of Mind', IV; in *Moralia*, Loeb edn, vol. VI (London and Cambridge, Mass., 1962), pp. 176–9). See also Juvenal X, 168, and a set of variations on the theme in the Elder Seneca, *Suasoriae*, I. The version given by Swift and Fielding may be post-classical. I am indebted to Professors Ernst Badian and Charles Garton for information on this point.

54 See also *Temple Beau*, II, vii (*Works*, VIII, 124).

55 Swift, *Works*, I, 247, 107.

56 Fielding, *Works*, XVI, 77–84, esp. 82–3.

57 Henry Knight Miller, *Essays on Fielding's Miscellanies. A Commentary on Volume One* (Princeton, 1961), pp. 407–8. See Miller's whole study of this dialogue, pp. 386–409.

58 *Tout Ubu*, pp. 23, 69, 75, 78 ff., 83, 269.

59 This technique is discussed in *Quick Springs of Sense*, ed. Larry S. Champion (see above, n. 22).

60 *Works*, XV, 229. Cited (as is the passage from *Polly*) in Miller, p. 400 and n. 38.

61 *Works*, XV, 288–9. The passage is from Suetonius, *Caligula*, XLV–XLVII. Fielding owned a Suetonius edited by Samuel Pitiscus (Item 263 in the sale catalogue of his library, reprinted in E. M. Thornbury, *Henry Fielding's Theory of the Comic Prose Epic* (New York, 1966), p. 177). The 'celebrated verse of Virgil' is *Aeneid*, I, 207.

62 *Works*, XV, 291.

63 *Works*, XV, 292

64 For more gratuitous pranks by Caligula, see above, n. 50, and p. 201.

65 *Works*, XV, 289.

66 Camus's *Caligula* was written in the late 1930s, but not acted until 1945. I have used the revised text of the play, given in the Pléiade edition of Camus's *Théâtre, Récits, Nouvelles*, ed. Roger Quilliot (Paris, 1962).

67 See Raymond Gay-Crosier, *Les Envers d'un Echec. Etude sur le Théâtre d'Albert Camus* (Paris, 1967), pp. 66–7. For a modern historian's mention of Caligula's moon-fantasies, see J. P. V. D. Balsdon, *The Emperor Gaius (Caligula)* (Oxford, 1934), p. 161. On the question of the sea-shells, Balsdon does not accept Suetonius's account (pp. 88 ff., 91–3). But whatever reasons or meaning may be reconstructed for Caligula's behaviour, Suetonius, whom Fielding quotes, presents it as an example, among others, of Caligula's unpredictable and extravagant play-acting.

68 In a notebook entry of January 1937, Camus records an early plan to make Caligula reappear after the final curtain, saying that he is not dead, that he is inside every member of the audience, and that our epoch is dying for having believed in 'values': 'Non, Caligula n'est pas mort. Il est là, et là. Il est en chacun de vous. Si le pouvoir vous était donné, si vous aviez du coeur, si vous aimiez la vie, vous le verriez se déchaîner, ce monstre ou cet ange que vous portez en vous. Notre époque meurt d'avoir cru aux valeurs et que les choses pouvaient être belles et cesser d'être absurdes. Adieu, je rentre dans l'histoire où me tiennent enfermé depuis si longtemps ceux qui craignent de trop aimer' (*Carnets Mai 1935–Février 1942* (Paris, 1962), p. 43).

69 *Tout Ubu*, p. 20.

70 *Théâtre, Récits, Nouvelles*, ed. Roger Quilliot (Paris, 1962), p. 1727. This was said in the Preface to the American edition of *Caligula and three Other Plays* (New York, 1958).

71 See Gay-Crosier, op. cit., pp. 72–3 and n. 31; 77. As Gay-Crosier shows, Camus is more particularly involved with Nietzschean thought. For an exploration of connections between Nietzsche, a political aestheticism (like that of Camus's Caligula) and a fascist tendency, see Thomas Mann, 'Nietzsche's Philosophy in the Light of Recent History', *Last Essays*, esp. pp. 157–9, and Denis Donoghue, *Yeats* (London, 1971), p. 125.

72 Gay-Crosier, op. cit., pp. 66–8.

73 Gay-Crosier, op. cit., pp. 75, 77.

74 *The Orators* (London, 1966), p. 8.

75 *Carnets*, p. 39: 'Aux confins—Et par-dessus: le jeu. . . . Question de volonté = pousser l'absurdité jusqu'au bout = je suis capable de . . .' (*sic*: the phrase is deliberately uncompleted), and 'Epurer le jeu par la conquête de soi-même—la sachant absurde'. On the theme of 'le jeu', see Gay-Crosier, op. cit., pp. 71–2, 76.

76 This closing cry is a striking theatrical transformation of an unhighlighted sentence near, not *at*, the end of Suetonius's biography, LVII, 3: 'As he lay upon the ground and with writhing limbs called out that he still lived, the others dispatched him with thirty wounds . . .'.

77 *Tout Ubu*, p. 23.

78 E.g. *Tout Ubu*, pp. 227–9.

79 Jensen, I, 251–2. Among many ancient references to this story, see, for a fullish account, Lucian, *Phalaris*, I, 11–13, and Diodorus Siculus, IX, 18–19.

80 Jensen, I, 250.

81 I mean by this only that Ubu was originally conceived as a satire against a schoolmaster, so that any disapproval would be against the tyrant-teacher and from the schoolboy's point of view. This pattern is partly present in the mature *Ubu* texts as we have them. But at the same time much of the disapproval is dissolved into a larger, more amoral and unselective sympathy for conqueror and victim alike: Ubu combines within himself the tyrant-pedagogue and schoolboy-anarchist.

82 André Breton, ed., *Anthologie de l'Humour Noir* (Paris, 1966), p. 361.

83 *Tout Ubu*, p. 23. For the identifications of Ubu with Jarry himself, see Perche, *Alfred Jarry*, pp. 56–7, 59 ff., 66, 100, 120.

84 See Breton's repudiation of 'L'intention satirique, moralisatrice' as inimical to 'l'humour à l'état pur', *Anthologie*, pp. 17–18.

85 *Tout Ubu*, pp. 23, 165.

86 Ronald Paulson and Thomas Lockwood, ed., *Henry Fielding. The Critical Heritage* (London and New York, 1969), pp. 103–4.

87 *Critical Heritage*, p. 104 and n. Fielding reverted to the burlesque acting of Alexander by '*Penkethman the Great*' in *Champion*, 20 November 1739 and 9 September 1740, adding on 16 September 1740 that the reference was not understood by his readers (*Criticism of Henry Fielding*, ed. Ioan Williams (London, 1970), pp. 60, 29, 340n. 12).

The reference remains elusive to this day. No exact record seems to have survived of performances by William Penkethman (or Pinkethman; d. 1725) or by his son of the same name (d. 1740) in the part of Alexander. The suggestion in *Critical Heritage*, p. 104 n., that Fielding was referring to the younger Penkethman, probably in some recent burlesque of Lee's *Rival Queens*, seems wrong. The passages from the *Champion* sound as though they refer to a distant rather than a recent event

('formerly', 'once'), that of 20 November 1739 adding that 'Dicky'
Norris (who died in 1730) played Statira to Penkethman's Alexander.
The phrase *Penkethman the Great* looks back to the heyday of the elder
Penkethman. In *Spectator*, No. 36, 11 April 1711, Steele humorously
mentioned 'The Petition of *William Bullock* to be *Hephestion* to
Penkethman the Great' in a putative operatic spectacle called *The Expedition
of Alexander*, which had been satirically discussed by Addison in
Spectator, No. 31, 5 April 1711. It was envisaged that Powell would
play Alexander and Penkethman King Porus. 'In the preceding summer
at Penkethman's Theatre . . . "Mr. Bullock, Jun." had played Hephestion
in *The Rival Queens*, with Powell as Alexander' (*The Spectator*, ed.
Donald F. Bond (Oxford, 1965), I. 150-1, 127-32, 151, n. 4; see also
Spectator, No. 599, 27 September 1714, *ed. cit.*, V. 47, for an allusion to
an unnamed comedian's desire to play Alexander.)

The production of Lee's *Rival Queens* at Penkethman's theatre at
Greenwich (6 July 1710, *London Stage 1660–1800*, Part 2, ed. Emmett
L. Avery (Carbondale, 1960), p. 226) was presumably a 'straight' one.
The most notable *burlesque* of Lee's play was Colley Cibber's *Rival
Queans, With the Humours of Alexander the Great*, first published in
Dublin in 1729, but probably written in 1703, and known to have
been performed on 29 June 1710, with Cibber himself as Alexander
(ed. William M. Peterson (Painesville, Ohio, 1965), pp. x–xi, xiii;
Peterson notes the practice in farce of casting men in female roles,
saying that Penkethman and Norris played such parts, but does not
report that Norris played Statira: Bullock Jr. was Statira in 1710). The
performance nearest the time of Fielding's remarks was at Drury Lane
on 17 May 1738, with Cross as Alexander (*London Stage*, Part 3, ed.
Arthur H. Scouten (Carbondale, 1961), p. 721). This is later than the
reference in *Common Sense*, 21 May 1737, but earlier than the references
in the *Champion*. It would be appropriate if Cibber were involved in
Fielding's allusion, not least because the Wild-Walpole-Alexander
connection ran alongside the not uncommon satiric association of
Walpole and Cibber (see above, ch. IV, n. 54). But the exact nature of
the allusion, if any, remains unclear.

If, as seems unlikely, Fielding was referring to the younger rather
than the elder Penkethman, then perhaps *Love and Jealousy: Or the
Downfall of Alexander the Great*, performed at the booth of Timothy
Fielding and John Hippisley at Bartholomew and Southwark Fairs in
1733, is involved in some way. According to the surviving play-bill
evidence, Penkethman Jr. was in the cast not of this play, but of the
ballad-opera which accompanied it in the double bill, namely, *A Cure
for Covetousness or the Cheats of Scapin*, a work which may also have a
peculiar relevance to *Jonathan Wild* (see above, ch. IV, n. 22).
Penkethman played Old Gripe. It is possible that on other occasions he

played Alexander in the companion-play (Sybil Rosenfeld, *The Theatre of the London Fairs in the 18th Century* (Cambridge, 1960), pp. 38, 94; *London Stage*, Part 3, p. 312; Henry Morley, *Memoirs of Bartholomew Fair* (London, 1892), pp. 322–3).

For another fairground version of the *Rival Queens* (1741), see Rosenfeld, pp. 127–8, 148; *London Stage*, Part 3, pp. 919–20. Alexander was played by Marshall. Penkethman Jr. had died in 1740.

88 *Dunciad*, pp. 256, 259.

89 *Works*, XII, 245–6.

90 *Works*, XVI, 11.

91 See above, n. 87.

92 See Martin C. Battestin, 'Fielding's Changing Politics and *Joseph Andrews*', *Philological Quarterly*, xxxix (1960), 39–55. A different view is expressed by W. B. Coley, 'Henry Fielding and the Two Walpoles', *Philological Quarterly*, xlv (1966), 157–78. See also Hugh Amory, 'Henry Fielding's *Epistles to Walpole:* A Reexamination', *Philological Quarterly*, xlvi (1967), 236–47.

93 I quote from an unpublished translation of the play by George Tabori, which was kindly made available to me by Messrs. Michael White Ltd. The translation is a free one, and the second line is an interpolation, but one which makes a very apt point.

94 *Works*, XII, 246.

95 David Hume, *Essays* (London and New York, New Universal Library, n.d.), p. 140.

96 John Dryden, letter to Sir Robert Howard prefixed to *Annus Mirabilis* (1667), *Of Dramatic Poesy and other Critical Essays*, ed. George Watson (London and New York, 1962), I, 101. For Dryden's distinction between comedy and farce, see Preface to *An Evening's Love* (1671), ed. cit., I, 145–6.

97 'A Defence of *An Essay of Dramatic Poesy*' (1668), ed. cit. I, 115. The context is a defence of verse in serious plays, because prose 'is too near the nature of converse: there may be too great a likeness'. The artist should heighten beauties and hide deformities. In *Bartholomew Fair* 'or the lowest kind of comedy, that degree of heightening is used which is proper to set off that subject: 'tis true the author was not there to go out of prose, . . . yet he does so raise his matter in that prose as to render it delightful' (I, 114–5). The term 'heightening' carries the sense of 'setting off' as well as of 'raising' (see definition (2) in H. J. Jensen's *Glossary of John Dryden's Critical Terms* (Minneapolis, 1969), p. 58).

98 'Of Heroic Plays: an Essay' (1672), ed. cit. I, 157.

99 Preface to *Miscellanies*, *Works*, XII, 244.

100 Swift, *Poems*, II, 650.

101 For an account of such entertainments, see Sybil Rosenfeld, *The Theatre of the London Fairs in the 18th Century* (Cambridge, 1960).

102 V. Barberet, *Lesage et le Théâtre de la Foire* (Slatkine Reprints, Geneva, 1970), pp. 227–32.

103 See the account of this piece and its staging in Rosenfeld, pp. 161 ff. Hogarth's *Southwark Fair* (1733), shows a booth with a large sign saying 'The Siege of Troy is here' (*Hogarth's Graphic Works*, ed. Ronald Paulson (New Haven and London, 1965), vol. I, p. 155 and II, Plate No. 137). *The Siege of Troy* was reprinted several times, and texts also survive of other such entertainments: for a selective list, see Rosenfeld, p. 135. For a full account of the connections of this work with Pope's *Dunciad*, see Pat Rogers, 'Pope, Settle and the Fall of Troy', forthcoming in *Studies in English Literature*.

104 Cited by Rosenfeld, op. cit., p. 162. And see Henry Morley, *Memoirs of Bartholomew Fair* (London, 1892), pp. 284 ff.

105 Rosenfeld, op. cit., pp. 136 ff.

106 Rosenfeld, op. cit., p. 144.

107 Arthur Murphy, review of Foote's *The Author*, *Literary Magazine*, No. 11, 15 February–15 March 1757, p. 78, in *Henry Fielding. The Critical Heritage*, pp. 397–8.

108 Louis Perche, *Alfred Jarry*, p. 21.

109 *Tout Ubu*, p. 153. Jarry was warning that his work was not funny as a complacent entertainment was funny, but in a sinister way which probed base instincts and showed the public 'son double ignoble'.

110 Yeats, *Autobiographies*, p. 349.

111 *Dunciad*, p. 257.

112 *Dunciad*, p. 258.

113 C. S. Lewis, *A Preface to Paradise Lost* (London, 1952), p. 93.

114 See Enid Welsford, *The Fool* (London, 1968), pp. 281 ff., 287 ff.; William Willeford, *The Fool and his Sceptre* (London, 1969), pp. xv–xvi, 89, 123 ff.; Robert H. Goldsmith, *Wise Fools in Shakespeare* (Liverpool, 1958), pp. 17 ff.; Winifred Smith, *The Commedia dell'Arte* (New York, 1964), pp. 10–11, 27. On the Devil in Punch and Judy shows, see George Speaight, *Punch & Judy. A History* (London, 1970), *passim*.

115 'The delight of an *Epique* Poem consisteth not in mirth, but admiration' (Thomas Hobbes, 'Answer . . . to . . . D'Avenant's Preface Before Gondibert' (1650), in *Critical Essays of the Seventeenth Century*, ed. J. E. Spingarn (Oxford, 1908–9), II, 64). See also Thomas Blackwell, *Enquiry into the Life and Writings of Homer* (1735), p. 67.

116 The example is suggested to me by Aldous Huxley's essay on 'Baudelaire', *Do What You Will* (London, 1939), pp. 175–6, a lively exploration of certain themes with which I am here concerned.

117 The parallel is noted in *The Poems and Songs of Robert Burns*, ed. James Kinsley (Oxford, 1968), III, 1129.

118 For a pertinent passage on the vanity of 'great men', see *Champion*, 3 May 1740 (*Works*, XV, 298).

119 Cf. Digeon's insight: 'I am inclined to think that the undeniably uncomfortable sensation which may still come over the modern reader of *Jonathan Wild* arises from the character of the book, which is at bottom purely anarchical' (*The Novels of Fielding*, p. 127). I believe in addition that in this anarchy there is a certain joy.

CHAPTER VII

FIELDING'S 'GOOD' MERCHANT: AN APPENDIX ON THE PROBLEM OF HEARTFREE AND OTHER 'GOOD' CHARACTERS IN FIELDING

> . . . I do not conceive my good man to be absolutely a fool or a coward . . .   (Preface to *Miscellanies*)

The moral world of *Jonathan Wild* depends principally on a linguistic polarization of the terms 'good' and 'great', and of the derivatives, semantic and moral, which these two terms acquire in Fielding's ironic scheme (e.g. 'weak' and 'silly' *vs.* 'heroic' and 'admirable', etc.). The ironic use of 'greatness', the pointed contrast with 'goodness', the ultimate ideal of 'true greatness' (which includes 'goodness' and is sometimes called the 'great-and-good'), were commonplace long before Fielding. One finds them in Swift, Congreve, Steele and many others, and they were part of the staple jargon of political (notably of anti-Walpole) pamphleteering. The disreputable sense of 'great' was commonly applied to despot-conquerors, ancient and modern, two favourite examples being Alexander and Louis XIV, both also nick-named 'the Great' (or 'le Grand') in positive praise. The positive connotations of 'great' which seem to have lent themselves most frequently to ironic exploitation were, first, that of heroic stature and achievement (often martial achievement and national leadership), and secondly, that of high social rank or office.[1] The two senses are inter-dependent, and a prime-ministerial figure like Walpole can readily be seen (whether straightforwardly or ironically) to combine aspects of both.[2] The second sense, moreover, easily shades from more or less grandiose conceptions of 'greatness' to a simple identification with 'persons of quality'. This usage is intrinsically neutral, becoming hostile when the user chooses to censure 'persons of quality', as Fielding often does. In such circumstances, however, the term 'great' becomes particularly open to moral ironies which expose the gap between moral character and social rank. Fielding speaks in *Amelia*, XI, v, of a 'little great man', and the same sarcasm is often implicit in his other references to the 'great'.

Such ironies of redefinition also occur in reverse. Just as Fielding, and others, sometimes describe as 'heroic' qualities pointedly not of martial aggressiveness or impressive leadership, but of tender fortitude in domestic affliction,[3] so also Fielding can use 'great' in a high and principally moral sense of, for example, Amelia's unfussy and deeply charitable attitude to her husband's amours with Miss Matthews.[4] Such positive praise of 'greatness' not only implies that the moral quality is a better thing than mere rank, but often contains a submerged hint that persons called 'great' because of their rank ought ideally to live up to the appellation in a moral sense. The hint is not primarily a levelling one, because Fielding's assumption is that it is more important for the highly-placed to fulfil the ideal responsibilities of their rank, than to relinquish their claims to high titles. The most impressively good man in the allegory of goodness and greatness in *A Journey from this World to the Next*, I, v, is in fact a king, and he says: 'I wonder not at the censure which so frequently falls on those in my station: but I wonder that those in my station so frequently deserve it'.[5] Fielding's list of the truly great at the end of the poem 'Of True Greatness' consists exclusively of noblemen and other public leaders. The poem's official theme tends towards freeing 'true greatness' from associations of rank:[6]

> To no profession, party, place confined,
> True greatness lives but in the noble mind.

But terms like 'noble mind' have a built-in tendency to bring notions of rank and virtue into mutual relation, creating overtones of subtle identification (not, of course, of crude equivalence) which will have particular force in an age still animated by aristocratic values. 'Noble mind' and similar phrases ('true greatness', 'natural gentility', etc.), as well as a whole range of stylistic *hauteurs* in Augustan satire, embody assumptions which are deeply ingrained in linguistic history and cultural tradition.[7] These assumptions will seem particularly meaningful to an author of aristocratic predisposition, like Fielding. It came naturally to him to feel that just as false greatness meant usually an unworthy exercise of high rank, so true greatness implies an ideal fusion of virtue and rank. That there was, in actual life, a wide gap between greatness and goodness, Fielding knew well. The painful irony was exacerbated by a deep personal attachment to the ideal, and the fact is reflected in many pained oscillations of usage.

One response (by no means unique to Fielding) is to insist that the combination of greatness and goodness is not confined to the socially 'great'. In a *Covent-Garden Journal* paper deploring snobbish contempt, Fielding speaks of 'a great and good Man . . . whether he be placed at the Top or Bottom of Life'.[8] In *Amelia*, III, vii, Booth exclaims:

> As it is no rare thing to see instances which degrade human nature in persons of the highest birth and education, so I apprehend that examples of whatever is really great and good have been sometimes found amongst those who have wanted all such advantages. In reality, palaces, I make no doubt, do sometimes contain nothing but dreariness and darkness, and the sun of righteousness hath shone forth with all its glory in a cottage.

Booth is replying to a comment by Miss Matthews about Atkinson: 'how astonishing is such behaviour in so low a fellow!' The fact is significant, because, as I argued in Chapter I, Atkinson is the subject of much class-conscious embarrassment in the novel, not least to Fielding himself, whose writing assumes a note of heavy patronizing affection when the sergeant appears.

The two usages from the *Covent-Garden Journal* and *Amelia* do not merely remind us of the inherent element of paradox, or of Fielding's consciousness of a mild verbal audacity (however commonplace), in the attribution of the 'great and good' to persons at the 'Bottom of Life'. They show also that some of Fielding's most important assertions of the purely moral conception of the 'great and good' occur in contexts in which he is explicitly preoccupied by the question of distinctions of rank. Certain characteristic tensions of tone are very obvious. The *Covent-Garden Journal* essay, while concerned to deplore all forms of mutual contempt, has several *hauteurs* in Fielding's best patrician manner. The passage from *Amelia*, on the other hand, has a fervid quality of sentimental overstatement, a rhetoric of beggars and princes and of suns shining with 'glory in a cottage', which also argues some failure of fully serious involvement. As I said in Chapter I, the sentiment is slightly undercut in context by Fielding's attitude to Booth's jargon about 'reigning passions', just as a similar discussion between Amelia and Mrs Bennet, also about Atkinson, is undercut by some mockery of Mrs Bennet.[9] At the same time, there is no real doubt in either place that Fielding passionately believes in the literal truth of the proposition that the qualities which form the 'great and good' are not confined to 'persons of the highest birth and education'. The fact that he tended both to oversentimentalize and to colour with ironic overtones his assertions of this must, however, be viewed together with moods in which he feels that the 'lowest degree' of men are worse than those classes in whom natural malignity has been refined and purged by a gentlemanly education.[10]

The oscillations of linguistic usage, in which the word 'great' slides between implications of rank, of 'heroic' prowess, and of moral excellence, or among varying combinations of these, are reflected in that part of the Preface to the *Miscellanies* which expounds what is sometimes thought of as the 'moral allegory' of *Jonathan Wild*.[11] They are further, I believe, compounded in both the Preface and the novel by uncertainties and at times by inconsistencies of emotional colouring not unlike those which I have just been describing. This fact makes the use of the Preface to explain the novel less straightforward than some critics assume. Paradoxically, the complications exist in spite of the fact that both the Preface and the novel make a show of formulaic precision, not to say patness.

The Preface makes explicit, as we should expect, that 'greatness' is wrongly attributed by the world to the highly-placed and the vicious, and that a moral redefinition is called for. 'True greatness of mind' is properly something 'in which we always include an idea of goodness'. In this redefinition, the association of 'greatness' with a quasi-heroic grandeur of 'parts' and 'courage' is explicitly retained, and its association with rank attenuated but not exorcized. Indeed, the heroic and the high-ranking are, not for the first time, in a curious if incomplete relation. Fielding has just been describing his ideal of the 'great and good' as, among other things, 'the Iliad of Nature', a quality attained 'in the highest degree' by a few sublime (not necessarily epic) personages like 'Socrates and Brutus; and perhaps . . . some among us'.[12] The last phrase has very much the air of alluding to those noble persons (Carteret, Chesterfield, Lyttelton etc.) who are celebrated by name at the end of the poem 'Of True Greatness', a poem included, incidentally, in the *Miscellanies*.[13] Heartfree, the 'good' hero of *Jonathan Wild*, is perhaps explicitly excluded, in the Preface, from the ranks of the 'great and good', if it is to him rather than to Fielding's generic type of 'goodness' that the Preface refers when it says that 'my good man . . . often partakes too little of parts or courage to have any pretensions to greatness'. 'Parts or courage' reassert criteria of personal accomplishment rather than social rank. But it may be apposite to recall that Heartfree was a tradesman, and that we have just had a hint, in 'some among us', of a residual identification of 'greatness' with distinguished rank as well as excellence. The names of Socrates and Brutus, as well as other state-ments in the Preface, make it clear that the class-identification is neither simple nor conclusive, and we should not expect it to be nakedly deliberate on Fielding's part. But all we know about Fielding suggests that it cannot be overlooked, and that an element of unconscious or self-concealed hauteur would be highly consistent with many overt features of his style.

In that part of the Preface to the Miscellanies which discusses *Jonathan Wild*, Fielding sometimes uses 'great' in the idiomatic sense of 'pertain-ing to high society': 'the great world', 'the splendid palaces of the great'. The usage is not of course neutral even here, and it modulates from time to time into various ironies of redefinition. The sarcasm as such, how-ever, is not a redefinition of the upper-class associations of the word 'great', but merely conveys Fielding's anger at the *mores* of high society. Wild is not great in *this* sense, and Fielding indicates that one irony of the novel is that he ought to be, since many highly placed persons are just as vicious as he is: 'without considering Newgate as no other than human nature with its mask off, which some very shameless writers have done, a thought which no price should purchase me to entertain, I think we may be excused for suspecting, that the splendid palaces of the great are often no other than Newgate with the mask on'. This (assum-ing that the Preface was written after the novel) is a variation of the reference to Newgate at the end of Book III as 'the place where most of the great men of this history are hastening as fast as possible; and, to confess the truth, it is a castle very far from being an improper or mis-becoming habitation for any great man whatever'. The difference is that the novel's formula takes for granted the moral perversion of the term 'great' and its applicability to Wild, whereas the Preface, which (though written last) the reader will read first, sets out to explain the novel in more literal terms and as it were from scratch. In the Preface it is made quietly obvious that Wild is not one of the 'great' in the social sense, whereas in the novel the distinction is deliberately blurred in a heavy routine of verbal equivalence, and in a host of mock-heroic grotesqueries. Yet in another sense the novel is full of comic reminders of Wild's ungenteel oafishness. The account of his conversations with Count La Ruse (himself a preposterous example of shifty underworld courtliness) shows up Wild's vulgarity in manner, language and dress (I, iv–vi). Even after Wild has entered 'into the world' and 'passed for a gentleman of great fortune in the funds', caressed by 'women of quality' and sought after by 'young ladies', the supposed gentility appears at best as a moneyed one, and the comic disparity between Wild and the world of polite accomplishments is always more vividly emphasized than any analogy. Indeed, some of the analogies deliberately highlight the difference, as when the young Wild is transported on a Grand Tour 'to his majesty's plantations in America' (I, vii: the disparity remains pointed even though part of the implication is a sarcasm of analogy at the expense of real grand tours). Even by the standards of that low parody of polite society in which he moves, where whores are the 'women of quality' and a spiv like La Ruse passes for a Count,[14] Wild is an ungenteel failure. As we have seen, his women deceive him with common beaux like Smirk; and when, after being defrauded by the Count, he rushes to the Count's house, he is compared to a footman and rebuffed by 'a well-dressed liveryman' (II, iv), a comic reduction which betrays Fielding's reluctance to take too seriously the proclaimed equivalence of Wild and the socially 'great'.

Wild's amusing unsuccess, here and in many other episodes, gives a special significance to the Preface's description of bad greatness (greatness without goodness) as a 'bombast' thing, like 'the false sublime in poetry'. Although Fielding seems to want to maintain, in both the Preface and the novel, that Wild's wickedness is no laughing matter, he does in both places effectively indicate (however deliberately) an important element of ridicule. Wild's comic dimension has already been fully discussed. Here, we may ask whether Fielding would have used words like 'bombast' and 'false sublime' in the Preface, if he had not felt that a comic impulse had run away with more explicit intentions? and whether in the novel the urgency of the moral ironist has not become unconsciously disarmed by the playful and uppish detachment of the gentleman novelist?

Corresponding gaps, both between Preface and novel, and, within the novel, between ostensible purposes and actual realization, exist in the treatment of Heartfree. If Fielding's seriousness about Wild's evil is attenuated by a comedy of uppish deflation, so his defence of Heartfree's 'goodness' is undermined by an opposite note of sentimental gravity. Heartfree has often been thought a failure of characterization. It seems conceivable that this failure may be due partly to the fact that, as a somewhat passively virtuous person and as a mere tradesman, Heartfree was someone whom Fielding found it easier to sentimentalize than to respect.[15] The more or less contemporary Joseph Andrews also combined a virtuous passiveness with (or so it seems in effect throughout most of the novel) non-gentility. Fielding treats Joseph with an open note of affectionate derision, amicably uppish over Joseph's rigidities of character, as well as his status as a footman. In some ways, this resembles the treatment of Wild rather than that of Heartfree, even though the humour about Wild is of course less amicable and perhaps less intentional than that about Joseph. In the case of Heartfree there is very little humour, and therefore no safety-valve for certain primary elements of Fielding's temperament: not only his tendency to uppishness, but a dislike of gravity, a scepticism of virtuous cant, and an authorial need to assert his emotional control of situations through rich feats of ironic modulation. The characterization of Heartfree may have been a victim of the oppressively simplifying demands of the ironic scheme. The character of Wild was in theory equally subject to these demands, but villains are not only notoriously easier to portray convincingly than the very virtuous ('for ill-nature adds great support and strength to faith', as Fielding explains in *Tom Jones*, VIII, i), but also probably easier to energize with an admixture of comedy. To have permitted a desolemnification of Heartfree would have entailed a grave risk of radically undermining 'goodness', in its difficult confrontation with 'greatness', especially where the latter has been more buoyantly portrayed. That Fielding was prepared to risk such desolemnification in *Joseph Andrews* may be the result of greater artistic maturity or confidence, and even of a realization of failure over Heartfree (this hypothesis, of course, would presuppose that a draft of *Jonathan Wild*, and especially the Heartfree element, was more or less finished before *Joseph Andrews*).[16] In *Joseph Andrews*, Fielding was also helped by the nature of his parodic purposes, which invited ironic play but did not burden it with starkly polarized issues of good and evil: a degree of comic deflation could be taken as good anti-Pamelaic fun, without diminishing Joseph beyond recovery.

In any event, Heartfree and his family seem to me the novel's main failure because Fielding could neither take their moral dignity entirely seriously, nor recognize this fact in himself. Recent attempts to see this failure of characterization as a deliberate indication of moral imperfection seem to me misguided. Allan Wendt is the chief proponent of this view, which has been widely accepted: 'Heartfree would seem to be an "imperfect" character not aesthetically, . . . but morally, as a part of Fielding's deliberate intent'.[17] Wendt's argument is based on the famous tripartite distinction, in the Preface to the *Miscellanies*, between 'the great, the good, and the great and good':[18]

The last of these is the true sublime in human nature. That

elevation by which the soul of man, raising and extending itself
above the order of this creation, and brightened with a certain
ray of divinity, looks down on the condition of mortals. This is
indeed a glorious object, on which we can never gaze with too
much praise and admiration. A perfect work! the Iliad of Nature!
ravishing and astonishing, and which at once fills us with love,
wonder, and delight.

The second falls greatly short of this perfection, and yet hath its
merit. Our wonder ceases; our delight is lessened, but our love
remains; of which passion, goodness hath always appeared to me
the only true and proper object. On this head I think proper to
observe, that I do not conceive my good man to be absolutely a
fool or a coward; but that he often partakes too little of parts or
courage to have any pretensions to greatness.

This passage is taken as making explicit a critique of Heartfree which is
genuinely embodied in the novel, and as implying that the novel is
concerned to advocate a combination of goodness and greatness in the
form of a 'golden mean'.[19]

The argument seems insensitive, first of all, to discrepancies of tone
and emphasis between the novel and the Preface. 'Golden means' are,
in a certain (paradoxical) sense, ideals of perfection. But the practical
union of caution with decency, of moderation and poise with generosity
of impulse, of self-interested energy with good-nature, which Wendt
has in mind (and of which Fielding also certainly approved), is hard to
reconcile with the tone of phrases like 'that elevation . . . brightened
with a certain ray of divinity . . . the Iliad of Nature! ravishing and
astonishing'. Heartfree would hardly be blamed, in the fabric of the
novel, for falling short of Socrates and Brutus, those two ancients who,
with 'perhaps . . . some among us', are listed in the Preface as embodying the true union of the great and good. In the novel as we read it,
there is no example of the great and good, no glorious Socrates nor even
a Swiftian Portuguese Captain, to set against the vices of Wild on the
one hand and the alleged deficiencies of Heartfree on the other. It
would be uncharacteristic of Fielding to write a work in which his
positives are not prominently emphasized. The ironic scheme of the
novel as we have it is so starkly polarized that Heartfree inevitably
presents himself as a positive foil (however clumsy or sentimentalized)
to Wild. The polarization is, of course, overtly rhetorical and formulaic.
It consciously pursues an antithesis to limits which would be inappropriate in the more literal-minded context of a Preface. The assertion of

incompatibility between greatness and goodness signposts itself as incomplete, even within the novel: 'while greatness consists in power, pride, insolence, and doing mischief to mankind—to speak out—while a great man and a great rogue are synonymous terms, so long shall Wild stand unrivalled on the pinnacle of GREATNESS' (IV, xv). Such a reminder that the irony is a verbal thing, depending on the language of a bad world rather than on the nature of things, also reminds us that in the here and now of this novel, 'great man' and 'great rogue' *are* 'synony-mous terms'. It is from time to time said in the novel, and notably both in its first and its last chapters, that Wild had a few weaknesses (i.e. virtues). But this concession is always minimal, and usually part of a playful 'realism', in which the mock-author assures us that he knows that no man is perfect, not even Wild. This hardly reduces the schemat-ism: it may indeed stiffen it by asserting that Wild was so wicked that he stopped just short of diabolism, or intensify the ironic sting by a momentary tactical softening or some other variation on the dominant formula (see, for example, I, i and IV, iv).

The novel is too firmly rooted in its bipartite formula for the Preface's third category to bear any live relation to it. The Preface reads more like an *ex post facto* elaboration, rationalizing an extremist fiction into more balanced ethical discourse, than as an account of the novel itself. The use of the Preface to interpret the novel is an understandable procedure on the part of the critics, but in a sense it is the novel which must be invoked to explain the Preface. Given the novel's schematism, Fielding might well, for example, have wished to clear himself from the suggestion of attacking *every* kind of 'great' man. It seems even likelier, moreover, that he would feel impelled, after the event, to make a statement allowing for some rather grander specimens of goodness than his long-suffering merchant had turned out to be. The trouble with Heartfree and his family most of the time is not that the novel seeks to introduce reservations about them, but that Fielding celebrates them with the overemphasis of an incomplete creative engagement:

> Mr. Thomas Heartfree ... was of an honest and open disposition. He was of that sort of men whom experience only, and not their own natures, must inform that there are such things as deceit and hypocrisy in the world ... He was possessed of several great weaknesses of mind, being good-natured, friendly, and generous to a great excess. He had, indeed, too little regard to common justice, for he had forgiven some debts to his acquaintance only because they could not pay him ... He was withal so silly a fellow

that he never took the least advantage of the ignorance of his customers, and contented himself with very moderate gains on his goods; which he was the better enabled to do, notwithstanding his generosity, because his life was extremely temperate, his expenses being solely confined to the cheerful entertainment of his friends at home, and now and then a moderate glass of wine, in which he indulged himself in the company of his wife, who, with an agreeable person, was a mean-spirited, poor, domestic, low-bred animal, who confined herself mostly to the care of her family . . .

To this silly woman did this silly fellow introduce the GREAT WILD . . . This simple woman no sooner heard her husband had been obliged to her guest than her eyes sparkled on him with a benevolence which is an emanation from the heart (II, i).[20]

This formal portrait is part of our first introduction to the Heartfrees.[21] The praise hardly seems undercut by deliberate authorial reservations. There are radical waverings of tone, but they do not seem to be wholly in Fielding's control. Fielding's serious-minded fervour, as in the praise of Heartfree's treatment of debtors, develops too easily into wooden cosiness or crude emotional rhetoric: the heavy detailing of 'cheerful entertainment', of the occasional 'moderate glass of wine' and similar frugalities (my quotation is abbreviated and selective), of the benevolent emanation from Mrs Heartfree's heart (to which may be added all the subsequent family-tableaux, the heart-rending separations and reunions, the tender tears and the faintings). The pervasive irony provides neither an overall cohesion, nor a saving detachment. It too oscillates, between a genuinely biting moral sarcasm ('He had, indeed, too little regard to common justice . . .'), and a rigorous but emotionally undisciplined schematism ('mean-spirited, poor, domestic, low-bred animal' 'silly woman', 'silly fellow'), whose topsy-turvy acerbities merely add a further dimension of coarse-grained sentimentality.

Nevertheless, the celebration of the Heartfrees is very definite. Fielding even shows some concern to describe Heartfree as not only judicious and moderate in his way of life, but as having also something of a positive and outgoing personality, especially generosity 'to a great excess'. In the paragraph preceding the formal portrait, we had also been told that he 'had married a very agreeable woman for love', a fact Fielding was later to note, at least twice, about Allworthy, as though wanting to stress an ardent nature in characters whose quiet virtue or judiciousness threatened to seem dull.[22] Like Allworthy, Heartfree is liable to be imposed upon, because men of an 'honest and open disposition' have no inner knowledge 'that there are such things as deceit and hypocrisy in the world', and must learn the fact from bitter experience. The theme is a favourite of Fielding's, and its formulation here makes Heartfree the exact antithesis of those bad men (like Wild cf. III, x), and those depraved students of human nature (cf. *Tom Jones*, VI, i), whose own bad hearts make it impossible for them to know that goodness can exist in others. Allworthy, older and more experienced than Heartfree, is also much imposed upon, and if he lacks a due measure of self-protecting (and self-regarding) prudence, he shares the lack with most of Fielding's sympathetic characters: the imprudence of benevolent men is something Fielding often complains of in principle, whilst actually suffusing its manifestations in the novels with an overriding warmth of affectionate approval. But Heartfree and Allworthy, unlike other impulsively imprudent characters such as Adams or Tom, are both presented with a certain awkwardness of tone, in which a tendency to ridicule is either unintended or not entirely under control. Allworthy happens, unlike Heartfree, to be 'great' as well as 'good'. In him, social status and a high sense of its responsibilities are combined with moral sensibility and intellectual power, 'true wisdom and philosophy'.[23] In the language of the Preface to the *Miscellanies*, he partakes of Socrates and the 'some among us', 'the true sublime in human nature'.[24] Yet this 'true sublime' comes perilously close to 'bombast greatness' in the rendering:[25]

> It was now the middle of May, and the morning was remarkably serene, when Mr. Allworthy walked forth on the terrace, where the dawn opened every minute that lovely prospect we have before described to his eye. And now having sent forth streams of light, which ascended the blue firmament before him, as harbingers preceding his pomp, in the full blaze of his majesty, rose the sun; than which one object alone in this lower creation could be more glorious, and that Mr. Allworthy himself presented; a human being replete with benevolence, meditating in what manner he might render himself most acceptable to his Creator, by doing most good to his creatures.

Whether or not this was meant to be funny, it goes wrong. Allworthy cannot be meant to be seriously subverted, yet he is. Instead of those assured witty complicities which Fielding sets up with the reader when describing Sophia or Tom, or the frankly extravagant comedy with which he presents Parson Adams, we have here a humour much more unsure of itself. Sophia, Tom and Adams have a vitality which enables them to compete with any mild humour at their expense, and emerge unscathed. Allworthy sinks ponderously. Grotesquely unassimilated shades of mock-heroic obtrude. The ponderously fussy image of the sun makes Allworthy, by an absurd logic, 'the Rival of his Beams'—like Pope's Belinda![26] 'Replete with benevolence' disconcertingly half-evokes the custard-crammed aldermanic figures of the *Dunciad*. Allworthy's 'true wisdom and philosophy' are invoked in *Tom Jones*, VI, iv, to account for his 'gravity', but gravity is seldom unscathed in Fielding, and Allworthy is residually tainted with a self-importance which is, precisely, aldermanic. One wonders whether the unintended deflation would have occurred if Fielding's real-life model had been, say, Lord Chesterfield rather than Ralph Allen. In theory, if Allworthy had been placed in *Jonathan Wild* instead of *Tom Jones*, he would have been an example of the 'great and good'. In practice, the self-made magnate might not have been any less vulnerable than the thrifty tradesman to Fielding's awkward mixture of sentimentalizing dullness and uncertainly focused ridicule.

The subversion of Allworthy by awkward humour and by an unintended dullness, and its bearing on the treatment of Heartfree, are thus partly outside the domain of a strictly *moral* allegory, and seem to involve an element of patronizing *hauteur*. This *hauteur* is implicit and unacknowledged, and must remain hypothetical, since all Fielding's avowed endeavours are to emphasize the moral aspects of 'goodness' and 'greatness'. If I am right that oscillations towards class-consciousness occur, they are much more evident with Heartfree than with Allworthy. There are good reasons for this. Heartfree, as a small tradesman, is lower and more vulnerable to patronizing than a great landowner like Allworthy. The humble origins of Allworthy's real-life original are in any case suppressed in the novel, where Allworthy enjoys great inherited wealth. In *Jonathan Wild*, moreover, but not in *Tom Jones*, the term 'greatness', with its unavoidable ambiguities, plays a central and very insistent part. In addition, the systematic ironic reversal in the earlier novel not only increases the general risk of uncertainties of nuance, but introduces further specific ambiguities when terms like 'mean' and 'low' are applied to the Heartfrees. Finally, the relative immaturity of Fielding's art in the earlier work would naturally account for a more uncertain handling of awkward implications than one would expect to find in an assured masterpiece like *Tom Jones*.

Fielding insisted very hard that Heartfree was not to be despised for *actual* silliness or 'lowness' of character, and especially not for excessive gullibility. Perhaps Fielding insisted too hard. But there seems no doubt that he wished to convince us. Good reasons why Heartfree should at first be very trusting of Wild are given time and again: their schoolboy friendship, the elaborate plausibility of Wild's strategies and arguments, and his persuasive composure of manner, as well as Heartfree's own decency, generosity of spirit, and youthful inexperience (II, i, ii, viii, ix; III, v, ix, etc.). Uncertainties clearly exist. We might feel that schoolboy memories might have put Heartfree on his guard sooner, and that he ought to have been more strongly and durably alerted to Wild's nature when, in III, v, Wild proposes to him a scheme involving murder. Fielding quickly smothers doubts on the first score in II, i, by insisting on Heartfree's indebtedness to Wild for favours during their boyhood (I shall return to these) and especially strongly on his inexperience and his generosity (in the formal portrait already quoted). The second doubt is partly dealt with in III, ix, when we are told that Heartfree had been 'unwilling to condemn his friend without certain evidence' but was now convinced of his villainy. Moreover, in III, v and III, x, Fielding diverts our attention from a possible momentary obtuseness in Heartfree to an undoubted and radical obtuseness in Wild, insisting on Wild's crazed inability to believe in the existence of goodness and to foresee that Heartfree would be antagonized by his crudely vicious proposal.

This refocusing of our attention onto Wild's oafish stupidity is Fielding's surest way of rescuing Heartfree from those uncertainties of irony which leave the impression that he is naïve to the point of foolishness, and contemptibly passive in other ways. Where Fielding's easy contempt for Wild is allowed free play, his *un*easiness over Heartfree can be powerfully countered by dramatic rather than merely verbal means. Where, on the other hand, direct attention has to be focused on Heartfree, the rescue operation is too often a matter of strenuous verbal insistence. This may take the form of disarming our doubts by wording them into the upsidedown irony, and thus identifying the doubts themselves with the anti-values of bad greatness-minded men:

> I am sensible that the reader, if he hath but the least notion of greatness, must have such a contempt for the extreme folly of this fellow, that he will be very little concerned at any misfortunes which may befall him in the sequel; for to have no suspicion that an old school-fellow, with whom he had, in his tenderest years, contracted a friendship, and who, on the accidental renewing of their acquaintance, had professed the most passionate regard for him, should be very ready to impose on him; in short, to conceive

that a friend should, of his own accord, without any view to his
own interest, endeavour to do him a service, must argue such
weakness of mind, such ignorance of the world, and such an artless,
simple, undesigning heart, as must render the person possessed of
it the lowest creature and the properest object of contempt
imaginable in the eyes of every man of understanding and
discernment (II, ii).

This works awkwardly, not only because the irony backfires through
over-insistence, so that some of the dispraise is taken literally, but also
because the reader has a legitimate doubt in the first place, so that there
is a gap between his real feelings, and those which Fielding wants him
to have. In other words, real and honest doubts merge, in the reader's
mind, with the more disreputable feelings which the irony imputes to
him, and the irony thus cannot disarm the reader by being simply
retranslated into its opposite. Wild had just suggested to Heartfree a
disreputable commercial proceeding, which Heartfree rejected 'not
without some disdain', while nevertheless agreeing to the seemingly
honest parts of the transaction and 'expressing much gratitude to his
friend for his recommendation'. This little drama of mixed implications
is encapsulated in a single long summarizing sentence, which immediately precedes the quoted passage. It shows Fielding needing to get
Heartfree duped by Wild, yet anxious to show him as too sensible and
decent to accept a dishonourable scheme. The balance is difficult to
achieve, because the reader has been made strongly aware of Wild's
nefarious scheming, although Heartfree has not; and because the deal
involves Count La Ruse, whom the reader knows but whom Heartfree,
again, does not. The 'dramatic irony' thus works against Heartfree not
only more strongly than the plot justifies, but also more strongly than
Fielding's moral scheme can comfortably bear.

Fielding's control of characterization, of plot-arrangement, and,
above all, of ironic modulation, is clearly not yet sufficiently developed
to accommodate such warring complexities or to bridge such debilitating gaps. The somewhat strenuous paragraph which I have quoted is
an attempt to recover the situation. This attempt, however, is itself not
fully under control and needs rectifying. In the next paragraph, before
returning from moral commentary to narrative action, Fielding makes
a further (and more successful) effort to rehabilitate Heartfree:

Wild remembered that his friend Heartfree's faults were rather
in his heart than in his head; that, though he was so mean a
fellow that he was never capable of laying a design to injure any

human creature, yet was he by no means a fool, nor liable to any
gross imposition, unless where his heart betrayed him. He therefore
instructed the count to take only one of his jewels at the first
interview.

This fresh start is in every way more satisfactory. It is briefer and more
to the point. The sentimental-ironic schematism is prevented from fussy
elaboration by the brisk return to factual narrative, as well as being in
itself more restrained (the revised edition's text, from which I am quoting, interestingly shows a slight toning-down of the original, the phrase
'so mean a fellow' replacing the first edition's 'an abject mean fellow').
The passage states what readers sometimes overlook and Wendt's article
denies,[27] that Heartfree has a 'good head' as well as a 'good heart'. It is
true that Fielding often warned that 'good hearts' may mislead 'good
heads', but wrong to suppose that he invariably regarded this as a mainly
culpable (if endearing) debility. As he said in *Amelia*, viii, ix, with the
heroine herself in mind:

> it is not want of sense, but want of suspicion, by which innocence
> is often betrayed. Again, we often admire the folly of the dupe,
> when we should transfer our whole surprise to the astonishing
> guilt of the betrayer. In a word, many an innocent person hath
> owed his ruin to this circumstance alone, that the degree of villainy
> was such as must have exceeded the faith of every man who was
> not himself a villain.

The point is missed in Heartfree, but not for want of reminders. Various
authorial uncertainties, including the fact that Wild turns out to be
much less diabolical than the verbalizing of his 'greatness' suggests,
prevent the effective realization of Heartfree as no more foolish than
other men. If we are made more vividly aware of Heartfree's 'good
head' on the present occasion, it may be because Fielding has mediated
the observation through Wild, who ought to know, thus rescuing the
author himself from the undermining disbelief which the crude ironic
reversals have induced in the reader.

Many reminders exist, in later novels, that those decent and innocent
characters who are duped by a villain are not fools. Most are delivered
in a more or less authorial voice, and carry greater conviction than the
earlier, *un*mediated comment about Heartfree. Not all have the plain
and impassioned completeness of the comment about Amelia, a comment which I believe to be exactly appropriate to the *intended* moral
effect of *Jonathan Wild*. There is the laconic sarcasm with which, at the

end of *Amelia*, x, iv, Fielding accepts that some readers will feel that the good Dr Harrison was 'too easy a dupe to the gross flattery' of a false old sycophant: 'If there be any such critics, we are heartily sorry, as well for them as for the doctor'. In *Amelia*, xii, v, there is by contrast a full circumstantial explanation of how Dr Harrison came unwittingly to employ a dishonest attorney. Such rebukes to readers who judge too hastily sometimes explicitly raise the question of 'dramatic irony', that disproportion between what the reader knows and what the character knows which we have seen to work to Heartfree's disadvantage. The nettle is eloquently grasped when Allworthy's tolerance of Thwackum comes up for comment:[28]

> the reader is greatly mistaken, if he conceives that Thwackum appeared to Mr. Allworthy in the same light as he doth to him in this history; and he is as much deceived, if he imagines, that the most intimate acquaintance which he himself could have had with that divine, would have informed him of those things which we, from our inspiration, are enabled to open and discover. Of readers who from such conceits as these, condemn the wisdom or penetration of Mr. Allworthy, I shall not scruple to say, that they make a very bad and ungrateful use of that knowledge which we have communicated to them.

An author must be very confident indeed, not only of what he has given to the reader but of his own established authority within the work, to carry off such a statement with success. It may be that, in the larger economy of the novel, such confidence is not fully justified. The disreputability of Thwackum, like that of Wild and La Ruse, has been made very vivid. Allworthy, on the other hand, and for that matter Dr Harrison (who exercises a similar aldermanly chairmanship over the action of *Amelia*), are problematic cases, and Fielding's disclaimers cannot in the end efface a certain impression of stuffy impercipience. It is even arguable that something must have gone amiss for the disclaimers to be called for, and we have already seen that the portrayal of Allworthy shares some weaknesses with that of Heartfree. Yet the passage I have quoted comes as near to total success as a disclaimer can. For one thing, any element of disconnection between the passage and the larger movement of the novel is outweighed not only by the passage's own eloquent blend of moral fervour and ironic judiciousness, but also by the sharply vivid validation provided by its immediate periphery. There we learn of Thwackum's good reputation 'for learning, religion and sobriety of manners', of the fact that he was vouched for by a close and trusted friend of Allworthy's, of his seeming amiability and of the real qualities which Allworthy had eventually to weigh against such infirmities as became evident later, of Allworthy's calculation that his and Square's 'contrary errors' would counteract one another in a fashion salutary to their two pupils. These paragraphs are in a style of crisp summarizing adjudication which Fielding handles masterfully, and if Allworthy's calculation about the 'contrary errors' seems implausible from our knowledge of Thwackum and Square, Fielding is master of that fact also: 'If the event happened contrary to his expectations, this possibly proceeded from some fault in the plan itself; which the reader hath my leave to discover, if he can: for we do not pretend to introduce any infallible characters into this history'. The entire passage has the kind of brilliant firmness which makes even the disclaimers and sub-disclaimers have more life as creative contributions than as correctives, not only relying on but furthering that sense of easy authorial domination of the reader, and of the action, which animates the novel.

But perhaps the most instructive parallel with Heartfree is a passage about Sophia at the end of *Tom Jones*, VII, iii. She has just failed to press a tactical advantage with her father over Mrs Western:

> Women who, like Mrs. Western, know the world, and have applied themselves to philosophy and politics, would have immediately availed themselves of the present disposition of Mr. Western's mind; by throwing in a few artful compliments to his understanding at the expence of his absent adversary; but poor Sophia was all simplicity. By which word we do not intend to insinuate to the reader, that she was silly, which is generally understood as a synonimous term with simple: for she was indeed a most sensible girl, and her understanding was of the first rate; but she wanted all that useful art which females convert to so many good purposes in life, and which, as it rather arises from the heart, than from the head, is often the property of the silliest of women.

The passage relies to some extent on the same ironic contrast as in *Jonathan Wild* between the language of 'the world' and that of a truer morality, and issues the usual reminder that innocence and integrity are not to be confused with stupidity. Like the passage describing Wild's misconception about Heartfree, this passage insists that a good heart and a good head may co-exist. It offers, indeed, a still further reversal, in which the low cunning which the world calls wisdom is identified not with 'the head' but with 'the heart', as a product of bad or shallow spontaneities rather than of shrewdness, and consistent with stupidity. This does not mean that Sophia's *good* heart, her warm and tender decency, are ever open to doubt, and the passage celebrates, as with Heartfree, the co-existence of a sound 'understanding' with a certain innocence in matters of self-interest.

The essential differences are of conviction, not of substance. If the disclaimer in *Jonathan Wild* worked better when mediated through Wild's point of view than when it proceeds from the narrator's ironic voice, Fielding is (other things being equal) normally at his best in a more direct presence, where authorial wisdom and authorial irony can freely flower. The authorial command of *Tom Jones* and, to a lesser degree, of Fielding's other two novels, has to be earned not only by the narrator's near-ubiquity, but by a continuous and vital plasticity of relationship between moral urgency and urbane detachment. In *Jonathan Wild*, on the other hand, the rigidity of the main ironic reversal allows little play to the awareness of nuance and the mastery of ironic modulation on which such a plasticity partly depends (it needs a negative vision like Swift's to come fully alive in an upsidedown scheme, say the *Tale of a Tub*'s). The rigidity of reversal becomes counter-productive, the mock-blame tending to acquire *literal* force, not only through over-insistence, but because no decent or sensible point of view is given a direct hearing. This means that Wild, being at least a personality involved in the consequences of whatever Heartfree's character may turn out to be, will provide a greater pertinence of vision than the sarcastic automaton officially telling the story.

In addition, disclaimers about Sophia or Amelia, and even about Allworthy or Harrison, have a reality absent from those about Heartfree, because these personages, unlike Heartfree, are treated as real characters, not as formulaic counters in a verbal irony. With Heartfree, we have nothing but his innocence, and the novel's insistence upon it. There is nothing sufficiently solid for a complicating disclaimer to modify. The fact that he is constantly gulled to the sound of repeated refrains upon his weakness and his silliness remains more real than the proper view we are invited to take. The much greater vitality of the character of Wild compounds this effect, not only by setting Heartfree's lifelessness into still sharper relief, but because, as we have seen, Wild's vitality is often that of a comic clumsy rogue rather than of a diabolical Machiavel, which makes Heartfree seem even sillier for being taken in.

But all the evidence is that Fielding wants to rescue him from this. The sentimental inflation with which he and his wife are normally

presented is, as I suggested, a rather awkward sign of Fielding's earnestness on the point. We have seen that the schematic sarcasms do not, in
such situations, provide a saving element of hard-headed detachment.
For Fielding to say that, after Heartfree's incarceration by Snap, Heartfree and his wife 'passed an hour in a scene of tenderness too low and
contemptible to be recounted to our great readers' (II, vii), is to increase,
not to reduce, its crude emotionalism. The scene itself has many of the
standard routines of pathos, 'sudden joy' and agonized despair, anxiety
for the 'little family' and stout-hearted moments of practicality-in-
distress, without any touch of the kind of humour which often qualifies
the 'high' moments in the other novels. If at times Fielding seems to be
trying, however unconsciously, to control the unruly sentimental
rhetoric, he does so less by comic deflations than by straightforward
soberings. When Mrs Heartfree first hears of the incarceration, just
before the 'scene of tenderness', she 'raved like one distracted', but
almost immediately 'applied herself to all possible means to procure her
husband's liberty'. The line between this and a more fondly elaborated
practicality-in-distress in other parts of the same chapter is rather fine,
but there is here a momentary note of serious-minded efficiency, made
convincing by a crispness in the writing. Its relative success in subduing
the hysteria and enabling us to take a respectful and uninflated view of
his heroine for a tiny instant, adds to our feeling that some part of
Fielding wanted to rescue the Heartfrees from his own sentimentalization of them, but was unwilling to risk a joking deflation. A more
creatively engaged Fielding would have been more confident that they
would survive the deflation, and be revitalized by it: one thinks of
Parson Adam's intensities of grief and joy in *Joseph Andrews*, IV, viii, or
of the freshness with which Sophia emerges from the ranting extravagance of *Tom Jones*, IV, ii.

Parson Adams is a good test case, being more nearly contemporary in
date with Heartfree than the other characters with whom we have
compared him, and closest to him in many details. The fact has often
been noted, and W. R. Irwin has said well that 'Heartfree and the good
clergyman have so much in common . . . that the former might almost
be considered a humorless and imperfect version of the latter'.[29]
Particularly apposite are these two passages, from the formal portraits
which introduce these characters in each novel. Heartfree, we have seen:

> was of that sort of men whom experience only, and not their own
> natures, must inform that there are such things as deceit and
> hypocrisy in the world . . . He was possessed of several great

weaknesses of mind, being good-natured, friendly, and generous to a great excess (*J.W.*, II, i).

Adams also:

was generous, friendly, and brave to an excess; but simplicity was his characteristic: he did, no more than Mr. Colley Cibber, apprehend any such passions as malice and envy to exist in mankind (*J.A.*, I, iii)

The obvious immediate difference between the two passages is the allusion in the second to Colley Cibber, a tiny joke which deftly lifts the discourse out of solemnity into a domain of humour. The sentence in fact parodies a remark in the first chapter of Cibber's *Apology*, and as it happens differs mainly from the parallel sentence from *Jonathan Wild* in taking up some of Cibber's vocabulary ('malice and envy' rather than 'deceit and hypocrisy'). This use of parody to desolemnify without deflating a character of his own (perhaps yet another variant aspect of that distinction between burlesque of diction, and mockery of 'sentiments and characters', which Fielding discussed in the Preface to *Joseph Andrews*), is something which Fielding did not risk with Heartfree. With the single special exception of Mrs Heartfree's travels,[30] the Heartfrees are rigorously insulated from the comic transformation which parody so often effects elsewhere in Fielding (and in much other Augustan writing). The mock-heroic element in *Jonathan Wild* is allowed to work its chemistry only on the villains (especially on Wild himself), where Fielding did not feel inhibited by the dangers of deflation, and where (as I argued in earlier chapters) an oddly comic and highly significant softening of Wild's character results, perhaps unintentionally.

Parody is not the only, nor even the main, agent of the humour which distinguishes the treatment of Adams from that of Heartfree. If we compare the whole of the two introductory portraits from which I have quoted the parallels only, we find that Adams is celebrated with a touch of humorous extravagance (cf. his polyglot prowess, or the pedantic enthusiasm with which he quizzed Joseph on the scriptures), whereas Heartfree is sentimentally frozen in a few virtuous postures (kindness, temperance and the 'moderate glass of wine', model tableaux of family life). Nevertheless, the touches of parody in *Joseph Andrews* are important to the difference, and the fact seems worth stressing especially because *Joseph Andrews* is the less systematically parodic, as a whole, of the two novels. The parallel portraits call Heartfree 'good-natured, friendly, and generous', and Adams 'generous, friendly, and brave'. That Heartfree is not here said to possess the 'heroic' virtue of 'bravery' is, I believe, entirely fortuitous. But it acquires a lucky aptness in the context of Fielding's statement in the Preface to the *Miscellanies* that the 'good man' tends to lack the 'parts or courage' for becoming 'great', and Allan Wendt notes that Heartfree's passivity must be contrasted with Adams's 'willingness to wade into a fight'.[31] This lucky aptness is, however, misleading. Heartfree is not unwilling to fight if he needs to. When a brutal officer of the law tries to take Heartfree's 'little one rudely from his knees ... Heartfree started up, and catching the fellow by the collar, dashed his head so violently against the wall, that, had he had any brains, he might possibly have lost them by the blow' (III, xii). There is a parallel in *Joseph Andrews*, II, ix, where Adams fights with a man who had attacked Fanny, and where the same joke about the brainlessness of heroes occurs:[32]

> lifting up his crabstick, he immediately levelled a blow at that part of the ravisher's head where, according to the opinion of the ancients, the brains of some persons are deposited, and which he had undoubtedly let forth, had not Nature (who, as wise men have observed, equips all creatures with what is most expedient for them) taken a provident care (as she always doth with those she intends for encounters) to make this part of the head three times as thick as those of ordinary men, who are designed to exercise talents which are vulgarly called rational, and for whom, as brains are necessary, she is obliged to leave some room for them in the cavity of the skull; whereas, those ingredients being entirely useless to persons of the heroic calling, she hath an opportunity of thickening the bone, so as to make it less subject to any impression, or liable to be cracked or broken; and, indeed, in some who are predestined to the command of armies and empires, she is supposed sometimes to make that part perfectly solid.

The passage continues for as long again and more, with similes and other 'Homerican' elaborations, notably an Iliadic particularity in the detailing of the fight. As so often, moreover, the mock-epic is laced with a strong element of mock-romance, for Adams is after all rescuing a damsel in distress, and also with a touch of mock-learned garrulity. It is even, in a way, more like the mock-heroic of *Jonathan Wild* than the corresponding passage from *Jonathan Wild* itself, in its elaborate use of mock-heroic inflation and its reference to commanders of 'armies and empires'. That, indeed, is a crucial detail, for it shows how much readier Fielding is to use *Wild*ian bombast in a passage about Adams than in one about Heartfree. The difference between Heartfree and Adams is not, as Wendt believes, that Heartfree is unwilling to 'wade in with his fists', but that Fielding describes the wading in with a flatly earnest efficiency instead of giving it all the heaving honours of parodic elaboration.

But if Heartfree's bravery is denied the leaven of humorous elaboration, it is, like much else about him and in spite of Fielding's purposes, susceptible to diminution by the effects of the upside-down irony. When Wild first meets him in the novel, many years after their intimate friendship as schoolboys, we read:

> It hath been thought that friendship is usually nursed by similitude of manners, but the contrary had been the case between these lads; for whereas Wild was rapacious and intrepid, the other had always more regard for his skin than his money; Wild therefore had very generously compassionated this defect in his schoolfellow, and had brought him off from many scrapes, into most of which he had first drawn him, by taking the fault and whipping to himself. He had always indeed been well paid on such occasions; but there are a sort of people who, together with the best of the bargain, will be sure to have the obligation too on their side; so it had happened here: for this poor lad had considered himself in the highest degree obliged to Mr. Wild, and had contracted a very great esteem and friendship for him; the traces of which an absence of many years had not in the least effaced in his mind (II, i).

Heartfree's 'more regard for his skin than his money' is, I think, the only place in the novel where his courage may be felt to have actually been brought into question. The impression is, however, so uncertain and fleeting that Wendt himself does not refer to the passage. This is our very first glimpse of Heartfree, and although we have reason to feel that he will be important to the story, we cannot help thinking of him, especially at this initial stage, as a figure whose main role it is to extend our understanding of Wild's villainy. We come to him immediately after Wild's latest bullying trickery has been mentioned ('Wild, having shared the booty in much the same manner as before, *i.e.*, taken three-fourths of it, amounting to eighteen-pence, was now retiring to rest, in no very happy mood, when by accident he met with a young fellow . . .'). We have no cause to individualize him yet. He has not even been named, and he is presented in any case through the filter of an irony which, purporting to be on the side of Wild's values, in a sense gives us Wild's own perspective. If Heartfree's 'regard for his skin' echoes schoolboy slang more than the heroic idiom of 'greatness', the variation is particularly apt, and it is by no means the only time in the novel when the heroic theme acquires schoolboy overtones, even outside a context of school memories. What remains certain is that we do not take the 'regard for his skin' *straight*, but as somehow distorted by the pseudo-heroic view, just as we take Heartfree's readiness to pay out money not as a simple gullibility, nor as a spendthrift folly (everything we learn later about Heartfree shows him to be frugal in his way of life), but as seeming these things to Wild. By the end of the paragraph, we are beginning to see Heartfree in a stronger positive light, and the next paragraph consists of the formal portrait (already quoted) which opens with the remark that Heartfree is still innocent and inexperienced enough to be unaware that 'deceit and hypocrisy' exist. (It is noted that he is only twenty-five, and will doubtless overcome this inexperience: Parson Adams, whom Wendt cites as an example of the more active kind of goodness, is, according to the parallel portrait, at least fifty, and thus presumably incurable!).

But if our very first glimpse of Heartfree is rapidly modified, and if he is relatively easily cleared of the charge of foolish gullibility, a slight difficulty still remains about the courage. Although we are invited by the irony to translate the schoolboy cowardice into something less discreditable, the irony is not in full control of the escape-routes. We see Heartfree tricked into situations where he has to pay Wild to protect him, and we are told that all aspects of these situations have been engineered by Wild: but we are also left with a picture of Heartfree in the unsporting and pusillanimous role of letting a fellow schoolboy take the whippings which were meant for him. The prose sense behind the irony is damagingly unclear. The passage permits the commonsense inference that nothing more is suggested about Heartfree than a decent shrinking from unpleasantness and violence and hazardous enterprises. But the inference, or any similar inference, has to be willed on to the passage by the reader, because although the irony tells us that some such explanation must exist, it does not guide us firmly towards it.

The example proves that Fielding was in a sense right to be cautious of allowing irony to get too close to his presentation of Heartfree. Unfortunately, he succeeded too well in withholding the kind of comic transformation which might have permitted him to transcend the weaknesses of characterization, whilst he remained trapped by the formulaic scheme into letting an element of the more mechanical and more damaging kind of sarcasm survive where, I believe, he did not want it. But it seems very unlikely from the novel as we have it that Fielding set out with the notion of casting doubt on Heartfree's wisdom and bravery, and of exposing the insufficiencies of mere 'goodness'. On the other hand, Fielding seems to have realized after the event that his portrayal of the Heartfrees was open to misapprehension on these points, and in the revised second edition of the novel he made efforts to correct this. Not only is the passage about Heartfree's 'regard for his skin', as I have quoted it from the revised version, an elaboration with saving elements of a much starker original, but several other passages in the revised version are clearly aimed at reducing any impression of undue timorousness or passive gullibility in the Heartfrees.[33] If Fielding was already conscious of this problem when he wrote the Preface to the *Miscellanies* (which discusses the novel's *first* version), he might well have felt inclined, in a context of expository prose, to dissociate his sober moral outlook from the unintentionally diminished and unimpressive portrayals of 'goodness' in the novel. It is likely that some such consideration prompted the statement in the Preface 'that I do not conceive my good man to be absolutely a fool or a coward; but that he often partakes too little of parts or courage to have any pretensions to greatness'.[34] If, however, the character of Heartfree contributed to Fielding's need to issue this caution, it is not certain that the phrase 'my good man' refers specifically to Heartfree himself, as Wendt assumes.[35] The immediate context is a generalizing disquisition on the characteristics of 'greatness', 'goodness' and the 'great and good', and it seems entirely possible that 'my good man' mainly means 'my category of good man' or 'the good man in my definition'. Since the merely 'good' person is being distinguished from that rare thing, 'A perfect work! the Iliad of Nature', the 'good man' is entitled to feel that he is being called nothing worse than an ordinary mortal.

The reservations about good men in the Preface may, therefore, be thought of partly as the product of failures of characterization in the novel; and partly as an assertion that, in Fielding's ordinary rational view, outside the special formulaic world of this novel, it is better to talk in terms of three categories and not two. It seems wrong, however, to extrapolate the Preface's rational view and to impose it on the novel. In the novel, Fielding is interested in Heartfree mainly as a foil to Wild, and seems in most ways to be resisting from within those subversive or deadening tendencies in his portrayal of Heartfree which later helped to bring about the cautions of the Preface, and which finally made recent critics like Wendt complete the circle by reinterpreting the novel through the Preface.

The novel is both more and less of a 'moral allegory' than Wendt suggests: more, because the nominal scheme is more rigidly bipartite, and less, because the novel keeps running away from its scheme, in success (in the enrichments of mock-heroic fantasy and in the treatment of Wild), and in failure (in the deadenings and oscillations over Heartfree, which awkwardly burst through schematic boundaries, whether these distinguish between two or three categories). Robert H. Hopkins has said, in a useful corrective to Wendt, that 'To read *Wild* as primarily a moral allegory is . . . to take it too seriously on one level and to stifle its comic possibilities on the other'.[36] It is Wendt, the exponent of an ironically diminished Heartfree, who finds himself in a grossly over-solemn posture when he comes to discuss the ending of the novel: 'Like Dante, Fielding ends his allegory with a vision of the multifoliate rose' ![37] When one thinks of the hanging of Wild, that triumph of oafish magniloquence, or the Heartfrees' dully and routinely registered happy ending, the extent to which Wendt has lost touch with the feeling of the work becomes vividly apparent. His comment says both too little and too much, inflating the novel into an inappropriate and simplifying sublimity, as he had earlier flattened it into a neat ideological essay, like the Preface. Yet his swing from an ironically criticized Heartfree to a justly rewarded one is in the right direction, and meets the truth somewhere near the latter end. Wendt makes undue fuss over the technical distinctions in theology between rewards on earth and rewards in heaven, but he is right (a) that Heartfree is and is meant to be justly rewarded, (b) that Fielding is not saying thereby that the virtuous are always rewarded in this life, and (c) that the happy ending (like most happy endings, I imagine) relates to some ideal notion of an 'ultimate and eternal justice of the universe'[38] where the bad fare badly and the good well, rather than to a verifiable experience of everyday life. These points might seem obvious, but Wendt needs to reassert them because he argues that in another sense Heartfree does not deserve reward, since his 'goodness' lacks the 'parts and courage' necessary to success.

The latter view, we may add, reads Fielding with a special pair of spectacles. It attributes to Fielding doctrines of the 'survival of the fittest' whose real affinities are with the success-ethos of a later commercial civilization, and whose particular tang goes well beyond the commonsense recommendations of prudence which Fielding did make. Wendt more or less unwittingly reveals this when he describes the outcome of the Heartfree story as presenting 'the eighteenth-century equivalent of "The world owes me a living" '.³⁹ Ironically, this is not even true on its own terms, since Heartfree ends up rich through the good commercial virtues of hard work and thrift: 'He now set up again in his trade; . . . and he hath, by industry joined with parsimony, amassed a considerable fortune' (IV, xv). The first edition had read 'an immense fortune', and the later change may perhaps be taken as a small further emphasis on commercial solidity, as against the economic cloudcuckooland of romance happy endings and the ideal hugeness of their financial settlements. At all events, Heartfree is the only one of Fielding's protagonists to end up in trade. The others all inherit or marry into great estates, or at least, like Joseph, pursue a rural occupation on their own (if relatively modest) property.

Here, as elsewhere in the novel, Heartfree is Fielding's sentimental tribute to the virtuous tradesman. It is a sincere tribute, but one which involved for Fielding certain ambiguities of feeling whose effect, as I have suggested, was to bring certain serious celebrations to the brink of subversion by unconscious humour, while keeping a potentially saving element of real comic transformation at bay. Robert H. Hopkins is one of the few critics who have understood that comic play is genuinely present in other parts of the novel, and his commentary on Wendt's deficiencies in this matter is particularly apt. But he errs in an opposite direction when he argues that the ending of the novel is a joke at the Heartfrees' expense.⁴⁰ He reads Heartfree's 'industry joined with parsimony' as ironic, apparently assuming that the pejorative sense of 'parsimony' (avarice, niggardliness) rather than the good or neutral sense (thrift, frugality) is here used by Fielding. He almost questions, with an engaging injustice to poor Mrs Heartfree, whether the diamond of 'prodigious value' which enabled Heartfree to set up in business again was earned, after all, by wholly chaste means; and then suggests that Fielding was, alternatively, mocking Mrs Heartfree's puritanism. Hopkins also draws attention to the fact that the Heartfrees 'never had another child', and points to the absurdity with which the novel describes the future of the younger of their existing daughters:

she never would listen to the addresses of any lover, not even of a young nobleman, who offered to take her with two thousand pounds, which her father would have willingly produced, and indeed did his utmost to persuade her to the match; but she refused absolutely, nor would give any other reason when Heartfree pressed her, than that she had dedicated her days to his service, and was resolved no other duty should interfere with that which she owed to the best of fathers, nor prevent her from being the nurse of his old age (IV, xv).

Hopkins sees this as mockery of 'fastidious asceticism and prudery', and it must be admitted that the passage sorely stimulates the modern reader's sense of ridicule. I can only say that I think the display of filial abnegation (very much in a familiar convention of sentimental rhetoric in prose fiction and domestic drama) invites us to read it not only straight, but if possible with a tender tear. Similarly, the girl's refusal of the young nobleman and the dowry of £2,000 suggests a deliberate straining by Fielding to assert the staunch merchant integrity which he chose to identify with the Heartfree plot. It seems to scorn the class-desertion of those children of merchants who marry their way into a title with their money. And the fact that no nobleman seemed to the younger daughter to be as good as her merchant father is balanced by the fact that the elder daughter marries a man who then becomes the father's 'partner in trade'.

Joseph Andrews's Fanny was also offered £2,000, and what is more, by no less unexpected or preposterous a donor than her new found brother-in-law Mr Booby, husband of Pamela—and she accepts! These details suffuse with a sufficient touch of comic fantasy the commonplace sentimental-domestic conclusion, in which Joseph uses the money to buy 'a little estate in the same parish with his father, which he now occupies . . .; and Fanny presides with most excellent management in his dairy; where, however, she is not at present very able to bustle much, being, as Mr. Wilson informs me in his last letter, extremely big with her first child'. The humour and the domestic tableau coexist under Fielding's full control. The happy-ever-after union of the lovers is, in the final chapter as a whole, streaked with rich touches of comedy: Fanny wearing at her wedding a shift with 'an edging of lace round the bosom', given to her by Pamela; Adams rebuking Booby and Pamela for laughing during the ceremony; and Adams himself overeating at the reception. In the final paragraphs of *Tom Jones*, a similar interplay exists between a festive sweetness of sentiment, and warm rich humour (mostly provided by Squire Western), and the coexistence similarly teaches us that what is absent in the happy ending of the Heartfrees is the element of humour which Hopkins's reading seeks to supply. The lack may partly be ascribed to an as yet incomplete command of the novelist's art (even though the Heartfrees may not have been Fielding's first novelistic attempt; on the dating see n. 16). But incomplete maturity as a novelist is complicated by the fact that Fielding was celebrating in

Heartfree a character unique among the protagonists of his fiction, and having to do so with a certain willed emphasis that betrays a special unease. It may well be that greater artistic maturity itself actually prevented him from trying to write a serious novel about a merchant again.

❋

NOTES

1 See the ironic systematization of this (or rather of a somewhat similar) semantic pairing in *J.W.*, IV, iv, where Wild speaks of a 'first class of greatness, the conquerors of mankind' and of 'that second order of greatness, the ministerial'.

2 The threefold identification Wild/Walpole/Great Man was of course common: see W. R. Irwin, *The Making of Jonathan Wild*, esp. pp. 22 ff.

3 *Amelia*, III, ii; *Voyage to Lisbon*, p. 44.

4 *Amelia*, XII, ii. The virtues of a more personal or domestic sensibility are often, in this period, pointedly set against heroic codes. When Fielding says in *J.A.*, III, xi, that Joseph's tears at the supposed loss of Fanny 'would have become any but a hero', he implies 'so much the worse for heroes'. Since epic heroes do in fact weep, the irony may seem blurred at the edges, but the generalized downgrading of the heroic ethos comes through clearly. The particular comment devalues heroic fortitude into mere hard-heartedness, whereas Amelia's fortitude, or that of Mrs Fielding in the *Voyage*, are called heroic in a redefined and favourable sense (see above, n. 3). Both ironies come to the same thing, however, in demoting traditional heroic values in favour of a humbler ethos of personal and domestic decency. The assertion of a humbler redefinition of the heroic ideal, away from associations of grandeur and prowess, is not confined to Fielding. Swift (and others) redefined heroism into a rational moderation (Martin Price, *Swift's Rhetorical Art* (New Haven, 1953), pp. 103 ff.), Richardson into an ethos of virtuous contentment and the 'feeling heart' (*Correspondence*, ed. A. L. Barbauld (London, 1804), II, 252). These two redefinitions are never mutually exclusive, and Fielding combines elements of both when he describes the high virtue of good-nature as heroic. This virtue is (in the semi-technical parlance of the day) 'amiable' rather than 'admirable' (see *C.-G.J.*, No. 16, 25 February 1752, Jensen, I, 232). Wild's greatness is 'admirable' (e.g. *J.W.*, IV, xv), but Amelia's heroic forgiveness of her husband appears in 'so amiable and great a light' (*Amelia*, XII, ii). For the use of 'heroic' and 'great' in contrast with 'amiable', see the last two paragraphs of Johnson's *Rambler*, No. 89, 22 January 1751.

5 *Works*, II, 236.
6 *Works*, XII, 256.
7 A crude but commonplace example is this line from Joseph Mitchell's
Poems on Several Occasions (1729), cited in Henry Knight Miller's *Essays
on Fielding's Miscellanies*, p. 48, n. 17: 'The Man, whose Vertues shew his
noble Blood . . .' Fuller evidence of the points made in this and the next
two paragraphs is given in ch. I above.
8 *C.-G.J.* No. 61, 29 August 1752, Jensen, II, 92.
9 *Amelia*, VII, x. See above, pp. 9, 23.
10 *Voyage to Lisbon*, p. 45. See above, pp. 18 ff.
11 *Works*, XII, 242–6.
12 *Works*, XII, 245. The phrase 'in the highest degree' seems to suggest that
what is rare might be not the combination, but only its highest forms.
On the other hand, no such qualification seems to govern the description
of the 'great and good', on the same page, as 'the true sublime in human
nature . . . A perfect work! the Iliad of Nature!'. The shift or oscillation
between the two emphases might itself be a sign of Fielding's uneasiness
in wrestling with a definition whose class-conscious implications he
perhaps wished to disguise from himself.
13 *Works*, XII, 249–57.
14 For such 'Mock Counts', see Howson, *Thief-Taker General*, pp. 44, 183.
15 The ambiguity of Fielding's attitude is real. He emphatically asserted the
usefulness of trade, and the right of the productive and public-spirited
merchant to the title of 'true greatness' (e.g. 'Of True Greatness', *Works*,
XII, 253). The jeweller Heartfree, moreover, may have been created as a
tribute to the dramatist and jeweller Lillo, author of *The London Merchant*
(A. Digeon, *The Novels of Fielding*, p. 121; W. R. Irwin, *The Making of
Jonathan Wild*, pp. 73 ff.) Fielding deplored 'the disdain with which
the great and fine world look down on a middle state' (*Champion*, 26
February 1739/40, *Works*, XV, 218), as he always deplored all forms of
snobbish contempt. There is no doubt, on the other hand, that his own
attitude to merchants, especially in moods when he feels hostile towards
them, is streaked with patrician *hauteur* (see H. K. Miller, *Essays on
Fielding's Miscellanies*, pp. 186, 188).
16 The dates of composition of the various parts of *Jonathan Wild* are
speculative. Dudden, who provides a good summary of the possibilities,
argues that the Heartfree plot, with the exception of Mrs Heartfree's
travels, was composed after *Joseph Andrews* had appeared in February 1742,
but that the travels and the main Wild section were both written as
separate pieces before *Joseph Andrews* was begun, possibly in 1740 (see
above, ch. V, n. 1). It seems possible to me that the Heartfree portions were
also written earlier, and then welded with the rest, with topical additions
and adjustments, in late 1742. Either way, the patchwork nature of
composition might have been a contributory cause of compensating
rigidity in the superimposed great-good schematism. Both the patchwork

and the schematism might well reduce authorial confidence and impair the ease and flexibility of Fielding's manner, especially at this early stage of his career as an author of prose fiction. Moreover, even if *Joseph Andrews* had in fact been written earlier than *Jonathan Wild*, or at least than its Heartfree portion, the fact would not necessarily imply that Fielding would be able, as early as this, to repeat a first success at will.

17 Allan Wendt, 'The Moral Allegory of *Jonathan Wild*', *ELH. A Journal of English Literary History*, xxiv (1057), 309.

18 *Works*, XII, 245–6.

19 Wendt, op. cit., p. 319.

20 The idiom of such passages as this may be, in some sense, mock-Mandevillian (e.g. *Fable of the Bees*, ed. F. B. Kaye (Oxford, 1966), I, 104: 'Frugality is like Honesty, a mean starving Virtue'; and see Martin Price, *To the Palace of Wisdom*, p. 128).

21 It comes immediately after the paragraph which describes the first meeting of Wild and Heartfree since their schooldays, and which gives a slightly problematical glimpse (discussed later in this chapter) of their schoolboy friendship.

22 *T.J.*, I, ii, and, especially, VI, iv.

23 *T.J.*, VI, iv.

24 *Works*, XII, 245.

25 *T.J.*, I, iv. The passage has echoes, and almost hints at unconscious parody, of the celebration of the 'great and good' which I quoted earlier from the Preface to the *Miscellanies* (above, pp. 234–5). The odd and surprising verbal resemblances speak for themselves, but a word about the Preface's description of the 'great and good' as 'A perfect work! the Iliad of Nature' seems appropriate here. 'Iliad of Nature' merely means 'very excellent', in apposition to 'A perfect work'. But Allworthy does as it happens conform to a definite Augustan conception of Homeric benevolence, as is suggested by the author of the *Critical Remarks on Sir Charles Grandison, Clarissa and Pamela* (London, 1754), pp. 18–20, who connects Allworthy with Eumaeus in *Odyssey*, XIV ff. The Twickenham editors of Pope's Homer note that Pope added to Eumaeus's benevolence a specific eighteenth-century flavour, and that this is even truer of Pope's treatment of Axylus near the beginning of *Iliad*, VI (*Twickenham Edition of the Poems of Alexander Pope*, vol. VII (London and New Haven, 1967), pp. ccxxvii and n. 2, ccxxvi–ccxxix). The Twickenham editors also note R. A. Brower's insight, that Pope's version of the lines on Axylus seem particularly applicable to a man like Ralph Allen—who was, of course not only a friend of both Fielding and Pope, but also the real-life model of Allworthy (and the dedicatee of *Amelia*). Fielding, moreover, used the pseudonym Axylus for several essays dealing partly or wholly with benevolence and good-nature in the *C.-G.J.* (Nos. 16, 20, 29), in one of which he praises Allen as 'that first of human Kind, the glorious Patron of Amelia' (No. 29, 11 April 1752, Jensen, I, 306). Axylus seems to have

interested both Pope and Fielding beyond what his almost complete insignificance in Homer might lead us to expect; he occurs in *Amelia* IX, viii, and he is again referred to in the *Voyage to Lisbon*, pp. 105–6, as a pattern of benevolence who, 'living by the highway, erected his hospitality . . . in favour of land-travellers'. The meaning of this is in Homer, and it may be unwarranted to sense a verbal resemblance to a sentence in Pope's note to *Iliad*, VI, 16: Axylus's 'manner of keeping House near a frequented Highway, and relieving all Travellers, is agreeable to that ancient Hospitality which we now only read of'. (See also Pope's self-identification with this, in a letter to Hugh Bethel, 9 August 1726, *Correspondence*, ed. G. Sherburn (Oxford, 1956), II, 386). The character of Allworthy is thus at several points indirectly involved in the Homeric personage as reimagined by Fielding and Pope, and is certainly the embodiment of the kind of benevolence which both authors (and presumably many eighteenth-century readers) would read into the original Axylus. The resemblance of the quoted paragraph about Allworthy's resplendent benevolence to the description of 'the Iliad of Nature' in the Preface to the *Miscellanies* acquires an added, if fortuitous, aptness.

26 *Rape of the Lock*, II, 3. The closeness to parody in the spectacle of Allworthy, walking about his estate 'meditating' projects of benevolence, is reinforced by its accidental resemblance to a passage in *A Popp upon Pope* (1728), where Pope, 'a great Poet (as we are inform'd)', is satirically pictured 'walking in *Ham-Walks*, meditating Verses for the Publick Good' (J. V. Guerinot, *Pamphlet Attacks on Alexander Pope 1711–1744* (London, 1969), p. 115).

27 Wendt, op. cit., p. 319.

28 *T.J.*, III, v.

29 *The Making of Jonathan Wild*, pp. 126–7, n. 141.

30 The chapters recounting these travels (IV, vii–ix, xi, in the revised edition) are often described as parodies of extravagant travel-books and improbable romances. In fact, Fielding spoke in the Preface to the *Miscellanies* of only one chapter as burlesque, and of all the rest as 'within the rules of probability': 'except in one chapter, which is visibly meant as a burlesque on the extravagant accounts of travellers, I believe I have not exceeded [probability]' (*Works*, XII, 244; the distinction between 'probability' and 'burlesque' occurs in a better-known form in the Preface to *Joseph Andrews*). The chapter in question (IV, ix in the *first* edition) was removed in the revised final state of the novel. The other travel-chapters are largely sober narrative, especially by the standards of what they are alleged to be parodying, and not at all difficult to take straight. A few scattered amusing touches, like the appearance of the naked hairy hermit in IV, ix and the African magistrate in IV, xi who is nightly kicked on the 'posteriors' by his beadle as a ritual guard against self-importance, do relatively little to subvert the narrative, and

nothing at all to diminish Mrs Heartfree. Two or three small indications that Mrs Heartfree feels flattered by compliments made to her by pressing suitors are all the deflation she has to endure, and Fielding is avuncularly tolerant about this. Discrepancies are sometimes noted between the character of Mrs Heartfree in the travels, and in other parts of the novel. Thus Mrs Heartfree turns, in the travels, from a 'simple, retiring creature' into a woman of 'astonishing finesse' (Dudden, I, 478) when it comes to warding off her lecherous admirers. Chaste women have in novels to remain (as all Fielding's heroines remain) victorious against all onslaughts on their virtue, so that this difference should not be overemphasized. But it is also true that the travel-story is, anyway, almost certainly an interpolation patched on to the novel from separately composed material. It not only has a strong change of subject-matter and atmosphere, but introduces a large structural imbalance in the book as a whole, coming as it does in protracted anticlimax, after the suspense over Heartfree's fate has been removed by his exoneration, and before the grand finale of Wild's execution. Even if, therefore, a certain element of parody does exist, it scarcely touches Mrs Heartfree, and may not originally have been meant for any story concerning her.

31 *Works*, XII, 246; Wendt, op. cit., pp. 315, 308–9.
32 Such jokes about brainlessness seem to have been common in novelistic fight-scenes: see Smollett's *Peregrine Pickle*, chs. XV, XIX.
33 Aurélien Digeon, *Le Texte des Romans de Fielding* (Paris, 1923), pp. 29 ff.
34 *Works*, XII, 245–6.
35 Wendt, op. cit., p. 307.
36 Robert H. Hopkins, 'Language and Comic Play in Fielding's *Jonathan Wild*', *Criticism*, viii (1966), 214.
37 Wendt, op. cit., p. 310.
38 Wendt, op. cit., p. 310.
39 Wendt, op. cit., p. 309.
40 Hopkins, op. cit., p. 228.

INDEX

INDEX

Lee, N., 213, 223–5
Lehmann, A. G., 142
Lesage, Alain René, 138, 226
Lewis, C. S., 215
Lewis, Wyndham, 147, 169–70, 174
Life of Jonathan Wild, by 'H. D.', 137
Lillo, George, 256
Lockwood, T., 66, 223
Loftis, John, 144
Louis XIV, 210, 228
Love and Jealousy: or the Downfall of Alexander the Great, 224
Lucian, 62, 223
Lyttelton, George, Lord, 231

Mabbe, James, 117, 138
Machiavelli, N., 137, 139
Mack, Maynard, 144, 169
Mackenzie, Henry, 5 (cited), 91
Maecenas, 193
Mailer, Norman, 64, 147–8
Malkoff, Karl, 41
Mandeville, Bernard, 257
Mann, Thomas, 117, 133, 142–3, 146, 216, 222; *Confessions of Felix Krull*: 114ff., ch. IV, *passim*, 200, 216
Martial, 80
Mason, John E., 34
Meikle, Susan, 132 (cited), 134 (cited)
Mendès, Catulle, 190
Meyer, H., 143
Miller, Henry Knight, 167–8, 195, 221, 256
Milton, John, 52, 105, 168, 215–16
Mist's Weekly Journal, 139, 167–8
Mitchell, Joseph, 256
Molière, 10, 113–14, 165
Moore, Edward, 17
Moore, J. R., 219
Morley, Henry, 225–6
Murphy, Arthur, 214
Musil, Robert, 133
Mylne, V., 138

Nepos, Cornelius, 149

Nero, 121, 191ff., 220–1
Nietzsche, F., 116, 141–2, 222
Norris, 'Dicky', 224
Norton, Charles Eliot, 65

Orwell, George, 79–80
Otway, Thomas, *Cheats of Scapin*, 113–14, 139, 165; *see also Cure for Covetousness*
Overbury, Thomas, 80–1

Parker, Alexander A., 138ff.
Parnell, Thomas, 85 (cited), 169
Paulson, R., 66, 223, 226
Penkethman, William, Sr. and/or Jr., 204, 208–9, 213, 223–5
Perche, Louis, 214, 220
Perillus, 202
Peterson, W. M., 224
Phalaris, 202, 223
Pitiscus, Samuel, 197, 222
Plato, 37, 181
Plutarch, 149–50, 156, 166–7, 189, 221
Poe, Edgar Allan, 142
Pope, Alexander: 10, 19, 22, 29, 36–8, 46–7, 50, 56, 83–6, 115, 150, 158–60, 165, 220, 226, 258; *Dunciad*, 41–3, 51–2, 82, 95, 102–3, 127, 144, 158–61, 163–4, 170, 175ff., 191, 205–6, 208, 215ff., 226, 239; *Essay on Criticism*, ix, 35, 38, 41–2, 52, 95; *Essay on Man*, 41, 43, 52, 159, 169; Homer, translation of, 65, 167–9, 257–8; *Imitations of Horace*, 35, 42; *Moral Essays*, 44; *Peri Bathous: or, Of the Art of Sinking in Poetry*, 51; *Rape of the Lock*, 42, 51, 94, 159, 239, 258; *Temple of Fame*, 169
Popp upon Pope, A, 258
Price, Martin, 51, 69, 71, 144, 255, 257
Purney, Thomas, 219
Pütz, H. P., 142

Quevedo, Francisco Gómez de, 183–4
Quilliot, Roger, 222

264

Rabelais, François, 190
Radin, Paul, 139
Ralph, James, 220
Rehearsal, The, 158
Retz, Cardinal de, 90
Richardson, Samuel, 6, 43, 88, 90–1, 95, 158, 167, 218, 255; *Clarissa*, 88, 95–6, 134; *Pamela*, 53–4, 58ff.; *Sir Charles Grandison*, 156, 158, 167
Robbins, A. F., 139
Roethke, Theodore, 40–1
Rogers, Pat, 226
Rosenfeld, Sybil, 139, 213, 220, 225–6
Rowlandson, Thomas, ix

Saillet, Maurice, 220
Sallust, 166
Sartre, Jean-Paul, 170
Scott, Sir Walter, 7, 101, 114
Scouten, A. H., 224
Seidlin, O., 143
Seneca the Elder, 221
Settle, Elkanah, 213, 226
Shakespeare, William, 116–17, 140–2, 191, 209–11, 221
Shea, Bernard, 137
Shellabarger, S., 30
Shelley, P. B., 39
Sheppard, Jack, 139
Sherburn, George, 30, 32, 94–5, 144, 258
Sidney, Sir Philip, 141
Smith, D. Nichol, 141–2
Smith, Winifred, 226
Smollett, Tobias: *Ferdinand Count Fathom*: 81–3, 114, 139; *Humphry Clinker*: 53–4; *Peregrine Pickle*: 259; *Roderick Random*: 54–5, 82; *Sir Launcelot Greaves*: 54–5
Socrates, 11, 140, 231ff.
Spanish Rogue, 113ff., 138, 165; *see also* Alemán, M.
Speaight, George, 226
Spectator, 224
Spingarn, J. E., 226

Stanford, W. B., 170
Stead, C. K., 39
Steele, Richard, 224, 228
Stephen, Leslie, 65
Sterne, Laurence, 91, 142–3
Stevens, Wallace, 39 (cited)
Stockdale, Percival, 83–4
Suetonius, 149, 193ff., ch. VI *passim*, 220
Swain, Barbara, 140
Swift, Jonathan, 19, 23, 44ff., 65–6, 83, 88, 110, 115–6, 128, 133, 134, 138, 142, 144–5, 157, 177, 183, 194, 203–4, 213, 216, 228, 235, 255; 'Beautiful Young Nymph Going to Bed': 80–1; *Epistle to a Lady*: 175; *Gulliver's Travels*: 46ff., 52, 56, 72–3, 194, 202, 235; 'Hints towards an Essay on Conversation': 142; *Mechanical Operation of the Spirit*: 142; 'On Good-Manners and Good-Breeding': 20–1; *On Poetry: A Rapsody*: 101, 213; *Project for the Advancement of Religion*: 122; *Sentiments of a Church-of-England Man*: 44ff.; *Short View of the State of Ireland*: 50–1; *Tale of a Tub*: 20, 43, 45–6, 48, 50, 115, 128, 132, 134, 142–4, 175–6, 245; 'Tritical Essay upon the Faculties of the Mind': 162, 194

Tacitus, 139, 168, 221
Tate, Nahum, 141
Temple, Sir William, 155, 167, 172
Thackeray, W. M., 85
Thomas, R. Hinton, 142, 145
Thornbury, E. M., 222
Tiberius, 192
Torchiana, Donald T., 32

Valéry, Paul, 36–40, 42–3
Vincent, Howard P., 144
Virgil, 94, 147ff., ch. V *passim*, 175, 197–8, 211, 222